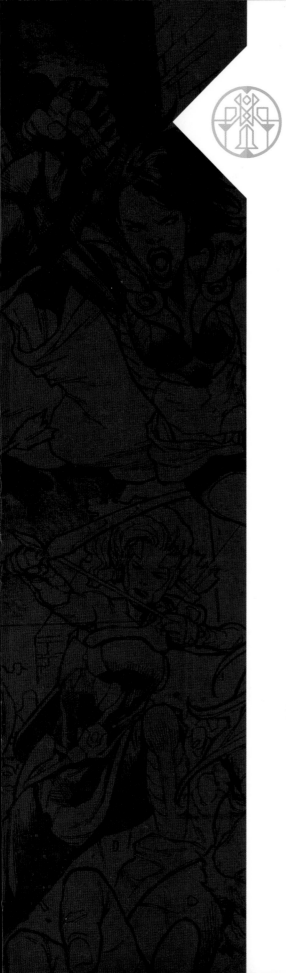

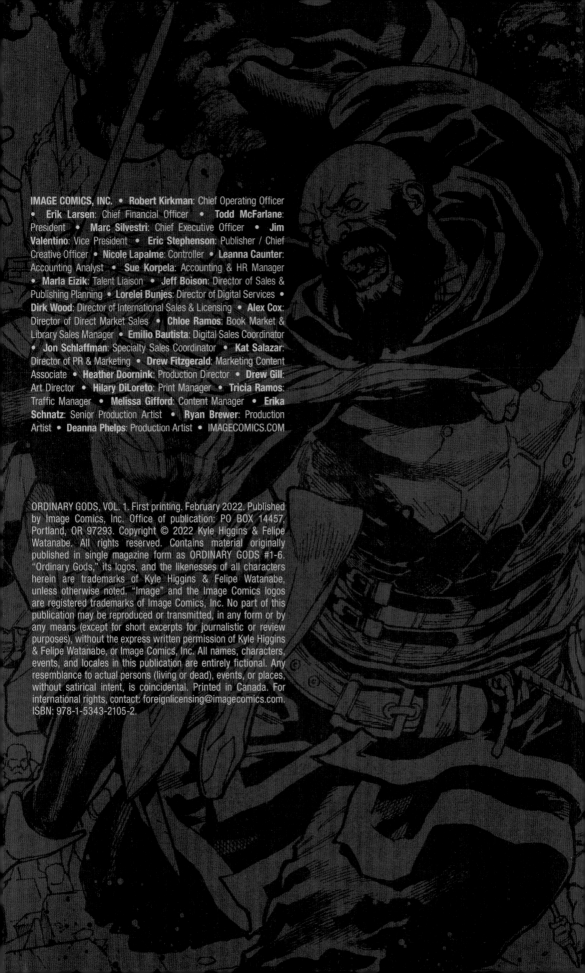

ORDINARY GODS, VOL. 1. First printing. February 2022. Published
by Image Comics, Inc. Office of publication: PO BOX 14457,
Portland, OR 97293. Copyright © 2022 Kyle Higgins & Felipe
Watanabe. All rights reserved. Contains material originally
published in single magazine form as ORDINARY GODS #1-6.
"Ordinary Gods," its logos, and the likenesses of all characters
herein are trademarks of Kyle Higgins & Felipe Watanabe,
unless otherwise noted. "Image" and the Image Comics logos
are registered trademarks of Image Comics, Inc. No part of this
publication may be reproduced or transmitted, in any form or by
any means (except for short excerpts for journalistic or review
purposes), without the express written permission of Kyle Higgins
& Felipe Watanabe, or Image Comics, Inc. All names, characters,
events, and locales in this publication are entirely fictional. Any
resemblance to actual persons (living or dead), events, or places,
without satirical intent, is coincidental. Printed in Canada. For
international rights, contact: foreignlicensing@imagecomics.com.
ISBN: 978-1-5343-2105-2.

Ordinary Gods

VOLUME ONE: GOD SPARK

WRITERS
Kyle Higgins
Joe Clark

ARTIST
Felipe Watanabe

COLORIST
Frank William

LETTERER
Clayton Cowles

BACKUP STORIES
Jana Tropper

LOGO DESIGNER
Rich Bloom

PRODUCTION ARTIST
Ryan Brewer

EDITOR & DESIGNER
Michael Busuttil

image

BLACK MARKET NARRATIVE

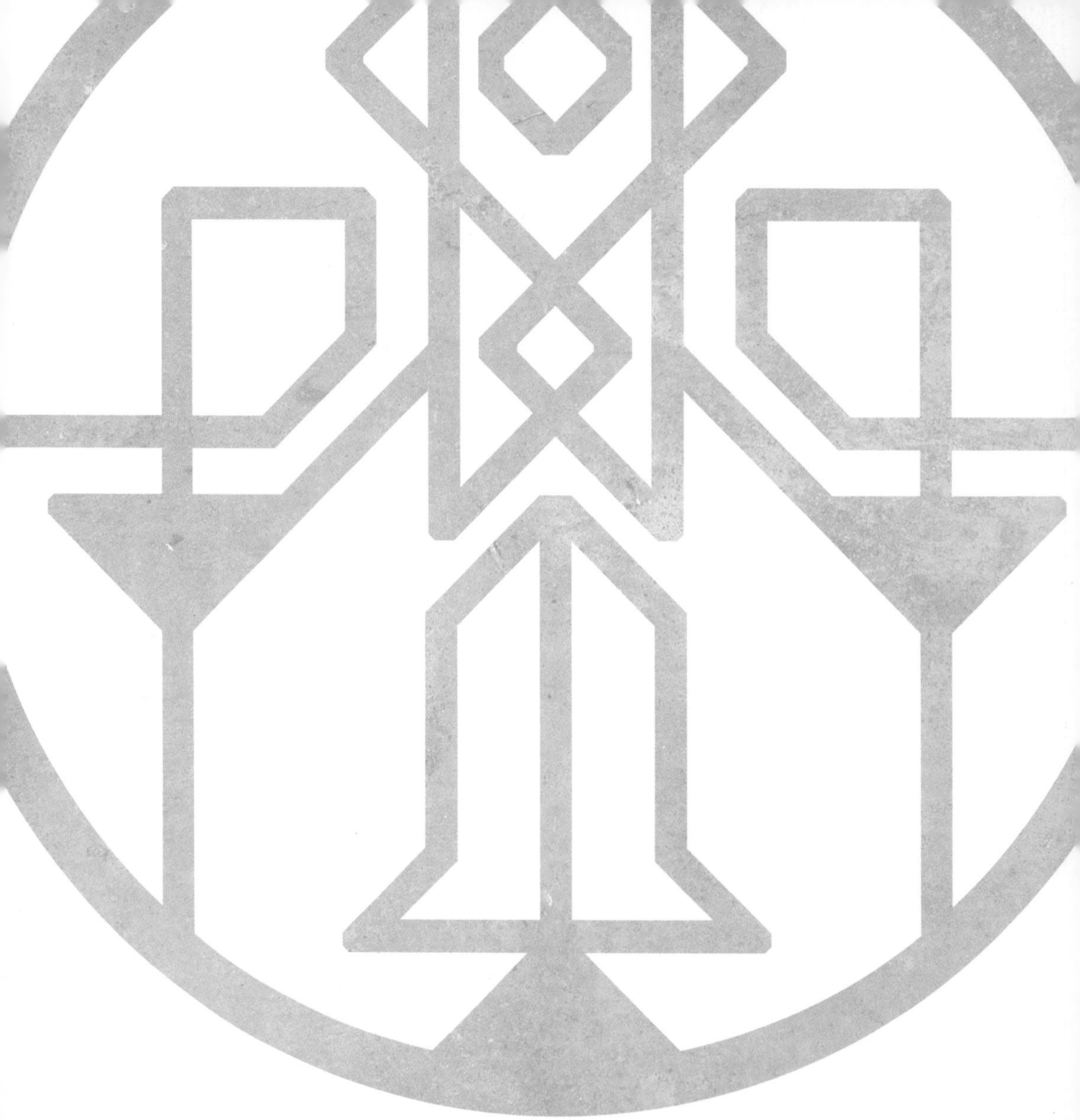

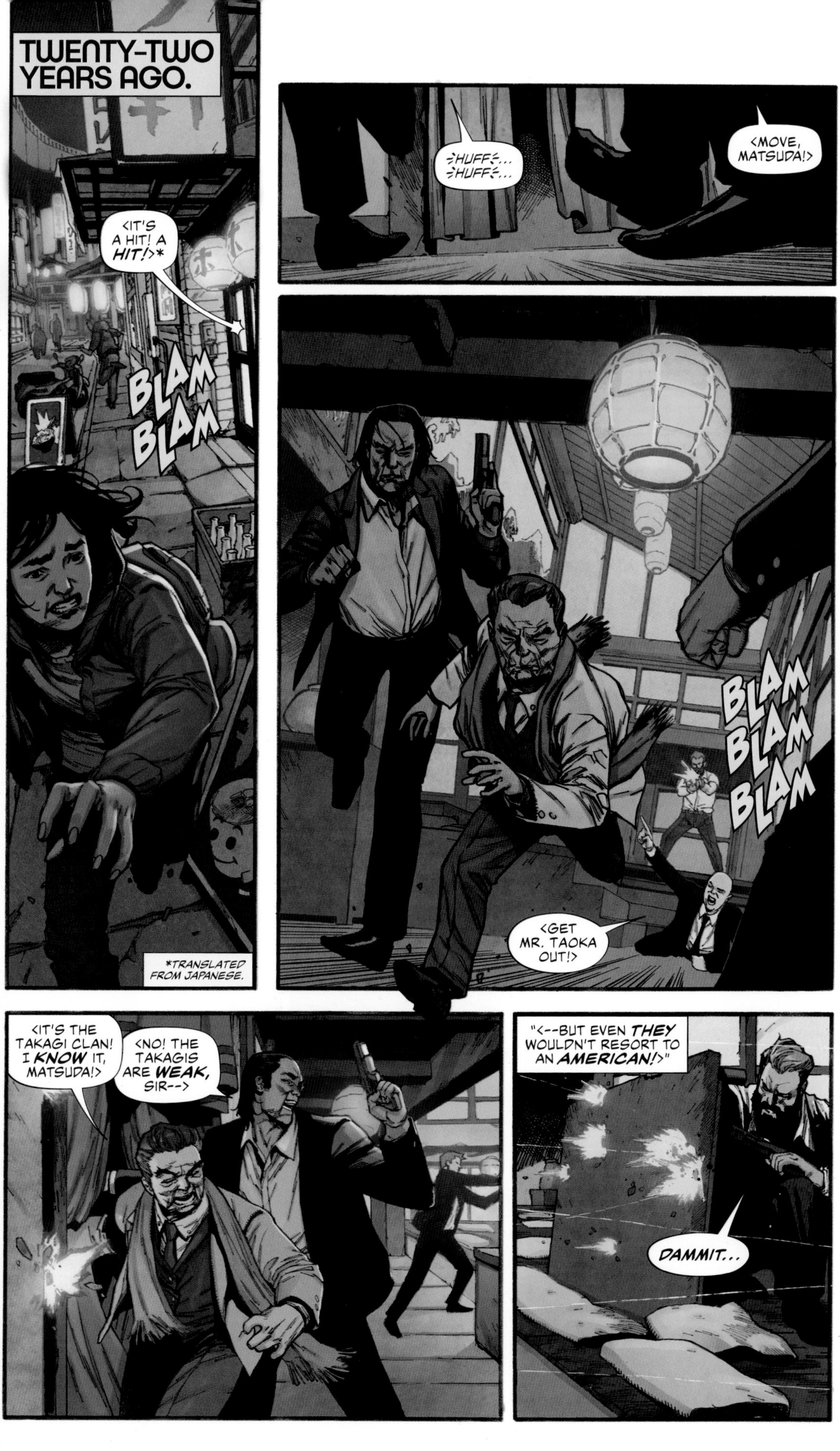
TWENTY-TWO YEARS AGO.
<IT'S A HIT! A HIT!>*
BLAM BLAM
*TRANSLATED FROM JAPANESE.
HUFF... HUFF...
<MOVE, MATSUDA!>
BLAM BLAM BLAM
<GET MR. TAOKA OUT!>
<IT'S THE TAKAGI CLAN! I KNOW IT, MATSUDA!>
<NO! THE TAKAGIS ARE WEAK, SIR-->
"<--BUT EVEN THEY WOULDN'T RESORT TO AN AMERICAN!>"
DAMMIT...

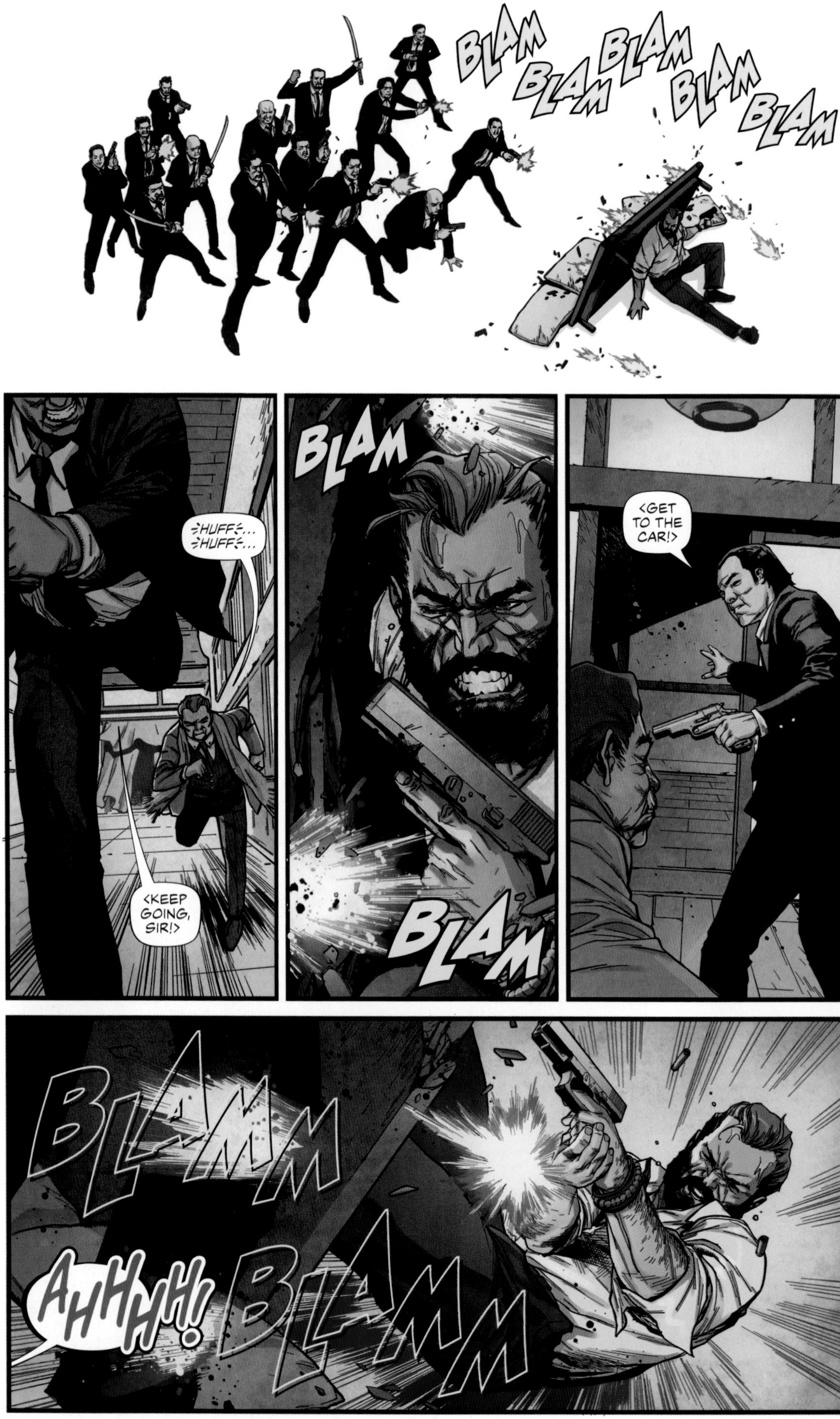
BLAM
BLAM
BLAM
BLAM
BLAM
HUFF... HUFF...
<KEEP GOING, SIR!>
BLAM
BLAM
<GET TO THE CAR!>
BLAMM
AHHHH!
BLAMM

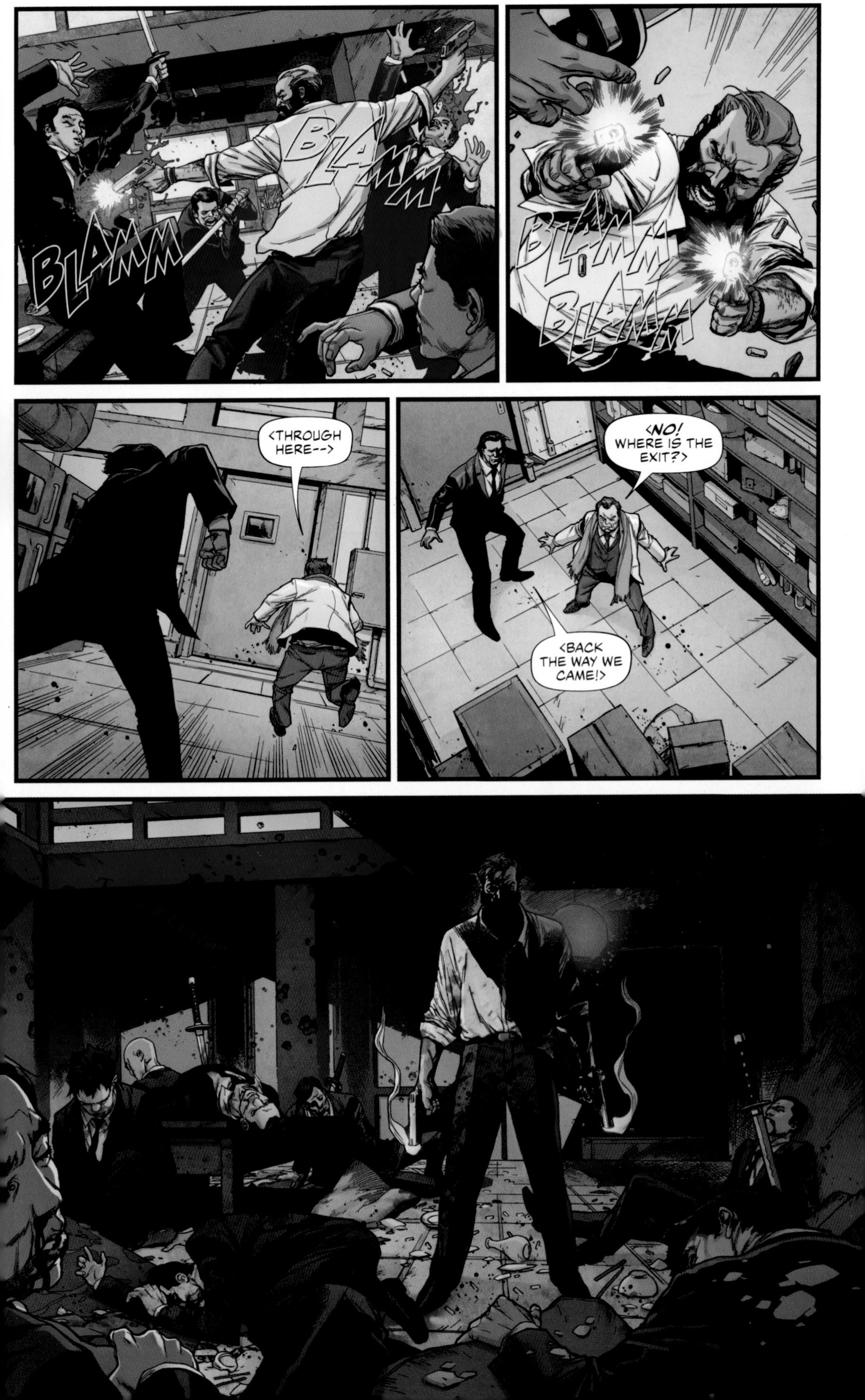
BLAMM
BLAMM
BLAMM
BLAMM
BLAMM
<THROUGH HERE-->
<NO! WHERE IS THE EXIT?>
<BACK THE WAY WE CAME!>

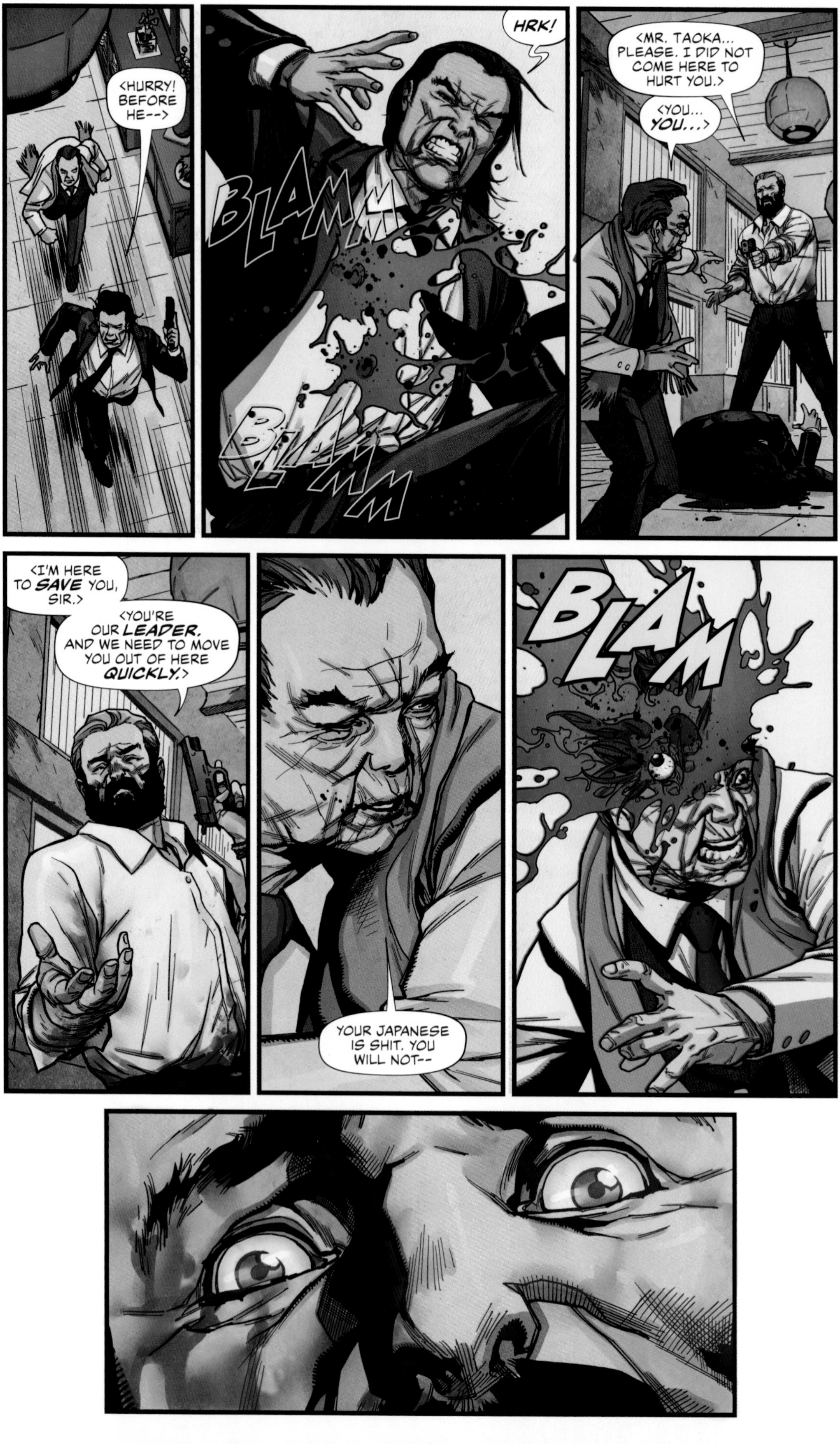

<HURRY! BEFORE HE-->
HRK!
BLAMM
BLAMM
<MR. TAOKA... PLEASE. I DID NOT COME HERE TO HURT YOU.>
<YOU... YOU...>
<I'M HERE TO SAVE YOU, SIR.>
<YOU'RE OUR LEADER, AND WE NEED TO MOVE YOU OUT OF HERE QUICKLY.>
YOUR JAPANESE IS SHIT. YOU WILL NOT--
BLAM

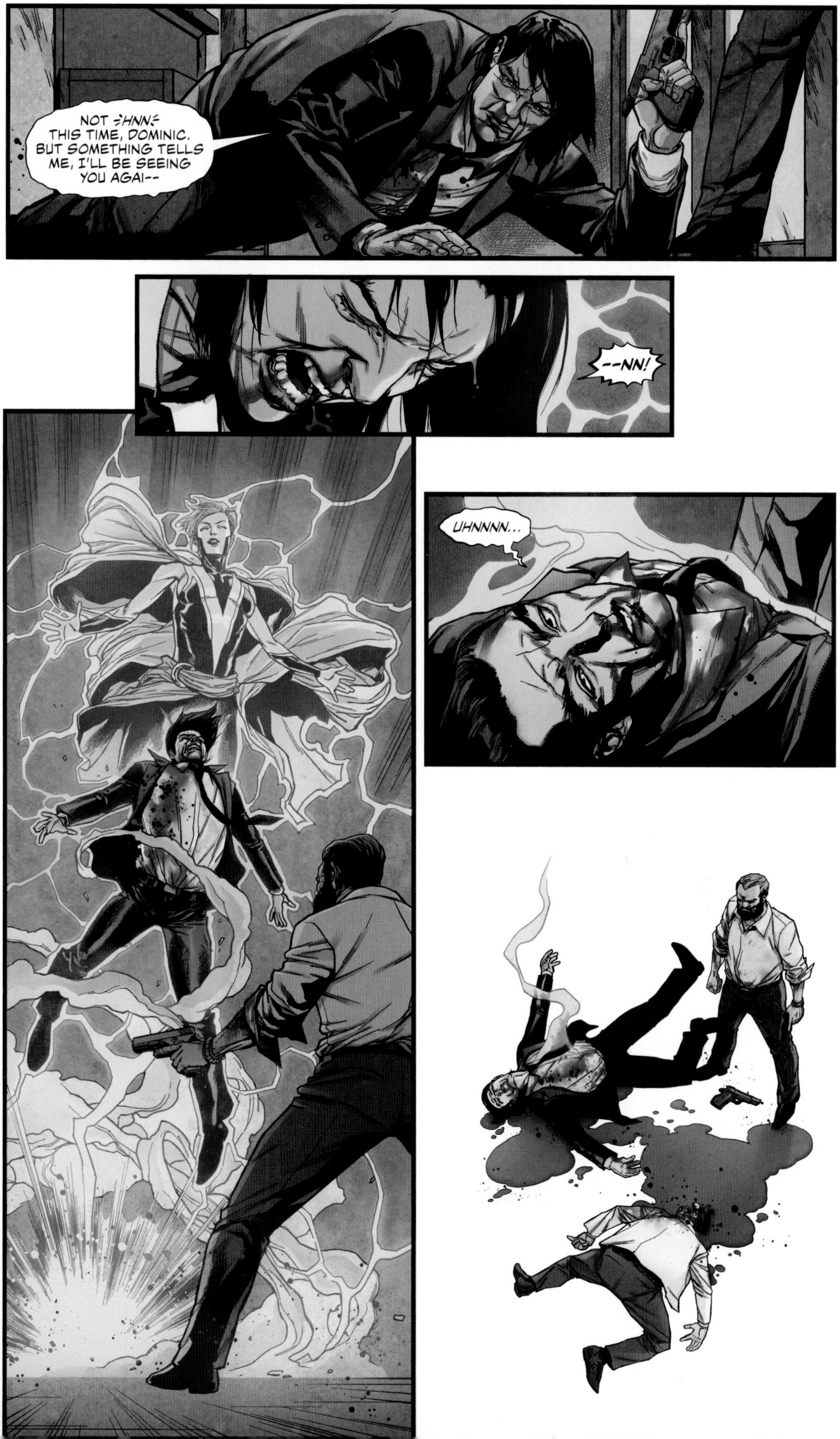
NOT -HNN- THIS TIME, DOMINIC. BUT SOMETHING TELLS ME, I'LL BE SEEING YOU AGAI--
--NN!
UHNNNN...

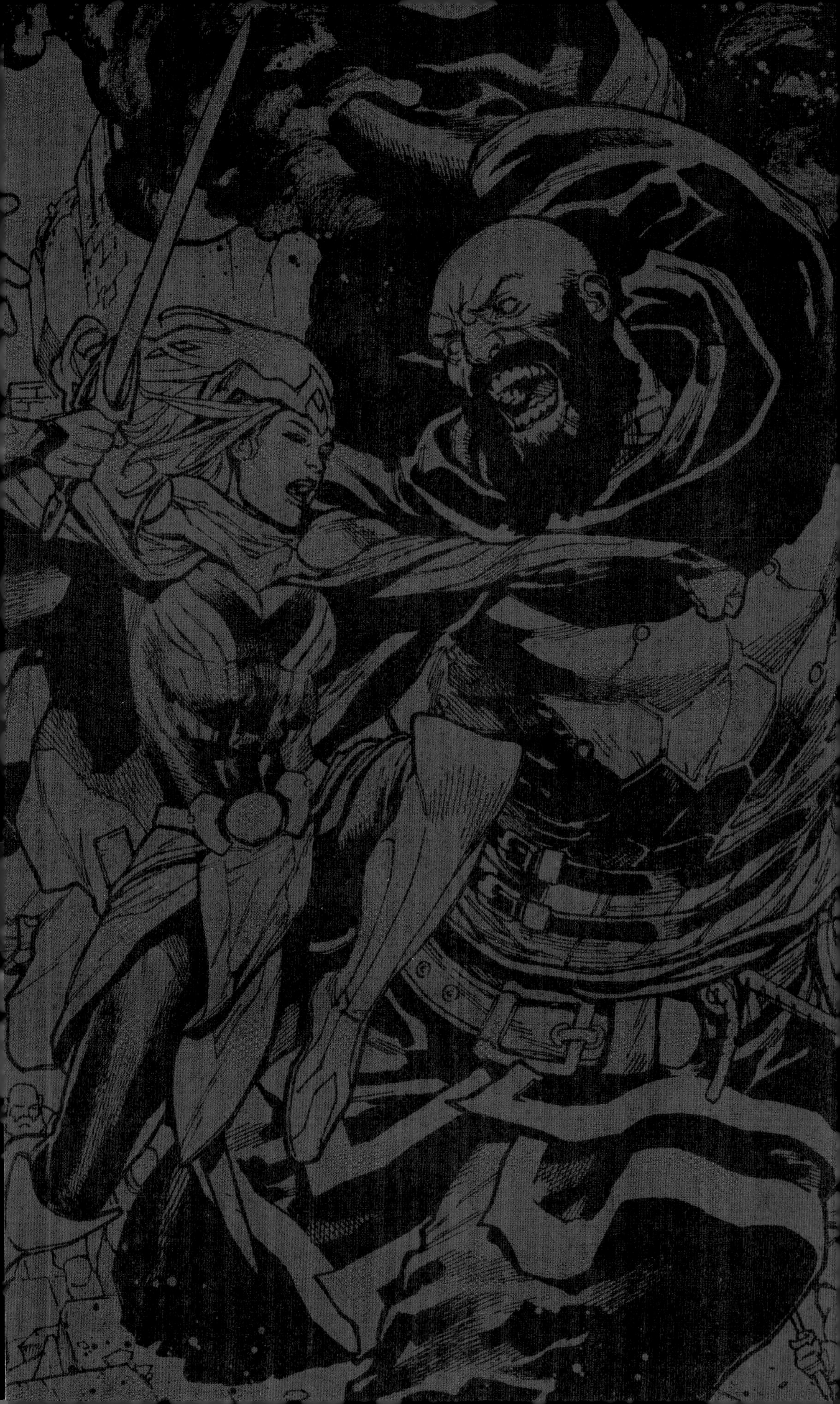

CHAPTER I
As The World Turns

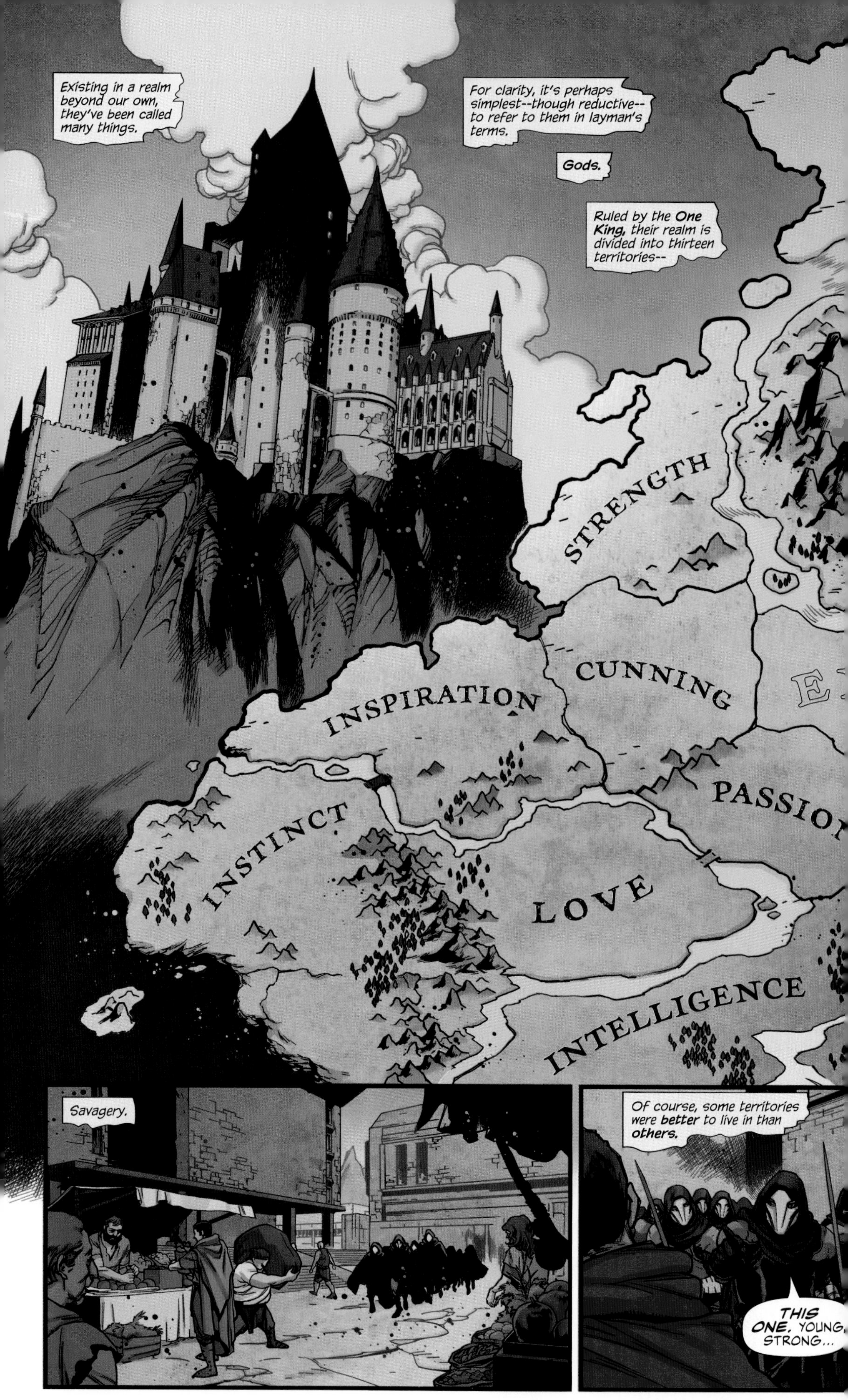

Existing in a realm beyond our own, they've been called many things.
For clarity, it's perhaps simplest--though reductive--to refer to them in layman's terms.
Gods.
Ruled by the One King, their realm is divided into thirteen territories--
STRENGTH
CUNNING
INSPIRATION
INSTINCT
LOVE
PASSIO
INTELLIGENCE
Savagery.
Of course, some territories were better to live in than others.
THIS ONE. YOUNG, STRONG...

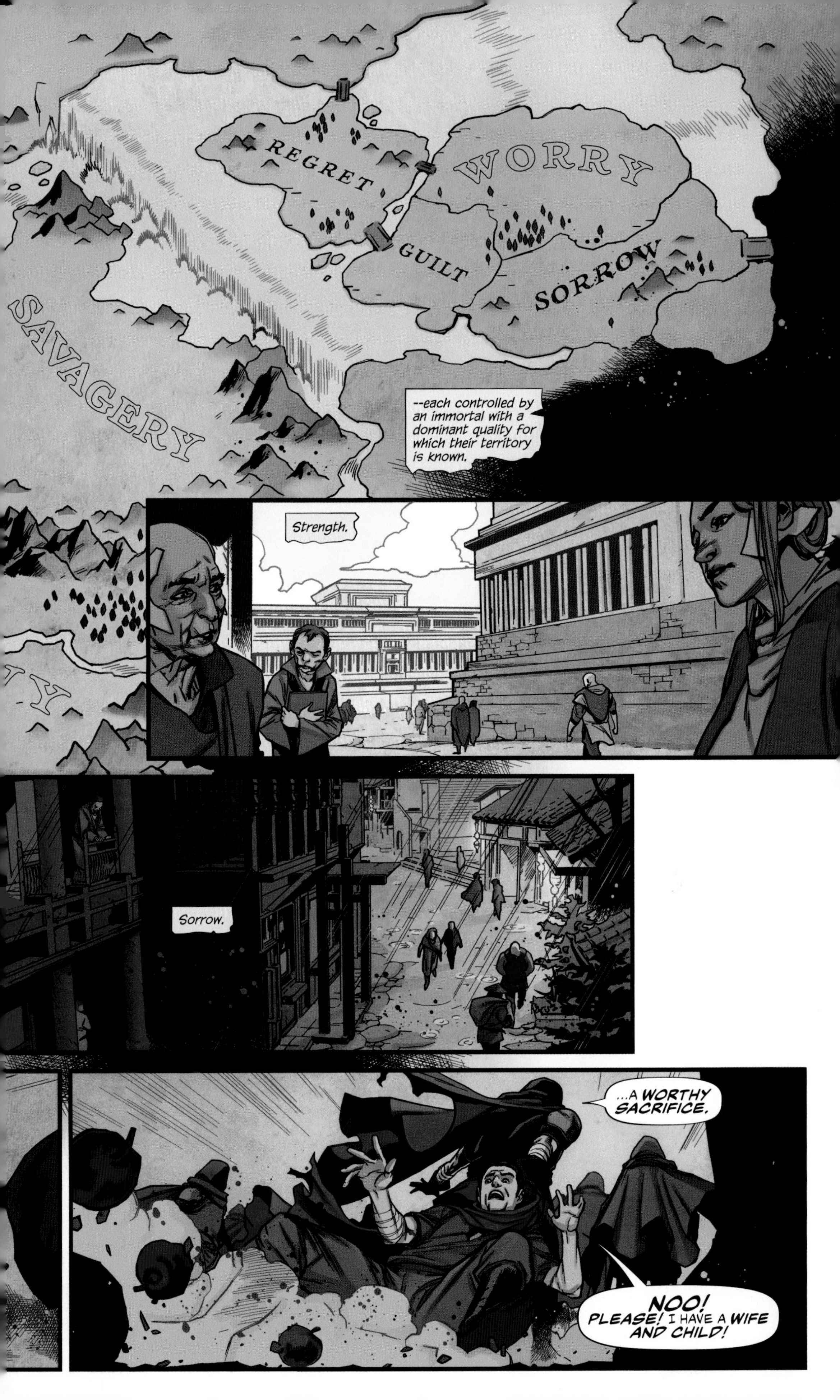

REGRET
WORRY
GUILT
SORROW
SAVAGERY
--each controlled by an immortal with a dominant quality for which their territory is known.
Strength.
Sorrow.
...A WORTHY SACRIFICE.
NOO! PLEASE! I HAVE A WIFE AND CHILD!

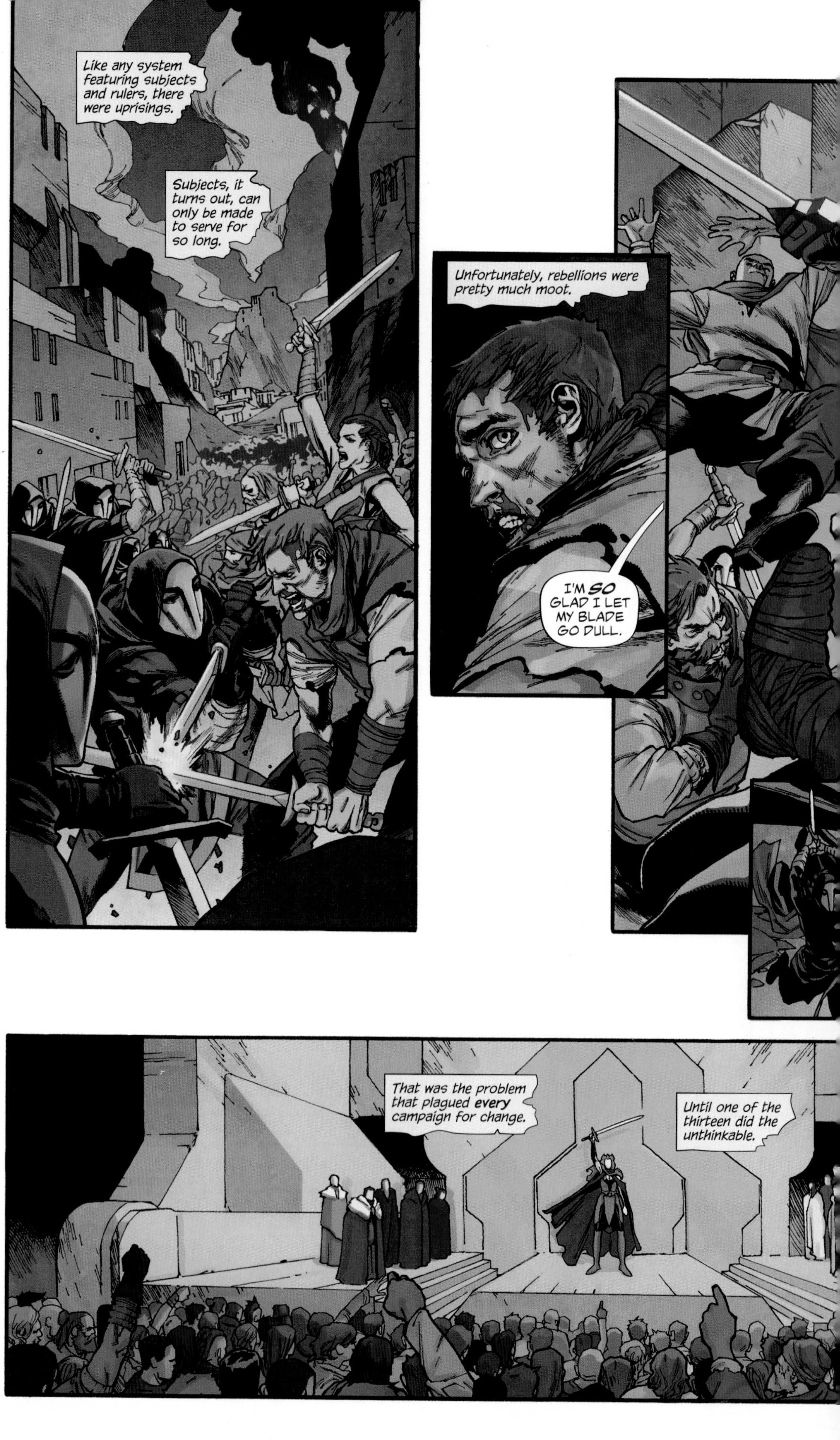
Like any system featuring subjects and rulers, there were uprisings.
Subjects, it turns out, can only be made to serve for so long.
Unfortunately, rebellions were pretty much moot.
I'M *SO* GLAD I LET MY BLADE GO DULL.
That was the problem that plagued **every** campaign for change.
Until one of the thirteen did the unthinkable.

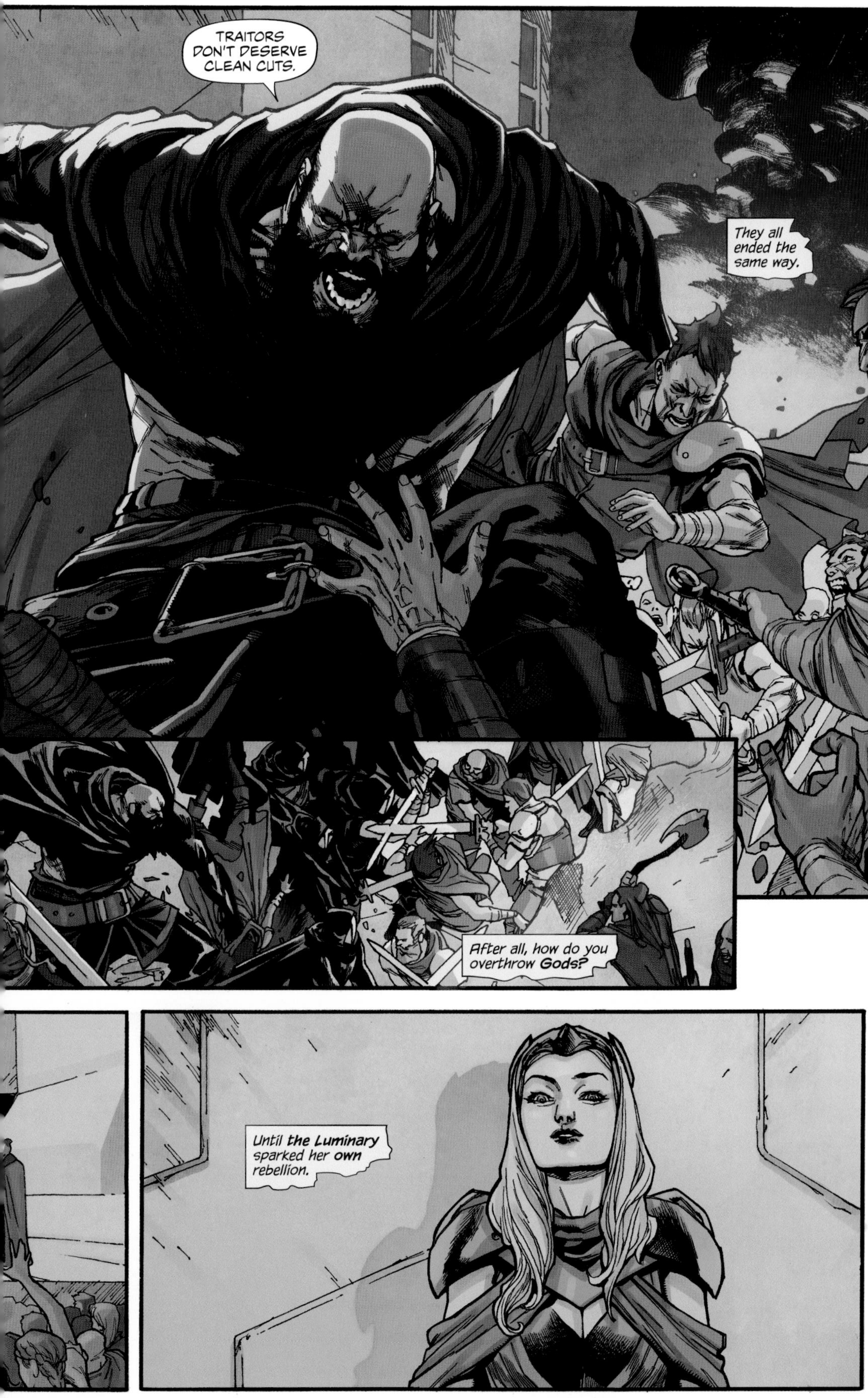
TRAITORS DON'T DESERVE CLEAN CUTS.
They all ended the same way.
After all, how do you overthrow Gods?
Until the Luminary sparked her own rebellion.

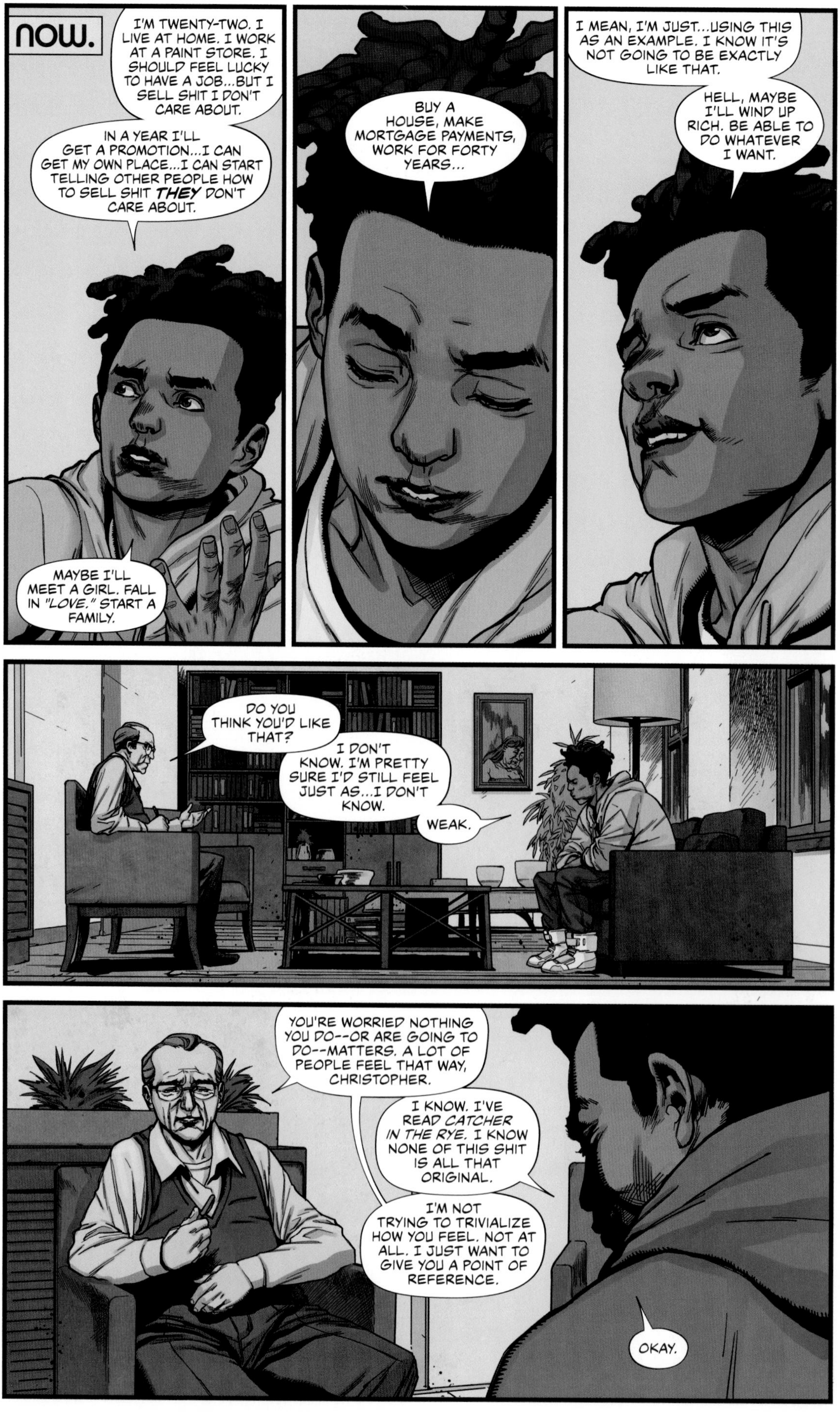
NOW.
I'M TWENTY-TWO. I LIVE AT HOME. I WORK AT A PAINT STORE. I SHOULD FEEL LUCKY TO HAVE A JOB...BUT I SELL SHIT I DON'T CARE ABOUT.
IN A YEAR I'LL GET A PROMOTION...I CAN GET MY OWN PLACE...I CAN START TELLING OTHER PEOPLE HOW TO SELL SHIT THEY DON'T CARE ABOUT.
MAYBE I'LL MEET A GIRL. FALL IN "LOVE." START A FAMILY.
BUY A HOUSE, MAKE MORTGAGE PAYMENTS, WORK FOR FORTY YEARS...
I MEAN, I'M JUST...USING THIS AS AN EXAMPLE. I KNOW IT'S NOT GOING TO BE EXACTLY LIKE THAT.
HELL, MAYBE I'LL WIND UP RICH. BE ABLE TO DO WHATEVER I WANT.
DO YOU THINK YOU'D LIKE THAT?
I DON'T KNOW. I'M PRETTY SURE I'D STILL FEEL JUST AS...I DON'T KNOW.
WEAK.
YOU'RE WORRIED NOTHING YOU DO--OR ARE GOING TO DO--MATTERS. A LOT OF PEOPLE FEEL THAT WAY, CHRISTOPHER.
I KNOW. I'VE READ CATCHER IN THE RYE. I KNOW NONE OF THIS SHIT IS ALL THAT ORIGINAL.
I'M NOT TRYING TO TRIVIALIZE HOW YOU FEEL. NOT AT ALL. I JUST WANT TO GIVE YOU A POINT OF REFERENCE.
OKAY.

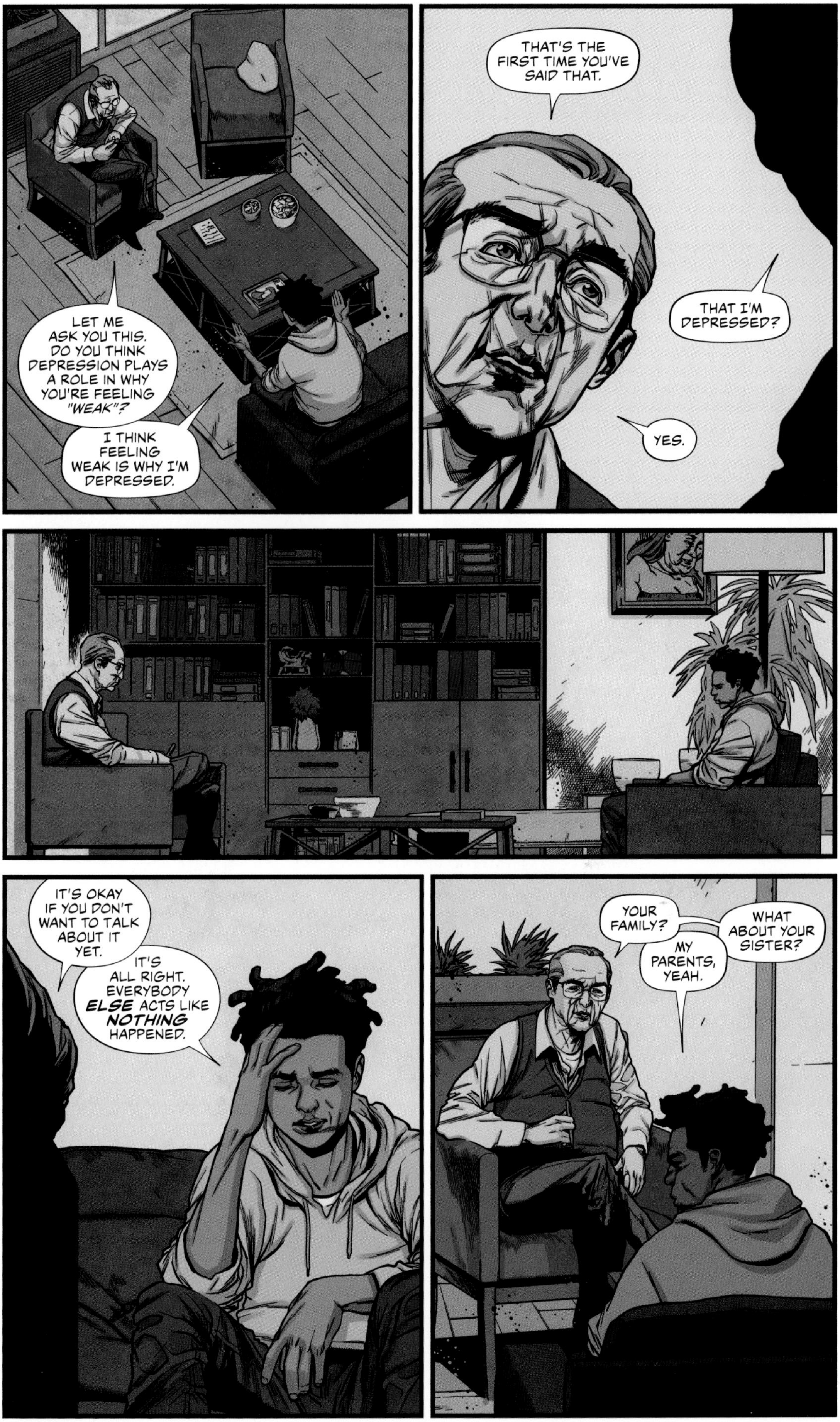
LET ME ASK YOU THIS. DO YOU THINK DEPRESSION PLAYS A ROLE IN WHY YOU'RE FEELING *"WEAK"*?
I THINK FEELING WEAK IS WHY I'M DEPRESSED.
THAT'S THE FIRST TIME YOU'VE SAID THAT.
THAT I'M DEPRESSED?
YES.
IT'S OKAY IF YOU DON'T WANT TO TALK ABOUT IT YET.
IT'S ALL RIGHT. EVERYBODY ***ELSE*** ACTS LIKE ***NOTHING*** HAPPENED.
YOUR FAMILY?
MY PARENTS, YEAH.
WHAT ABOUT YOUR SISTER?

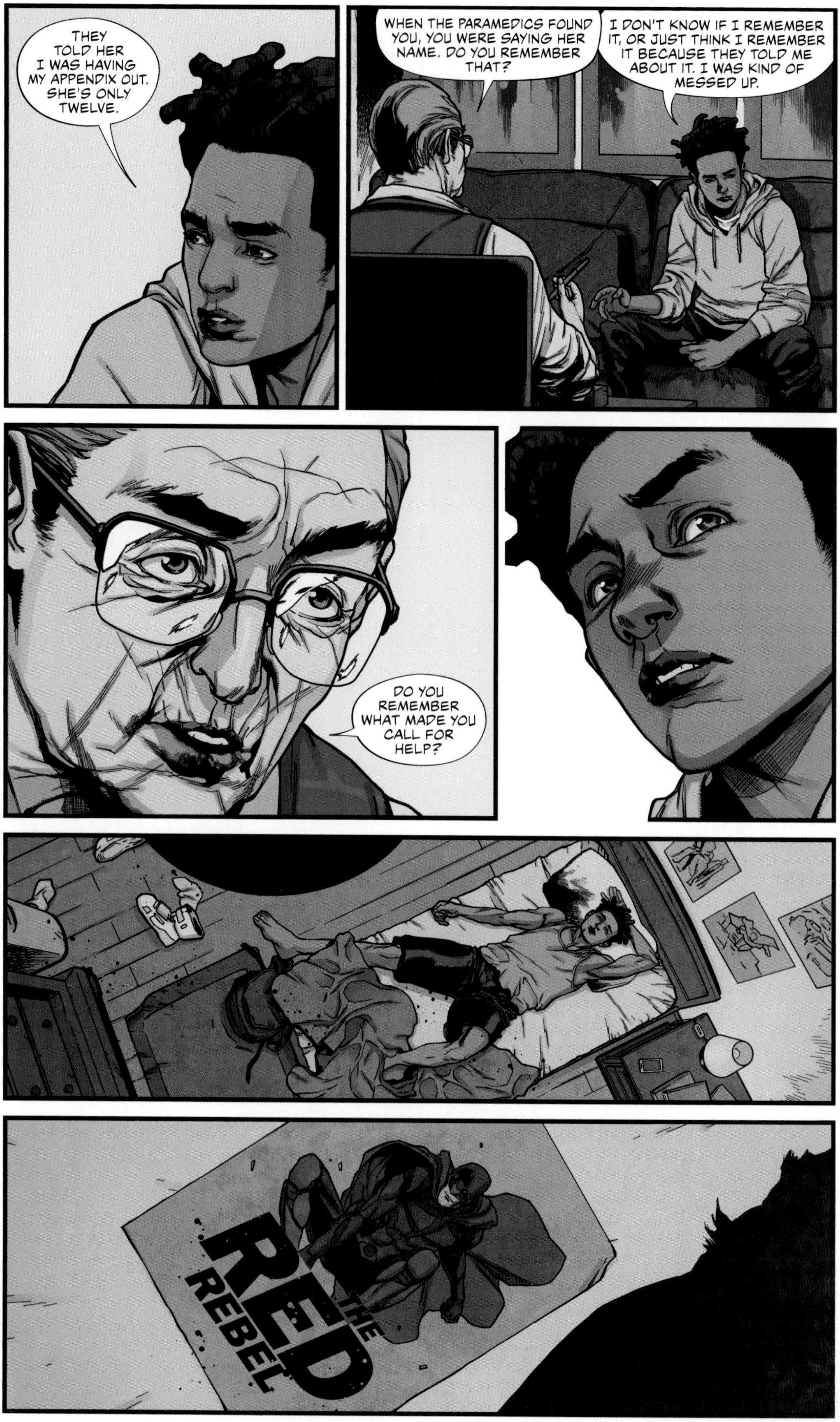
THEY TOLD HER I WAS HAVING MY APPENDIX OUT. SHE'S ONLY TWELVE.
WHEN THE PARAMEDICS FOUND YOU, YOU WERE SAYING HER NAME. DO YOU REMEMBER THAT?
I DON'T KNOW IF I REMEMBER IT, OR JUST THINK I REMEMBER IT BECAUSE THEY TOLD ME ABOUT IT. I WAS KIND OF MESSED UP.
DO YOU REMEMBER WHAT MADE YOU CALL FOR HELP?
THE RED REBEL

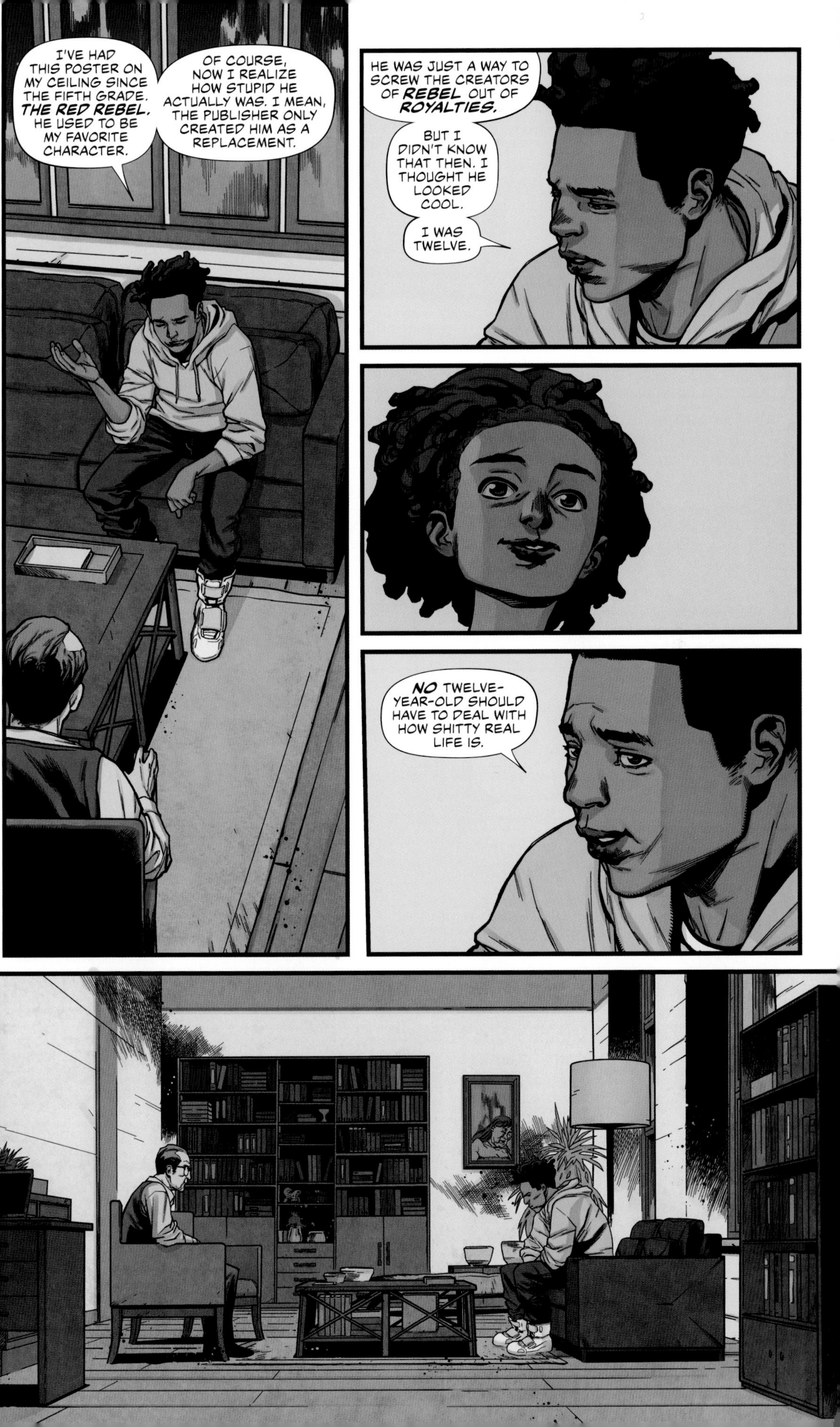
I'VE HAD THIS POSTER ON MY CEILING SINCE THE FIFTH GRADE. THE RED REBEL. HE USED TO BE MY FAVORITE CHARACTER.
OF COURSE, NOW I REALIZE HOW STUPID HE ACTUALLY WAS. I MEAN, THE PUBLISHER ONLY CREATED HIM AS A REPLACEMENT.
HE WAS JUST A WAY TO SCREW THE CREATORS OF REBEL OUT OF ROYALTIES.
BUT I DIDN'T KNOW THAT THEN. I THOUGHT HE LOOKED COOL.
I WAS TWELVE.
NO TWELVE-YEAR-OLD SHOULD HAVE TO DEAL WITH HOW SHITTY REAL LIFE IS.

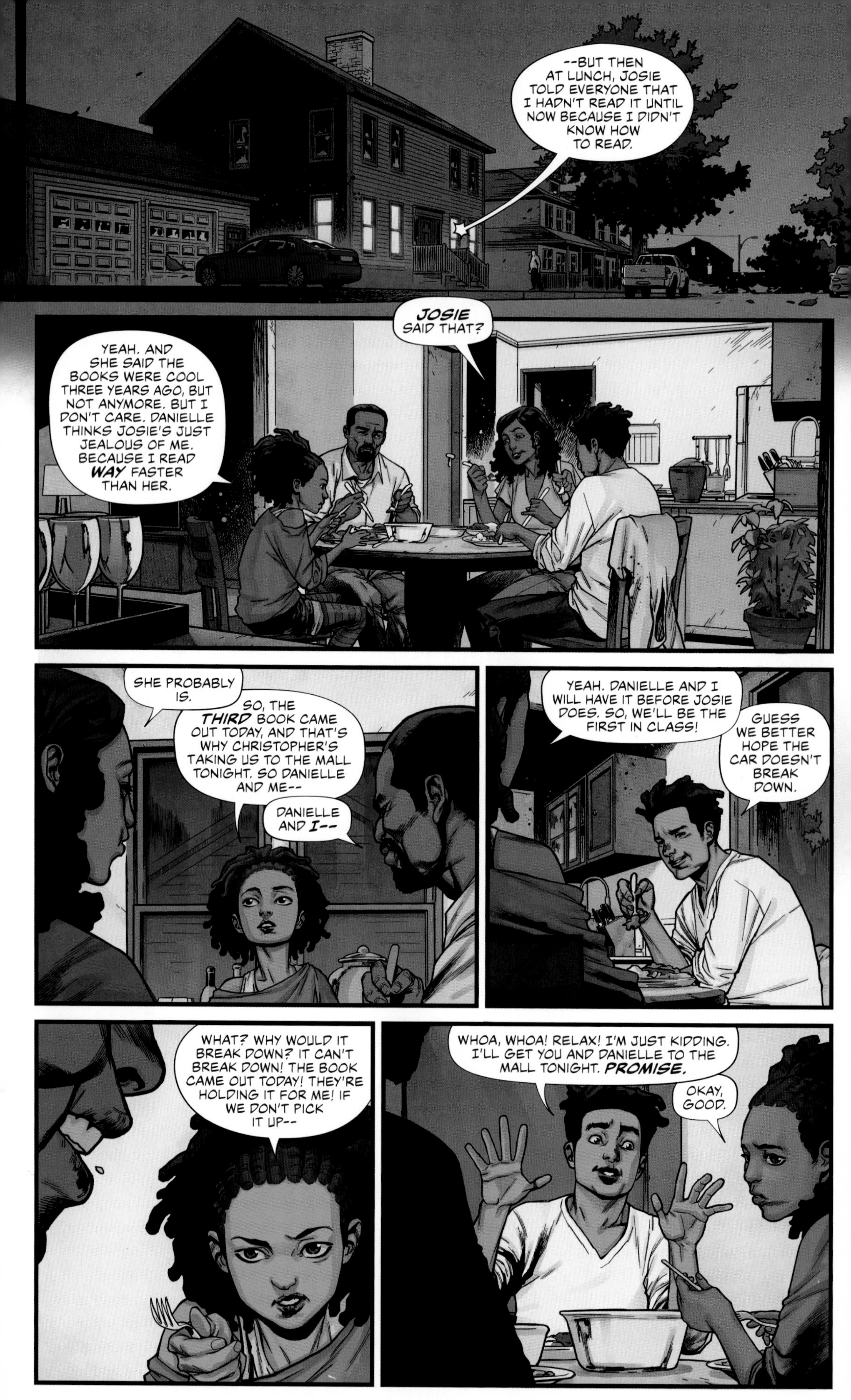
--BUT THEN AT LUNCH, JOSIE TOLD EVERYONE THAT I HADN'T READ IT UNTIL NOW BECAUSE I DIDN'T KNOW HOW TO READ.
JOSIE SAID THAT?
YEAH. AND SHE SAID THE BOOKS WERE COOL THREE YEARS AGO, BUT NOT ANYMORE. BUT I DON'T CARE. DANIELLE THINKS JOSIE'S JUST JEALOUS OF ME. BECAUSE I READ WAY FASTER THAN HER.
SHE PROBABLY IS.
SO, THE THIRD BOOK CAME OUT TODAY, AND THAT'S WHY CHRISTOPHER'S TAKING US TO THE MALL TONIGHT. SO DANIELLE AND ME--
DANIELLE AND I--
YEAH. DANIELLE AND I WILL HAVE IT BEFORE JOSIE DOES. SO, WE'LL BE THE FIRST IN CLASS!
GUESS WE BETTER HOPE THE CAR DOESN'T BREAK DOWN.
WHAT? WHY WOULD IT BREAK DOWN? IT CAN'T BREAK DOWN! THE BOOK CAME OUT TODAY! THEY'RE HOLDING IT FOR ME! IF WE DON'T PICK IT UP--
WHOA, WHOA! RELAX! I'M JUST KIDDING. I'LL GET YOU AND DANIELLE TO THE MALL TONIGHT. PROMISE.
OKAY, GOOD.

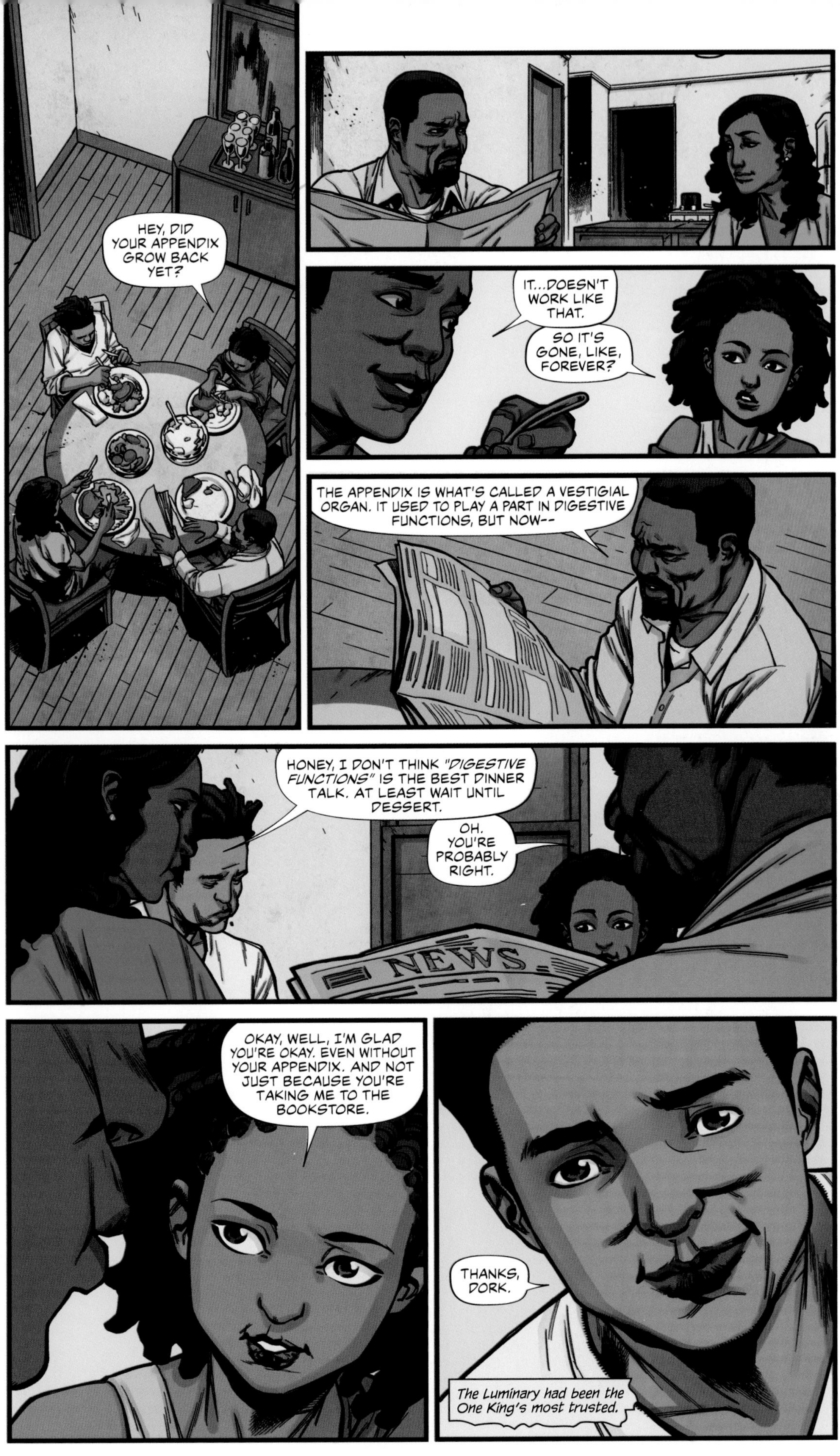
HEY, DID YOUR APPENDIX GROW BACK YET?
IT...DOESN'T WORK LIKE THAT.
SO IT'S GONE, LIKE, FOREVER?
THE APPENDIX IS WHAT'S CALLED A VESTIGIAL ORGAN. IT USED TO PLAY A PART IN DIGESTIVE FUNCTIONS, BUT NOW--
HONEY, I DON'T THINK "DIGESTIVE FUNCTIONS" IS THE BEST DINNER TALK. AT LEAST WAIT UNTIL DESSERT.
OH. YOU'RE PROBABLY RIGHT.
NEWS
OKAY, WELL, I'M GLAD YOU'RE OKAY. EVEN WITHOUT YOUR APPENDIX. AND NOT JUST BECAUSE YOU'RE TAKING ME TO THE BOOKSTORE.
THANKS, DORK.
The Luminary had been the One King's most trusted.

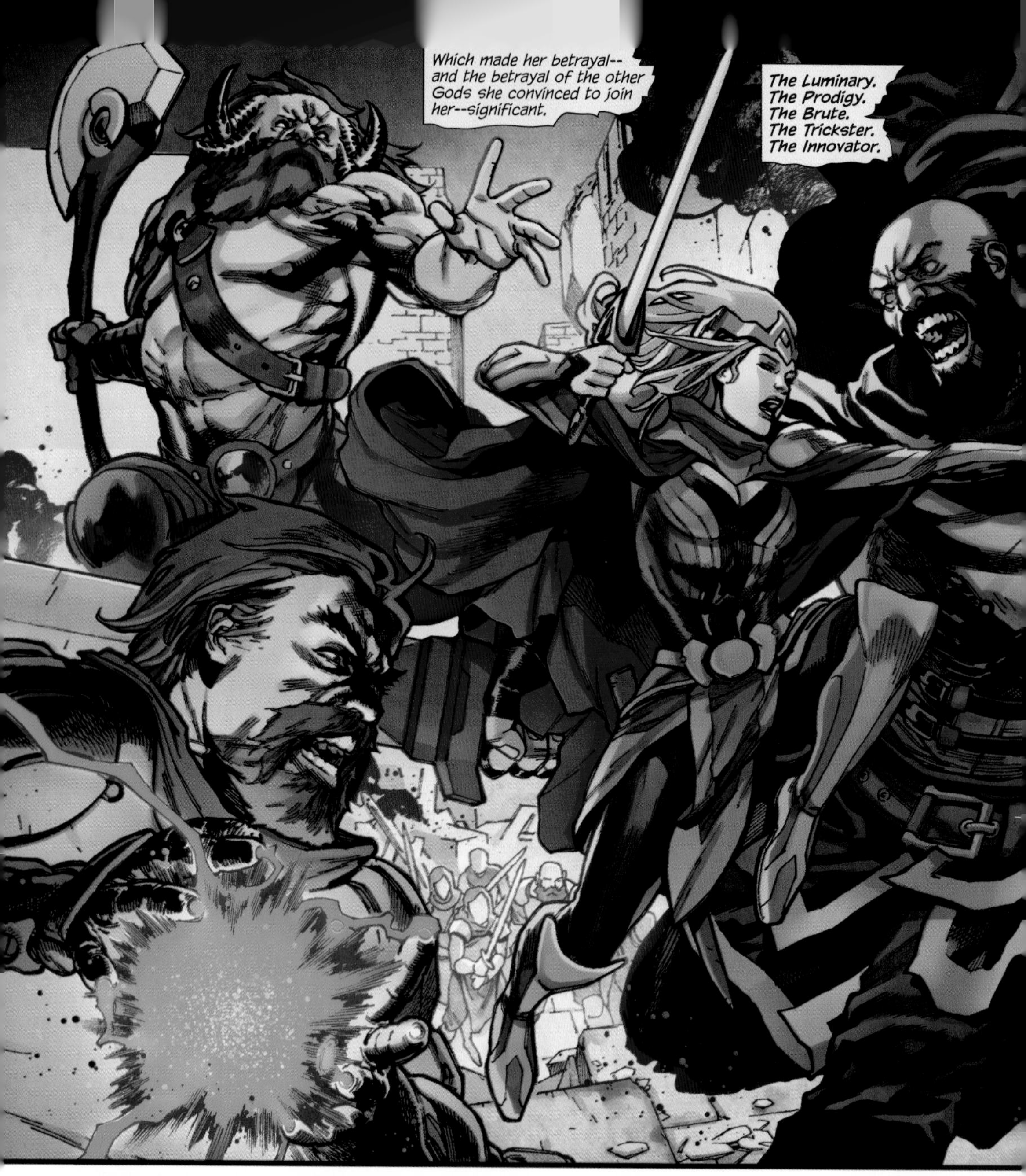
Which made her betrayal--and the betrayal of the other Gods she convinced to join her--significant.
The Luminary.
The Prodigy.
The Brute.
The Trickster.
The Innovator.

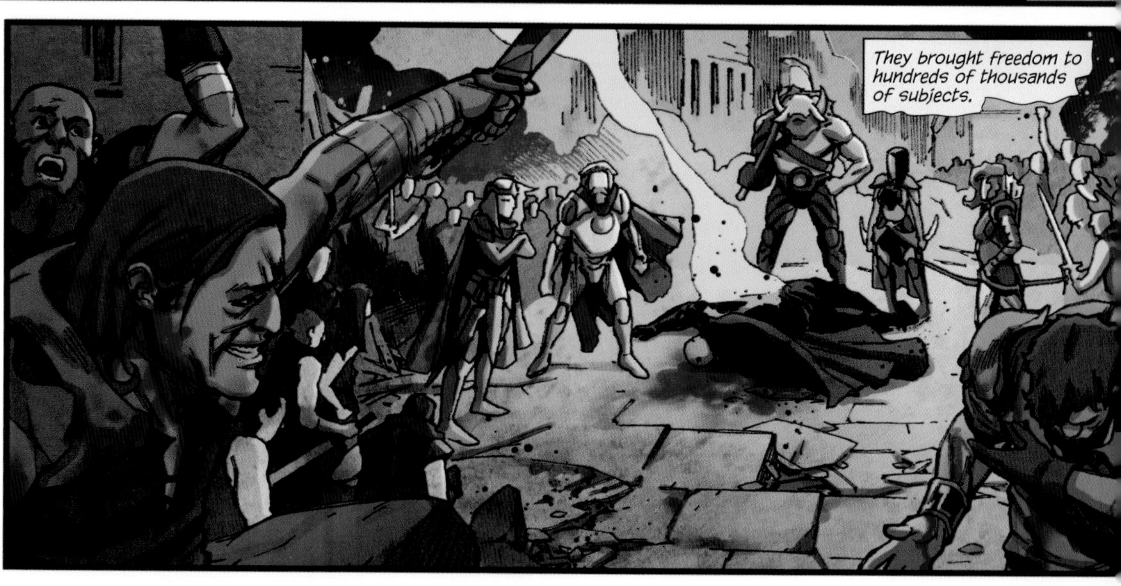
They brought freedom to hundreds of thousands of subjects.

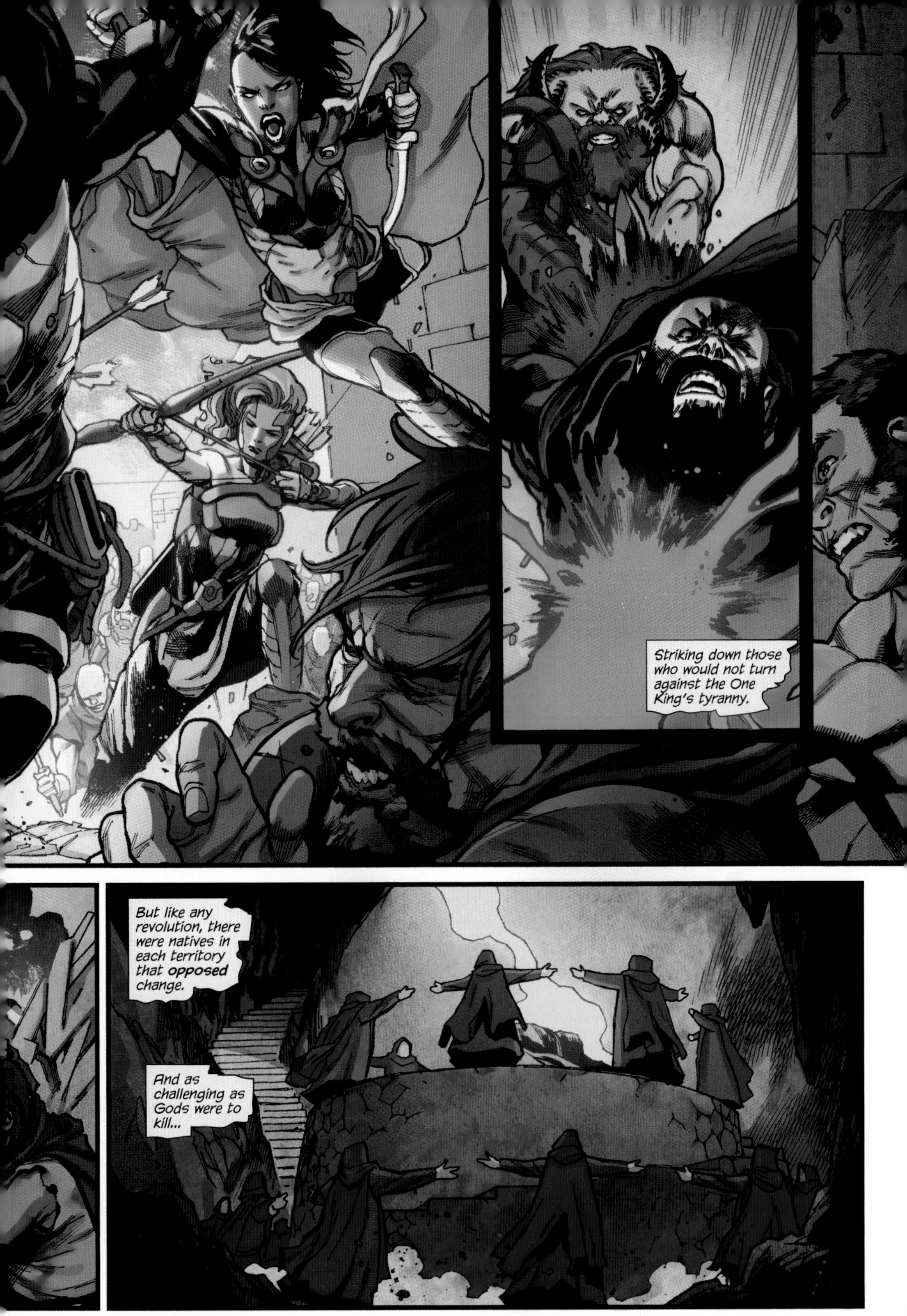
Striking down those who would not turn against the One King's tyranny.
But like any revolution, there were natives in each territory that **opposed** change.
And as challenging as Gods were to kill...

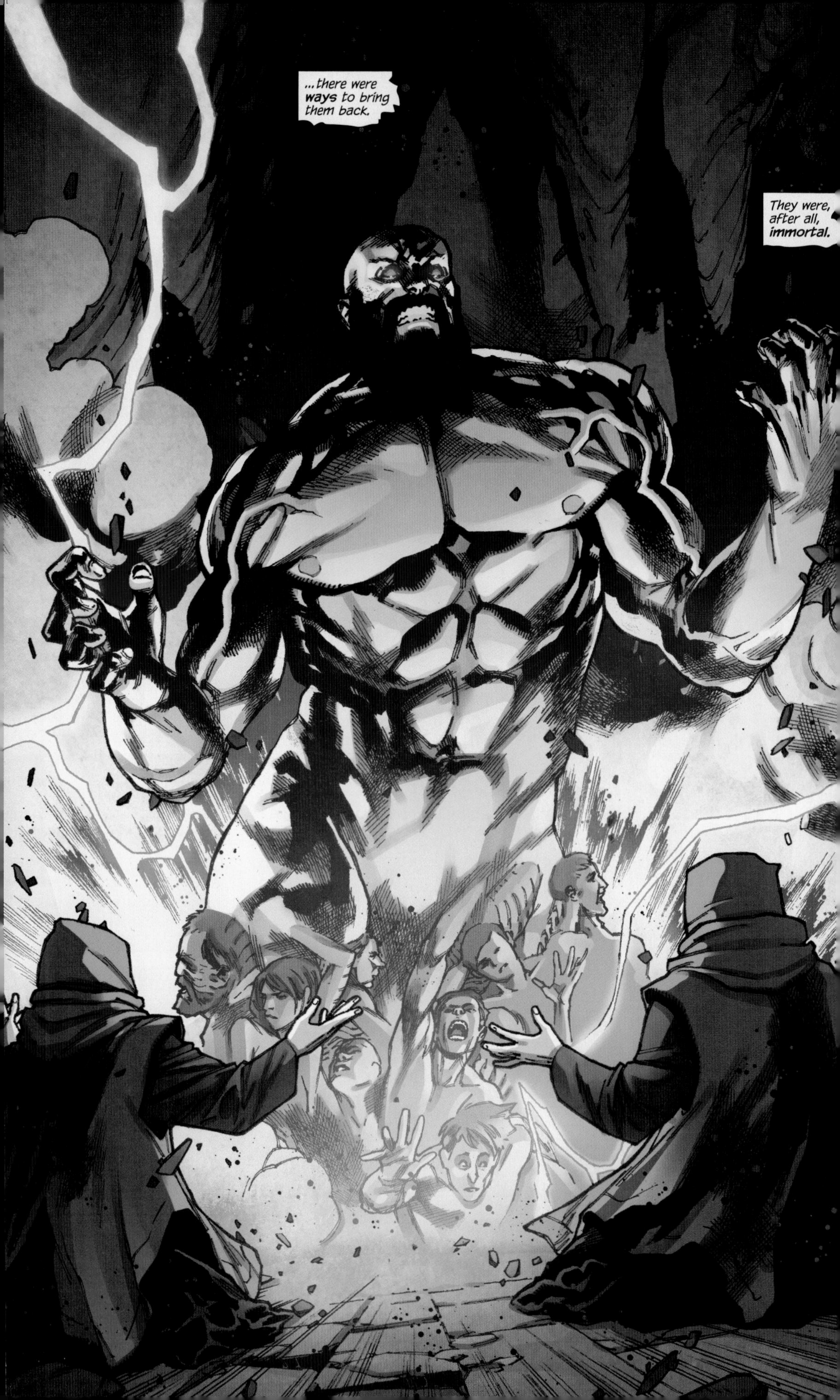
...there were ways to bring them back.
They were, after all, immortal.

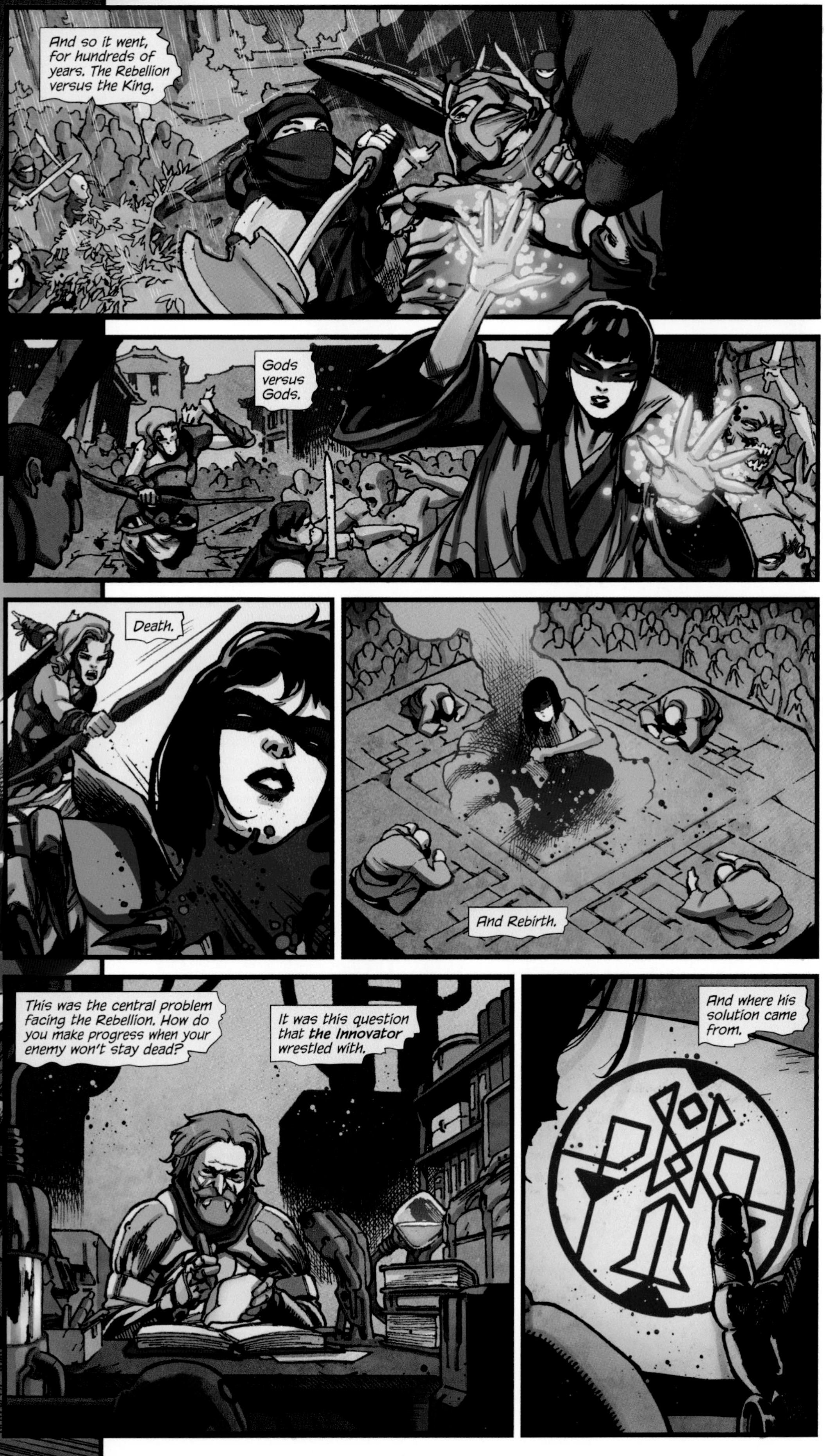
And so it went, for hundreds of years. The Rebellion versus the King.
Gods versus Gods.
Death.
And Rebirth.
This was the central problem facing the Rebellion. How do you make progress when your enemy won't stay dead?
It was this question that **the Innovator** wrestled with.
And where his solution came from.

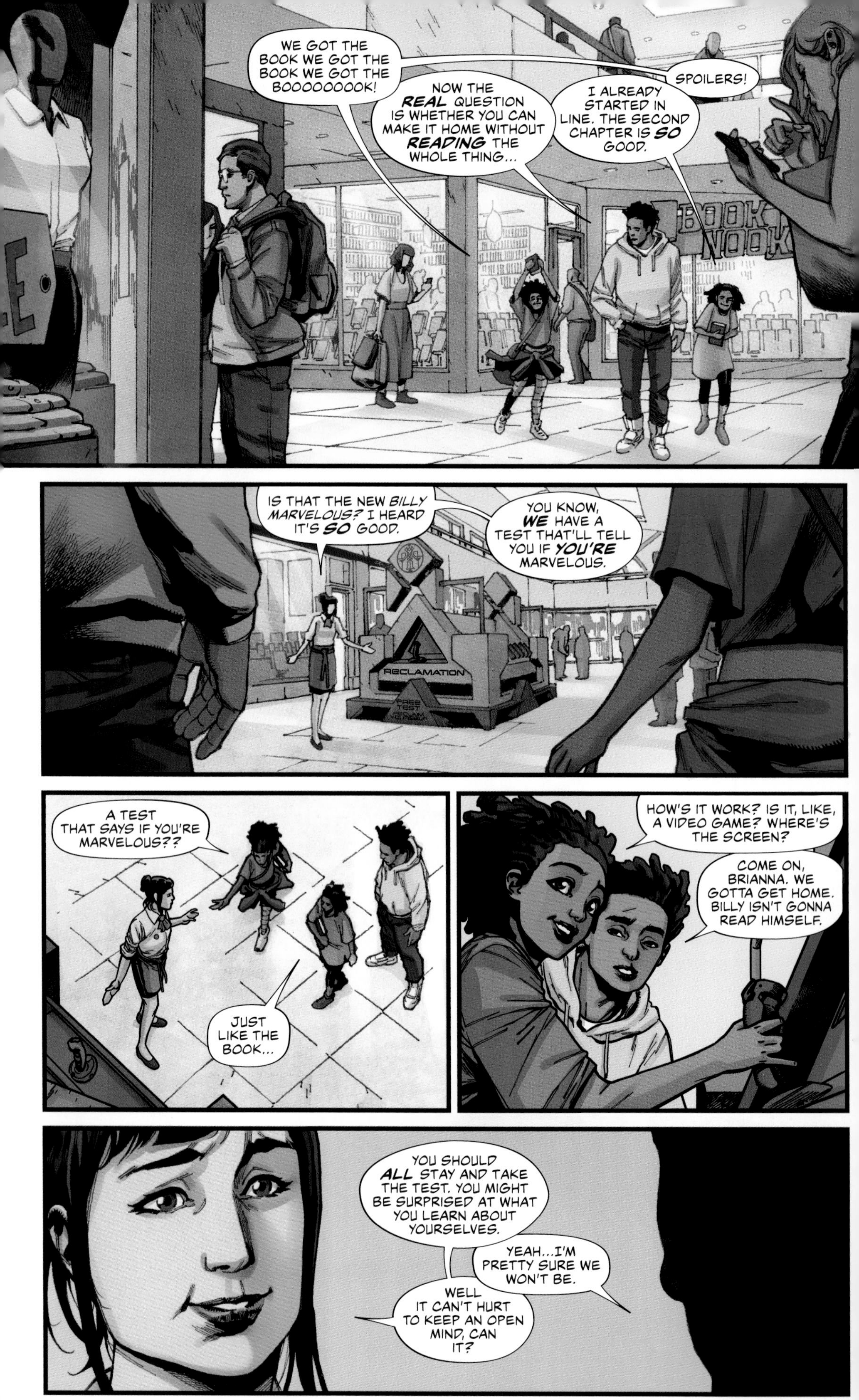

WE GOT THE BOOK WE GOT THE BOOK WE GOT THE BOOOOOOOOK!
SPOILERS!
NOW THE ***REAL*** QUESTION IS WHETHER YOU CAN MAKE IT HOME WITHOUT ***READING*** THE WHOLE THING...
I ALREADY STARTED IN LINE. THE SECOND CHAPTER IS ***SO*** GOOD.
BOOK NOOK
IS THAT THE NEW *BILLY MARVELOUS?* I HEARD IT'S ***SO*** GOOD.
YOU KNOW, ***WE*** HAVE A TEST THAT'LL TELL YOU IF ***YOU'RE*** MARVELOUS.
RECLAMATION
FREE TEST
A TEST THAT SAYS IF YOU'RE MARVELOUS??
JUST LIKE THE BOOK...
HOW'S IT WORK? IS IT, LIKE, A VIDEO GAME? WHERE'S THE SCREEN?
COME ON, BRIANNA. WE GOTTA GET HOME. BILLY ISN'T GONNA READ HIMSELF.
YOU SHOULD ***ALL*** STAY AND TAKE THE TEST. YOU MIGHT BE SURPRISED AT WHAT YOU LEARN ABOUT YOURSELVES.
YEAH...I'M PRETTY SURE WE WON'T BE.
WELL IT CAN'T HURT TO KEEP AN OPEN MIND, CAN IT?

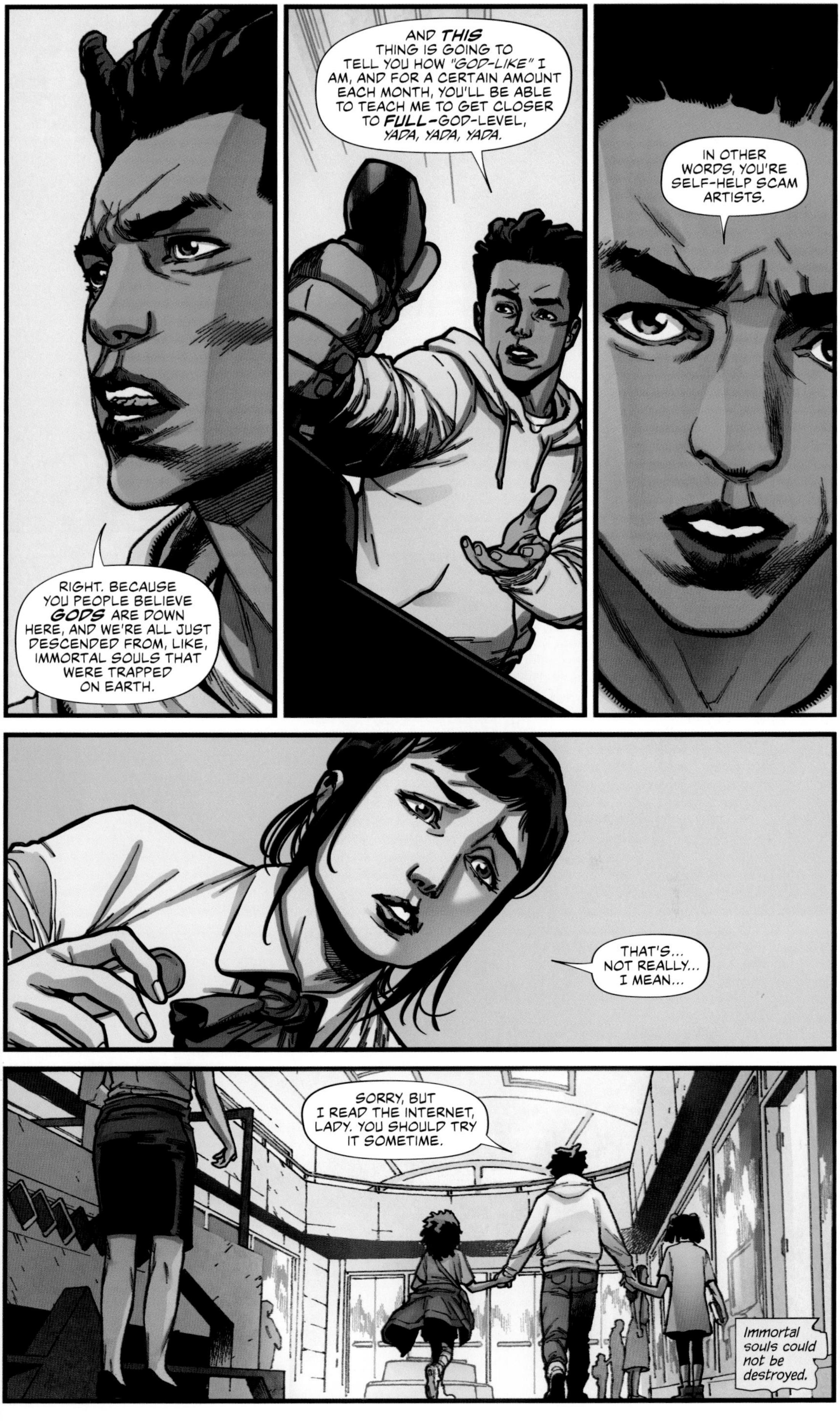
RIGHT. BECAUSE YOU PEOPLE BELIEVE GODS ARE DOWN HERE, AND WE'RE ALL JUST DESCENDED FROM, LIKE, IMMORTAL SOULS THAT WERE TRAPPED ON EARTH.
AND THIS THING IS GOING TO TELL YOU HOW "GOD-LIKE" I AM, AND FOR A CERTAIN AMOUNT EACH MONTH, YOU'LL BE ABLE TO TEACH ME TO GET CLOSER TO FULL-GOD-LEVEL, YADA, YADA, YADA.
IN OTHER WORDS, YOU'RE SELF-HELP SCAM ARTISTS.
THAT'S... NOT REALLY... I MEAN...
SORRY, BUT I READ THE INTERNET, LADY. YOU SHOULD TRY IT SOMETIME.
Immortal souls could not be destroyed.

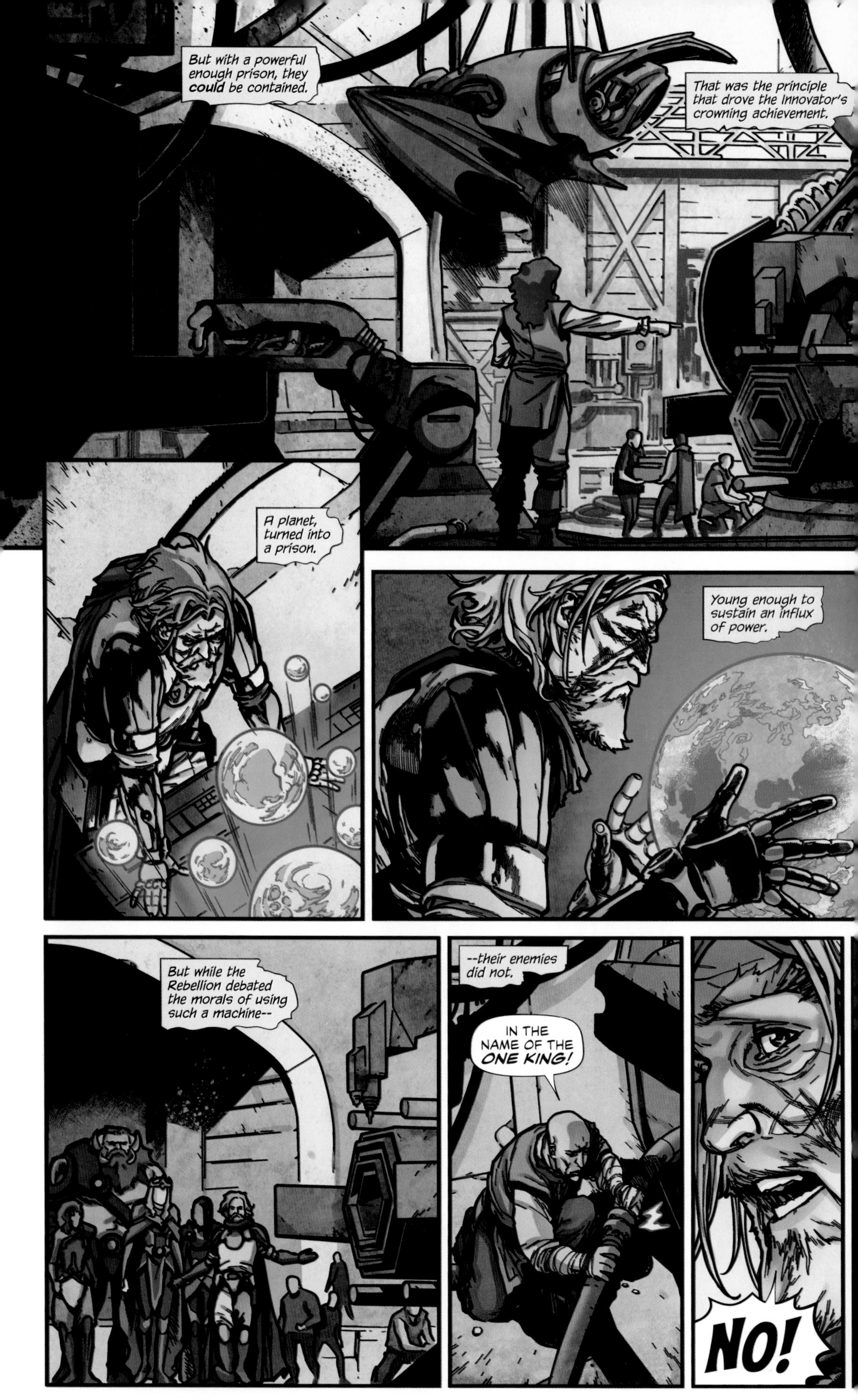

But with a powerful enough prison, they **could** be contained.
That was the principle that drove the Innovator's crowning achievement.
A planet, turned into a prison.
Young enough to sustain an influx of power.
But while the Rebellion debated the morals of using such a machine--
--their enemies did not.
IN THE NAME OF THE ONE KING!
NO!

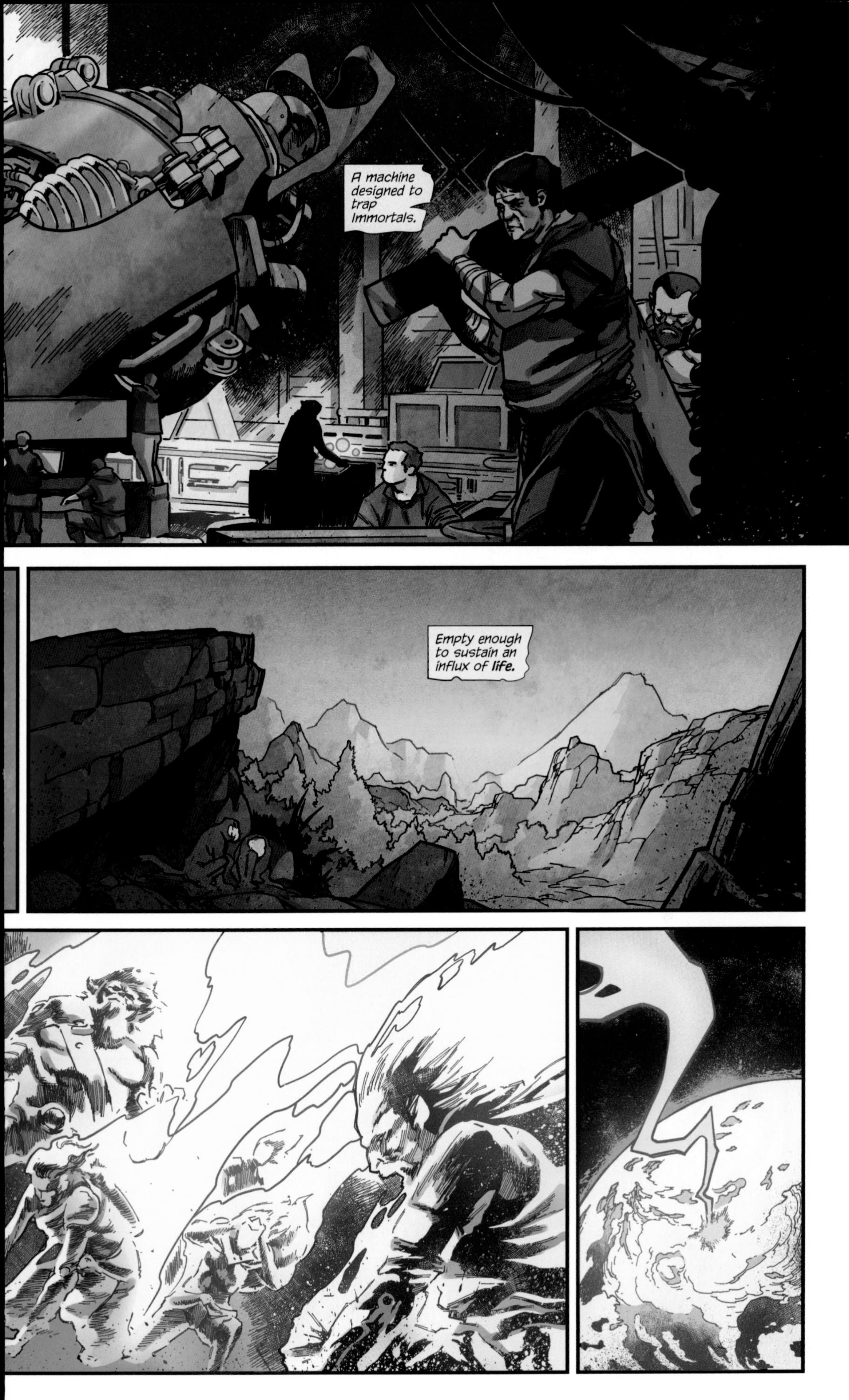
A machine designed to trap Immortals.
Empty enough to sustain an influx of life.

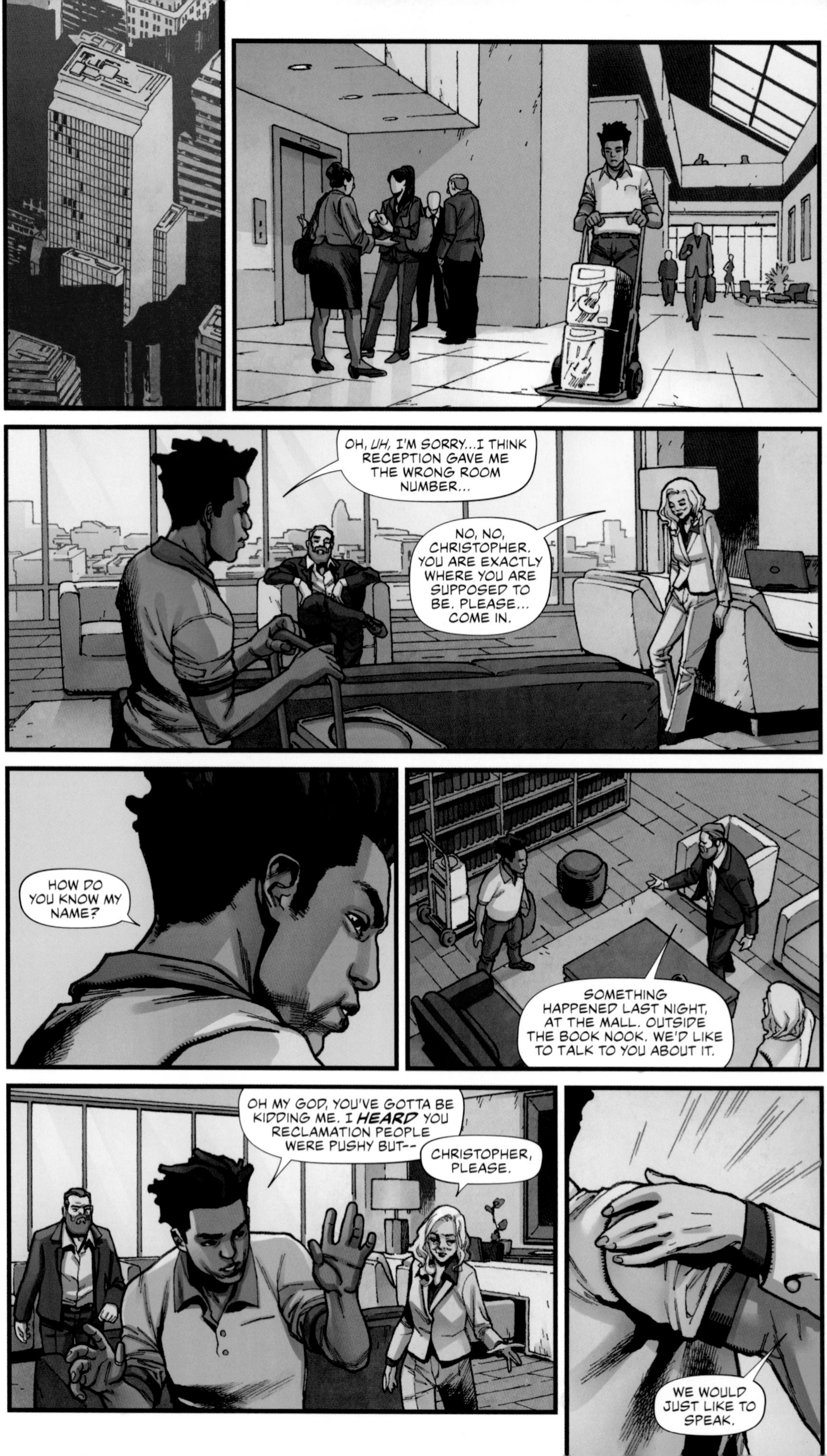
OH, UH, I'M SORRY...I THINK RECEPTION GAVE ME THE WRONG ROOM NUMBER...
NO, NO, CHRISTOPHER. YOU ARE EXACTLY WHERE YOU ARE SUPPOSED TO BE. PLEASE... COME IN.
HOW DO YOU KNOW MY NAME?
SOMETHING HAPPENED LAST NIGHT, AT THE MALL. OUTSIDE THE BOOK NOOK. WE'D LIKE TO TALK TO YOU ABOUT IT.
OH MY GOD, YOU'VE GOTTA BE KIDDING ME. I HEARD YOU RECLAMATION PEOPLE WERE PUSHY BUT--
CHRISTOPHER, PLEASE.
WE WOULD JUST LIKE TO SPEAK.

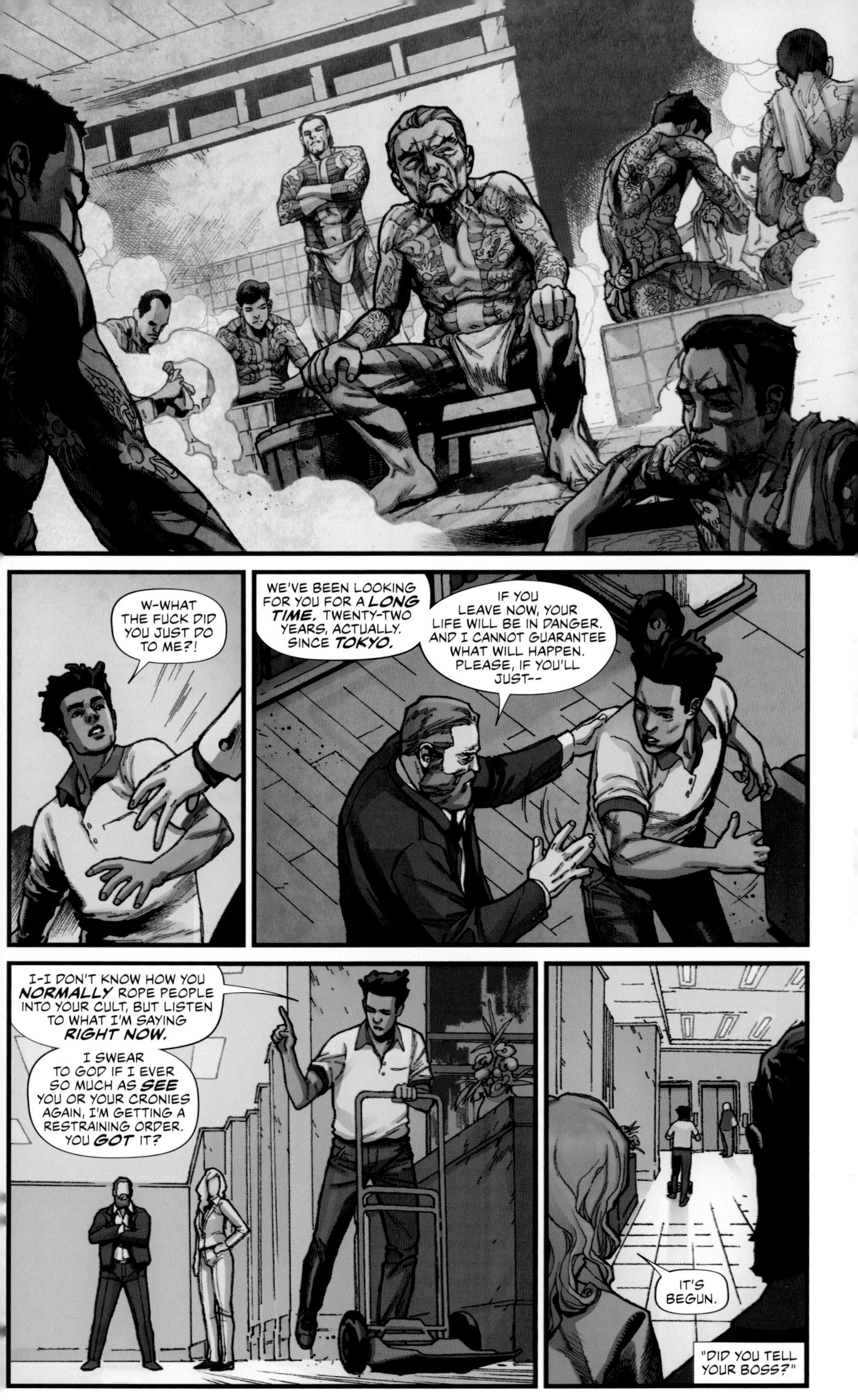

W-WHAT THE FUCK DID YOU JUST DO TO ME?!
WE'VE BEEN LOOKING FOR YOU FOR A LONG TIME. TWENTY-TWO YEARS, ACTUALLY. SINCE TOKYO.
IF YOU LEAVE NOW, YOUR LIFE WILL BE IN DANGER. AND I CANNOT GUARANTEE WHAT WILL HAPPEN. PLEASE, IF YOU'LL JUST--
I-I DON'T KNOW HOW YOU NORMALLY ROPE PEOPLE INTO YOUR CULT, BUT LISTEN TO WHAT I'M SAYING RIGHT NOW.
I SWEAR TO GOD IF I EVER SO MUCH AS SEE YOU OR YOUR CRONIES AGAIN, I'M GETTING A RESTRAINING ORDER. YOU GOT IT?
IT'S BEGUN.
"DID YOU TELL YOUR BOSS?"

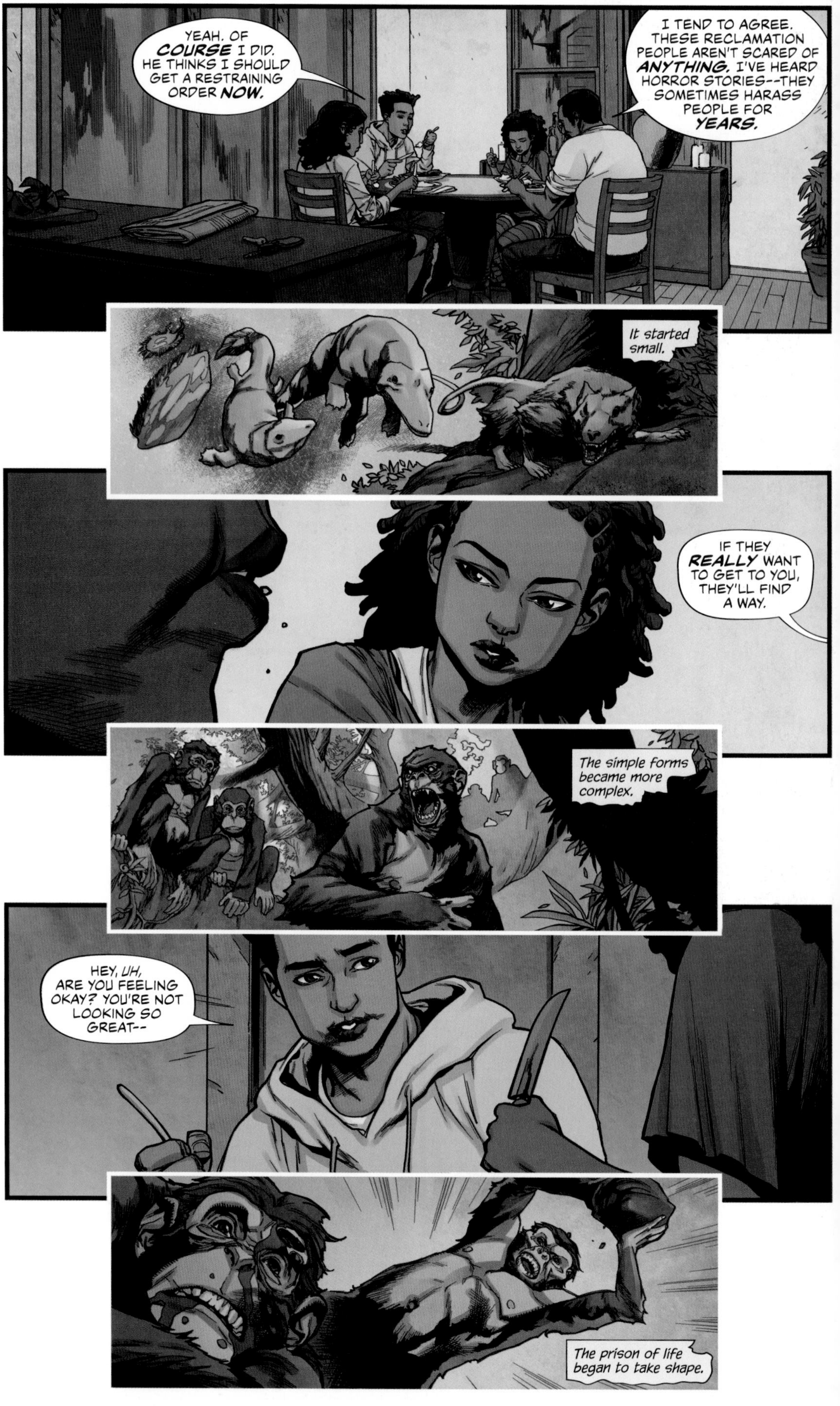
YEAH. OF COURSE I DID. HE THINKS I SHOULD GET A RESTRAINING ORDER NOW.
I TEND TO AGREE. THESE RECLAMATION PEOPLE AREN'T SCARED OF ANYTHING. I'VE HEARD HORROR STORIES--THEY SOMETIMES HARASS PEOPLE FOR YEARS.
It started small.
IF THEY REALLY WANT TO GET TO YOU, THEY'LL FIND A WAY.
The simple forms became more complex.
HEY, UH, ARE YOU FEELING OKAY? YOU'RE NOT LOOKING SO GREAT--
The prison of life began to take shape.

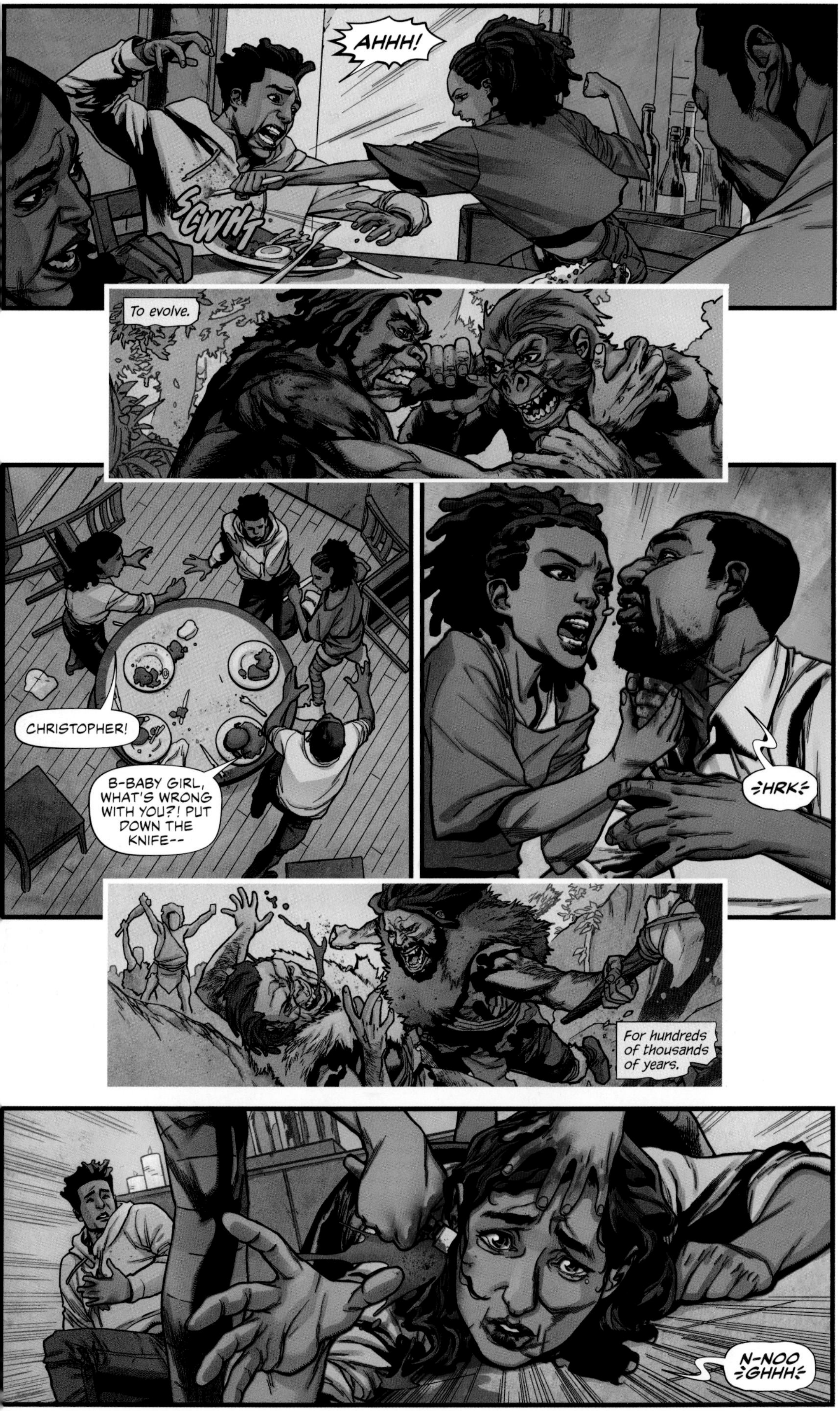
AHHH!
SCWHT
To evolve.
CHRISTOPHER!
B-BABY GIRL, WHAT'S WRONG WITH YOU?! PUT DOWN THE KNIFE--
HRK
For hundreds of thousands of years.
N-NOO GHHH

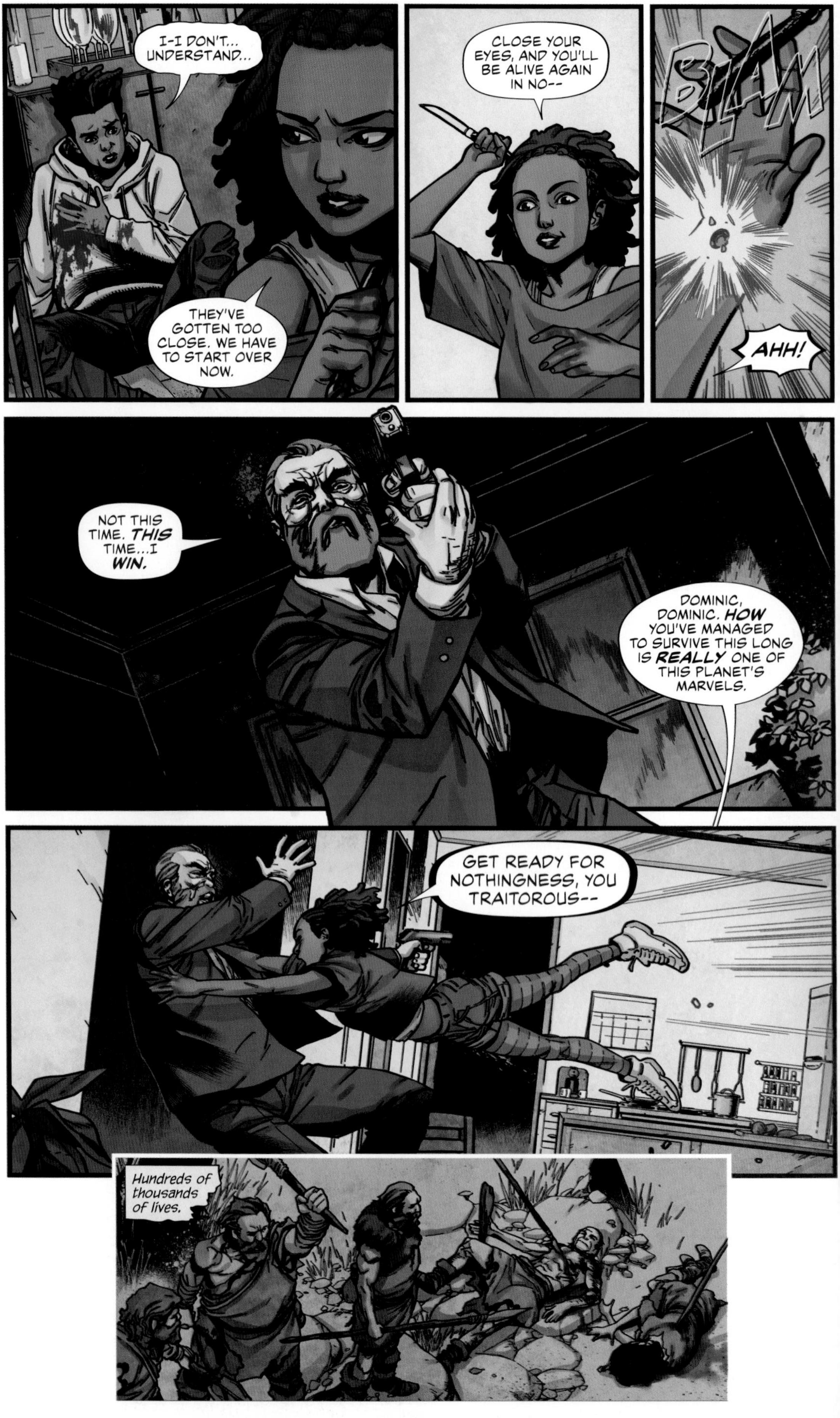
I-I DON'T... UNDERSTAND...
THEY'VE GOTTEN TOO CLOSE. WE HAVE TO START OVER NOW.
CLOSE YOUR EYES, AND YOU'LL BE ALIVE AGAIN IN NO--
BLAM
AHH!
NOT THIS TIME. THIS TIME...I WIN.
DOMINIC, DOMINIC. HOW YOU'VE MANAGED TO SURVIVE THIS LONG IS REALLY ONE OF THIS PLANET'S MARVELS.
GET READY FOR NOTHINGNESS, YOU TRAITOROUS--
Hundreds of thousands of lives.

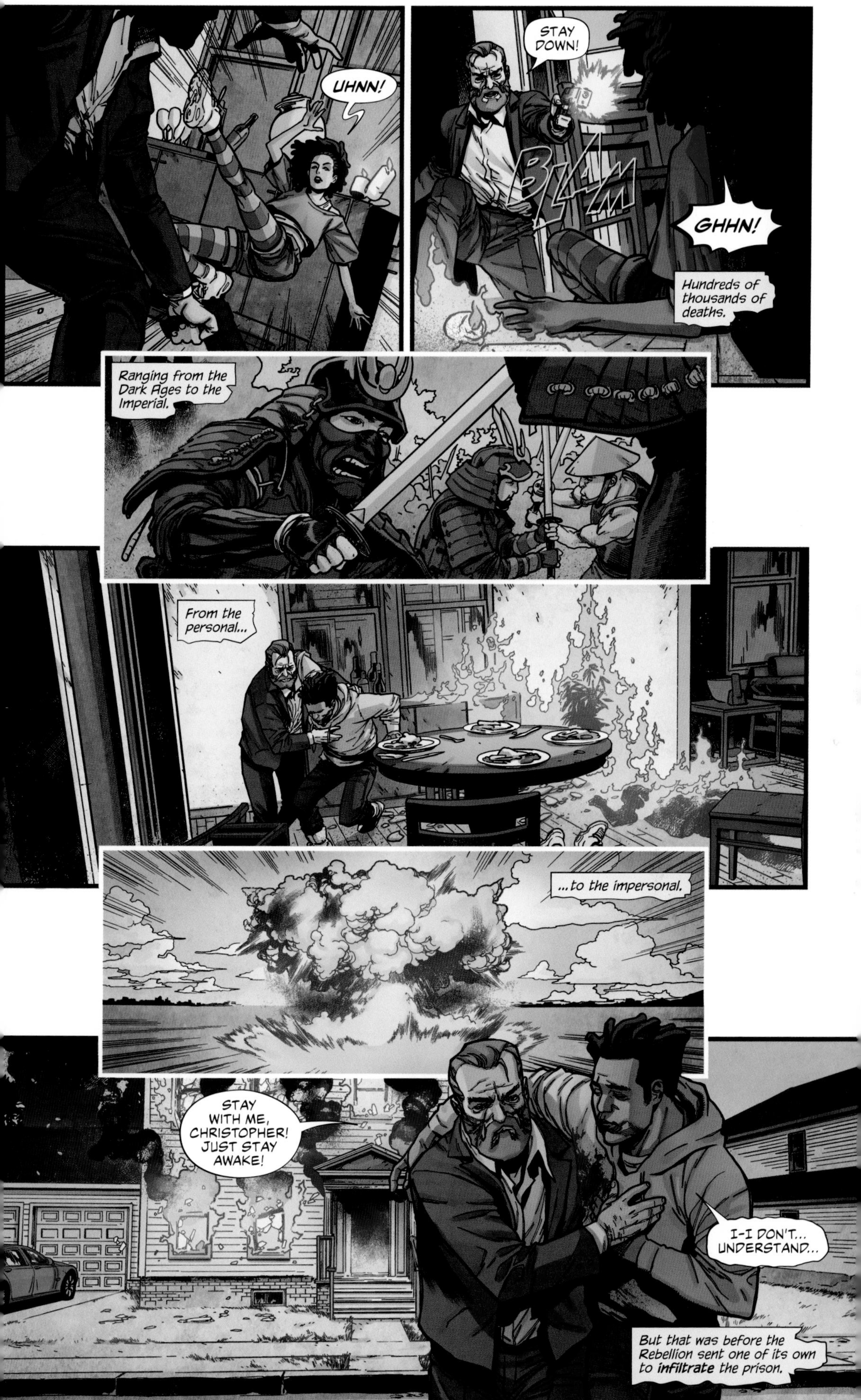
UHNN!
STAY DOWN!
BLAM
GHHN!
Hundreds of thousands of deaths.
Ranging from the Dark Ages to the Imperial.
From the personal...
...to the impersonal.
STAY WITH ME, CHRISTOPHER! JUST STAY AWAKE!
I-I DON'T... UNDERSTAND...
But that was before the Rebellion sent one of its own to **infiltrate** the prison.

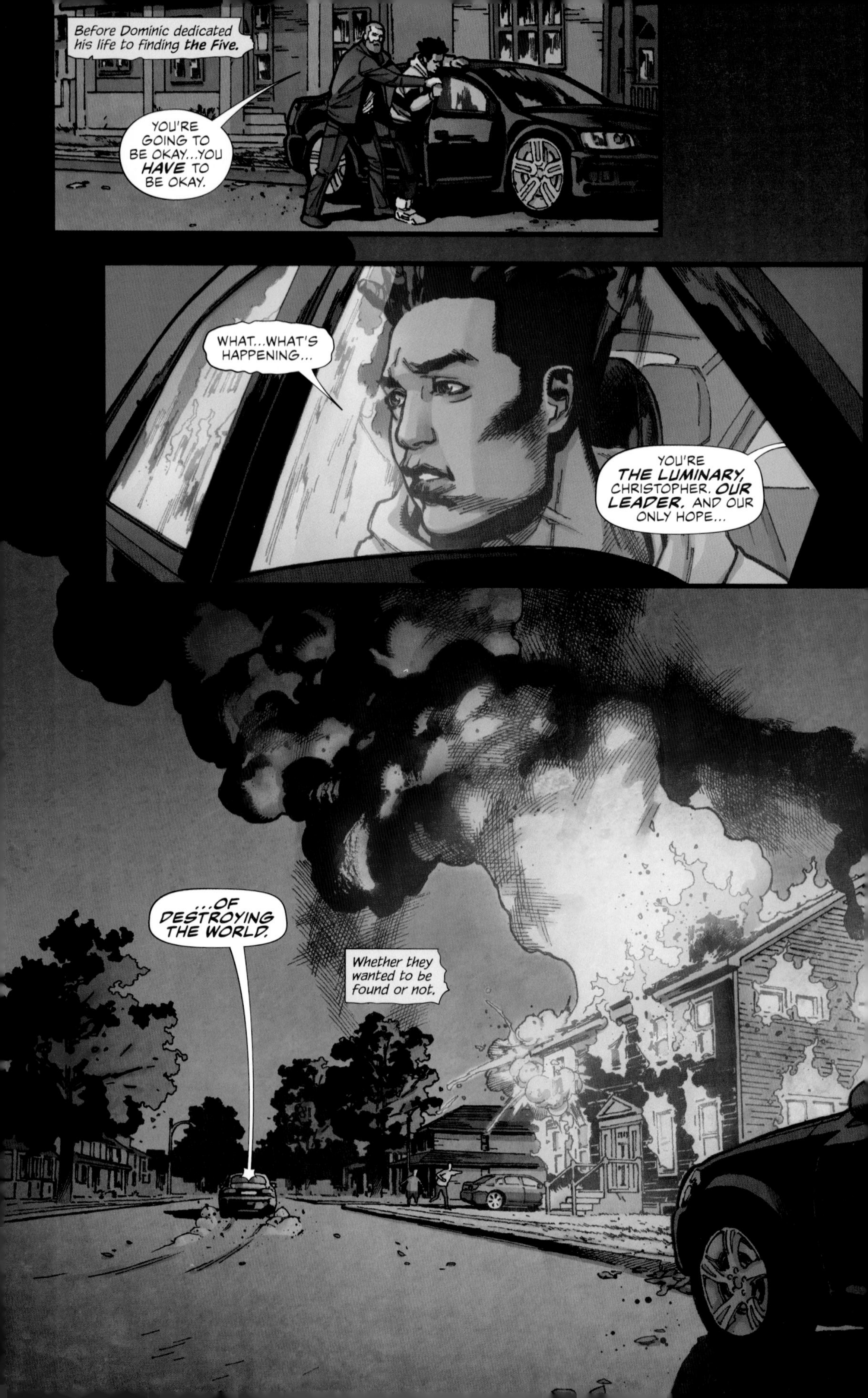
Before Dominic dedicated his life to finding the Five.
YOU'RE GOING TO BE OKAY...YOU HAVE TO BE OKAY.
WHAT...WHAT'S HAPPENING...
YOU'RE THE LUMINARY, CHRISTOPHER. OUR LEADER. AND OUR ONLY HOPE...
...OF DESTROYING THE WORLD.
Whether they wanted to be found or not.

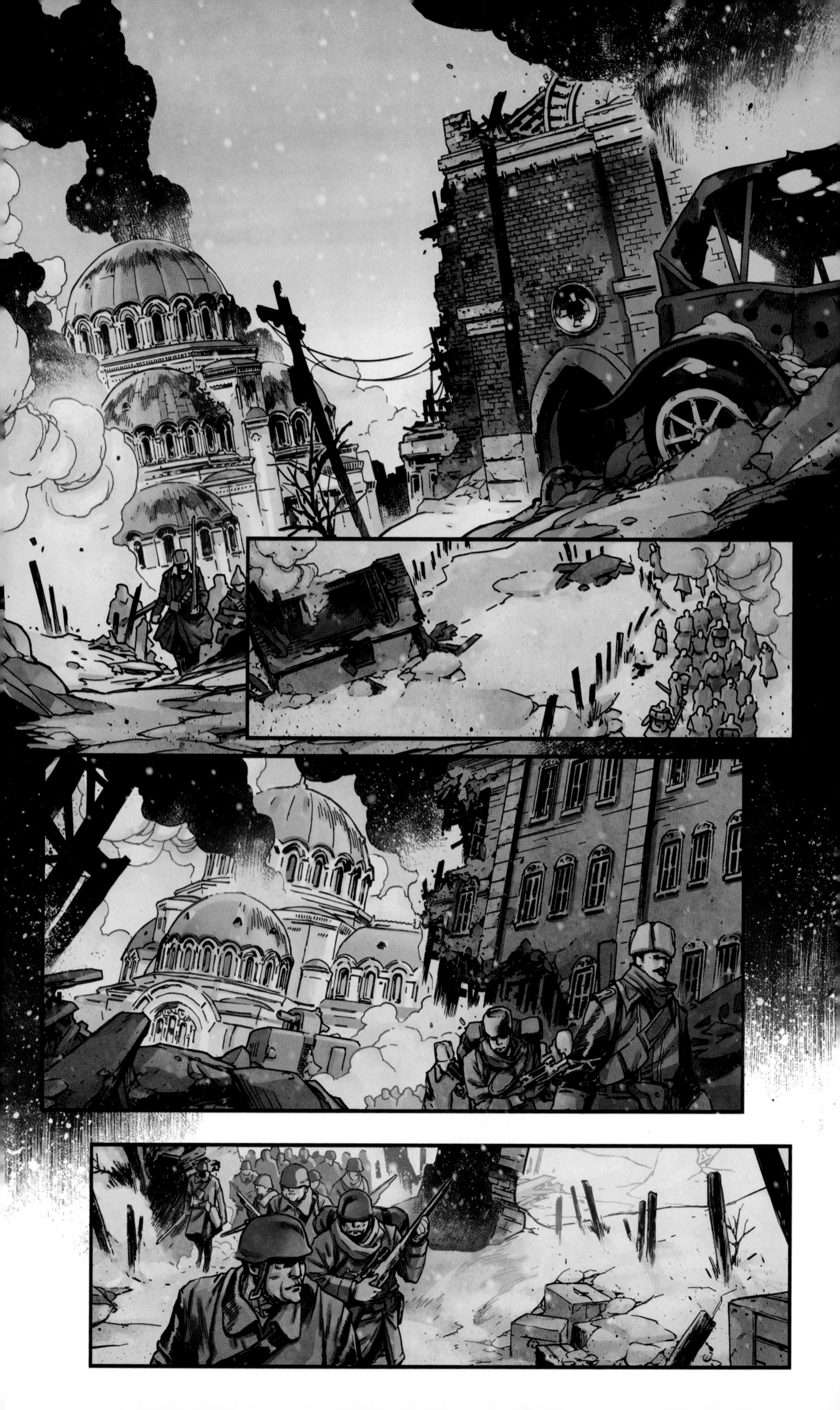

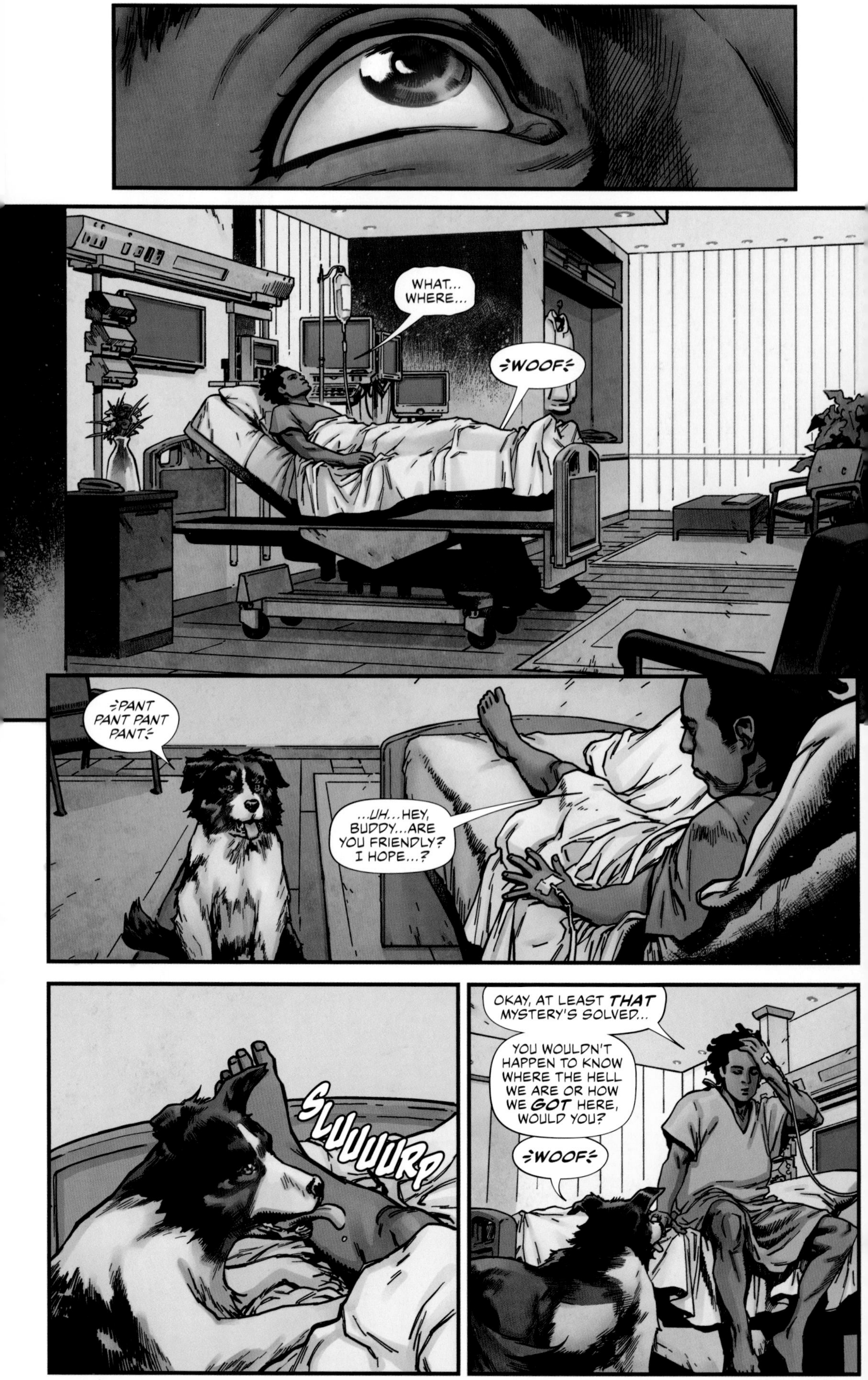
WHAT... WHERE...
WOOF
PANT PANT PANT PANT
...UH...HEY, BUDDY...ARE YOU FRIENDLY? I HOPE...?
SLUUUURP
OKAY, AT LEAST THAT MYSTERY'S SOLVED...
YOU WOULDN'T HAPPEN TO KNOW WHERE THE HELL WE ARE OR HOW WE GOT HERE, WOULD YOU?
WOOF

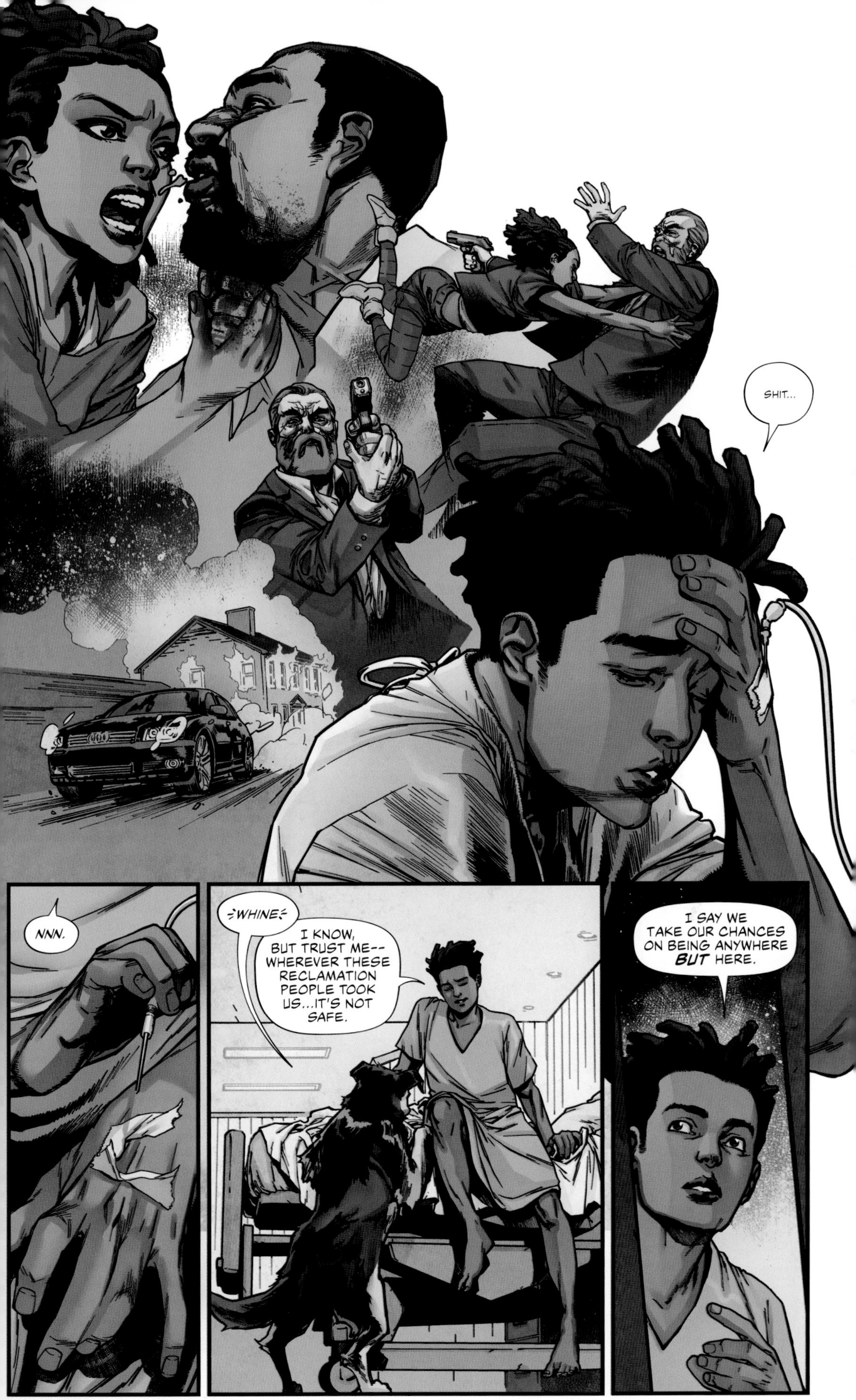
SHIT...
NNN.
WHINE
I KNOW, BUT TRUST ME-- WHEREVER THESE RECLAMATION PEOPLE TOOK US...IT'S NOT SAFE.
I SAY WE TAKE OUR CHANCES ON BEING ANYWHERE **BUT** HERE.

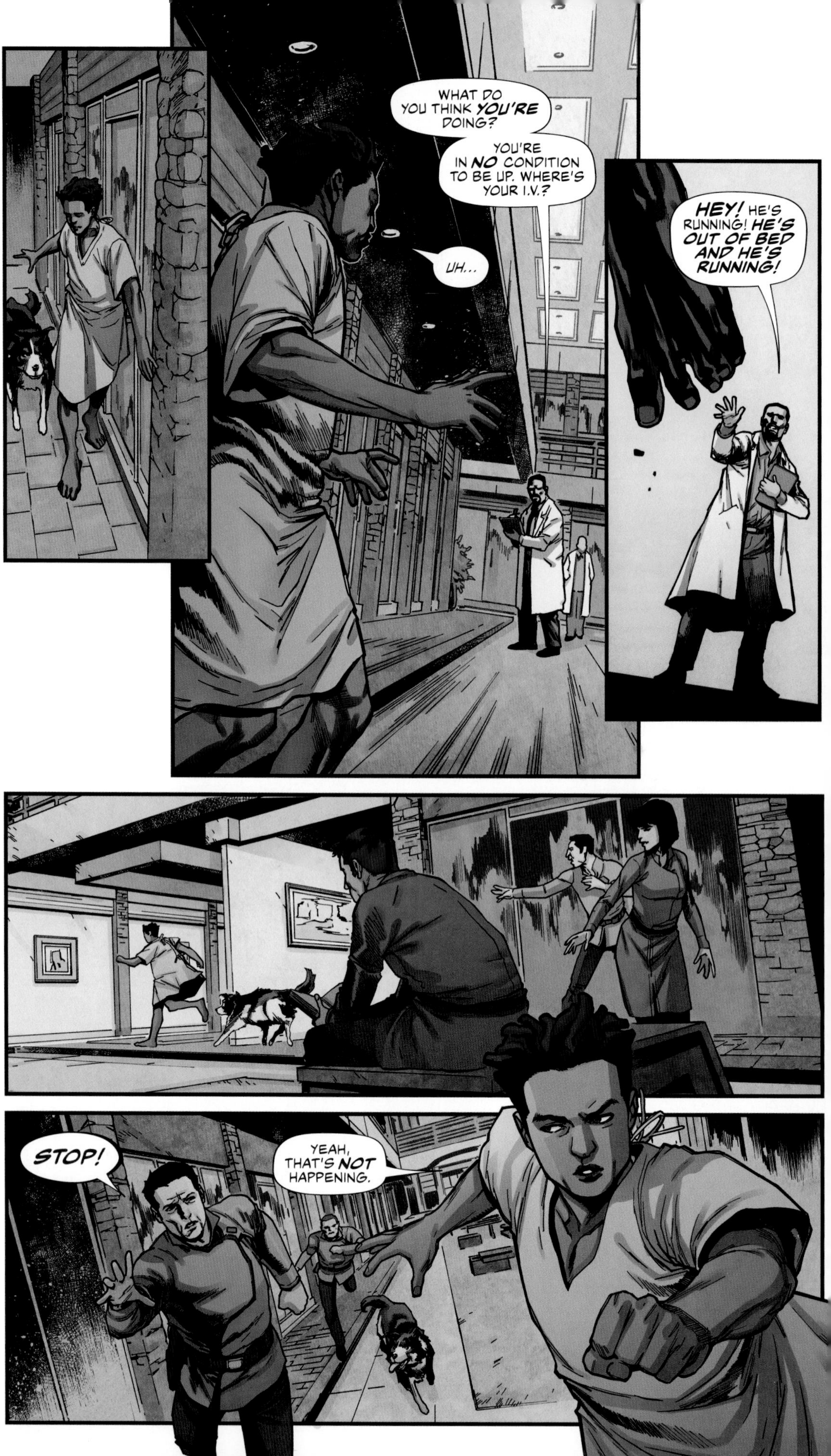
WHAT DO YOU THINK YOU'RE DOING?
YOU'RE IN NO CONDITION TO BE UP. WHERE'S YOUR I.V.?
UH...
HEY! HE'S RUNNING! HE'S OUT OF BED AND HE'S RUNNING!
STOP!
YEAH, THAT'S NOT HAPPENING.

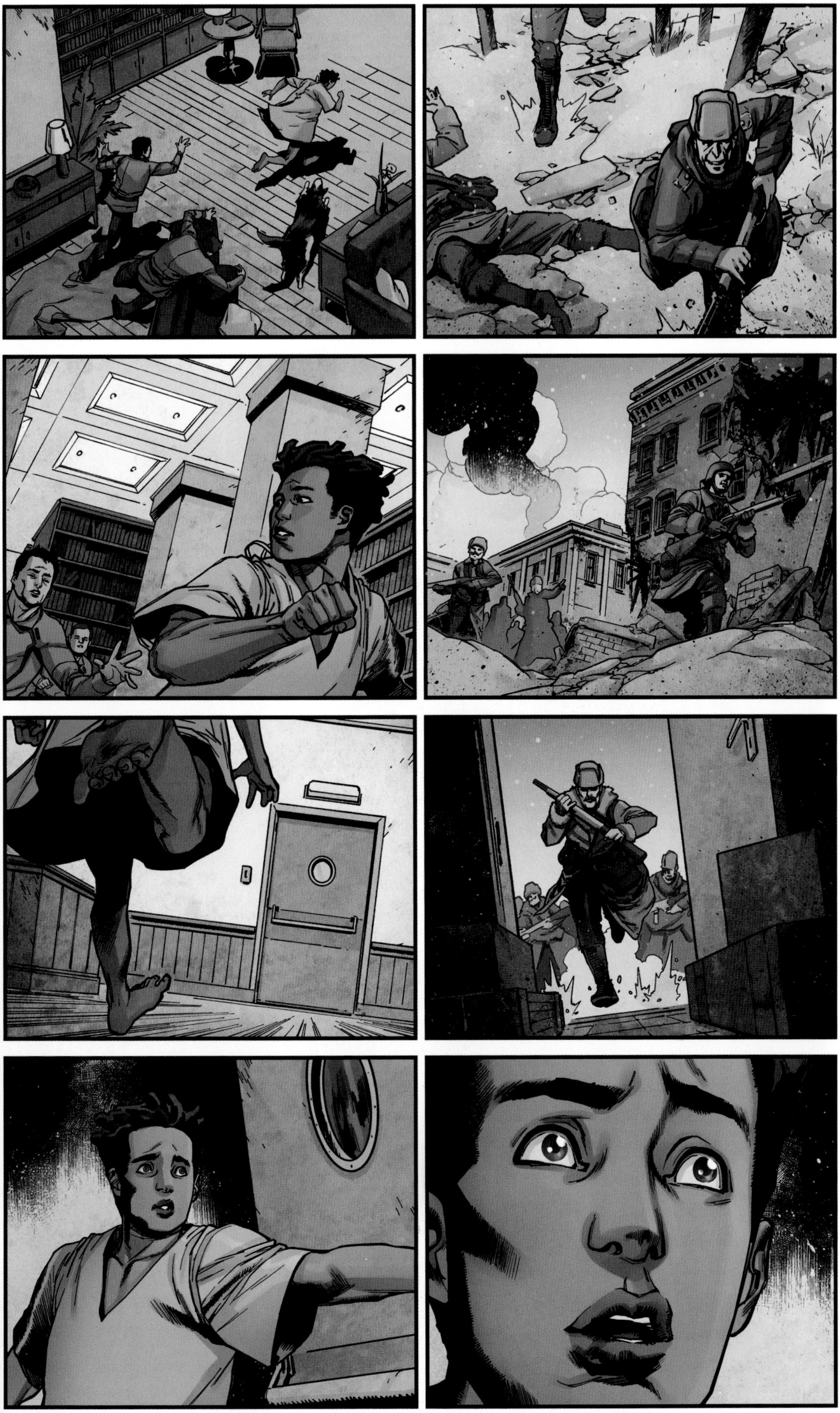

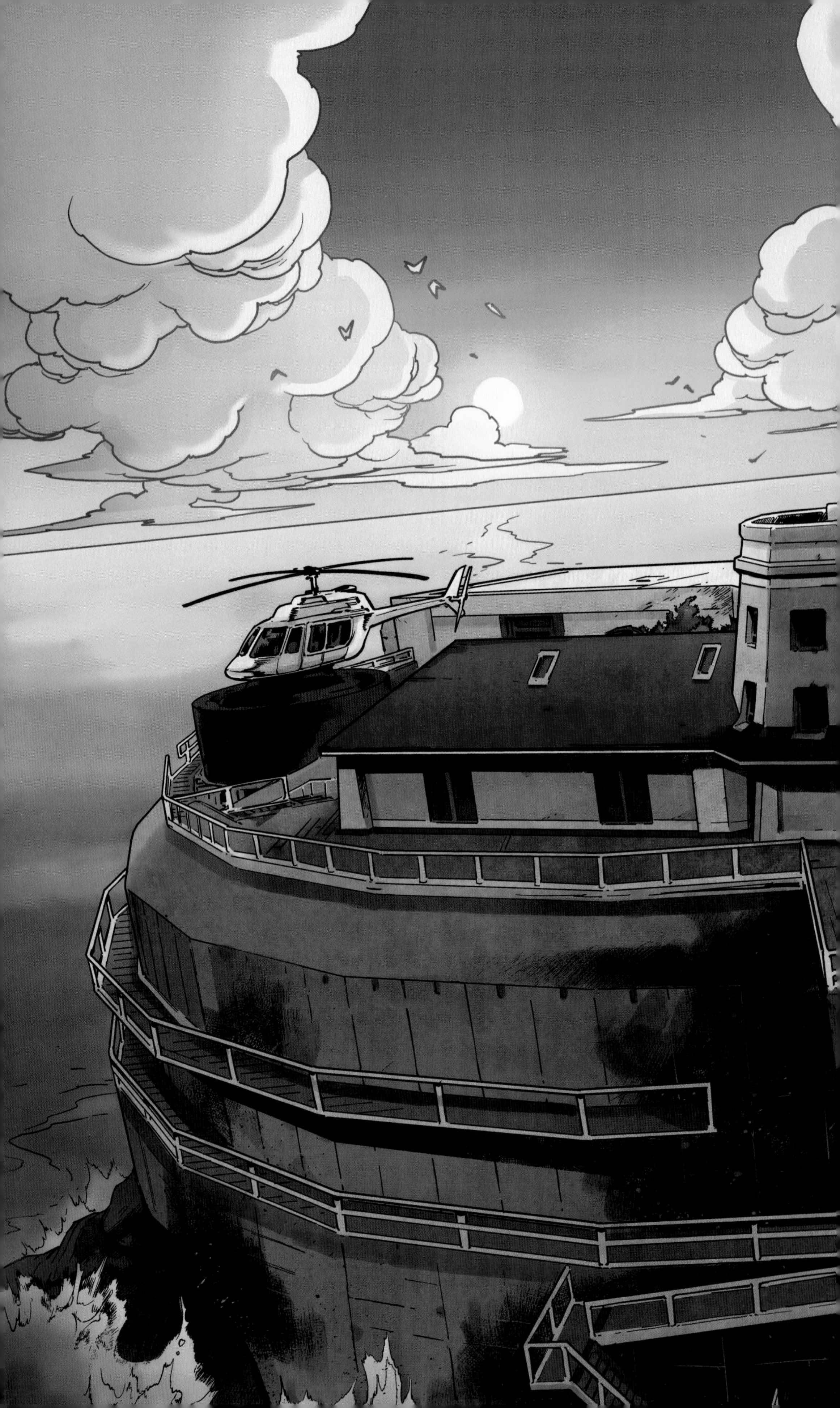

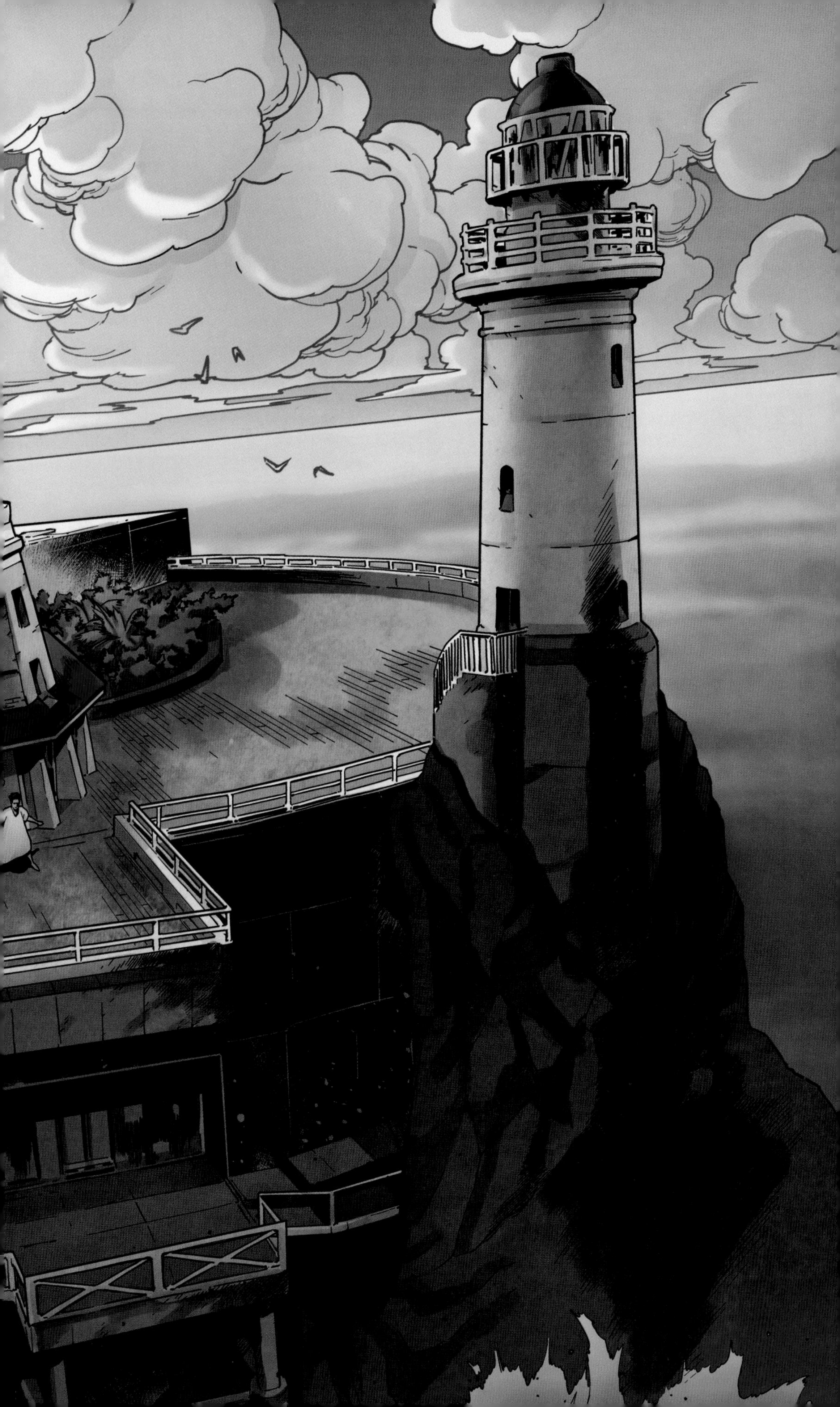

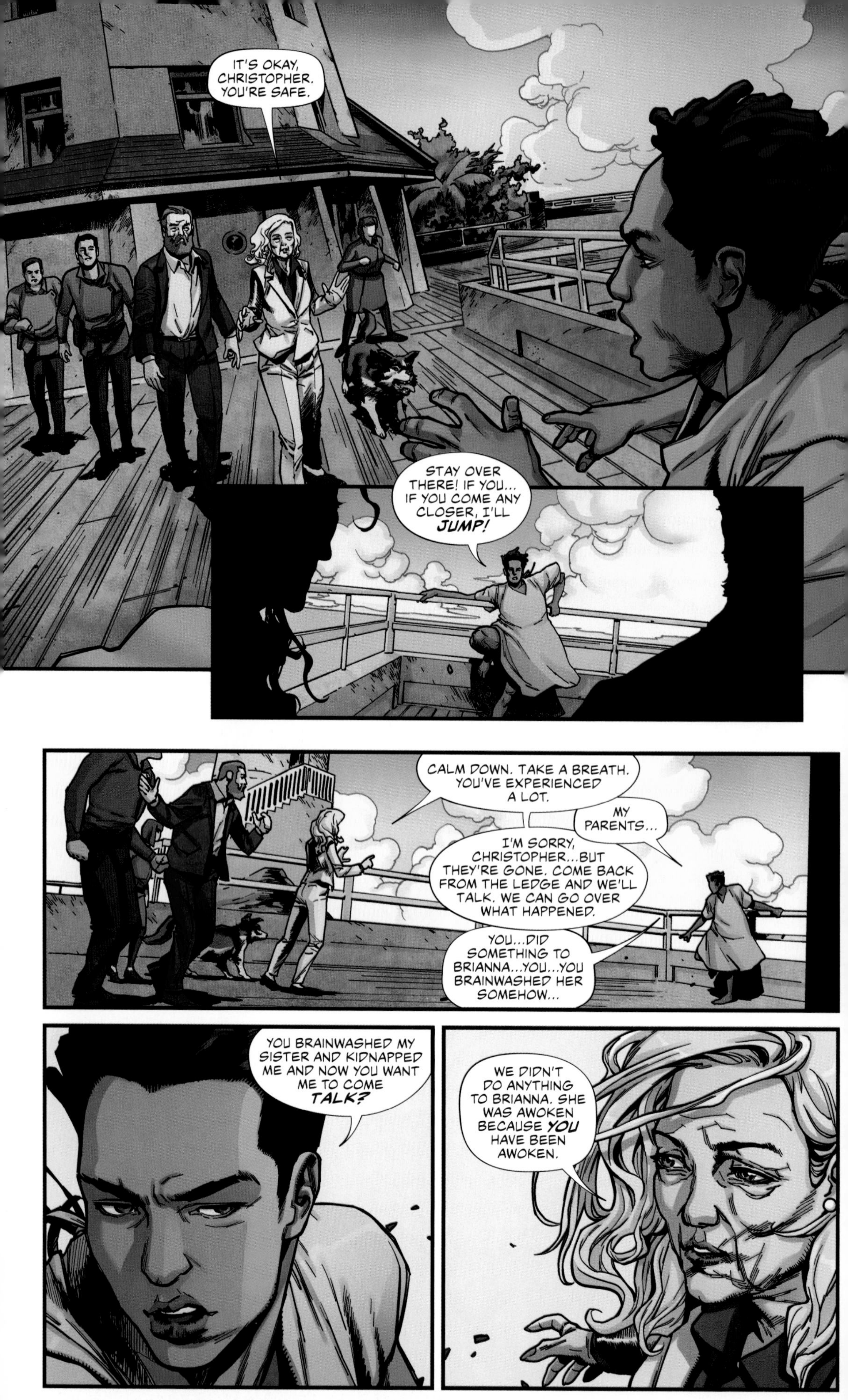
IT'S OKAY, CHRISTOPHER. YOU'RE SAFE.
STAY OVER THERE! IF YOU... IF YOU COME ANY CLOSER, I'LL JUMP!
CALM DOWN. TAKE A BREATH. YOU'VE EXPERIENCED A LOT.
MY PARENTS...
I'M SORRY, CHRISTOPHER...BUT THEY'RE GONE. COME BACK FROM THE LEDGE AND WE'LL TALK. WE CAN GO OVER WHAT HAPPENED.
YOU...DID SOMETHING TO BRIANNA...YOU...YOU BRAINWASHED HER SOMEHOW...
YOU BRAINWASHED MY SISTER AND KIDNAPPED ME AND NOW YOU WANT ME TO COME TALK?
WE DIDN'T DO ANYTHING TO BRIANNA. SHE WAS AWOKEN BECAUSE YOU HAVE BEEN AWOKEN.

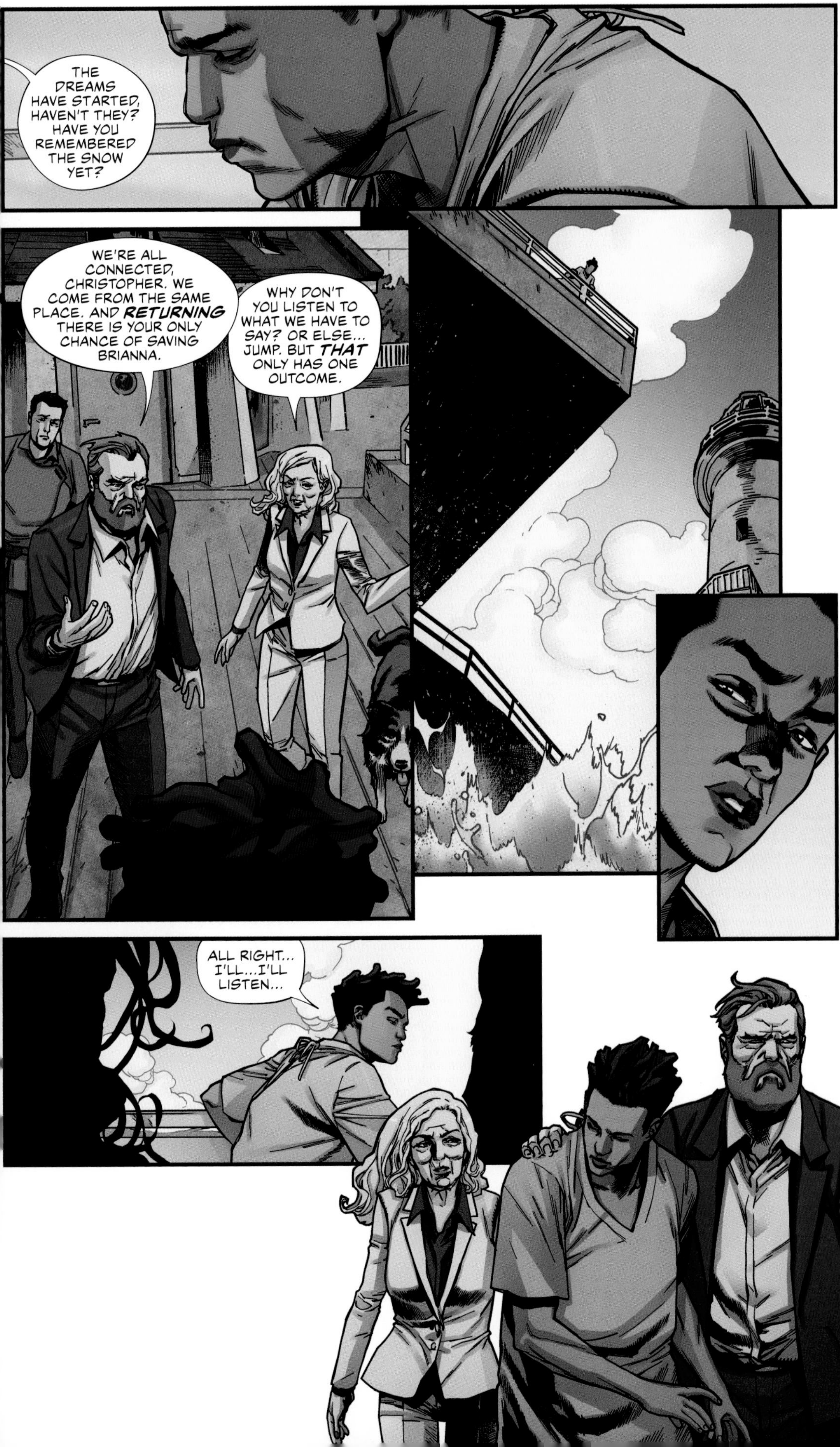
THE DREAMS HAVE STARTED, HAVEN'T THEY? HAVE YOU REMEMBERED THE SNOW YET?
WE'RE ALL CONNECTED, CHRISTOPHER. WE COME FROM THE SAME PLACE. AND RETURNING THERE IS YOUR ONLY CHANCE OF SAVING BRIANNA.
WHY DON'T YOU LISTEN TO WHAT WE HAVE TO SAY? OR ELSE... JUMP. BUT THAT ONLY HAS ONE OUTCOME.
ALL RIGHT... I'LL...I'LL LISTEN...

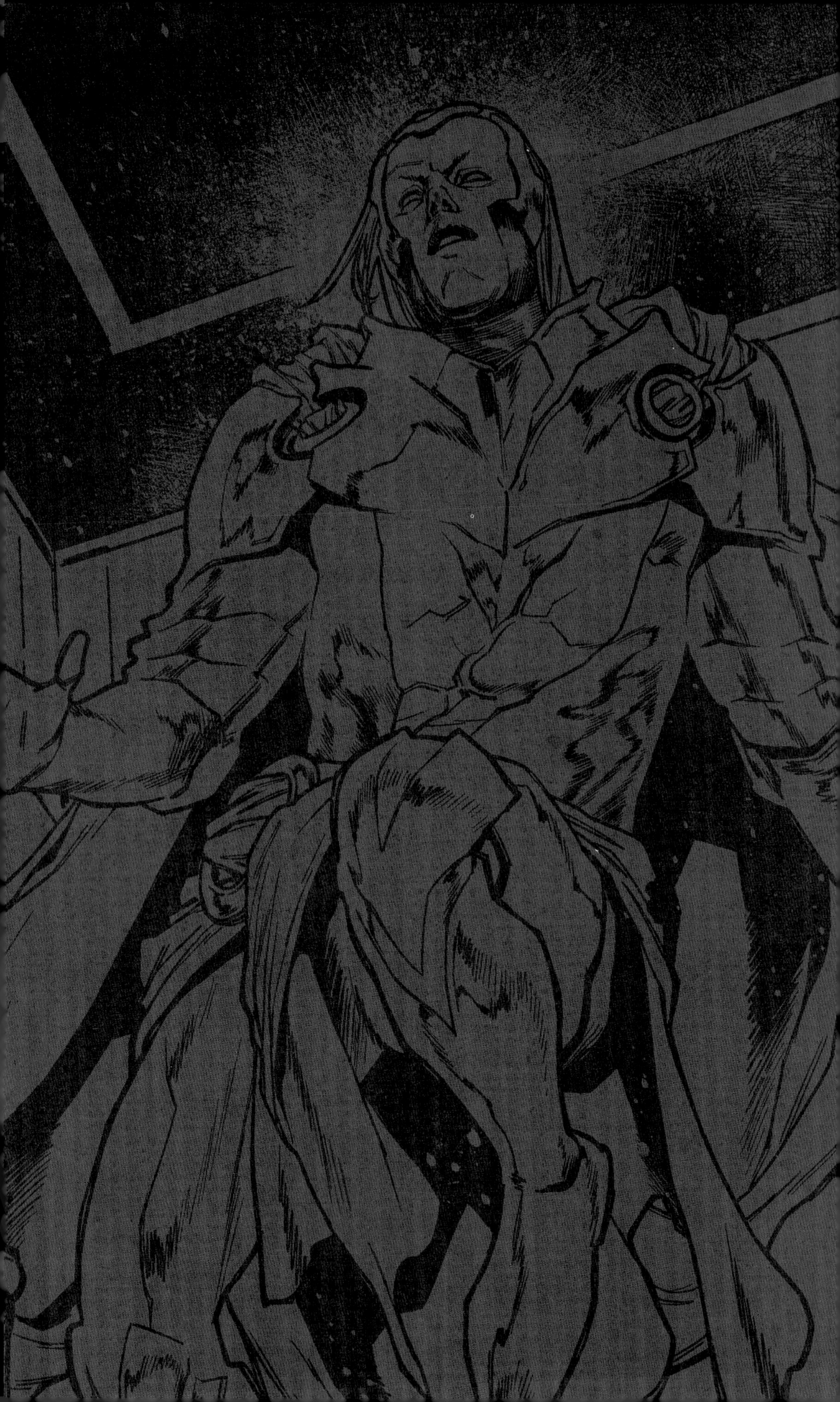

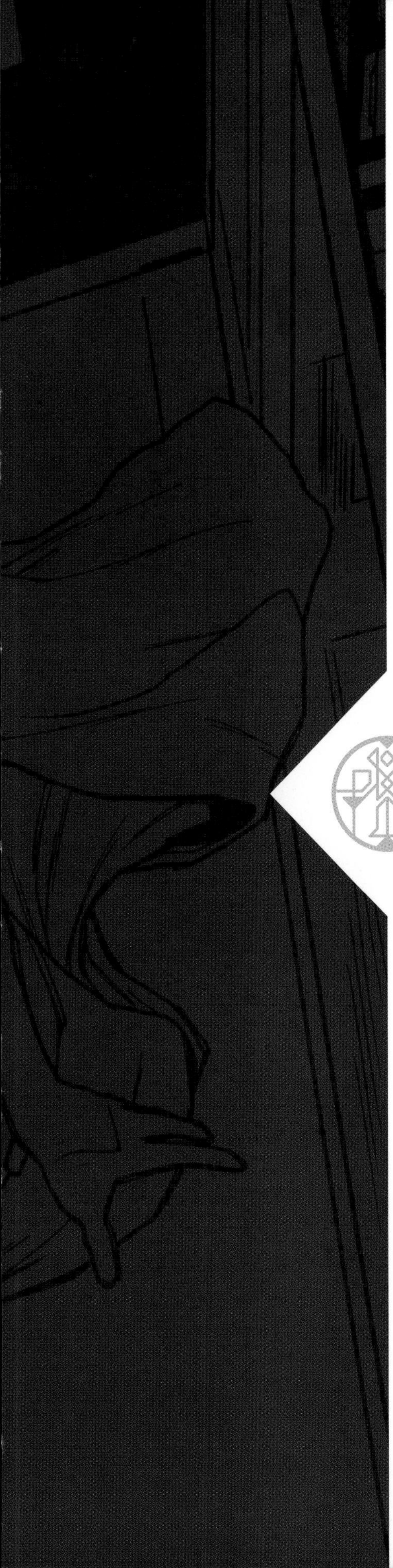

CHAPTER II

Black Light

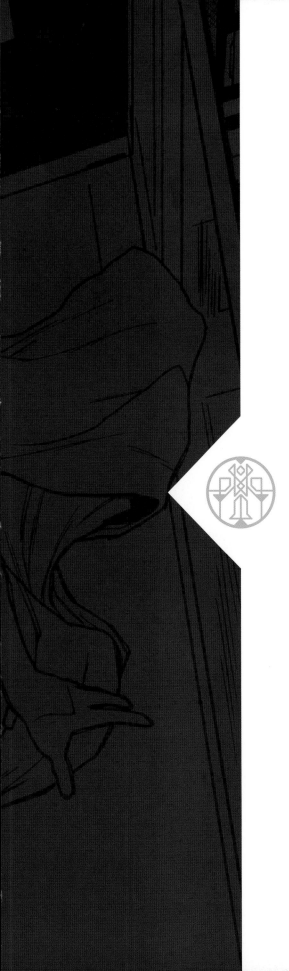

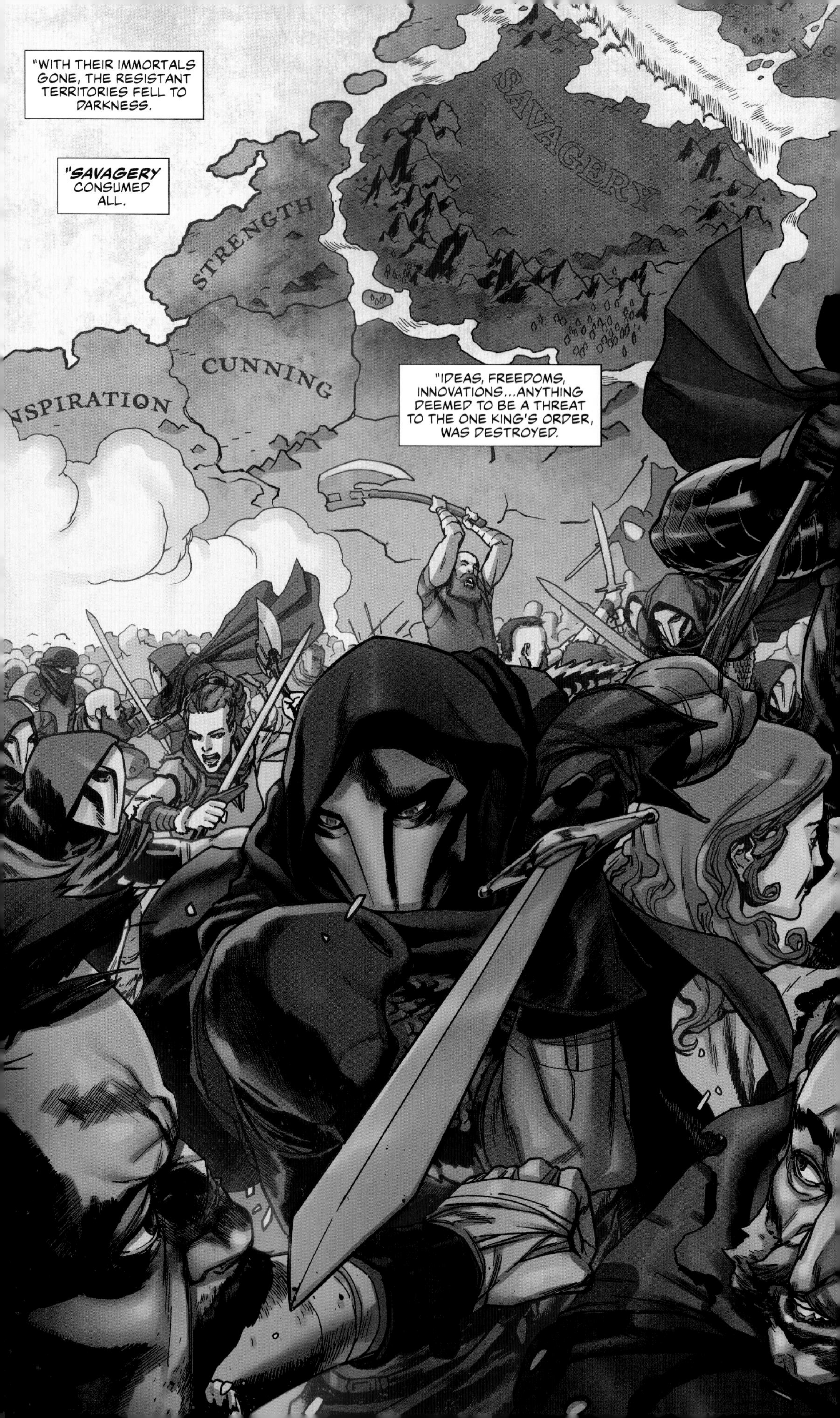
"WITH THEIR IMMORTALS GONE, THE RESISTANT TERRITORIES FELL TO DARKNESS.
"SAVAGERY CONSUMED ALL.
SAVAGERY
STRENGTH
CUNNING
NSPIRATION
"IDEAS, FREEDOMS, INNOVATIONS...ANYTHING DEEMED TO BE A THREAT TO THE ONE KING'S ORDER, WAS DESTROYED.

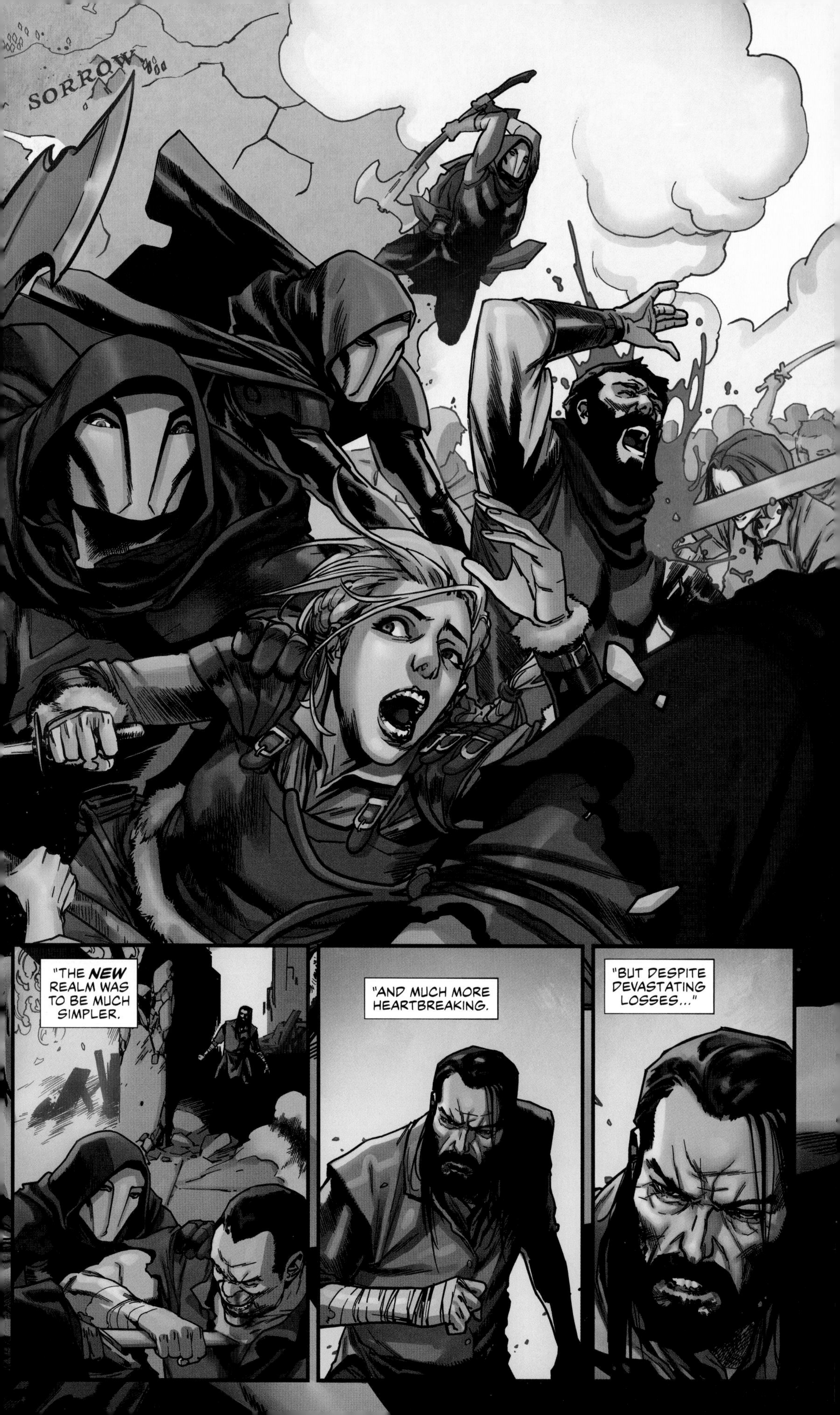
SORROW
"THE NEW REALM WAS TO BE MUCH SIMPLER.
"AND MUCH MORE HEARTBREAKING.
"BUT DESPITE DEVASTATING LOSSES..."

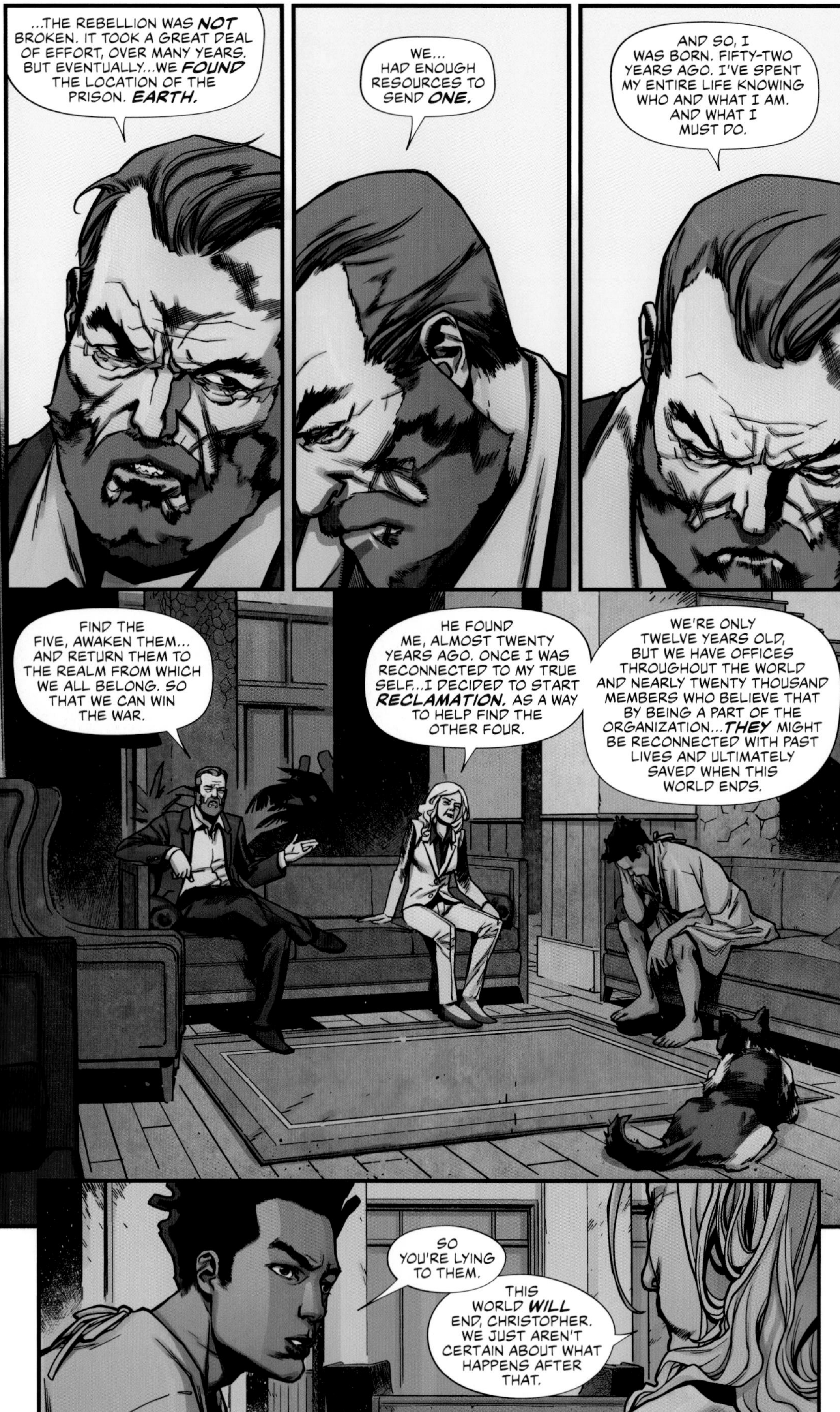

...THE REBELLION WAS NOT BROKEN. IT TOOK A GREAT DEAL OF EFFORT, OVER MANY YEARS. BUT EVENTUALLY...WE FOUND THE LOCATION OF THE PRISON. EARTH.
WE... HAD ENOUGH RESOURCES TO SEND ONE.
AND SO, I WAS BORN. FIFTY-TWO YEARS AGO. I'VE SPENT MY ENTIRE LIFE KNOWING WHO AND WHAT I AM. AND WHAT I MUST DO.
FIND THE FIVE, AWAKEN THEM... AND RETURN THEM TO THE REALM FROM WHICH WE ALL BELONG. SO THAT WE CAN WIN THE WAR.
HE FOUND ME, ALMOST TWENTY YEARS AGO. ONCE I WAS RECONNECTED TO MY TRUE SELF...I DECIDED TO START RECLAMATION, AS A WAY TO HELP FIND THE OTHER FOUR.
WE'RE ONLY TWELVE YEARS OLD, BUT WE HAVE OFFICES THROUGHOUT THE WORLD AND NEARLY TWENTY THOUSAND MEMBERS WHO BELIEVE THAT BY BEING A PART OF THE ORGANIZATION...THEY MIGHT BE RECONNECTED WITH PAST LIVES AND ULTIMATELY SAVED WHEN THIS WORLD ENDS.
SO YOU'RE LYING TO THEM.
THIS WORLD WILL END, CHRISTOPHER. WE JUST AREN'T CERTAIN ABOUT WHAT HAPPENS AFTER THAT.

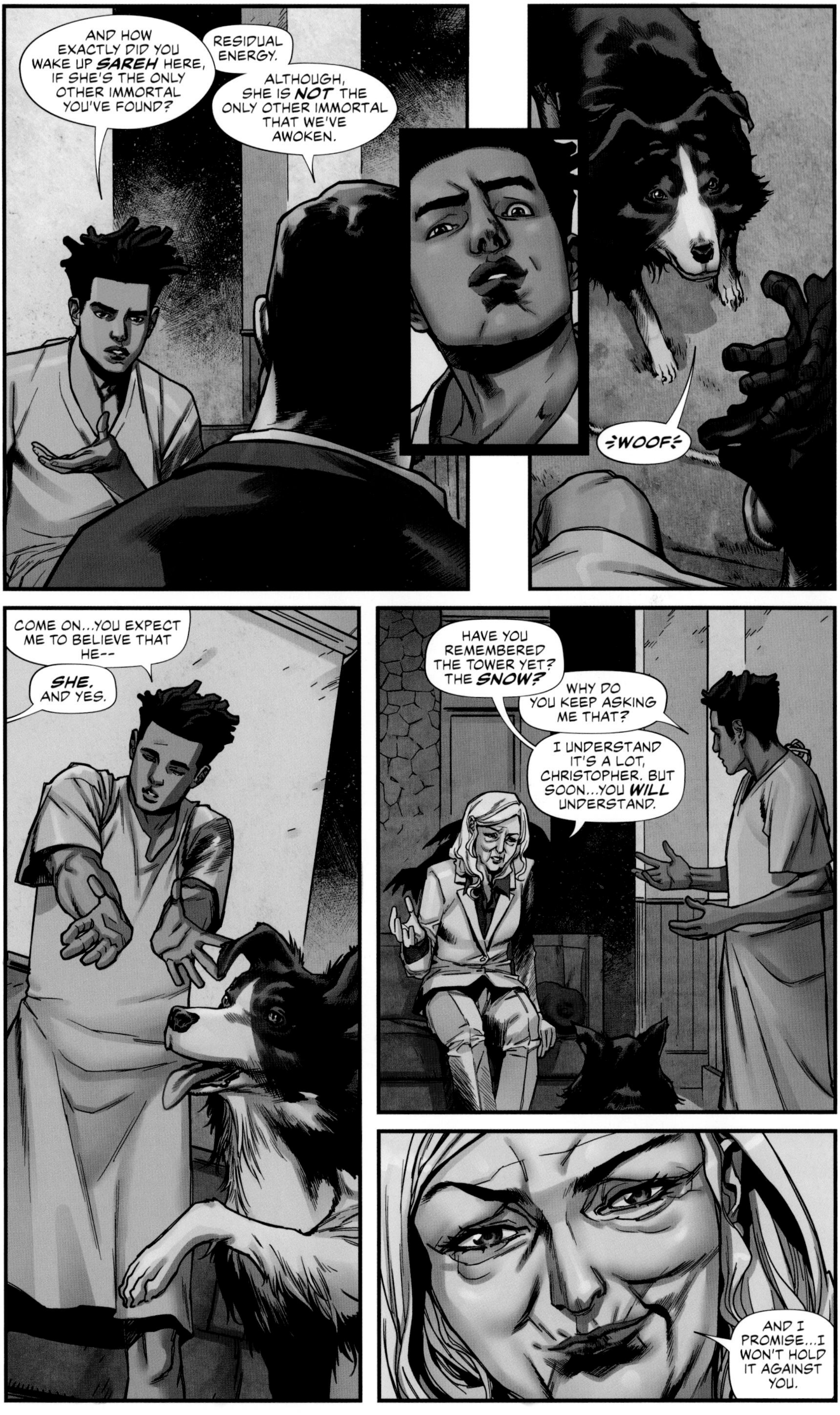

AND HOW EXACTLY DID YOU WAKE UP SAREH HERE, IF SHE'S THE ONLY OTHER IMMORTAL YOU'VE FOUND?
RESIDUAL ENERGY.
ALTHOUGH, SHE IS NOT THE ONLY OTHER IMMORTAL THAT WE'VE AWOKEN.
WOOF
COME ON...YOU EXPECT ME TO BELIEVE THAT HE--
SHE. AND YES.
HAVE YOU REMEMBERED THE TOWER YET? THE SNOW?
WHY DO YOU KEEP ASKING ME THAT?
I UNDERSTAND IT'S A LOT, CHRISTOPHER. BUT SOON...YOU WILL UNDERSTAND.
AND I PROMISE...I WON'T HOLD IT AGAINST YOU.

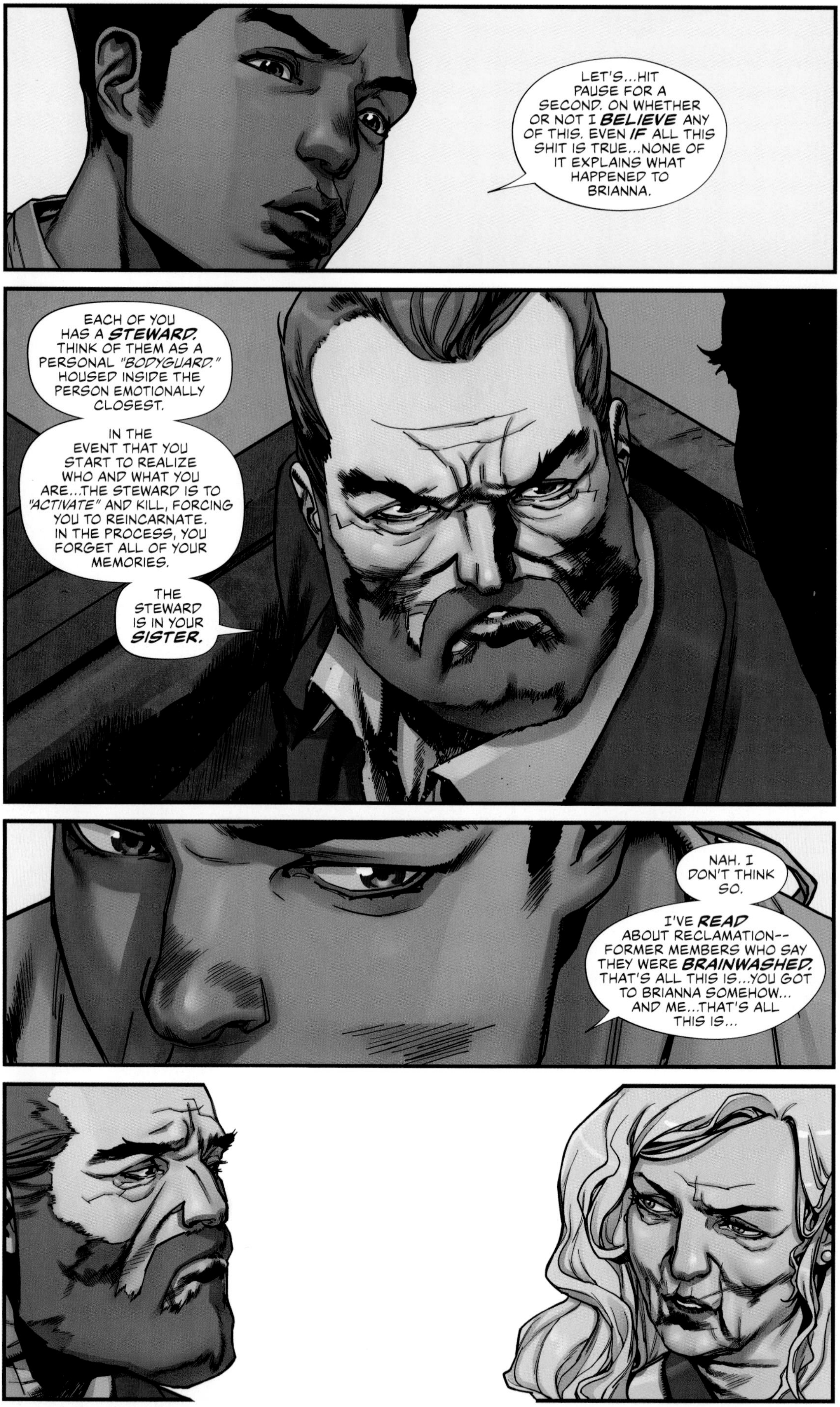
LET'S...HIT PAUSE FOR A SECOND. ON WHETHER OR NOT I BELIEVE ANY OF THIS. EVEN IF ALL THIS SHIT IS TRUE...NONE OF IT EXPLAINS WHAT HAPPENED TO BRIANNA.
EACH OF YOU HAS A STEWARD. THINK OF THEM AS A PERSONAL "BODYGUARD." HOUSED INSIDE THE PERSON EMOTIONALLY CLOSEST.
IN THE EVENT THAT YOU START TO REALIZE WHO AND WHAT YOU ARE...THE STEWARD IS TO "ACTIVATE" AND KILL, FORCING YOU TO REINCARNATE. IN THE PROCESS, YOU FORGET ALL OF YOUR MEMORIES.
THE STEWARD IS IN YOUR SISTER.
NAH. I DON'T THINK SO.
I'VE READ ABOUT RECLAMATION-- FORMER MEMBERS WHO SAY THEY WERE BRAINWASHED. THAT'S ALL THIS IS...YOU GOT TO BRIANNA SOMEHOW... AND ME...THAT'S ALL THIS IS...

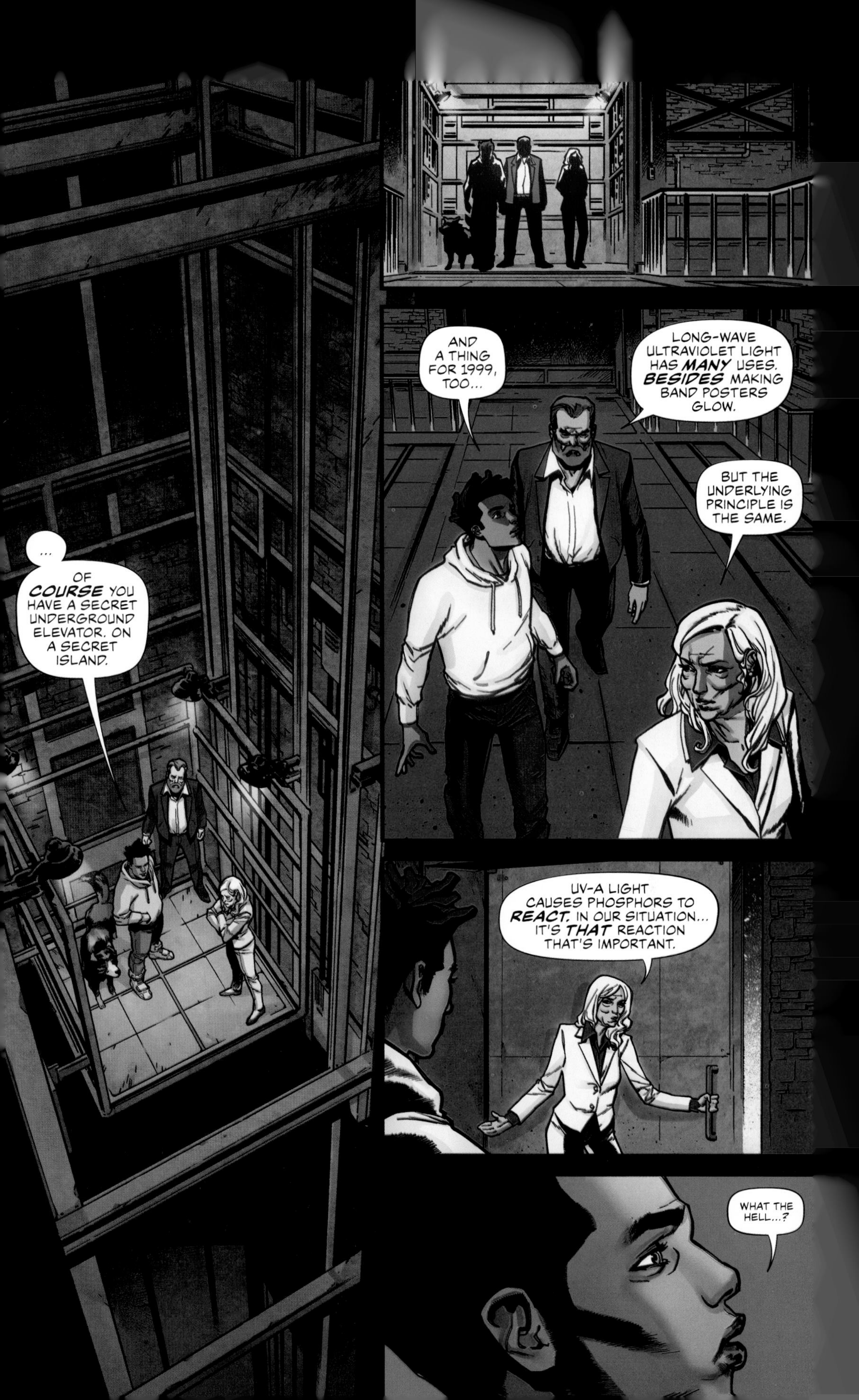
...
OF COURSE YOU HAVE A SECRET UNDERGROUND ELEVATOR. ON A SECRET ISLAND.
AND A THING FOR 1999, TOO...
LONG-WAVE ULTRAVIOLET LIGHT HAS MANY USES. BESIDES MAKING BAND POSTERS GLOW.
BUT THE UNDERLYING PRINCIPLE IS THE SAME.
UV-A LIGHT CAUSES PHOSPHORS TO REACT. IN OUR SITUATION... IT'S THAT REACTION THAT'S IMPORTANT.
WHAT THE HELL...?

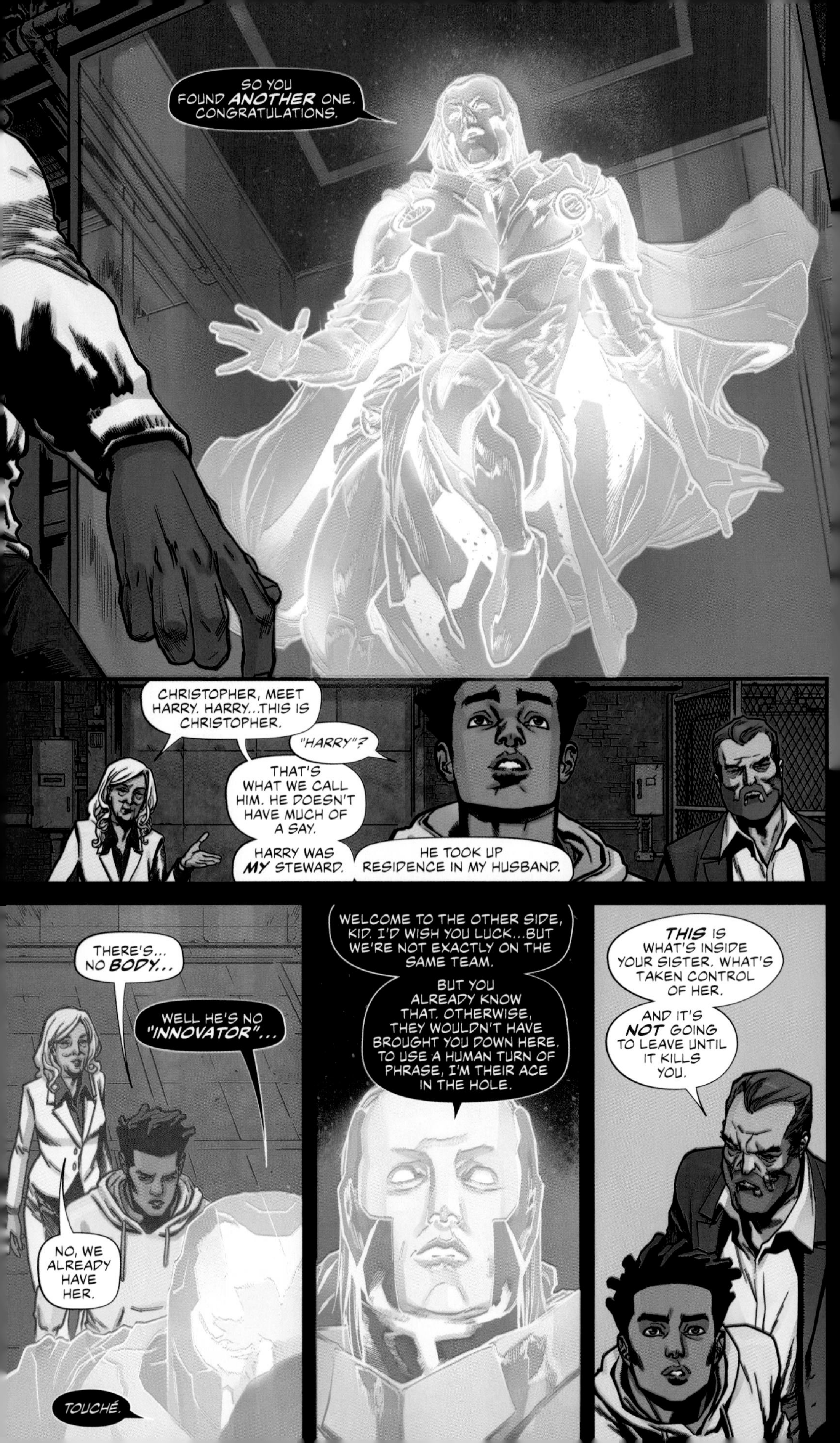
SO YOU FOUND ANOTHER ONE. CONGRATULATIONS.
CHRISTOPHER, MEET HARRY. HARRY...THIS IS CHRISTOPHER.
"HARRY"?
THAT'S WHAT WE CALL HIM. HE DOESN'T HAVE MUCH OF A SAY.
HARRY WAS MY STEWARD.
HE TOOK UP RESIDENCE IN MY HUSBAND.
THERE'S... NO BODY...
WELL HE'S NO "INNOVATOR"...
NO, WE ALREADY HAVE HER.
TOUCHÉ.
WELCOME TO THE OTHER SIDE, KID. I'D WISH YOU LUCK...BUT WE'RE NOT EXACTLY ON THE SAME TEAM.
BUT YOU ALREADY KNOW THAT. OTHERWISE, THEY WOULDN'T HAVE BROUGHT YOU DOWN HERE. TO USE A HUMAN TURN OF PHRASE, I'M THEIR ACE IN THE HOLE.
THIS IS WHAT'S INSIDE YOUR SISTER. WHAT'S TAKEN CONTROL OF HER.
AND IT'S NOT GOING TO LEAVE UNTIL IT KILLS YOU.

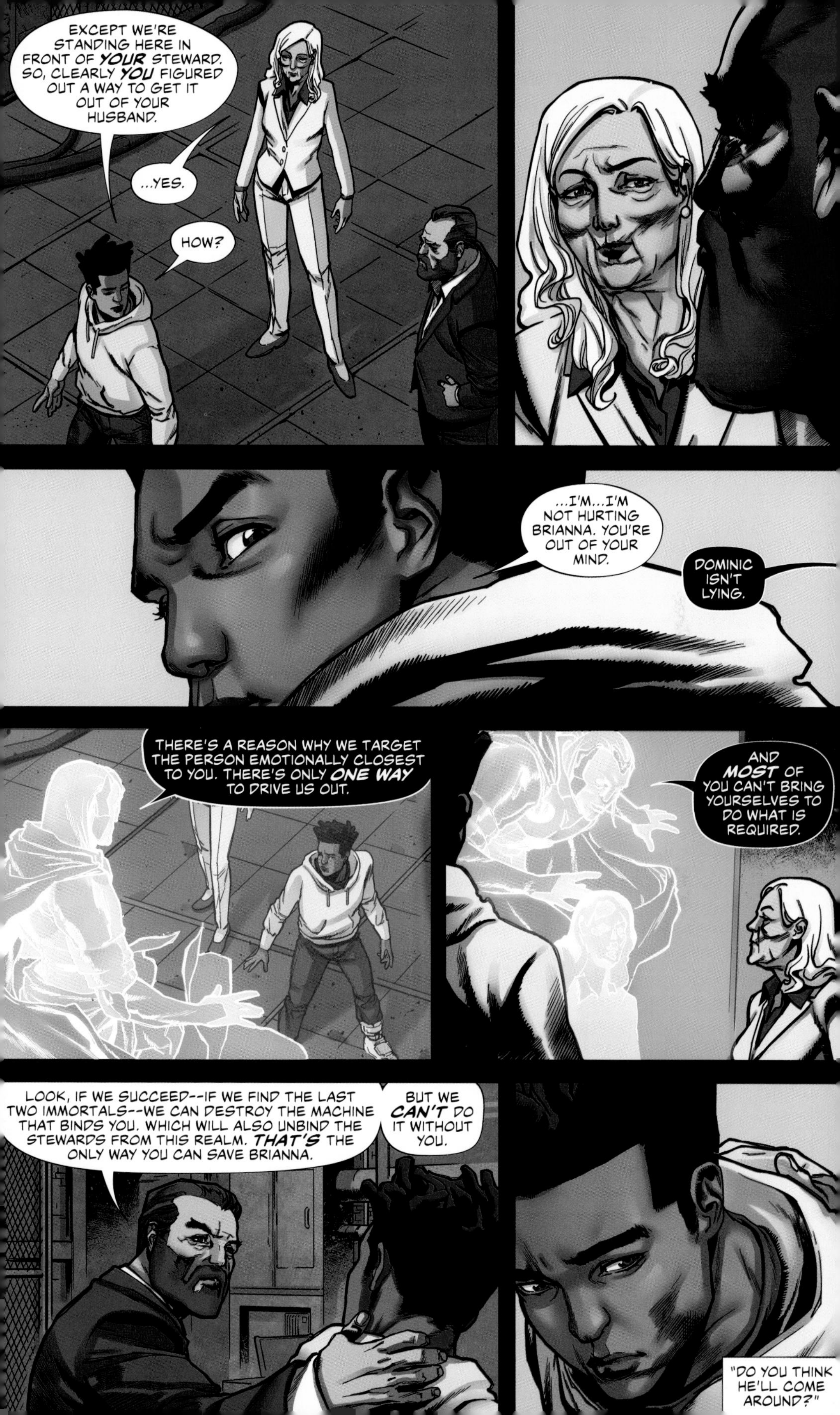

EXCEPT WE'RE STANDING HERE IN FRONT OF YOUR STEWARD. SO, CLEARLY YOU FIGURED OUT A WAY TO GET IT OUT OF YOUR HUSBAND.
...YES.
HOW?
...I'M...I'M NOT HURTING BRIANNA. YOU'RE OUT OF YOUR MIND.
DOMINIC ISN'T LYING.
THERE'S A REASON WHY WE TARGET THE PERSON EMOTIONALLY CLOSEST TO YOU. THERE'S ONLY ONE WAY TO DRIVE US OUT.
AND MOST OF YOU CAN'T BRING YOURSELVES TO DO WHAT IS REQUIRED.
LOOK, IF WE SUCCEED--IF WE FIND THE LAST TWO IMMORTALS--WE CAN DESTROY THE MACHINE THAT BINDS YOU. WHICH WILL ALSO UNBIND THE STEWARDS FROM THIS REALM. THAT'S THE ONLY WAY YOU CAN SAVE BRIANNA.
BUT WE CAN'T DO IT WITHOUT YOU.
"DO YOU THINK HE'LL COME AROUND?"

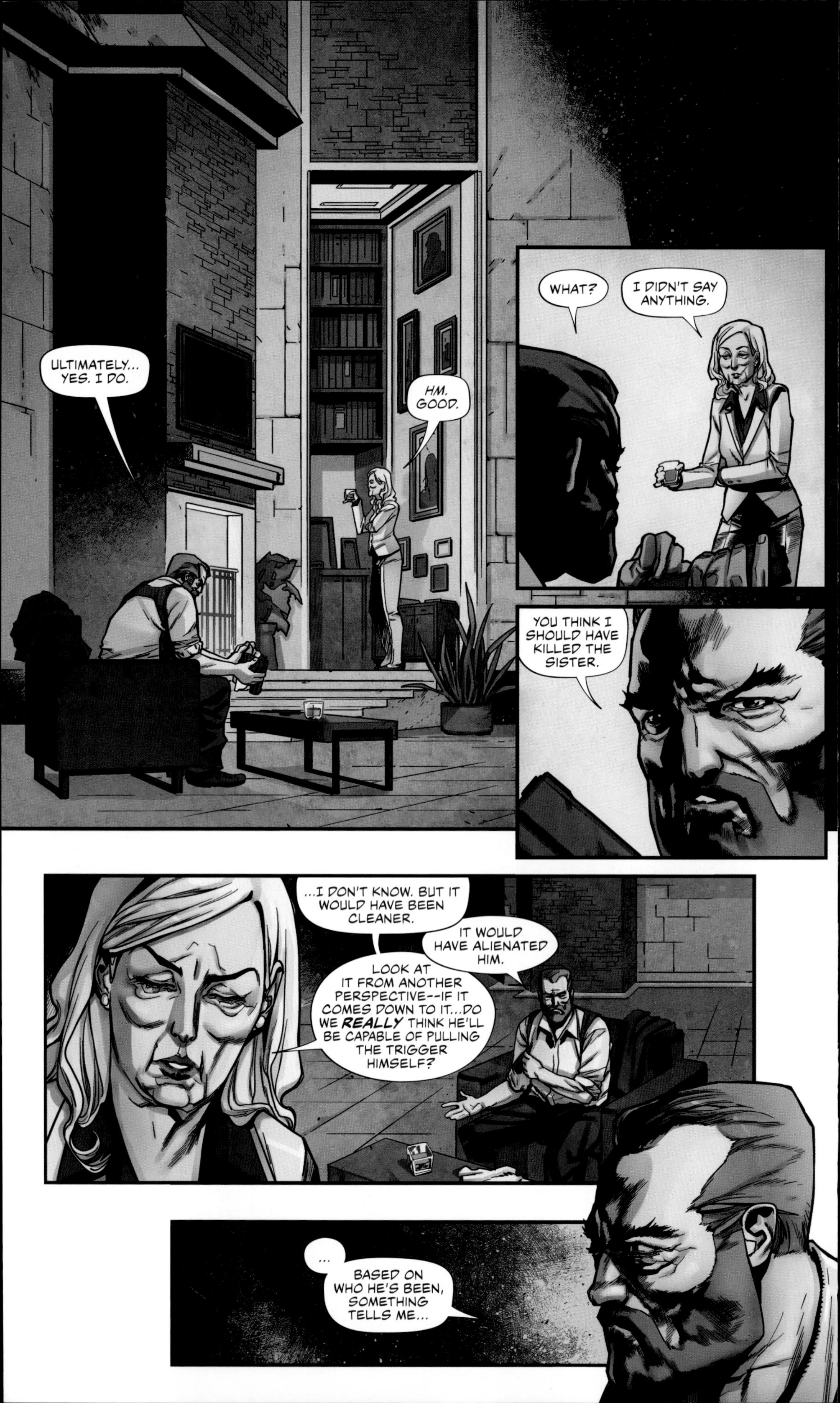
ULTIMATELY... YES. I DO.
HM. GOOD.
WHAT?
I DIDN'T SAY ANYTHING.
YOU THINK I SHOULD HAVE KILLED THE SISTER.
...I DON'T KNOW. BUT IT WOULD HAVE BEEN CLEANER.
IT WOULD HAVE ALIENATED HIM.
LOOK AT IT FROM ANOTHER PERSPECTIVE--IF IT COMES DOWN TO IT...DO WE REALLY THINK HE'LL BE CAPABLE OF PULLING THE TRIGGER HIMSELF?
...
BASED ON WHO HE'S BEEN, SOMETHING TELLS ME...

"...KILLING WON'T TAKE LONG TO GET USED TO."
--THE DECEASED HAVE BEEN IDENTIFIED AS DANIEL AND VICTORIA BECKER. A THIRD VICTIM, THEIR DAUGHTER BRIANNA, IS STILL IN THE HOSPITAL, THOUGH I'M TOLD HER CONDITION IS NOT LIFE-THREATENING.
WHAT ARE YOU HEARING FROM AUTHORITIES, GAIL? HAVE THE POLICE NARROWED DOWN ANY SUSPECTS?
WELL, WE'VE BEEN GIVEN NO OFFICIAL WORD, BUT I CAN TELL YOU THAT THE BECKERS' SON, CHRISTOPHER, HAS BEEN MISSING SINCE THE ATTACK.
WHETHER HE'S A SUSPECT OR NOT, I CAN'T SAY, BUT THE POLICE ARE LOOKING FOR HIM TO ASSIST IN THEIR INQUIRIES.
BY THE SOUNDS OF IT, AUTHORITIES BELIEVE HE'S SOMEHOW CONNECTED TO THIS TRAGEDY...
HRRRRN
...YEAH... =SNIFFLE= I DON'T KNOW HOW THE HELL--
"<THE CITY IS SECURE.>"

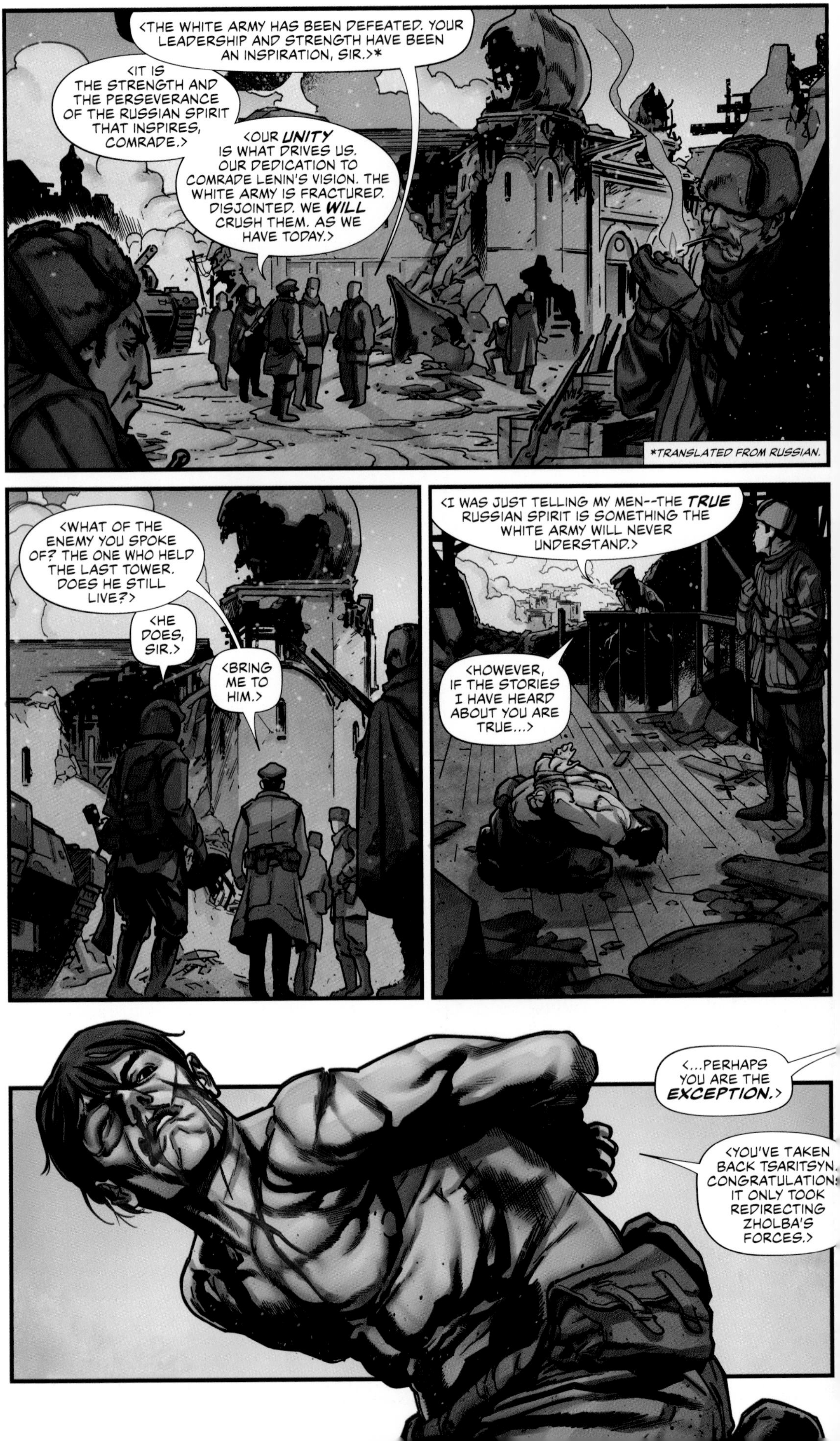
<THE WHITE ARMY HAS BEEN DEFEATED. YOUR LEADERSHIP AND STRENGTH HAVE BEEN AN INSPIRATION, SIR.>*
<IT IS THE STRENGTH AND THE PERSEVERANCE OF THE RUSSIAN SPIRIT THAT INSPIRES, COMRADE.>
<OUR *UNITY* IS WHAT DRIVES US. OUR DEDICATION TO COMRADE LENIN'S VISION. THE WHITE ARMY IS FRACTURED. DISJOINTED. WE *WILL* CRUSH THEM. AS WE HAVE TODAY.>
*TRANSLATED FROM RUSSIAN.
<WHAT OF THE ENEMY YOU SPOKE OF? THE ONE WHO HELD THE LAST TOWER. DOES HE STILL LIVE?>
<HE DOES, SIR.>
<BRING ME TO HIM.>
<I WAS JUST TELLING MY MEN--THE *TRUE* RUSSIAN SPIRIT IS SOMETHING THE WHITE ARMY WILL NEVER UNDERSTAND.>
<HOWEVER, IF THE STORIES I HAVE HEARD ABOUT YOU ARE TRUE...>
<...PERHAPS YOU ARE THE *EXCEPTION.*>
<YOU'VE TAKEN BACK TSARITSYN. CONGRATULATION: IT ONLY TOOK REDIRECTING ZHOLBA'S FORCES.>

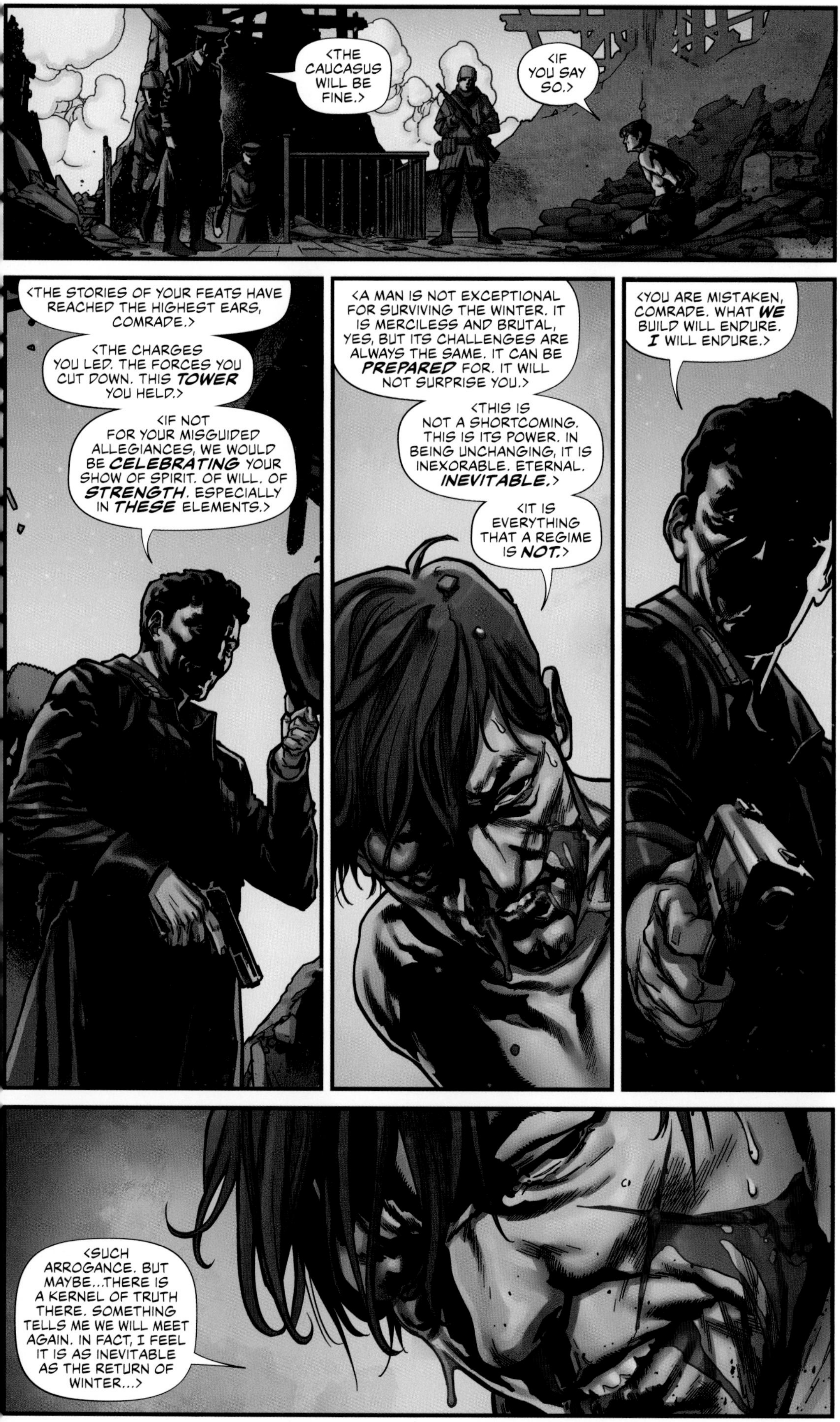
<THE CAUCASUS WILL BE FINE.>
<IF YOU SAY SO.>
<THE STORIES OF YOUR FEATS HAVE REACHED THE HIGHEST EARS, COMRADE.>
<THE CHARGES YOU LED. THE FORCES YOU CUT DOWN. THIS TOWER YOU HELD.>
<IF NOT FOR YOUR MISGUIDED ALLEGIANCES, WE WOULD BE CELEBRATING YOUR SHOW OF SPIRIT. OF WILL. OF STRENGTH. ESPECIALLY IN THESE ELEMENTS.>
<A MAN IS NOT EXCEPTIONAL FOR SURVIVING THE WINTER. IT IS MERCILESS AND BRUTAL, YES, BUT ITS CHALLENGES ARE ALWAYS THE SAME. IT CAN BE PREPARED FOR. IT WILL NOT SURPRISE YOU.>
<THIS IS NOT A SHORTCOMING. THIS IS ITS POWER. IN BEING UNCHANGING, IT IS INEXORABLE. ETERNAL. INEVITABLE.>
<IT IS EVERYTHING THAT A REGIME IS NOT.>
<YOU ARE MISTAKEN, COMRADE. WHAT WE BUILD WILL ENDURE. I WILL ENDURE.>
<SUCH ARROGANCE. BUT MAYBE...THERE IS A KERNEL OF TRUTH THERE. SOMETHING TELLS ME WE WILL MEET AGAIN. IN FACT, I FEEL IT IS AS INEVITABLE AS THE RETURN OF WINTER...>

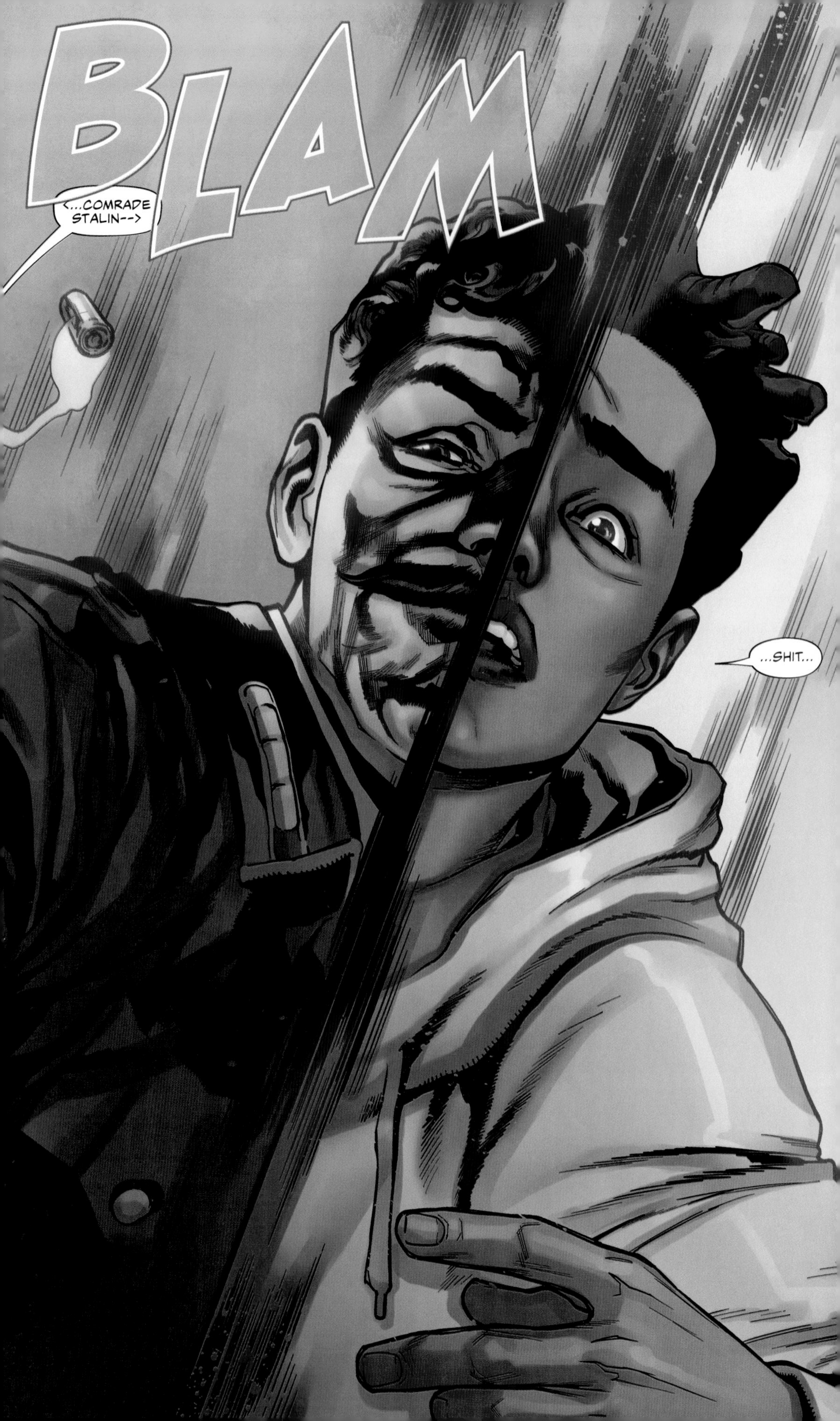
BLAM
<...COMRADE STALIN-->
...SHIT...

THERE.

MY LIEGE!

≈GULP≈

THE CITADEL IS IN SIGHT. NEARLY THERE!

THANK THE ONE KING, IT'S ABOUT TIME.

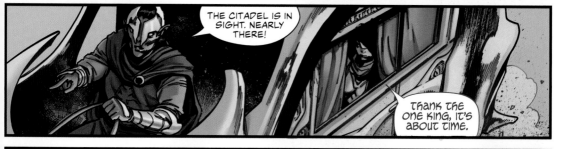

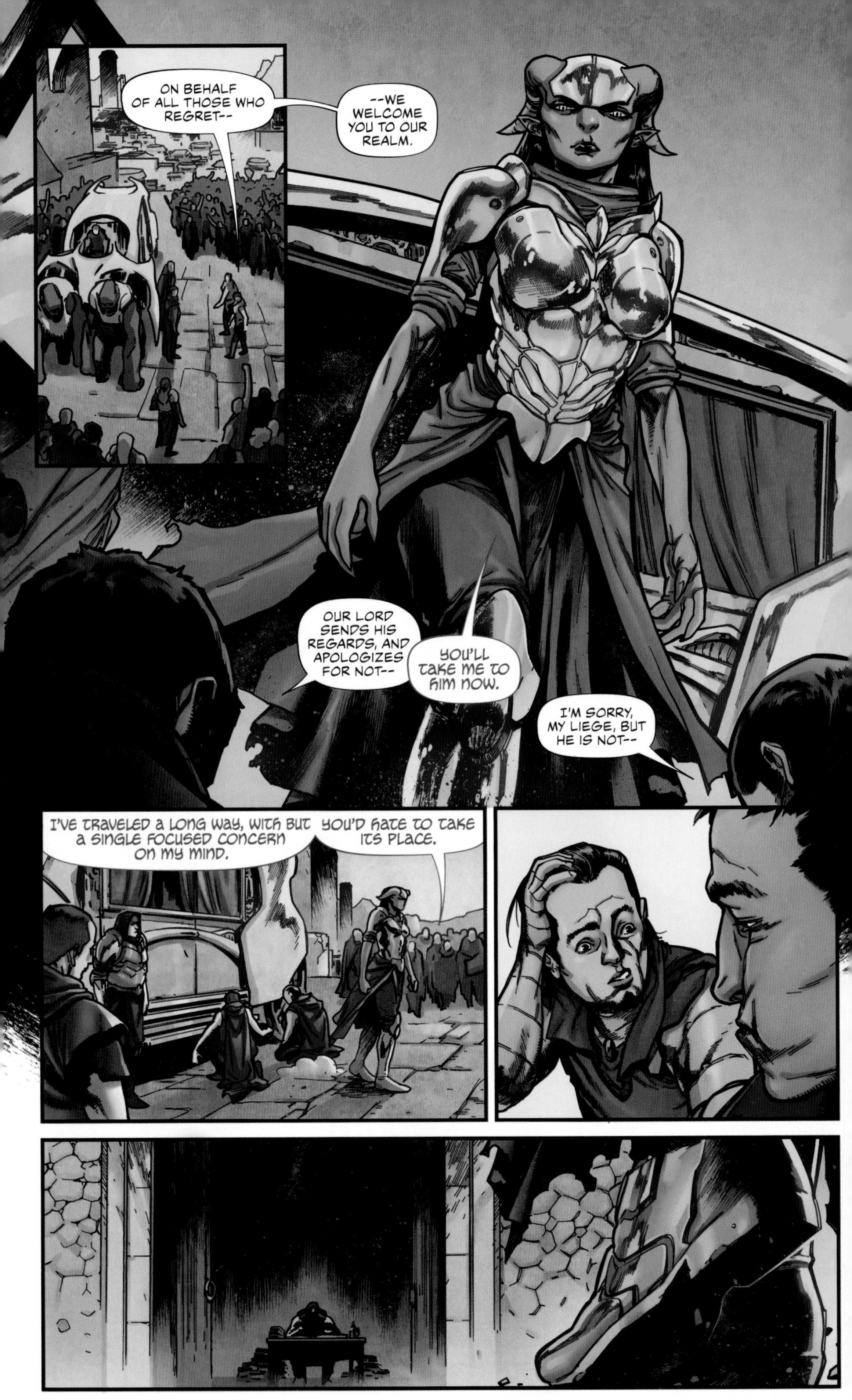

ON BEHALF OF ALL THOSE WHO REGRET--
--WE WELCOME YOU TO OUR REALM.
OUR LORD SENDS HIS REGARDS, AND APOLOGIZES FOR NOT--
YOU'LL TAKE ME TO HIM NOW.
I'M SORRY, MY LIEGE, BUT HE IS NOT--
I'VE TRAVELED A LONG WAY, WITH BUT A SINGLE FOCUSED CONCERN ON MY MIND.
YOU'D HATE TO TAKE ITS PLACE.

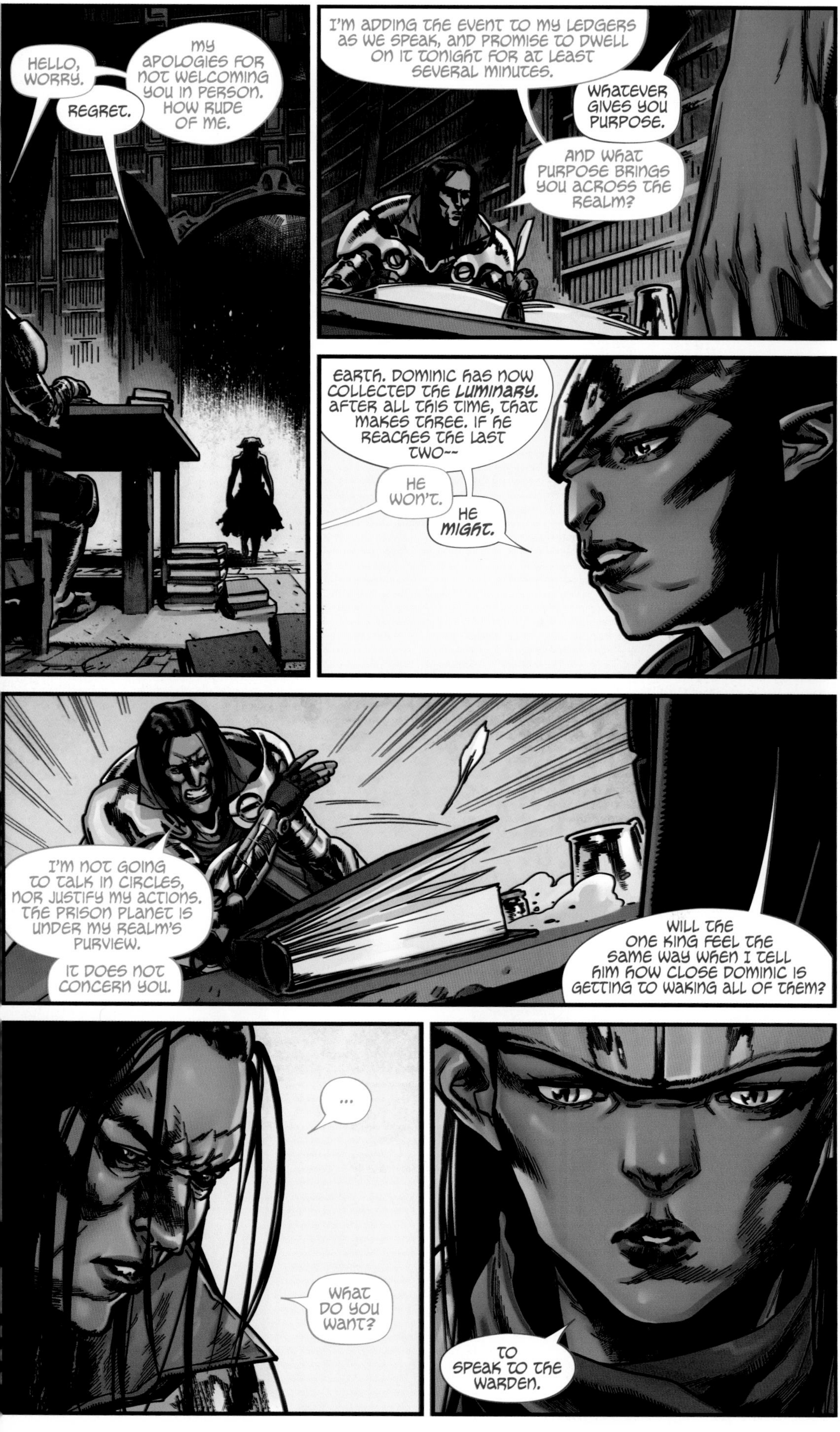

HELLO, WORRY.
REGRET.
MY APOLOGIES FOR NOT WELCOMING YOU IN PERSON. HOW RUDE OF ME.
I'M ADDING THE EVENT TO MY LEDGERS AS WE SPEAK, AND PROMISE TO DWELL ON IT TONIGHT FOR AT LEAST SEVERAL MINUTES.
WHATEVER GIVES YOU PURPOSE.
AND WHAT PURPOSE BRINGS YOU ACROSS THE REALM?
EARTH. DOMINIC HAS NOW COLLECTED THE *LUMINARY.* AFTER ALL THIS TIME, THAT MAKES THREE. IF HE REACHES THE LAST TWO--
HE WON'T.
HE *MIGHT.*
I'M NOT GOING TO TALK IN CIRCLES, NOR JUSTIFY MY ACTIONS. THE PRISON PLANET IS UNDER MY REALM'S PURVIEW.
IT DOES NOT CONCERN YOU.
WILL THE ONE KING FEEL THE SAME WAY WHEN I TELL HIM HOW CLOSE DOMINIC IS GETTING TO WAKING ALL OF THEM?
...
WHAT DO YOU WANT?
TO SPEAK TO THE WARDEN.

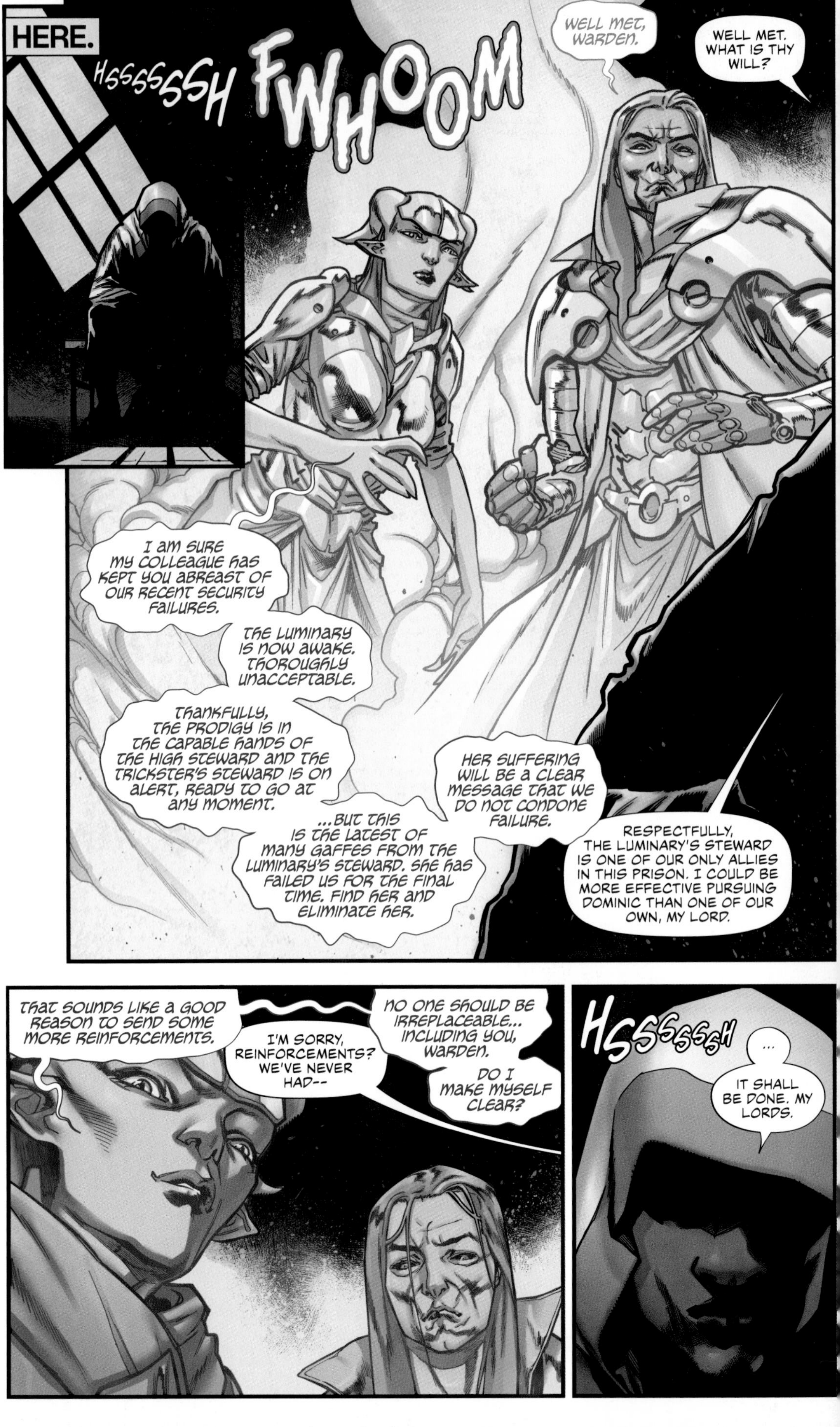
HERE.
HSSSSSSH FWHOOM
WELL MET, WARDEN.
WELL MET. WHAT IS THY WILL?
I AM SURE MY COLLEAGUE HAS KEPT YOU ABREAST OF OUR RECENT SECURITY FAILURES.
THE LUMINARY IS NOW AWAKE. THOROUGHLY UNACCEPTABLE.
THANKFULLY, THE PRODIGY IS IN THE CAPABLE HANDS OF THE HIGH STEWARD AND THE TRICKSTER'S STEWARD IS ON ALERT, READY TO GO AT ANY MOMENT.
...BUT THIS IS THE LATEST OF MANY GAFFES FROM THE LUMINARY'S STEWARD. SHE HAS FAILED US FOR THE FINAL TIME. FIND HER AND ELIMINATE HER.
HER SUFFERING WILL BE A CLEAR MESSAGE THAT WE DO NOT CONDONE FAILURE.
RESPECTFULLY, THE LUMINARY'S STEWARD IS ONE OF OUR ONLY ALLIES IN THIS PRISON. I COULD BE MORE EFFECTIVE PURSUING DOMINIC THAN ONE OF OUR OWN, MY LORD.
THAT SOUNDS LIKE A GOOD REASON TO SEND SOME MORE REINFORCEMENTS.
I'M SORRY, REINFORCEMENTS? WE'VE NEVER HAD--
NO ONE SHOULD BE IRREPLACEABLE... INCLUDING YOU, WARDEN.
DO I MAKE MYSELF CLEAR?
HSSSSSSH
...
IT SHALL BE DONE. MY LORDS.

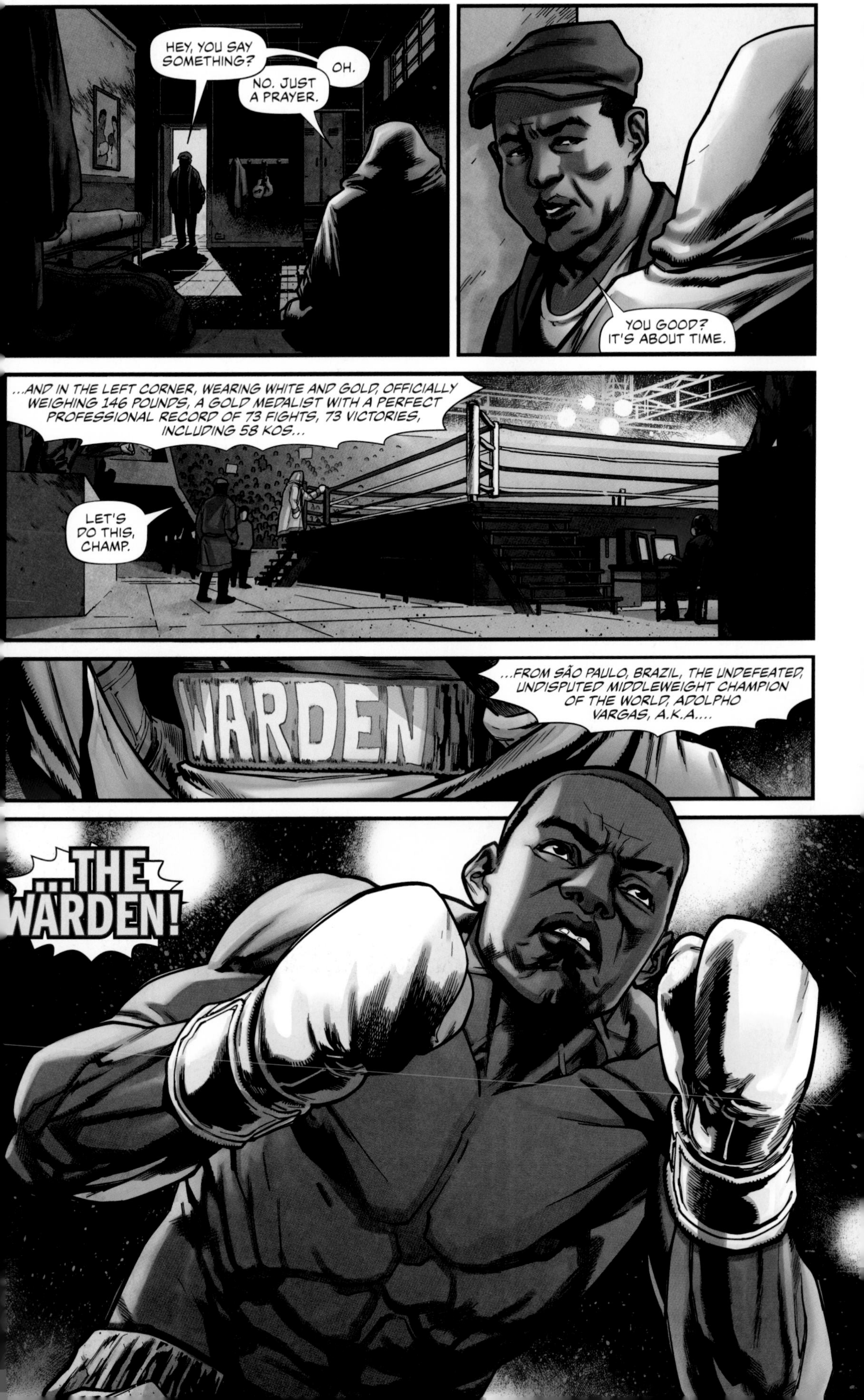
HEY, YOU SAY SOMETHING?
NO. JUST A PRAYER.
OH.
YOU GOOD? IT'S ABOUT TIME.
...AND IN THE LEFT CORNER, WEARING WHITE AND GOLD, OFFICIALLY WEIGHING 146 POUNDS, A GOLD MEDALIST WITH A PERFECT PROFESSIONAL RECORD OF 73 FIGHTS, 73 VICTORIES, INCLUDING 58 KOS...
LET'S DO THIS, CHAMP.
WARDEN
...FROM SÃO PAULO, BRAZIL, THE UNDEFEATED, UNDISPUTED MIDDLEWEIGHT CHAMPION OF THE WORLD, ADOLPHO VARGAS, A.K.A....
...THE WARDEN!

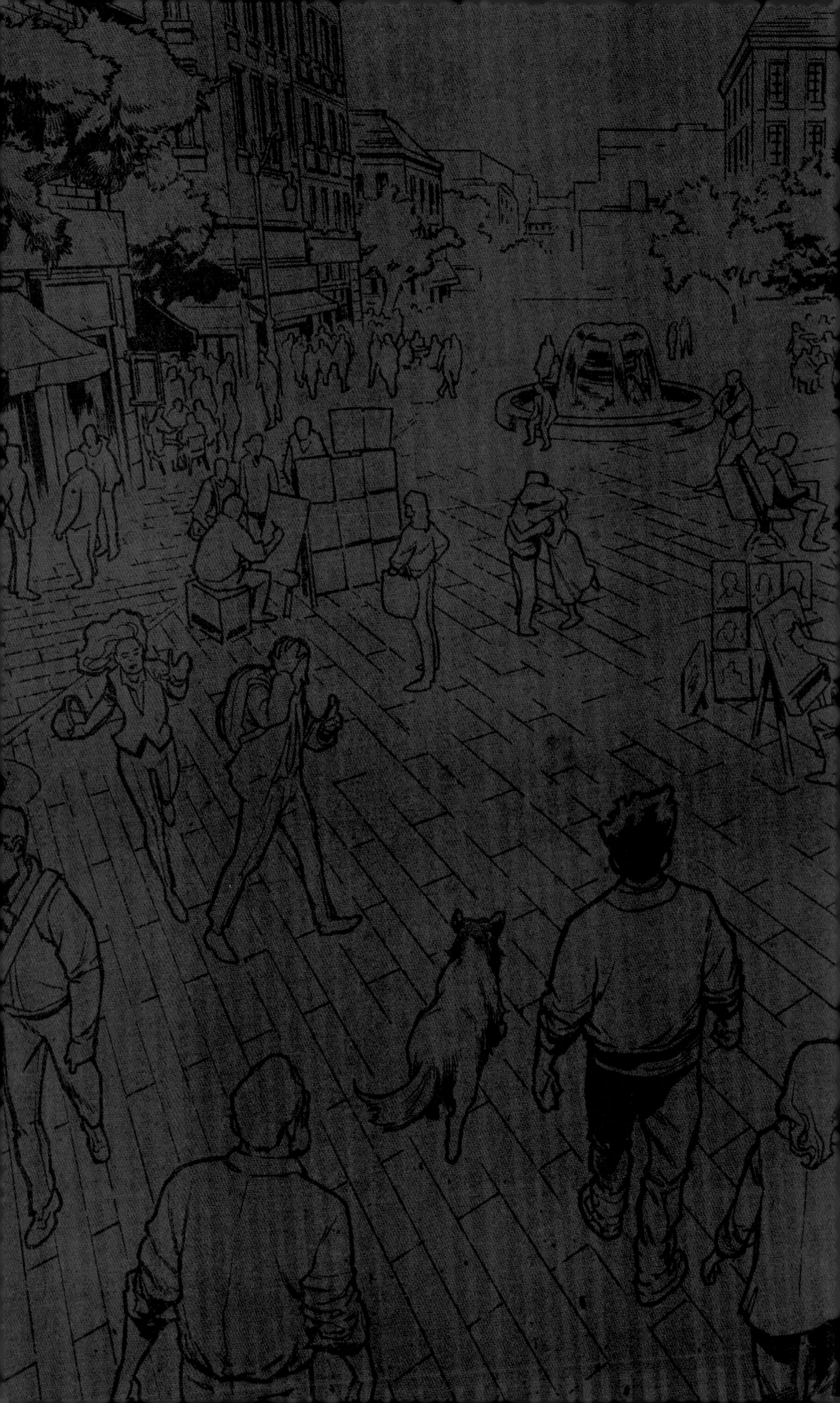

CHAPTER III
Ward

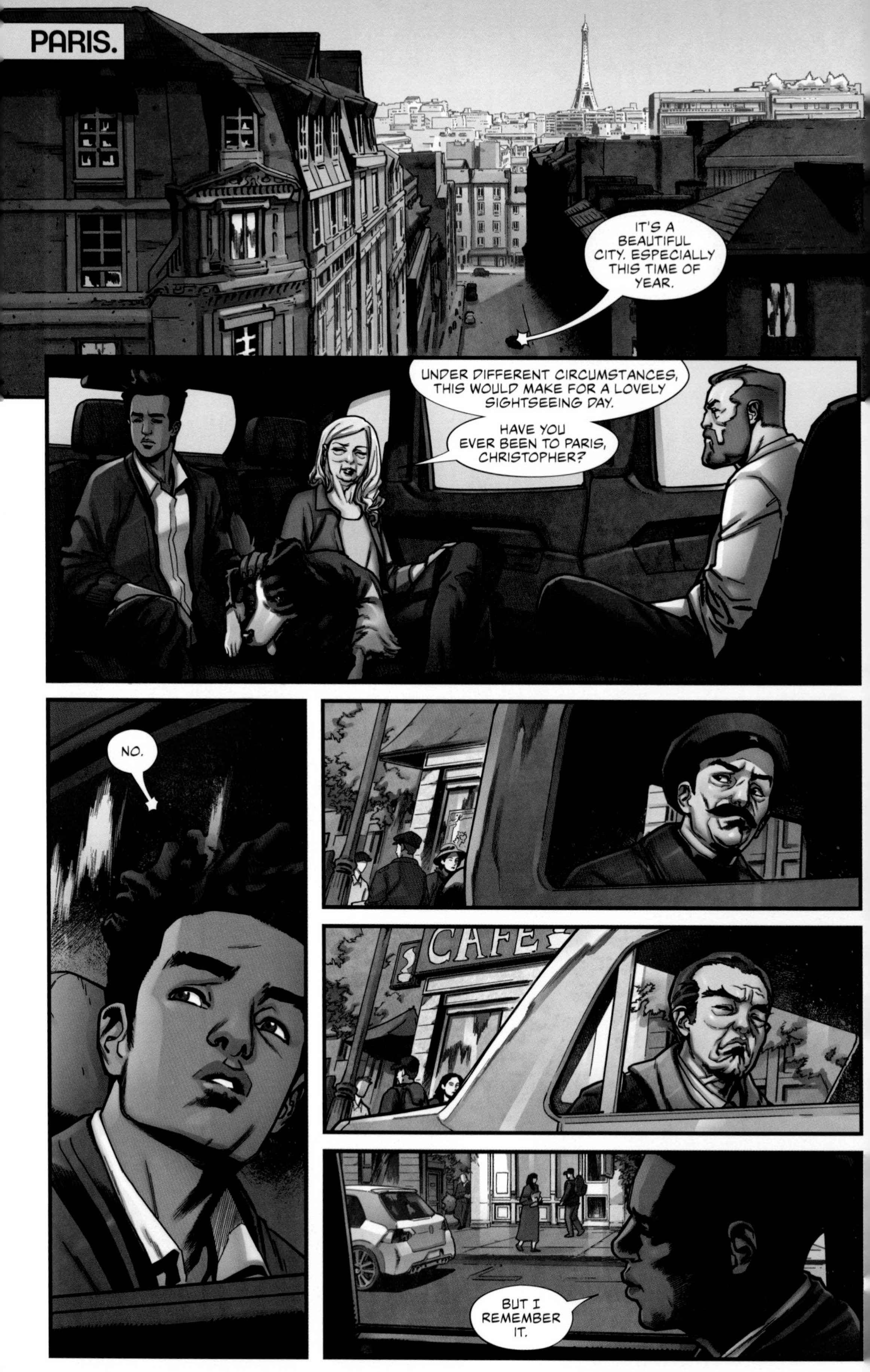
PARIS.
IT'S A BEAUTIFUL CITY. ESPECIALLY THIS TIME OF YEAR.
UNDER DIFFERENT CIRCUMSTANCES, THIS WOULD MAKE FOR A LOVELY SIGHTSEEING DAY.
HAVE YOU EVER BEEN TO PARIS, CHRISTOPHER?
NO.
CAFE
BUT I REMEMBER IT.

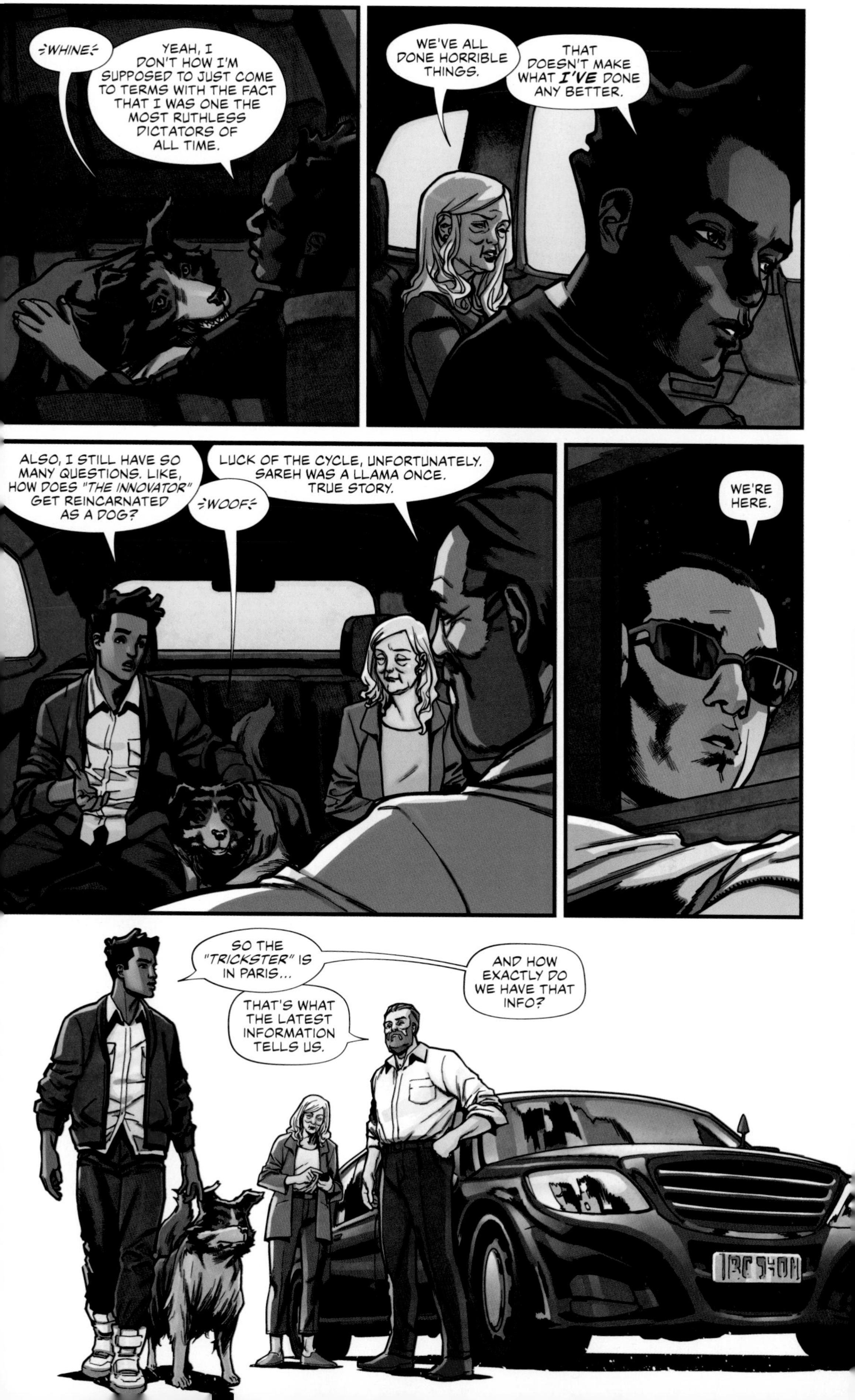
WHINE
YEAH, I DON'T HOW I'M SUPPOSED TO JUST COME TO TERMS WITH THE FACT THAT I WAS ONE THE MOST RUTHLESS DICTATORS OF ALL TIME.
WE'VE ALL DONE HORRIBLE THINGS.
THAT DOESN'T MAKE WHAT *I'VE* DONE ANY BETTER.
ALSO, I STILL HAVE SO MANY QUESTIONS. LIKE, HOW DOES "*THE INNOVATOR*" GET REINCARNATED AS A DOG?
WOOF
LUCK OF THE CYCLE, UNFORTUNATELY. SAREH WAS A LLAMA ONCE. TRUE STORY.
WE'RE HERE.
SO THE "*TRICKSTER*" IS IN PARIS...
THAT'S WHAT THE LATEST INFORMATION TELLS US.
AND HOW EXACTLY DO WE HAVE THAT INFO?

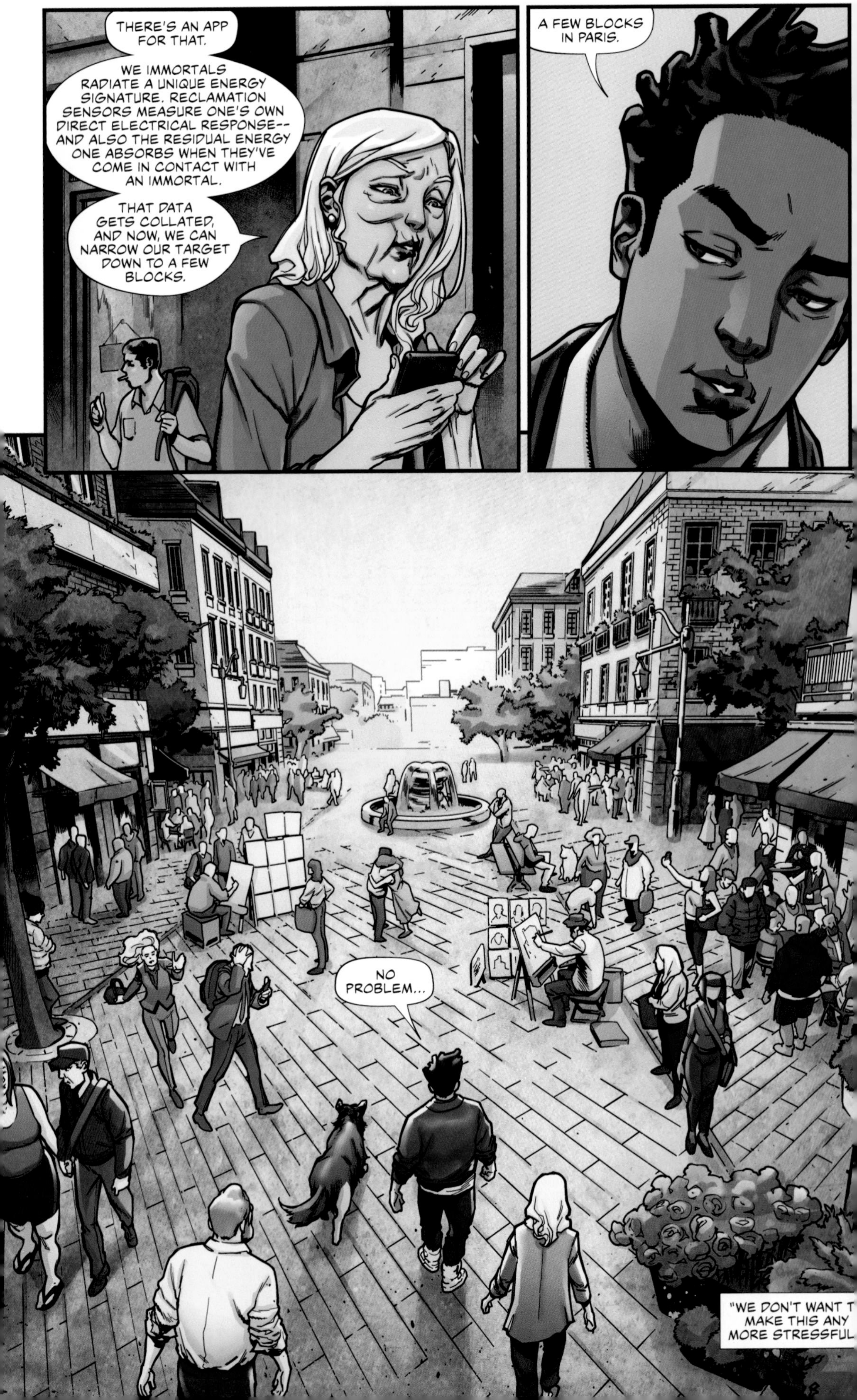
THERE'S AN APP FOR THAT.
WE IMMORTALS RADIATE A UNIQUE ENERGY SIGNATURE. RECLAMATION SENSORS MEASURE ONE'S OWN DIRECT ELECTRICAL RESPONSE-- AND ALSO THE RESIDUAL ENERGY ONE ABSORBS WHEN THEY'VE COME IN CONTACT WITH AN IMMORTAL.
THAT DATA GETS COLLATED, AND NOW, WE CAN NARROW OUR TARGET DOWN TO A FEW BLOCKS.
A FEW BLOCKS IN PARIS.
NO PROBLEM...
"WE DON'T WANT T
MAKE THIS ANY
MORE STRESSFUL

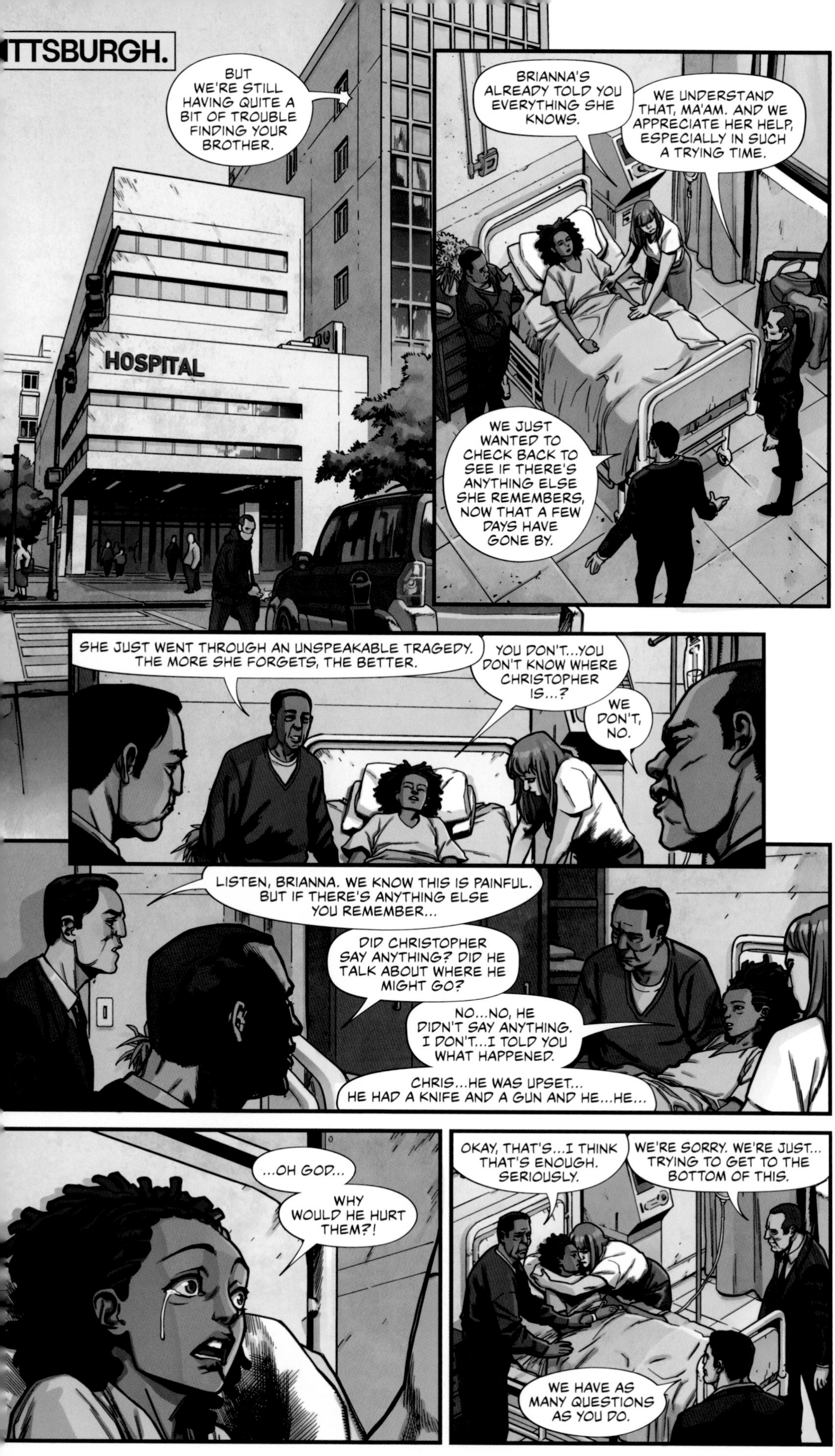

TTSBURGH.
BUT WE'RE STILL HAVING QUITE A BIT OF TROUBLE FINDING YOUR BROTHER.
BRIANNA'S ALREADY TOLD YOU EVERYTHING SHE KNOWS.
WE UNDERSTAND THAT, MA'AM. AND WE APPRECIATE HER HELP, ESPECIALLY IN SUCH A TRYING TIME.
WE JUST WANTED TO CHECK BACK TO SEE IF THERE'S ANYTHING ELSE SHE REMEMBERS, NOW THAT A FEW DAYS HAVE GONE BY.
SHE JUST WENT THROUGH AN UNSPEAKABLE TRAGEDY. THE MORE SHE FORGETS, THE BETTER.
YOU DON'T...YOU DON'T KNOW WHERE CHRISTOPHER IS...?
WE DON'T, NO.
LISTEN, BRIANNA. WE KNOW THIS IS PAINFUL. BUT IF THERE'S ANYTHING ELSE YOU REMEMBER...
DID CHRISTOPHER SAY ANYTHING? DID HE TALK ABOUT WHERE HE MIGHT GO?
NO...NO, HE DIDN'T SAY ANYTHING. I DON'T...I TOLD YOU WHAT HAPPENED.
CHRIS...HE WAS UPSET... HE HAD A KNIFE AND A GUN AND HE...HE...
...OH GOD...
WHY WOULD HE HURT THEM?!
OKAY, THAT'S...I THINK THAT'S ENOUGH. SERIOUSLY.
WE'RE SORRY. WE'RE JUST... TRYING TO GET TO THE BOTTOM OF THIS.
WE HAVE AS MANY QUESTIONS AS YOU DO.

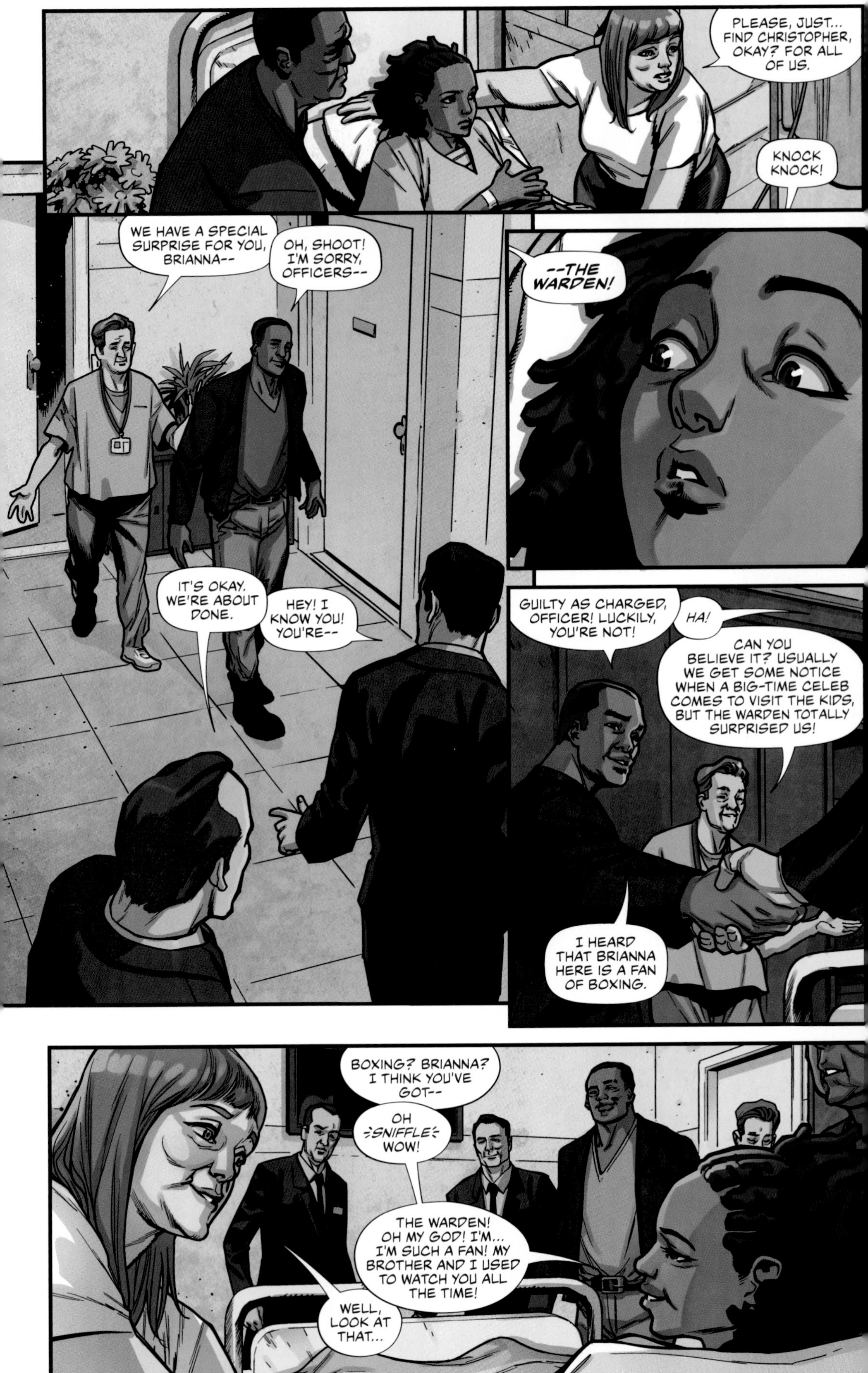
PLEASE, JUST... FIND CHRISTOPHER, OKAY? FOR ALL OF US.
KNOCK KNOCK!
WE HAVE A SPECIAL SURPRISE FOR YOU, BRIANNA--
OH, SHOOT! I'M SORRY, OFFICERS--
--THE WARDEN!
IT'S OKAY. WE'RE ABOUT DONE.
HEY! I KNOW YOU! YOU'RE--
GUILTY AS CHARGED, OFFICER! LUCKILY, YOU'RE NOT!
HA!
CAN YOU BELIEVE IT? USUALLY WE GET SOME NOTICE WHEN A BIG-TIME CELEB COMES TO VISIT THE KIDS, BUT THE WARDEN TOTALLY SURPRISED US!
I HEARD THAT BRIANNA HERE IS A FAN OF BOXING.
BOXING? BRIANNA? I THINK YOU'VE GOT--
OH *SNIFFLE* WOW!
THE WARDEN! OH MY GOD! I'M... I'M SUCH A FAN! MY BROTHER AND I USED TO WATCH YOU ALL THE TIME!
WELL, LOOK AT THAT...

TELL YOU WHAT, WE'RE GOING TO DUCK OUT AND TALK TO THE DETECTIVES HERE.

MAYBE GET SOME COFFEE? DO...YOU WANT ANYTHING, SIR?

COFFEE, PLEASE. BLACK. THAT WOULD BE FANTASTIC. IN THE MEANTIME...

...I'D LOVE TO LEARN MORE ABOUT MY BIGGEST FAN.

STEWARD. YOU SEEM...CALM.

THIS BODY WAS SHOT. BETTER TO RELAX THAN TO FIGHT IT.

I'M JUST SURPRISED YOU DIDN'T TAKE A NEW ONE. SURE, IT'S PAINFUL, BUT CONSIDERING THE SITUATION...I DIDN'T THINK YOU'D LET YOURSELF BE SO EASILY FOUND.

I'M SORRY, "THE SITUATION"?

YOU FAILED, STEWARD. THE LEADER IS AWAKE.

NOW THEY'RE CONSIDERING SENDING REINFORCEMENTS.

THEY'VE NEVER DONE THAT. NOT IN MILLENNIA.

AND YET...

I... I CAN FIX THIS. GIVE ME THE CHANCE.

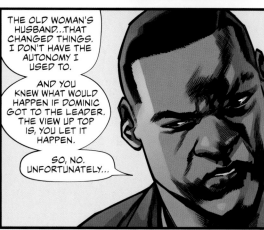

THE OLD WOMAN'S HUSBAND...THAT CHANGED THINGS. I DON'T HAVE THE AUTONOMY I USED TO.

AND YOU KNEW WHAT WOULD HAPPEN IF DOMINIC GOT TO THE LEADER. THE VIEW UP TOP IS, YOU LET IT HAPPEN.

SO, NO. UNFORTUNATELY...

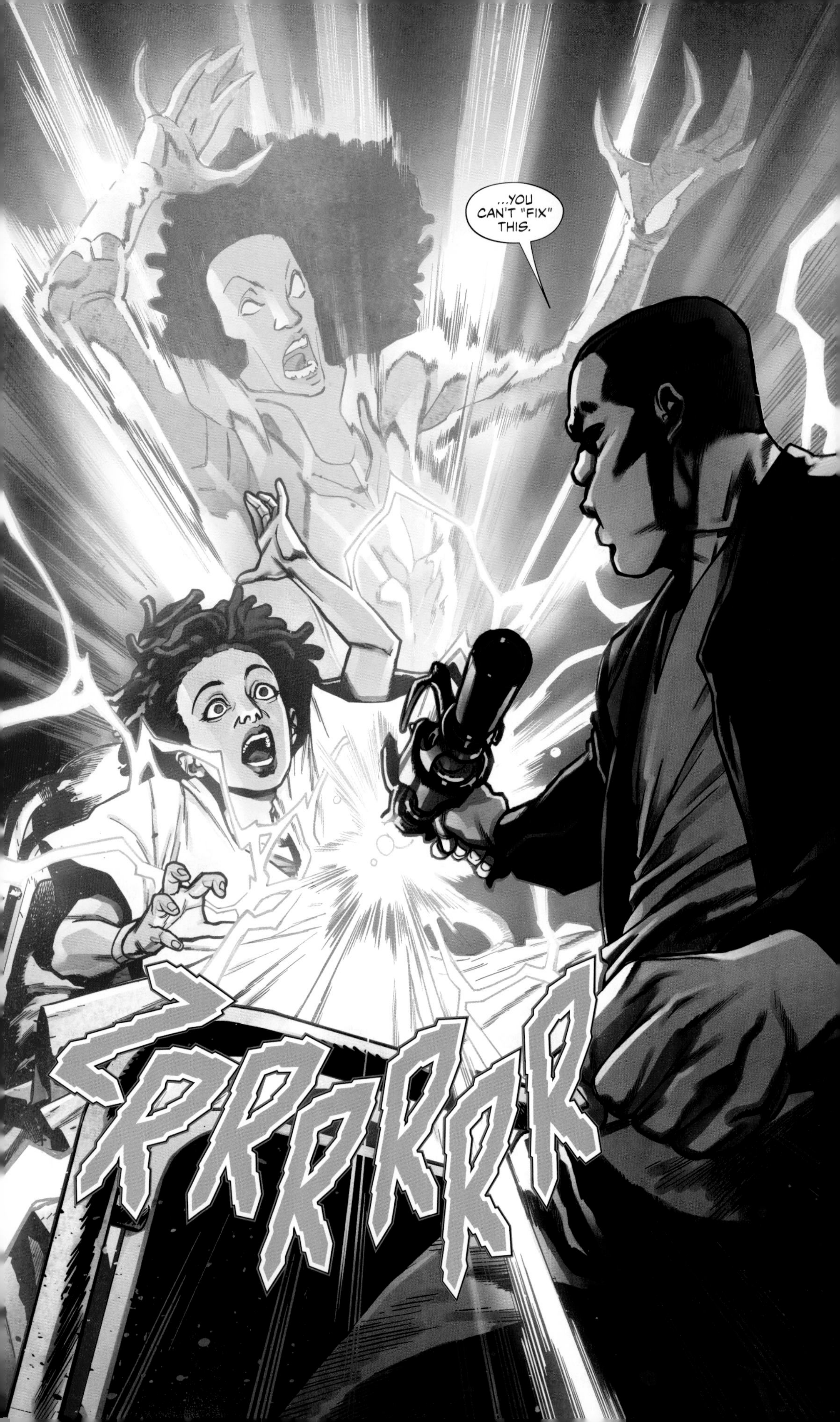
...YOU CAN'T "FIX" THIS.
KRRRRRR

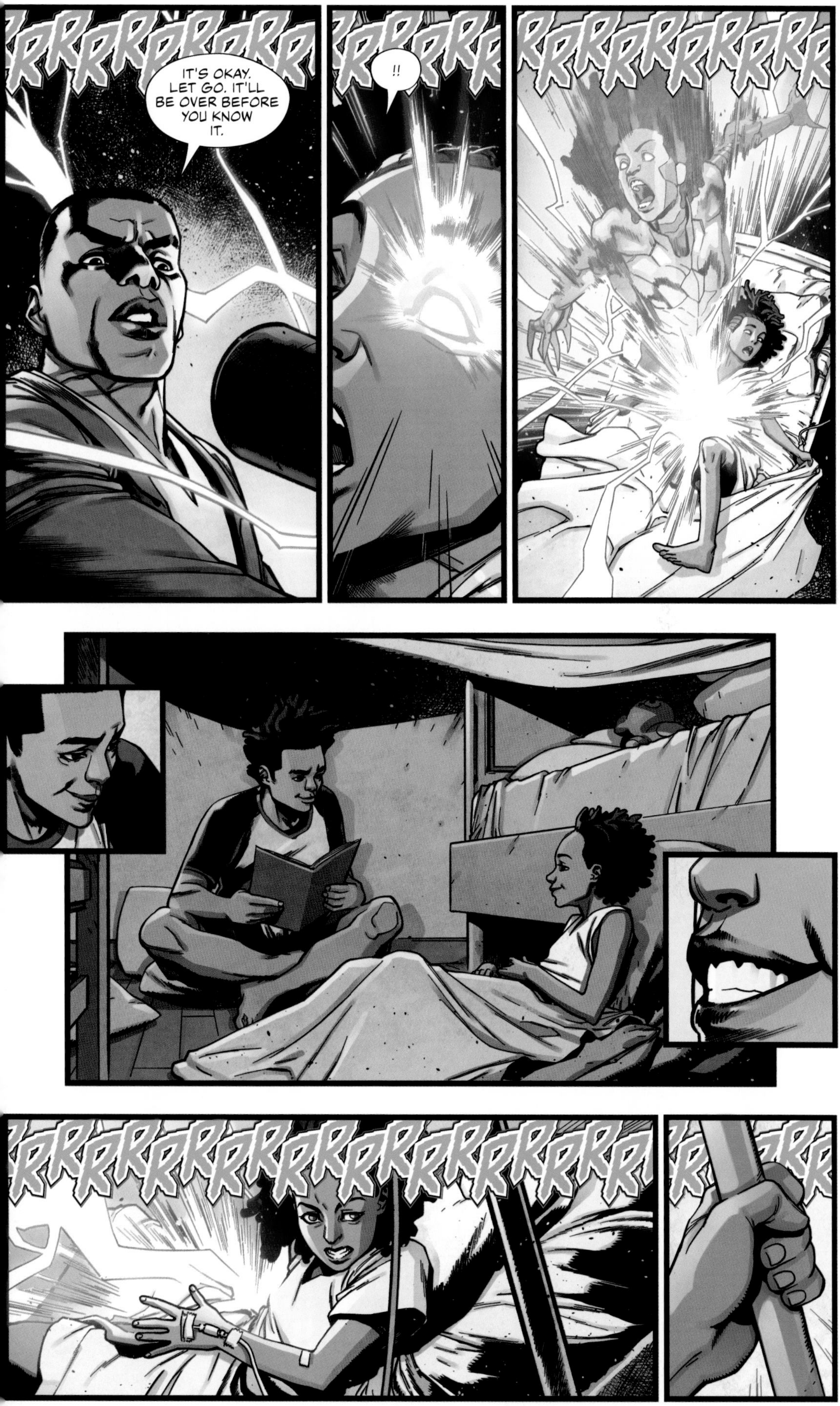
RRRRRRR
IT'S OKAY. LET GO. IT'LL BE OVER BEFORE YOU KNOW IT.
RRRRR
!!
RRRRRRRRR
RRRRRRRRRRRRRRRR
RRRR

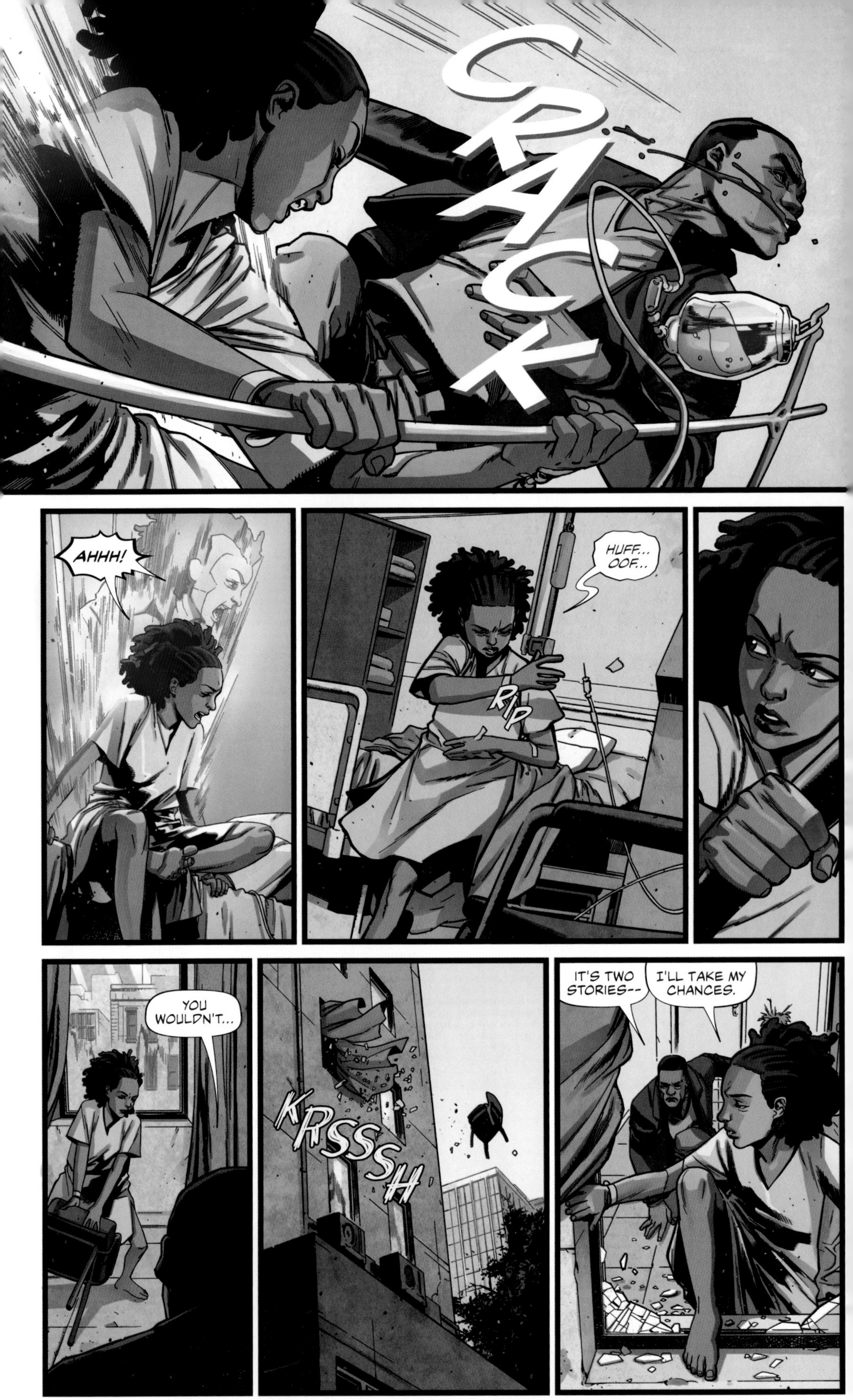
CRACK
AHHH!
HUFF... OOF...
RIP
YOU WOULDN'T...
KRSSSH
IT'S TWO STORIES--
I'LL TAKE MY CHANCES.

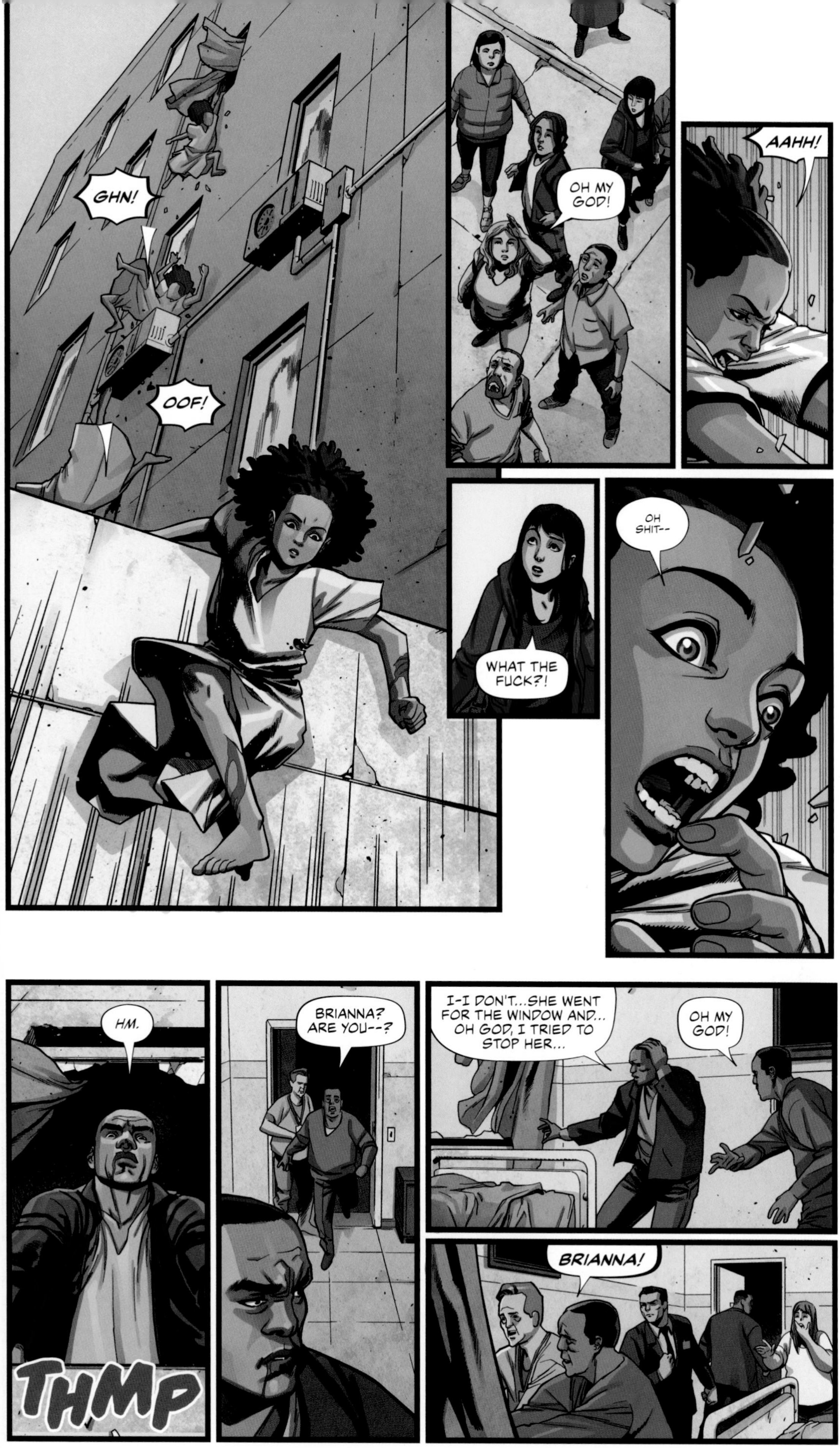
GHN!
OOF!
OH MY GOD!
AAHH!
WHAT THE FUCK?!
OH SHIT--
HM.
THMP
BRIANNA? ARE YOU--?
I-I DON'T...SHE WENT FOR THE WINDOW AND... OH GOD, I TRIED TO STOP HER...
OH MY GOD!
BRIANNA!

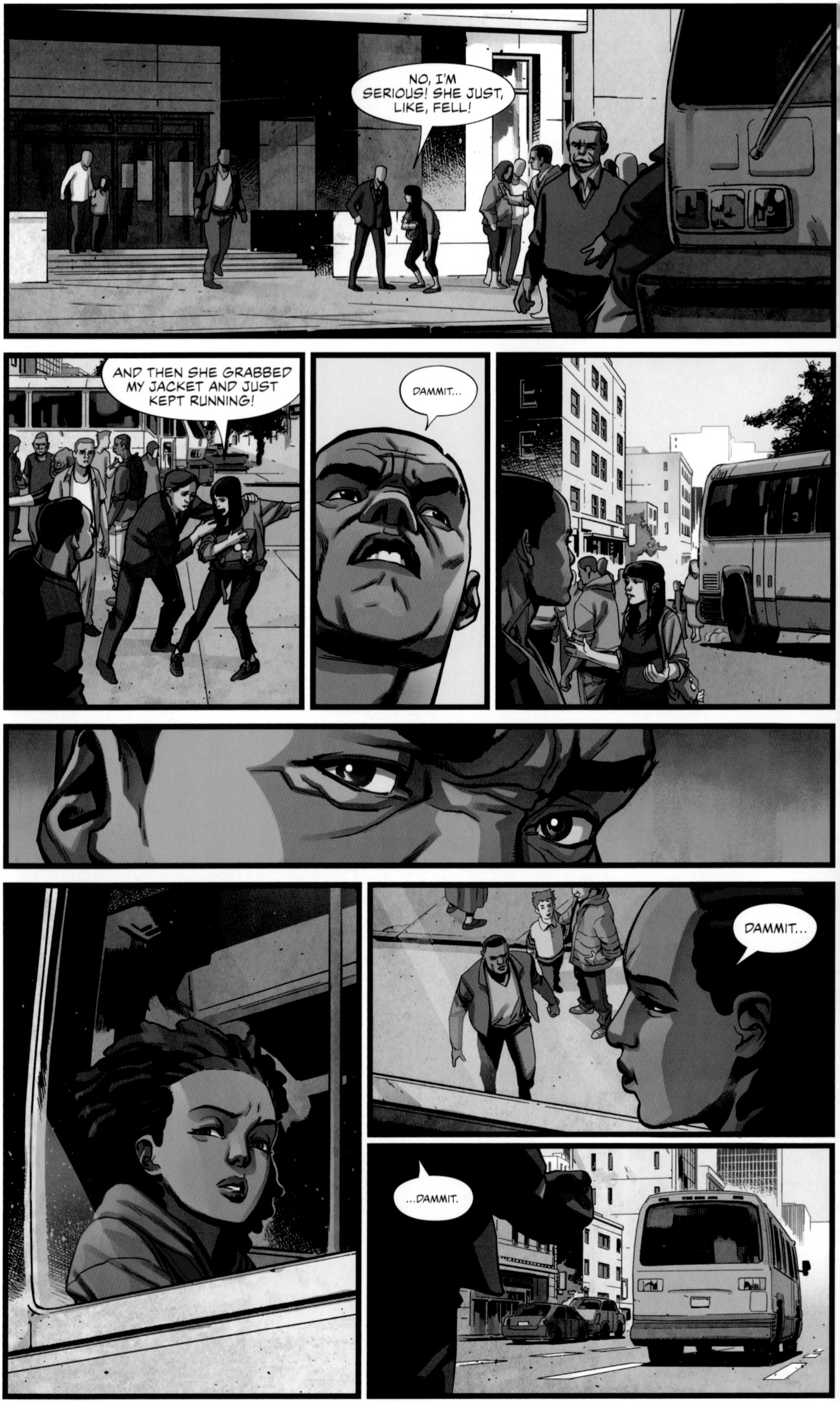
NO, I'M SERIOUS! SHE JUST, LIKE, FELL!
AND THEN SHE GRABBED MY JACKET AND JUST KEPT RUNNING!
DAMMIT...
DAMMIT...
...DAMMIT.

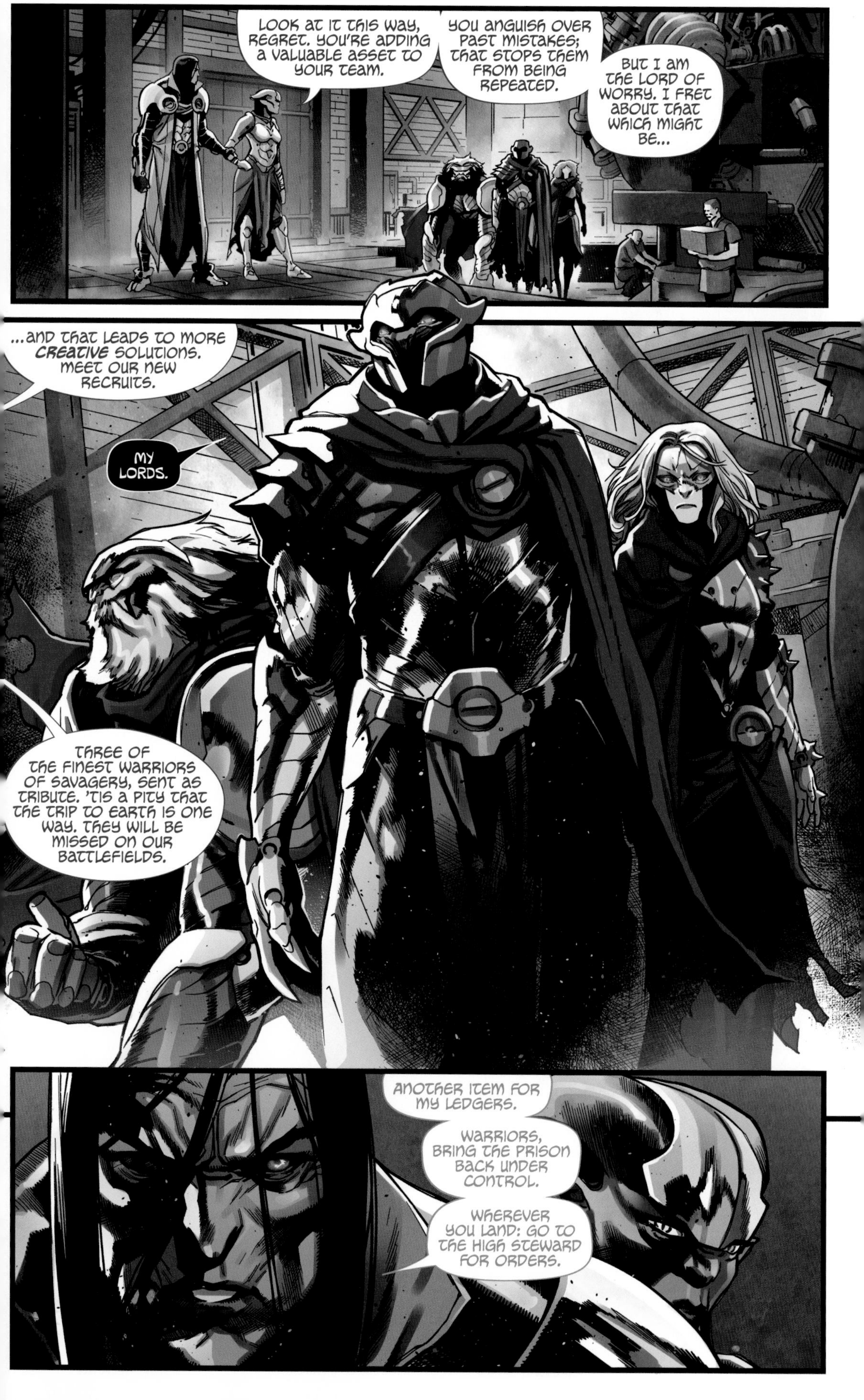

LOOK AT IT THIS WAY, REGRET. YOU'RE ADDING A VALUABLE ASSET TO YOUR TEAM.
YOU ANGUISH OVER PAST MISTAKES; THAT STOPS THEM FROM BEING REPEATED.
BUT I AM THE LORD OF WORRY. I FRET ABOUT THAT WHICH MIGHT BE...
...AND THAT LEADS TO MORE CREATIVE SOLUTIONS. MEET OUR NEW RECRUITS.
MY LORDS.
THREE OF THE FINEST WARRIORS OF SAVAGERY, SENT AS TRIBUTE. 'TIS A PITY THAT THE TRIP TO EARTH IS ONE WAY. THEY WILL BE MISSED ON OUR BATTLEFIELDS.
ANOTHER ITEM FOR MY LEDGERS.
WARRIORS, BRING THE PRISON BACK UNDER CONTROL.
WHEREVER YOU LAND: GO TO THE HIGH STEWARD FOR ORDERS.

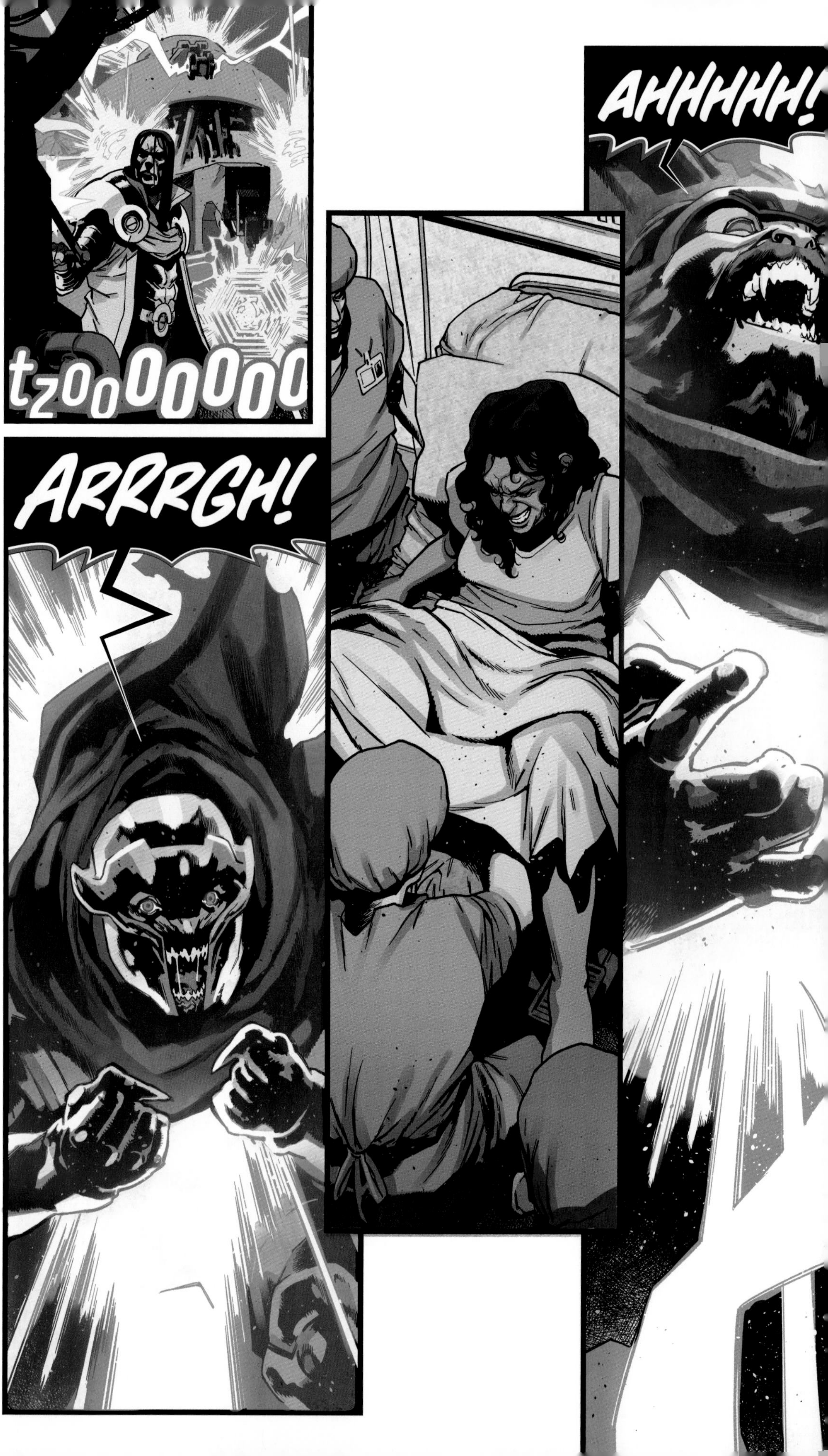
tzooOOOOOO
ARRRGH!
AHHHHH!

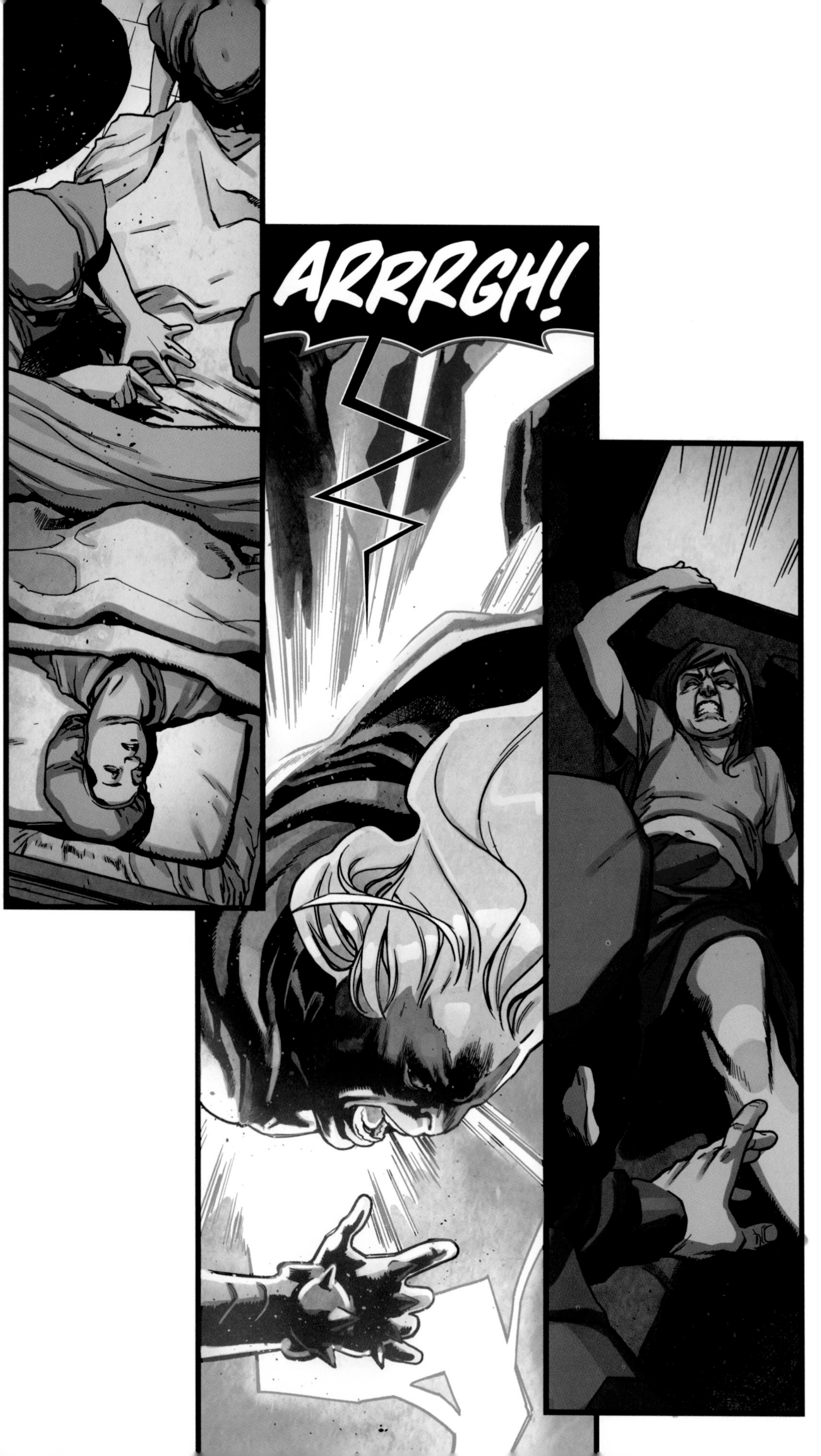
ARRRGH!

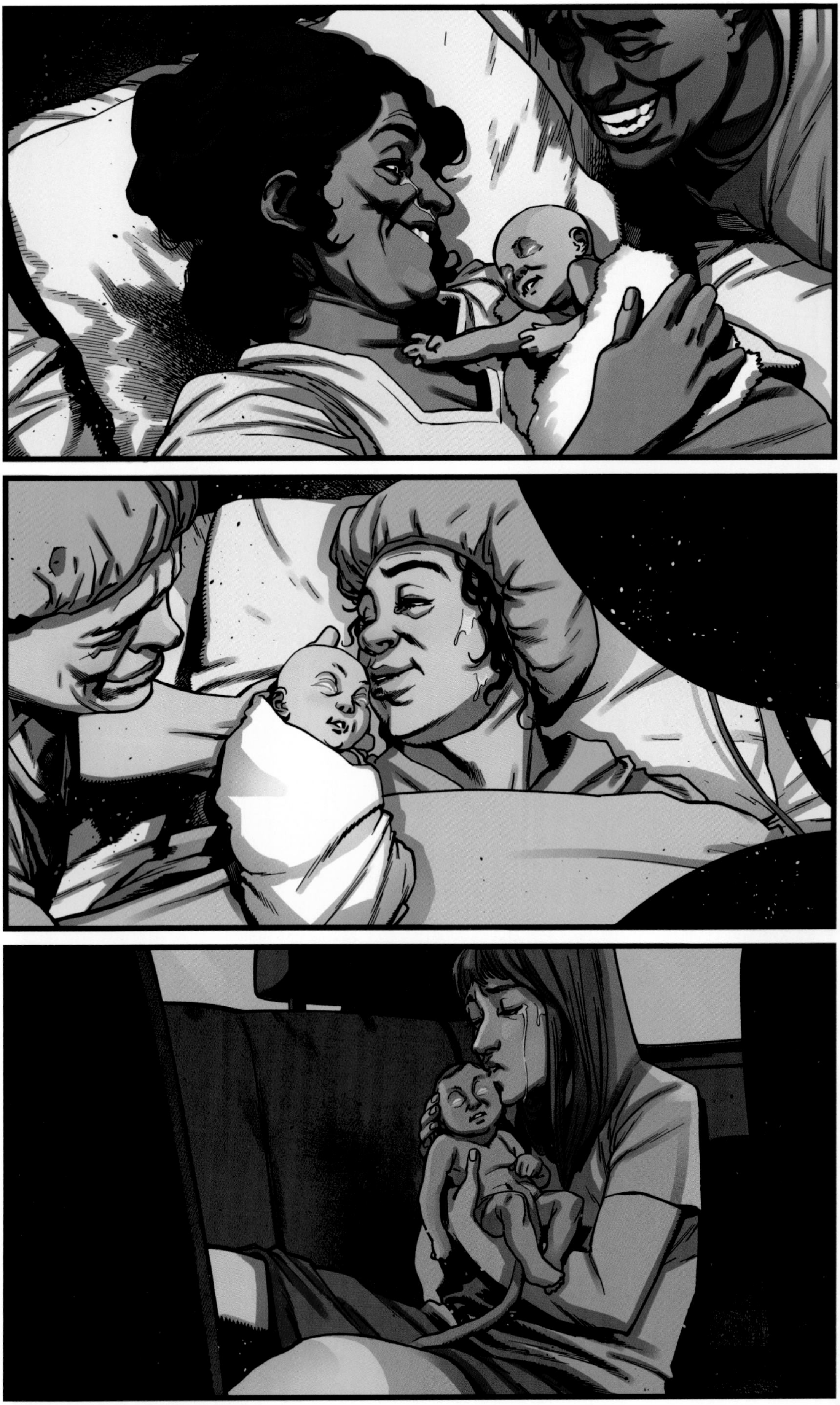

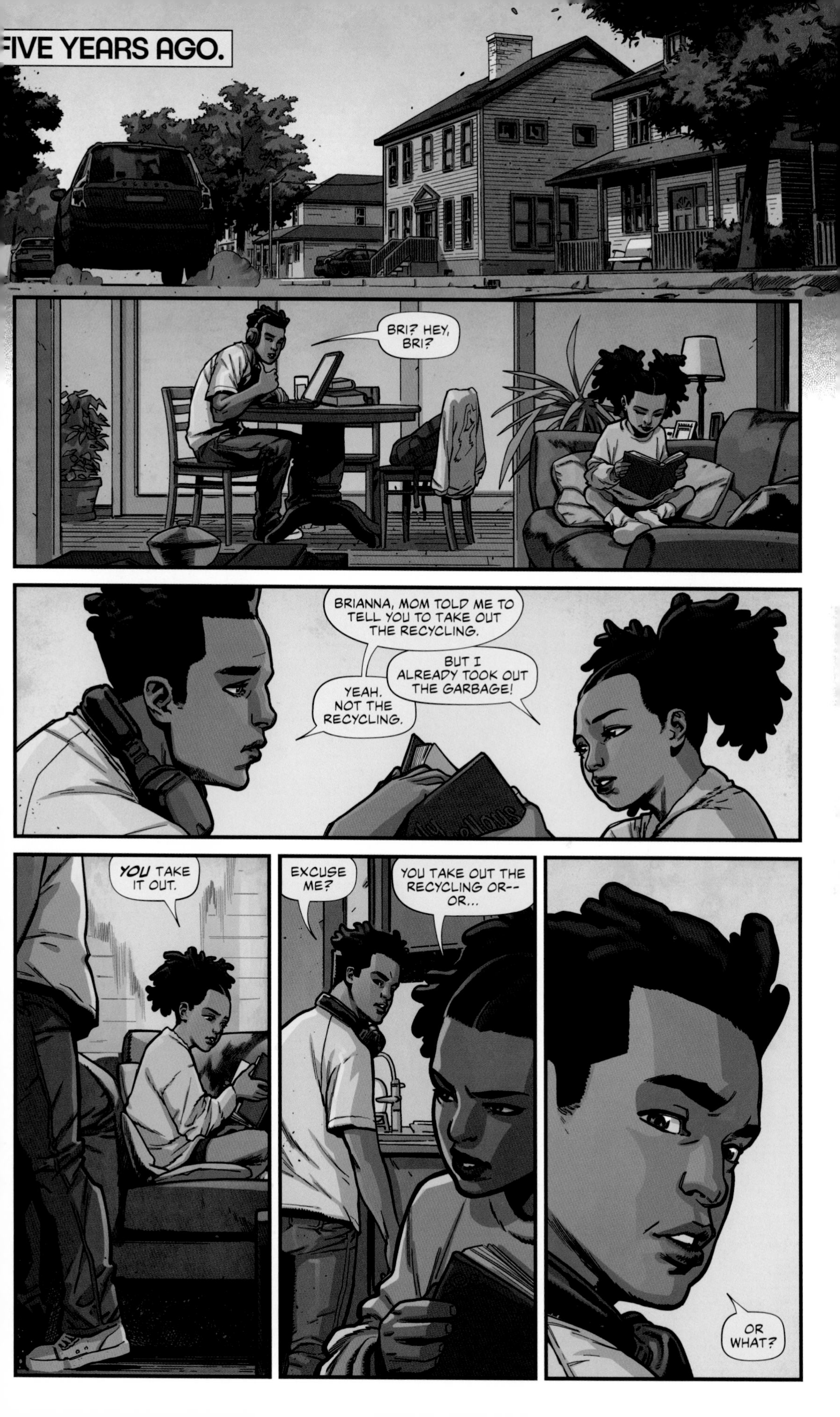

FIVE YEARS AGO.
BRI? HEY, BRI?
BRIANNA, MOM TOLD ME TO TELL YOU TO TAKE OUT THE RECYCLING.
BUT I ALREADY TOOK OUT THE GARBAGE!
YEAH. NOT THE RECYCLING.
YOU TAKE IT OUT.
EXCUSE ME?
YOU TAKE OUT THE RECYCLING OR-- OR...
OR WHAT?

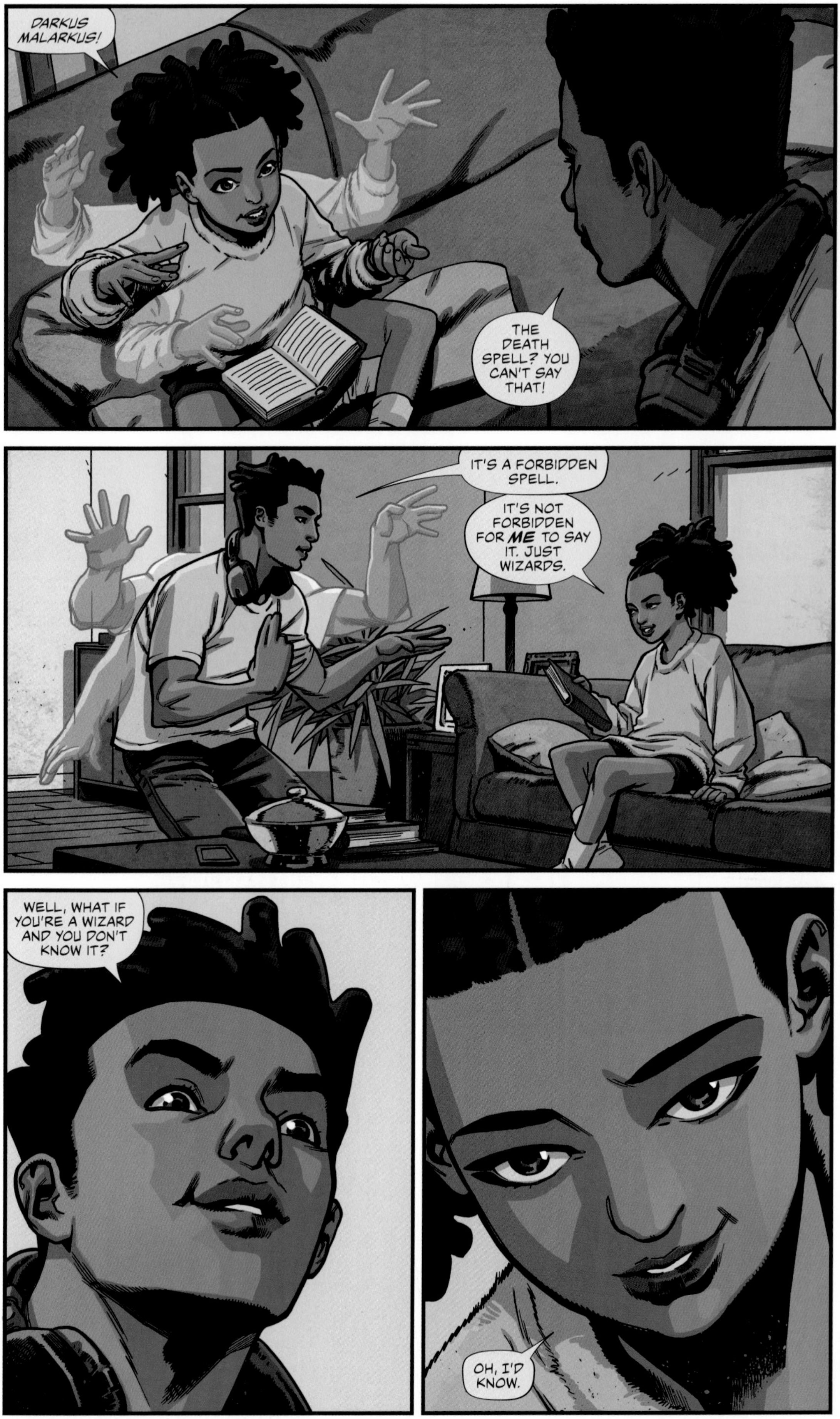
DARKUS MALARKUS!
THE DEATH SPELL? YOU CAN'T SAY THAT!
IT'S A FORBIDDEN SPELL.
IT'S NOT FORBIDDEN FOR *ME* TO SAY IT. JUST WIZARDS.
WELL, WHAT IF YOU'RE A WIZARD AND YOU DON'T KNOW IT?
OH, I'D KNOW.

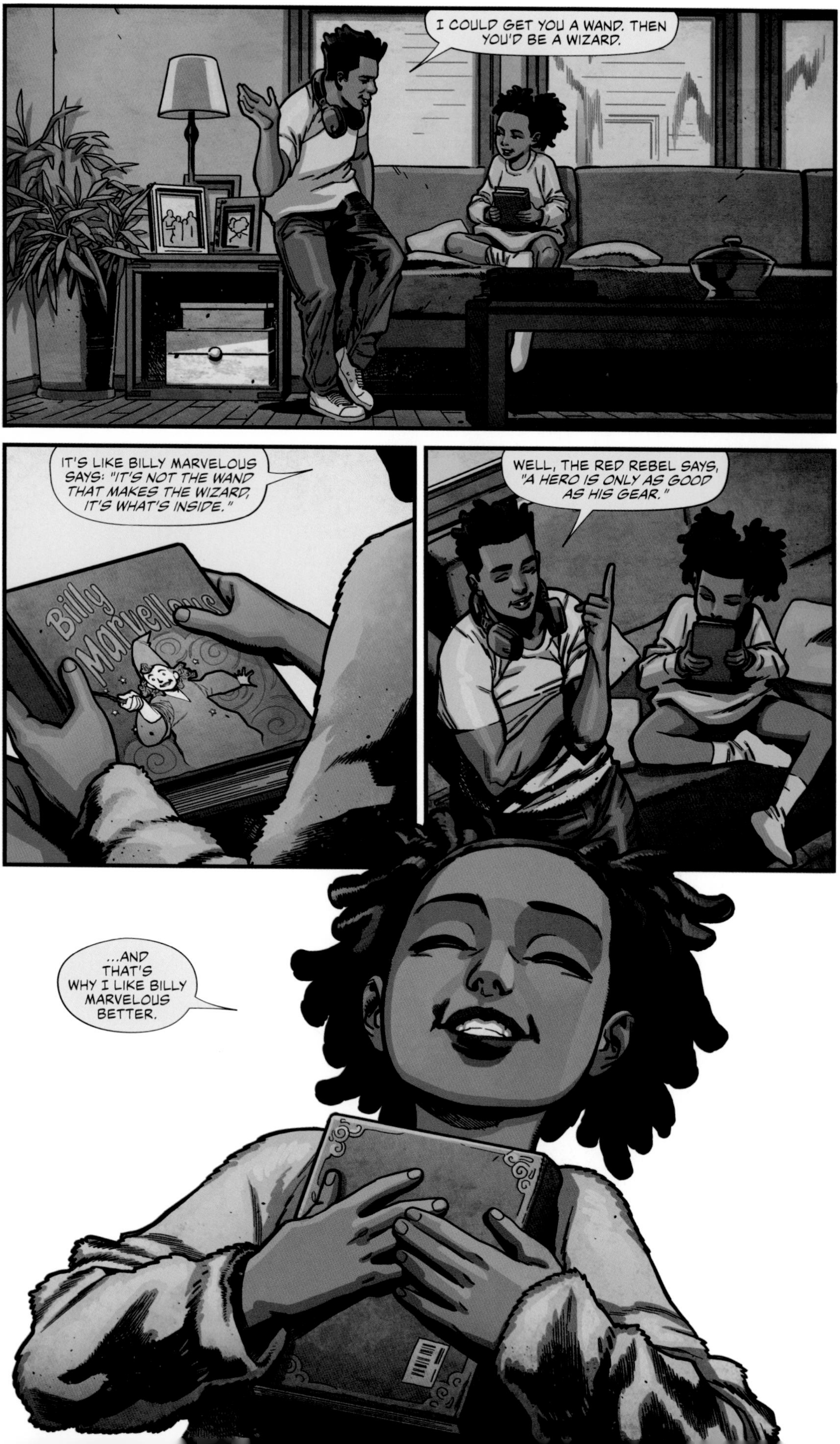

I COULD GET YOU A WAND. THEN YOU'D BE A WIZARD.
IT'S LIKE BILLY MARVELOUS SAYS: "IT'S NOT THE WAND THAT MAKES THE WIZARD, IT'S WHAT'S INSIDE."
Billy Marvelous
WELL, THE RED REBEL SAYS, "A HERO IS ONLY AS GOOD AS HIS GEAR."
...AND THAT'S WHY I LIKE BILLY MARVELOUS BETTER.

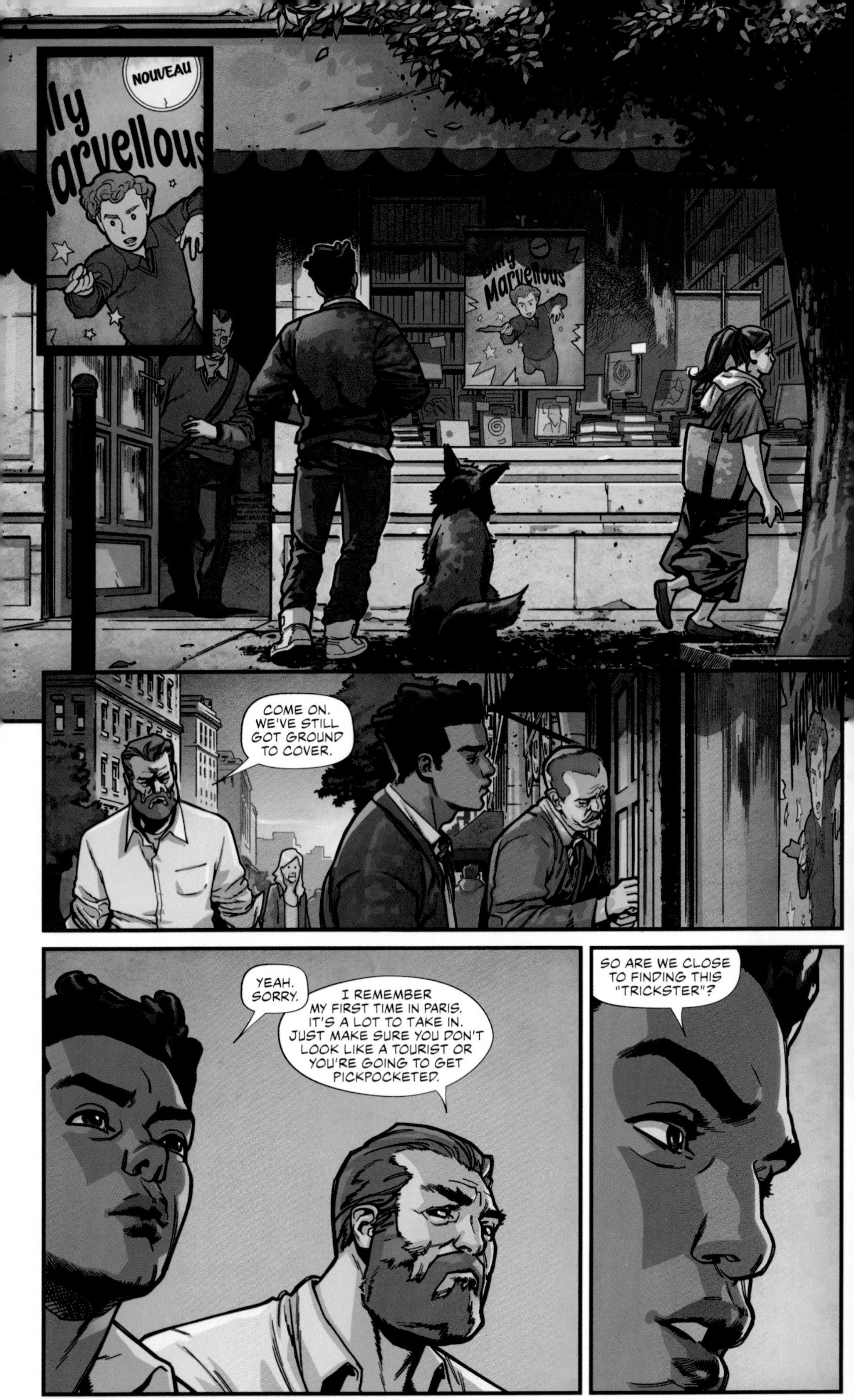
NOUVEAU
Billy Marvellous
Billy Marvellous
COME ON. WE'VE STILL GOT GROUND TO COVER.
YEAH. SORRY.
I REMEMBER MY FIRST TIME IN PARIS. IT'S A LOT TO TAKE IN. JUST MAKE SURE YOU DON'T LOOK LIKE A TOURIST OR YOU'RE GOING TO GET PICKPOCKETED.
SO ARE WE CLOSE TO FINDING THIS "TRICKSTER"?

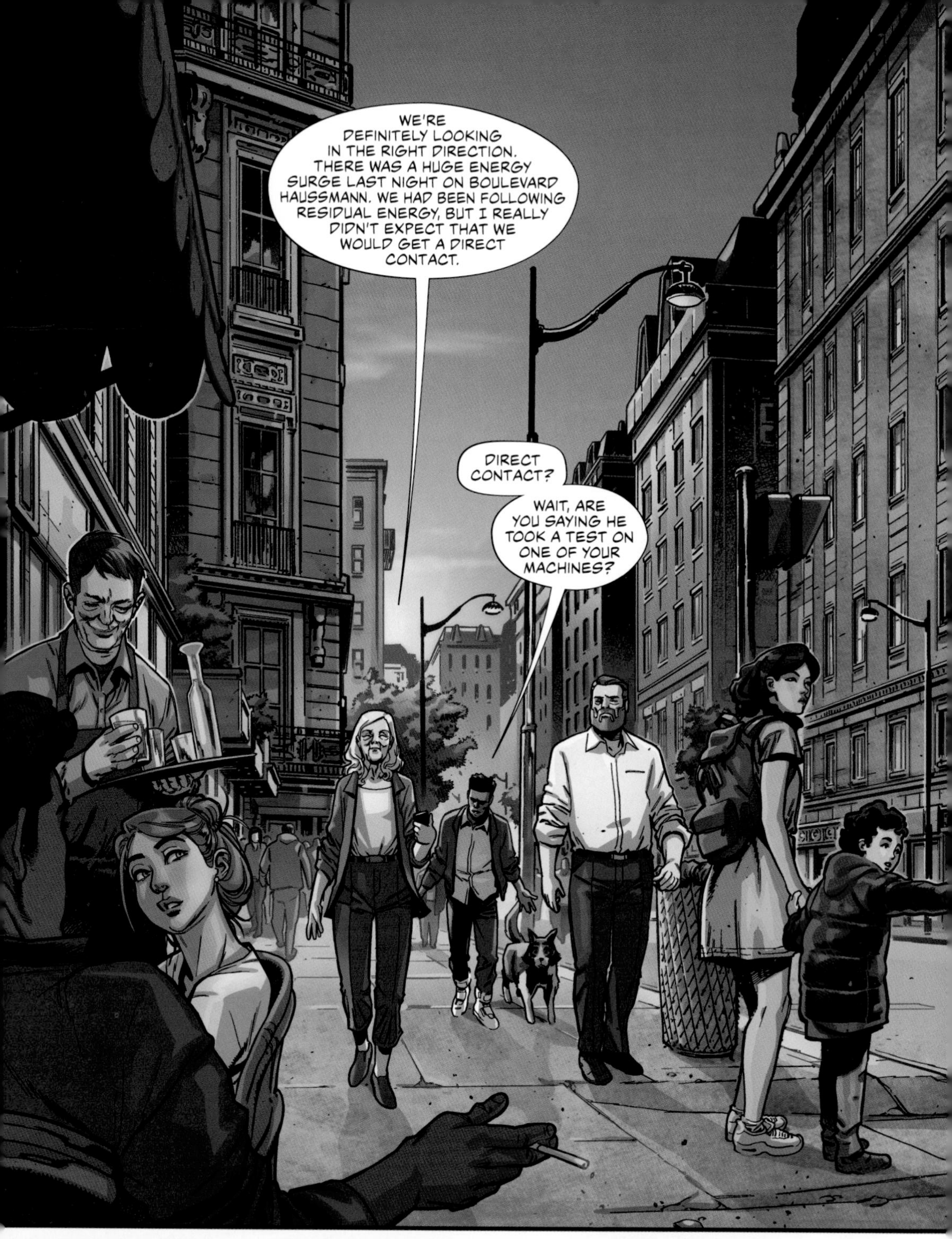
WE'RE DEFINITELY LOOKING IN THE RIGHT DIRECTION. THERE WAS A HUGE ENERGY SURGE LAST NIGHT ON BOULEVARD HAUSSMANN. WE HAD BEEN FOLLOWING RESIDUAL ENERGY, BUT I REALLY DIDN'T EXPECT THAT WE WOULD GET A DIRECT CONTACT.
DIRECT CONTACT?
WAIT, ARE YOU SAYING HE TOOK A TEST ON ONE OF YOUR MACHINES?

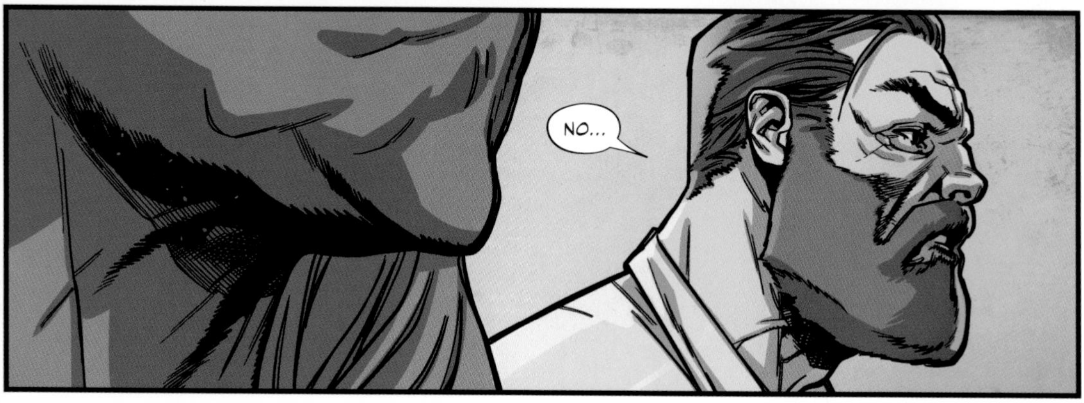
NO...

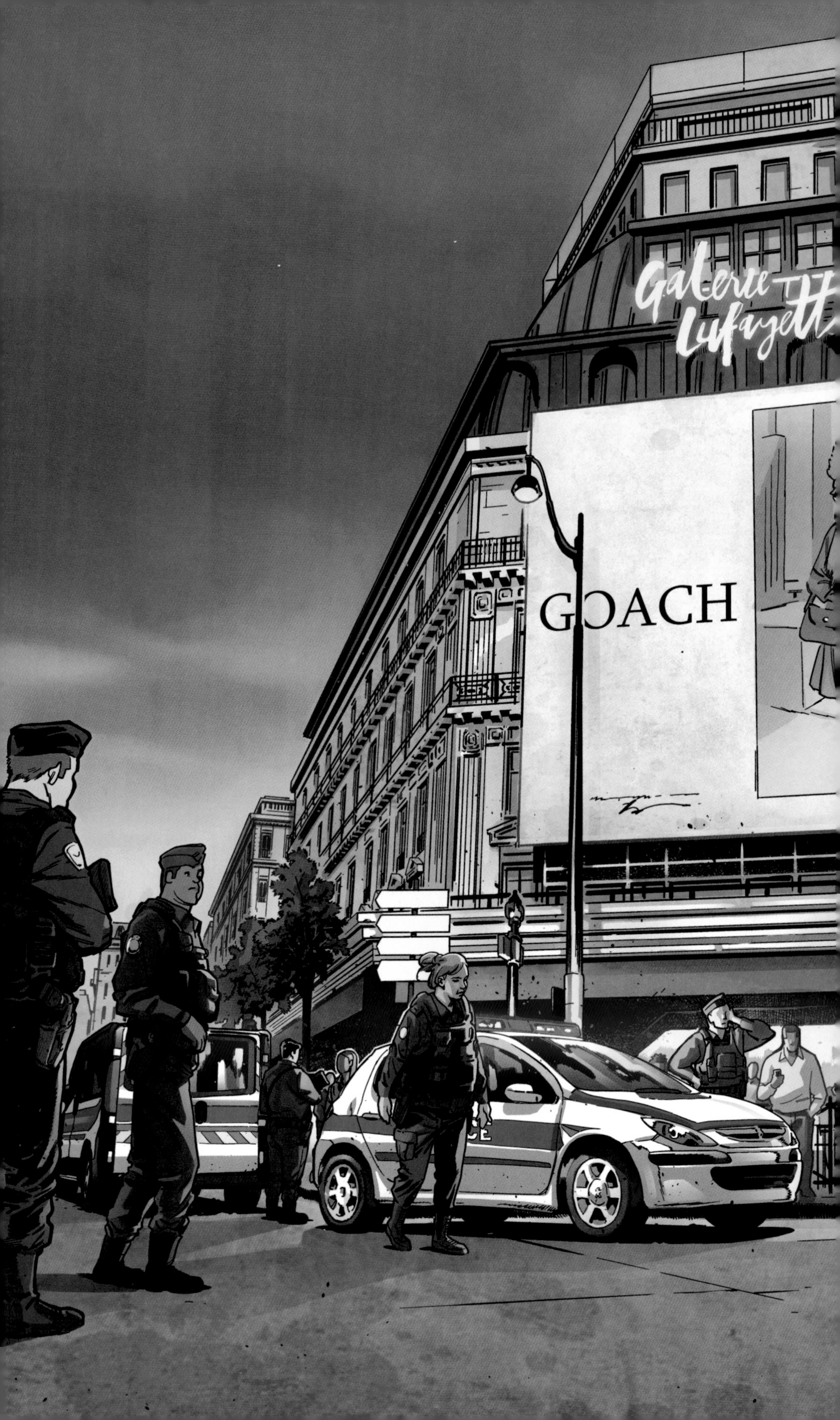
GOACH

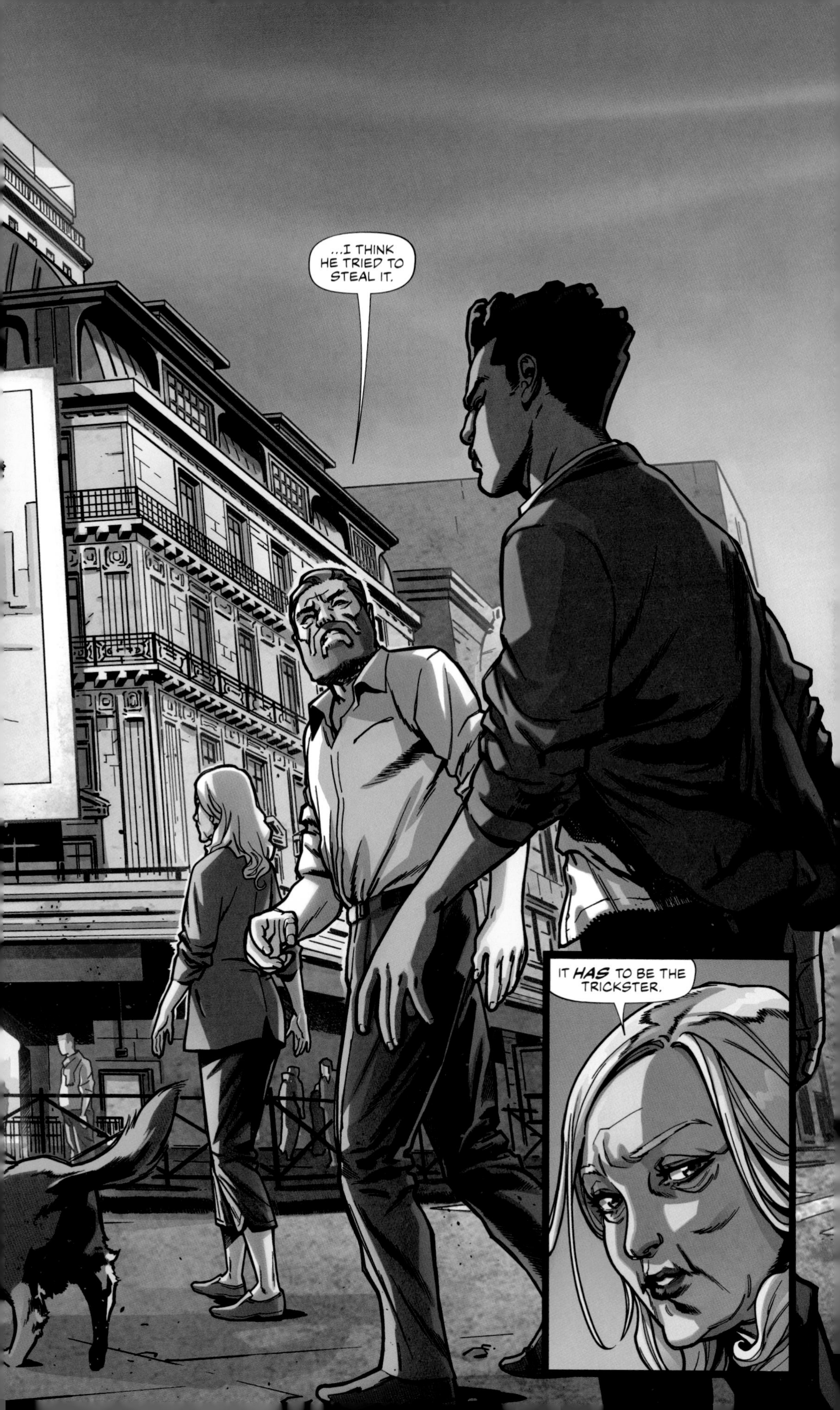

...I THINK HE TRIED TO STEAL IT.
IT HAS TO BE THE TRICKSTER.

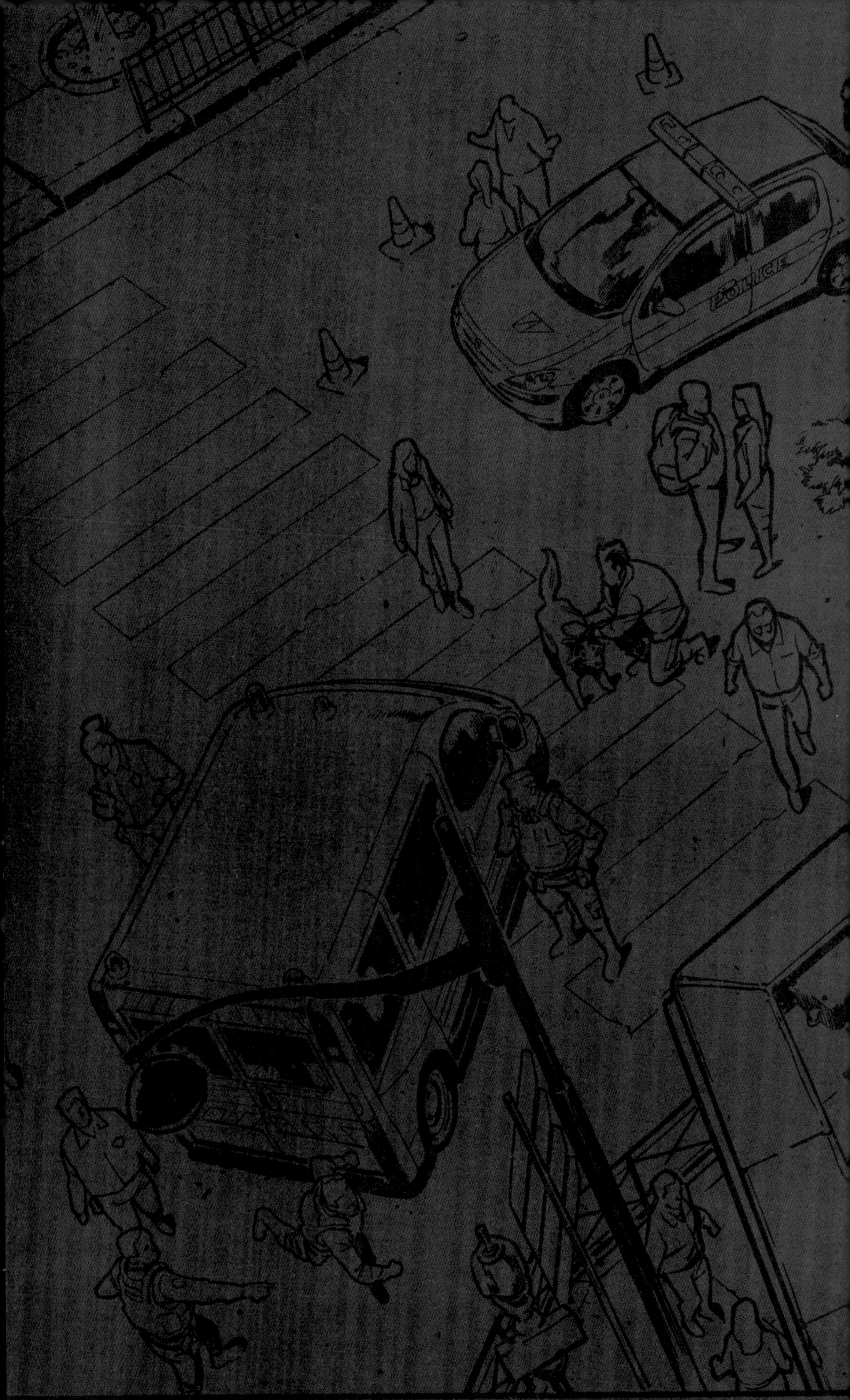
POLICE

CHAPTER IV
Magic Trick

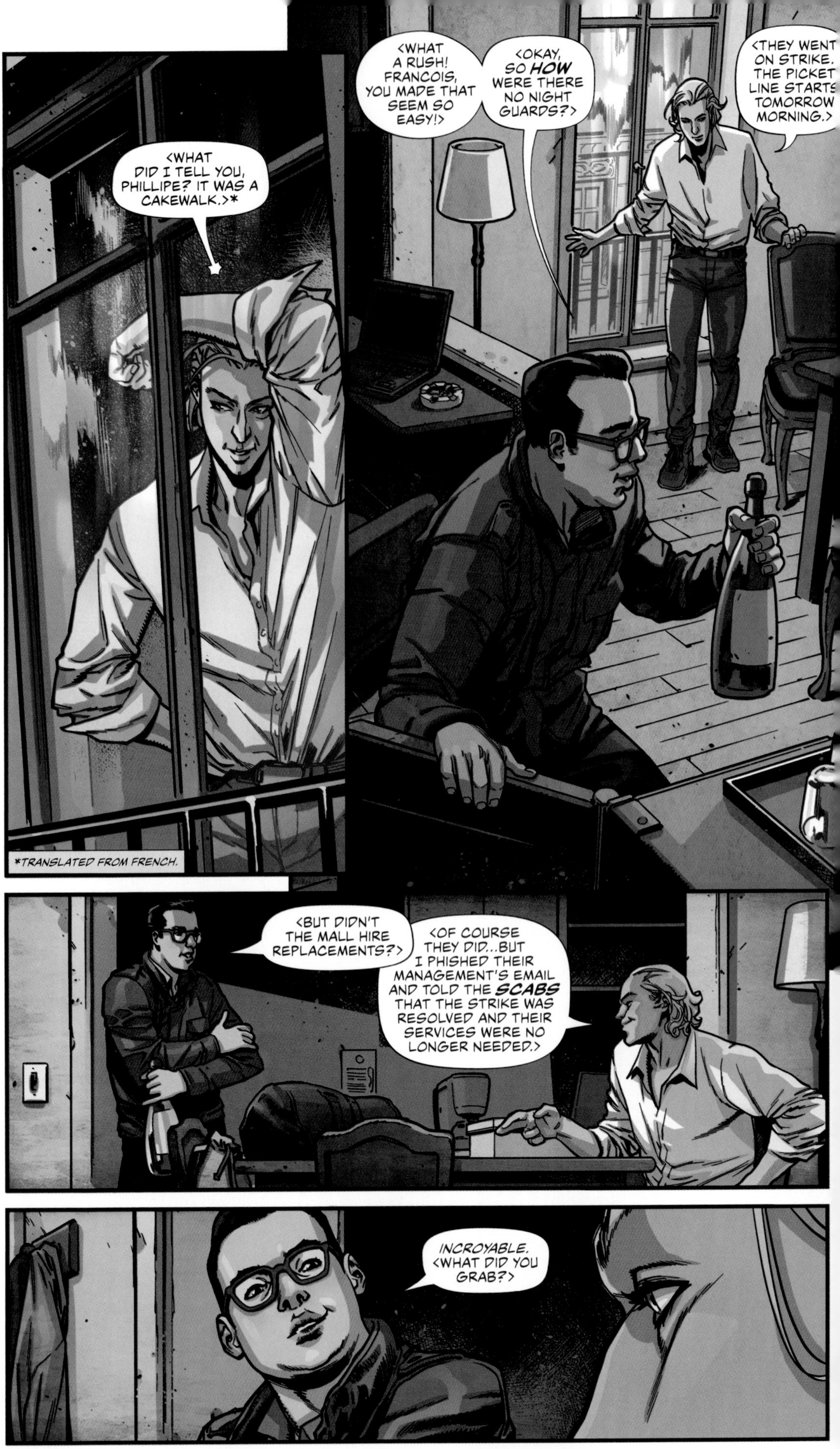
<WHAT DID I TELL YOU, PHILLIPE? IT WAS A CAKEWALK.>*
<WHAT A RUSH! FRANCOIS, YOU MADE THAT SEEM SO EASY!>
<OKAY, SO HOW WERE THERE NO NIGHT GUARDS?>
<THEY WENT ON STRIKE. THE PICKET LINE STARTS TOMORROW MORNING.>
*TRANSLATED FROM FRENCH.
<BUT DIDN'T THE MALL HIRE REPLACEMENTS?>
<OF COURSE THEY DID...BUT I PHISHED THEIR MANAGEMENT'S EMAIL AND TOLD THE SCABS THAT THE STRIKE WAS RESOLVED AND THEIR SERVICES WERE NO LONGER NEEDED.>
INCROYABLE. <WHAT DID YOU GRAB?>

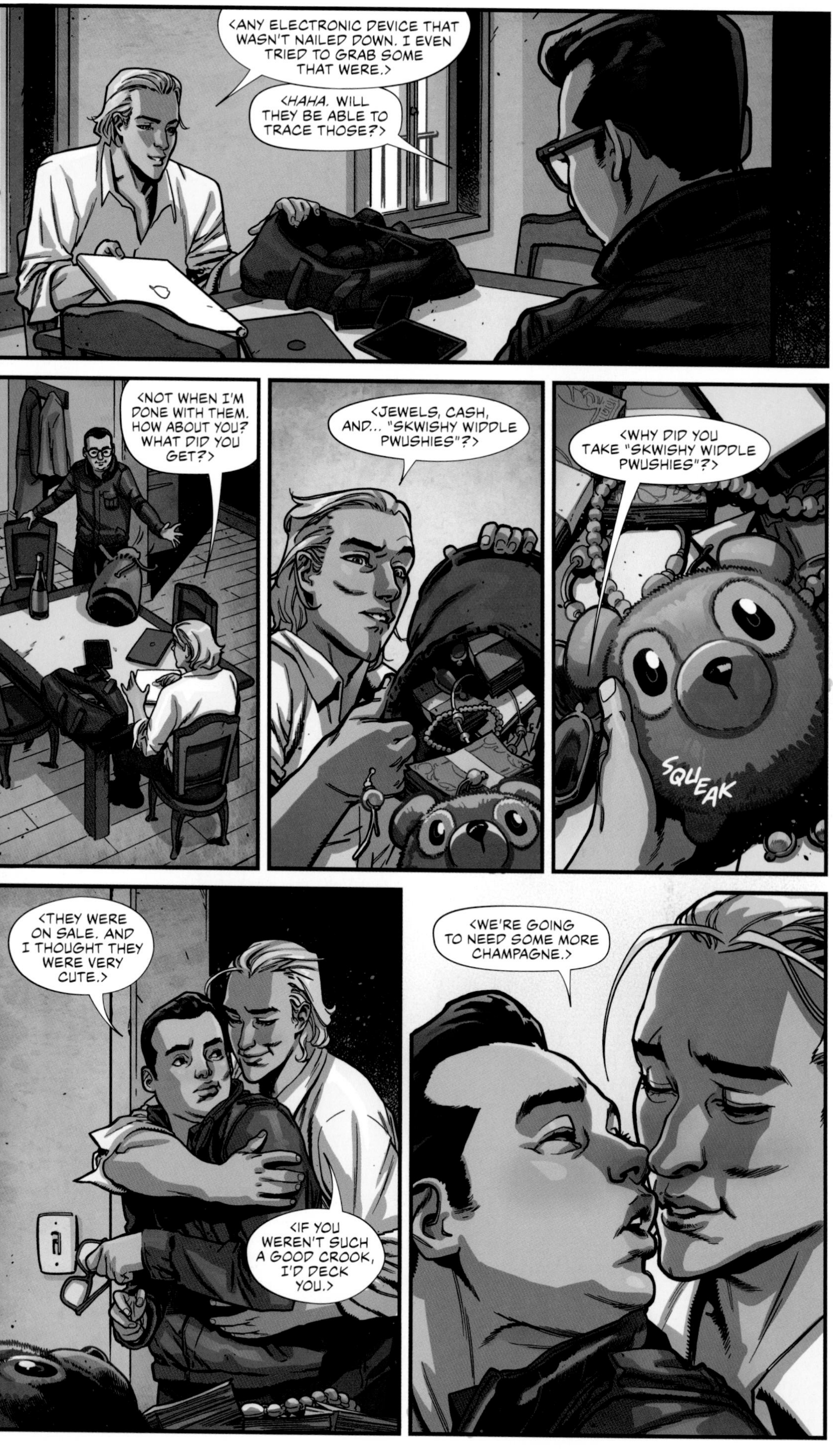
<ANY ELECTRONIC DEVICE THAT WASN'T NAILED DOWN. I EVEN TRIED TO GRAB SOME THAT WERE.>
<*HAHA.* WILL THEY BE ABLE TO TRACE THOSE?>
<NOT WHEN I'M DONE WITH THEM. HOW ABOUT YOU? WHAT DID YOU GET?>
<JEWELS, CASH, AND... "SKWISHY WIDDLE PWUSHIES"?>
<WHY DID YOU TAKE "SKWISHY WIDDLE PWUSHIES"?>
SQUEAK
<THEY WERE ON SALE. AND I THOUGHT THEY WERE VERY CUTE.>
<IF YOU WEREN'T SUCH A GOOD CROOK, I'D DECK YOU.>
<WE'RE GOING TO NEED SOME MORE CHAMPAGNE.>

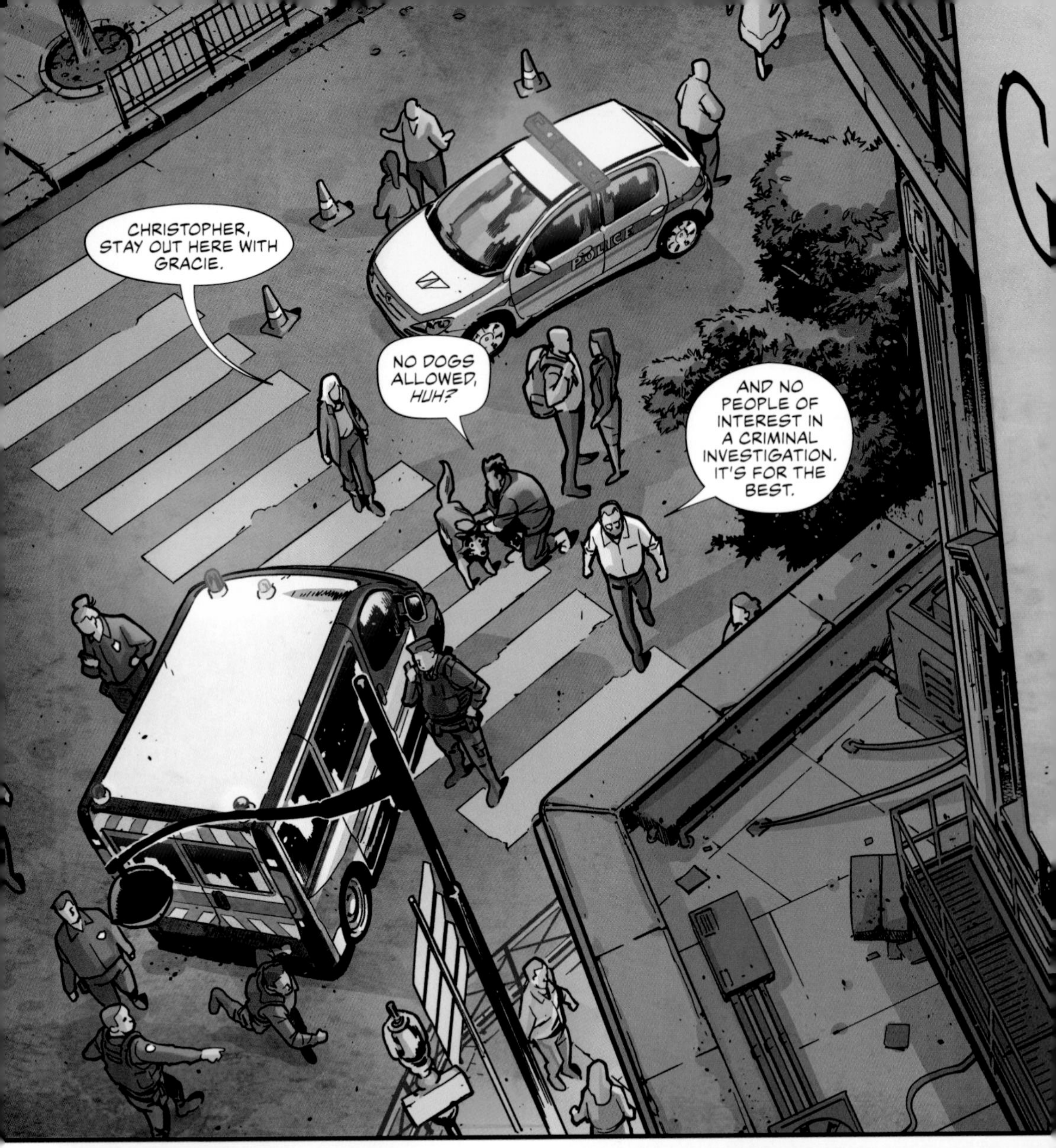
CHRISTOPHER, STAY OUT HERE WITH GRACIE.
NO DOGS ALLOWED, HUH?
AND NO PEOPLE OF INTEREST IN A CRIMINAL INVESTIGATION. IT'S FOR THE BEST.

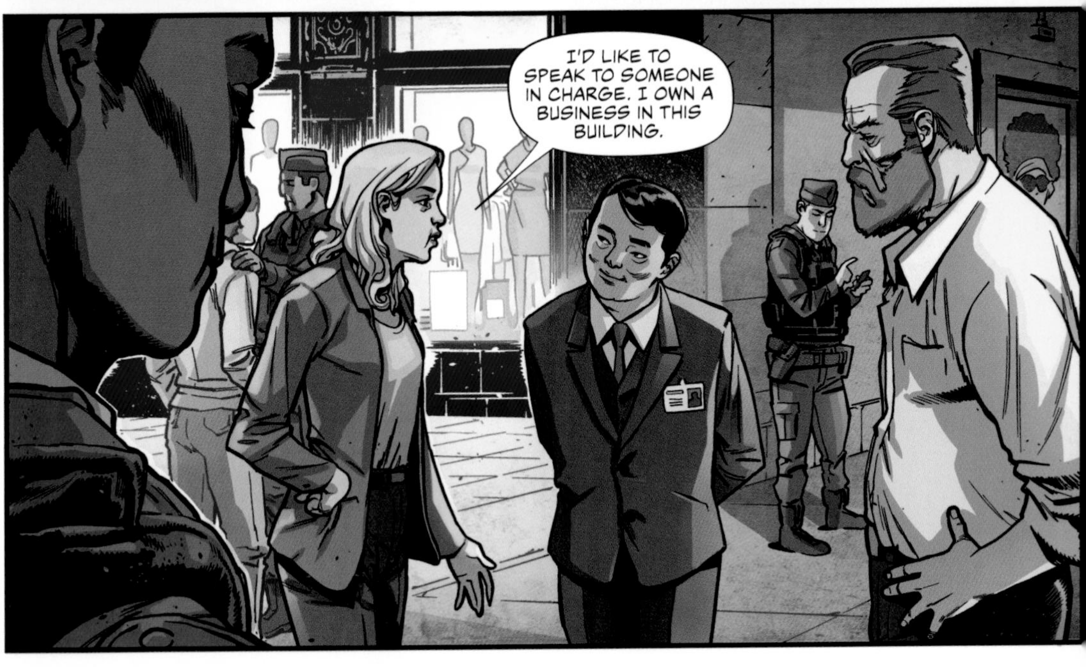
I'D LIKE TO SPEAK TO SOMEONE IN CHARGE. I OWN A BUSINESS IN THIS BUILDING.

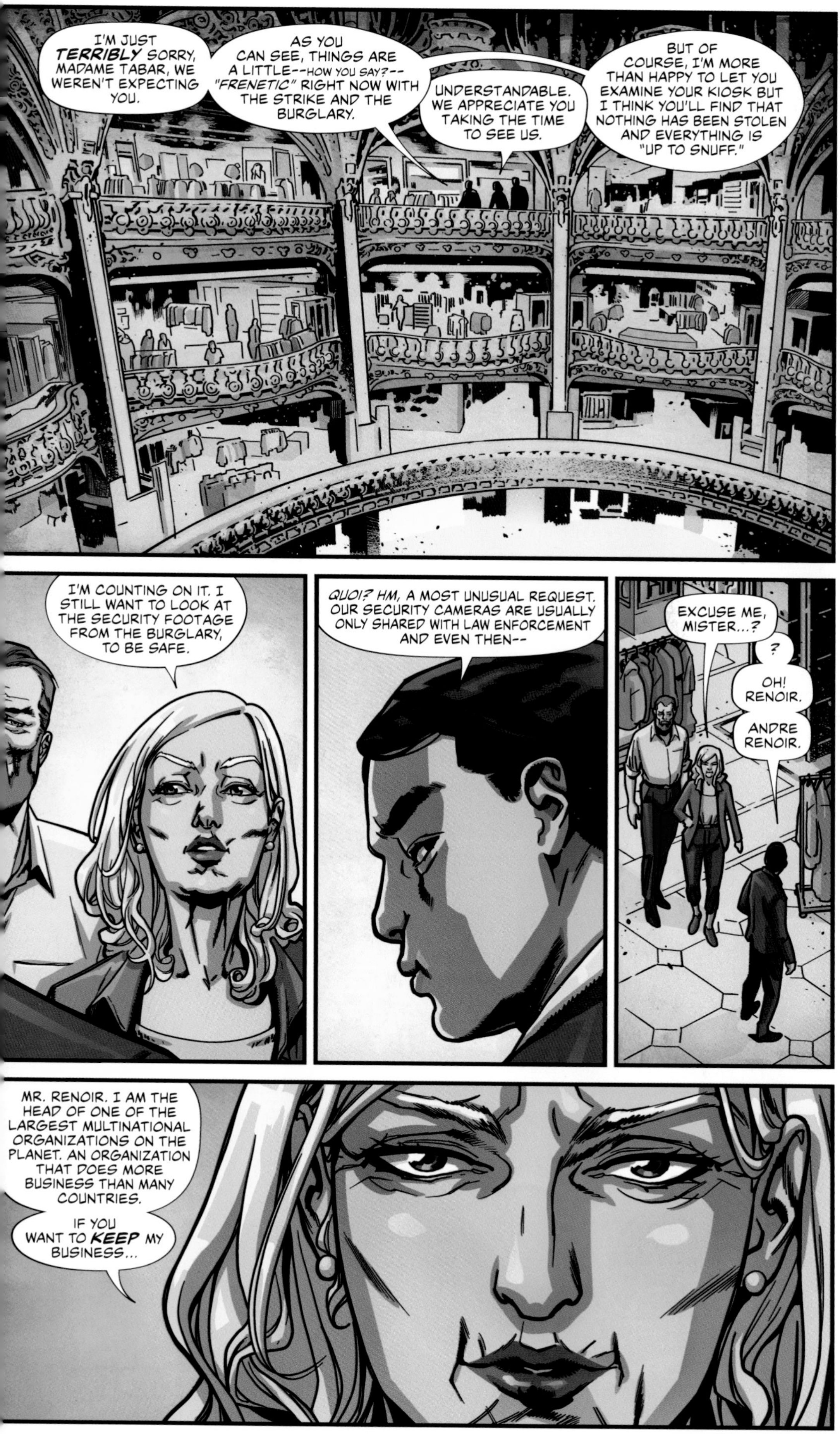
I'M JUST TERRIBLY SORRY, MADAME TABAR, WE WEREN'T EXPECTING YOU.
AS YOU CAN SEE, THINGS ARE A LITTLE--HOW YOU SAY?--"FRENETIC" RIGHT NOW WITH THE STRIKE AND THE BURGLARY.
UNDERSTANDABLE. WE APPRECIATE YOU TAKING THE TIME TO SEE US.
BUT OF COURSE, I'M MORE THAN HAPPY TO LET YOU EXAMINE YOUR KIOSK BUT I THINK YOU'LL FIND THAT NOTHING HAS BEEN STOLEN AND EVERYTHING IS "UP TO SNUFF."
I'M COUNTING ON IT. I STILL WANT TO LOOK AT THE SECURITY FOOTAGE FROM THE BURGLARY, TO BE SAFE.
QUOI? HM, A MOST UNUSUAL REQUEST. OUR SECURITY CAMERAS ARE USUALLY ONLY SHARED WITH LAW ENFORCEMENT AND EVEN THEN--
EXCUSE ME, MISTER...?
?
OH! RENOIR.
ANDRE RENOIR.
MR. RENOIR. I AM THE HEAD OF ONE OF THE LARGEST MULTINATIONAL ORGANIZATIONS ON THE PLANET. AN ORGANIZATION THAT DOES MORE BUSINESS THAN MANY COUNTRIES.
IF YOU WANT TO KEEP MY BUSINESS...

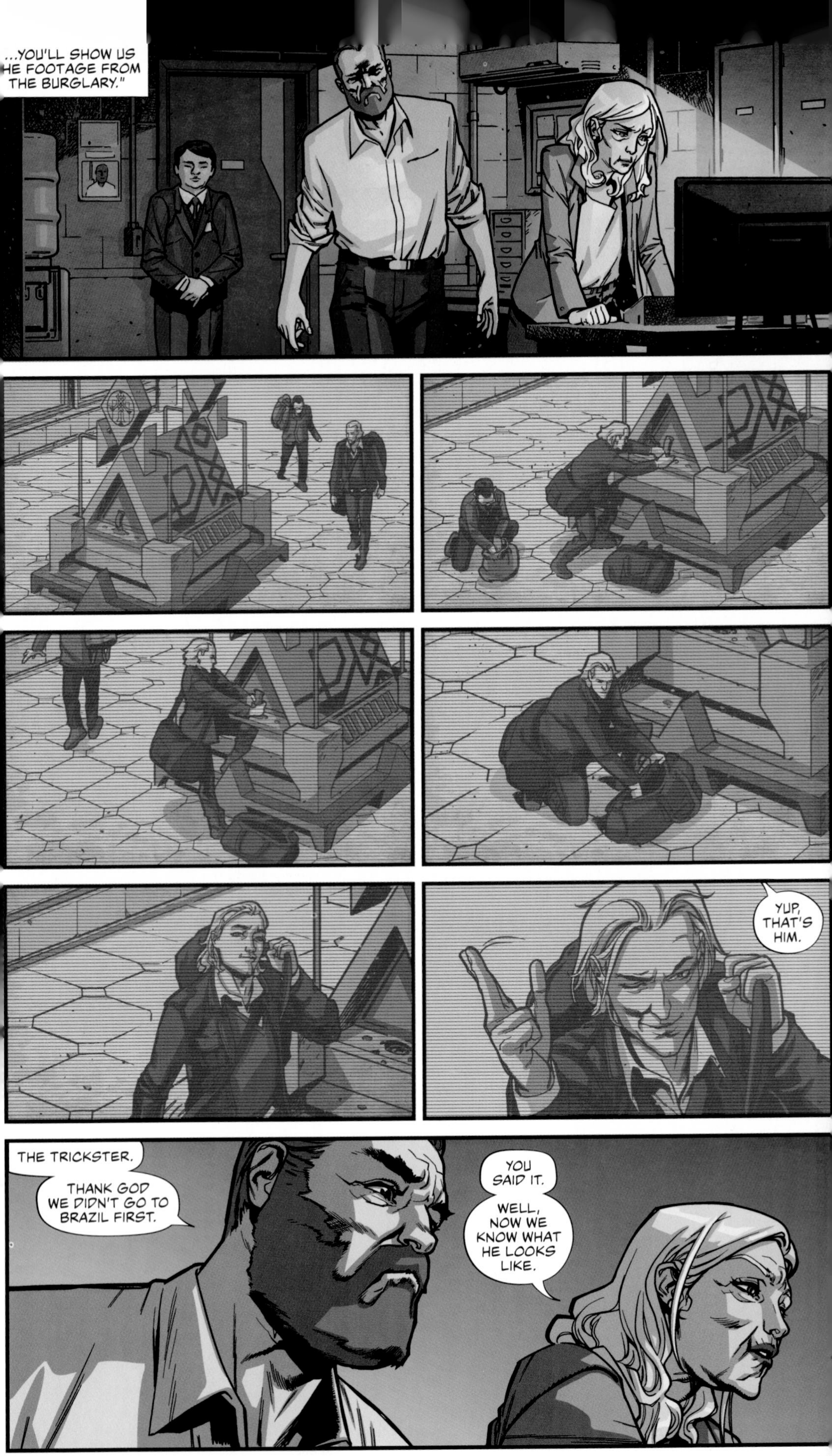
...YOU'LL SHOW US
HE FOOTAGE FROM
THE BURGLARY."
YUP, THAT'S HIM.
THE TRICKSTER.
THANK GOD WE DIDN'T GO TO BRAZIL FIRST.
YOU SAID IT.
WELL, NOW WE KNOW WHAT HE LOOKS LIKE.

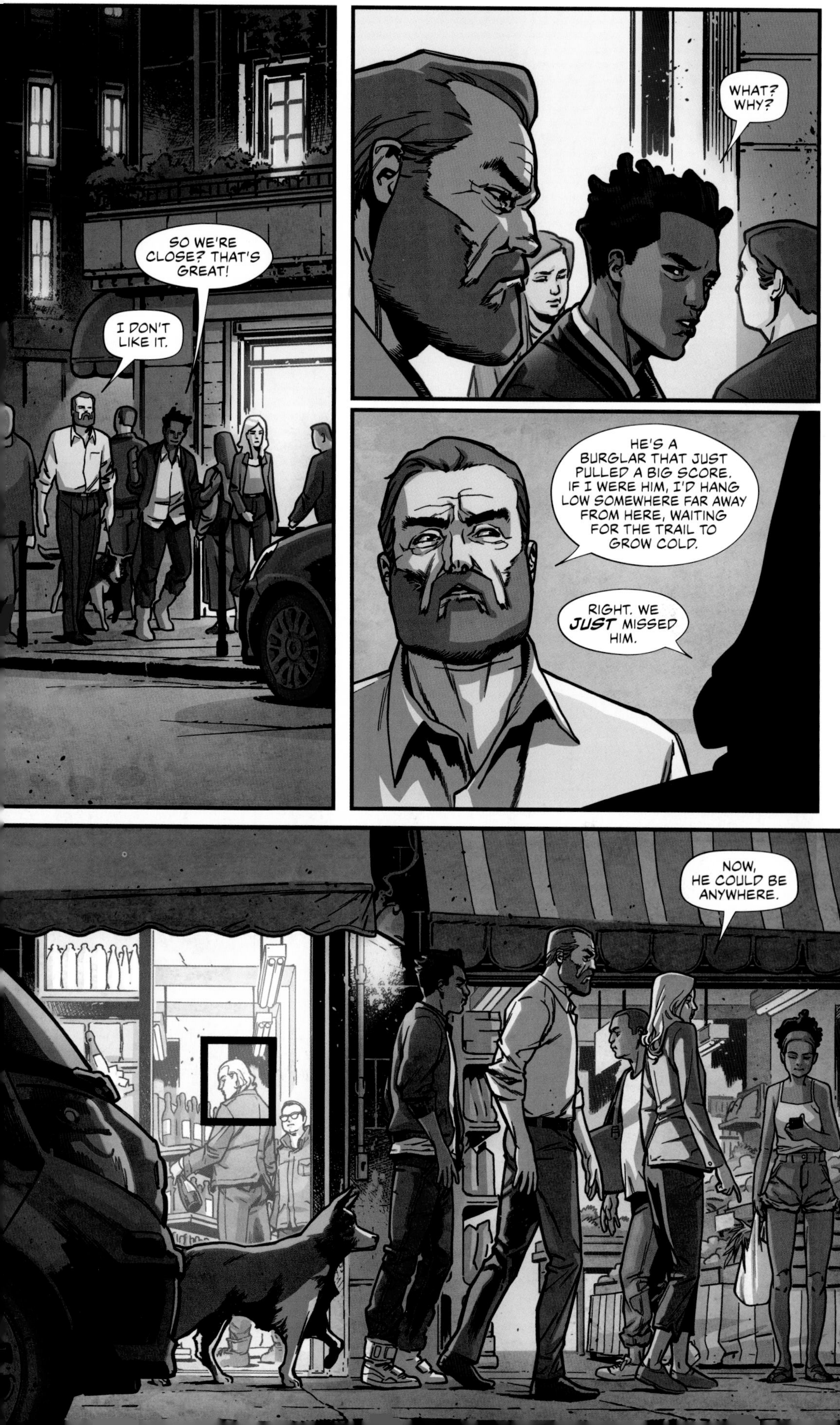

SO WE'RE CLOSE? THAT'S GREAT!
I DON'T LIKE IT.
WHAT? WHY?
HE'S A BURGLAR THAT JUST PULLED A BIG SCORE. IF I WERE HIM, I'D HANG LOW SOMEWHERE FAR AWAY FROM HERE, WAITING FOR THE TRAIL TO GROW COLD.
RIGHT. WE JUST MISSED HIM.
NOW, HE COULD BE ANYWHERE.

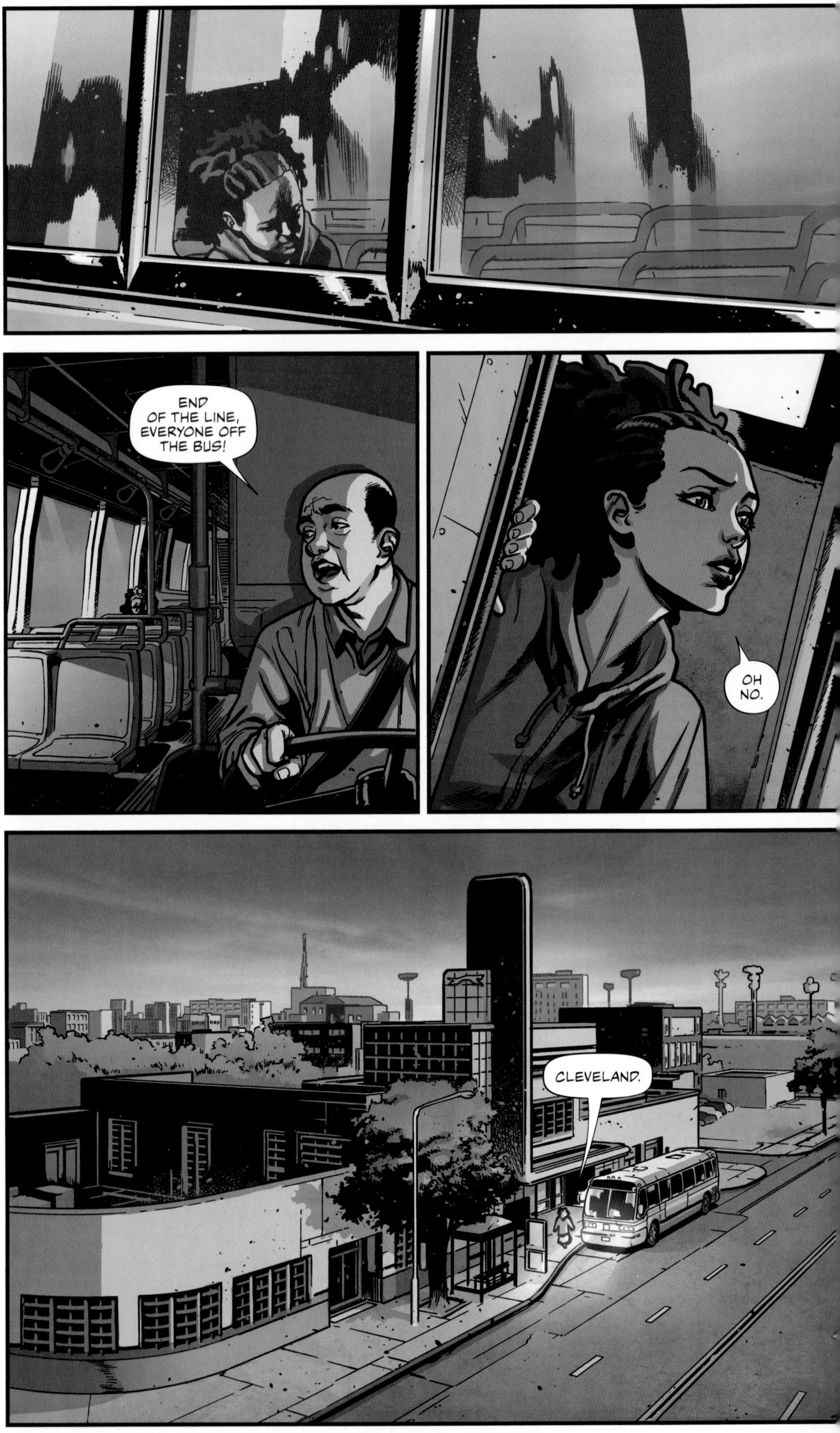
END OF THE LINE, EVERYONE OFF THE BUS!
OH NO.
CLEVELAND.

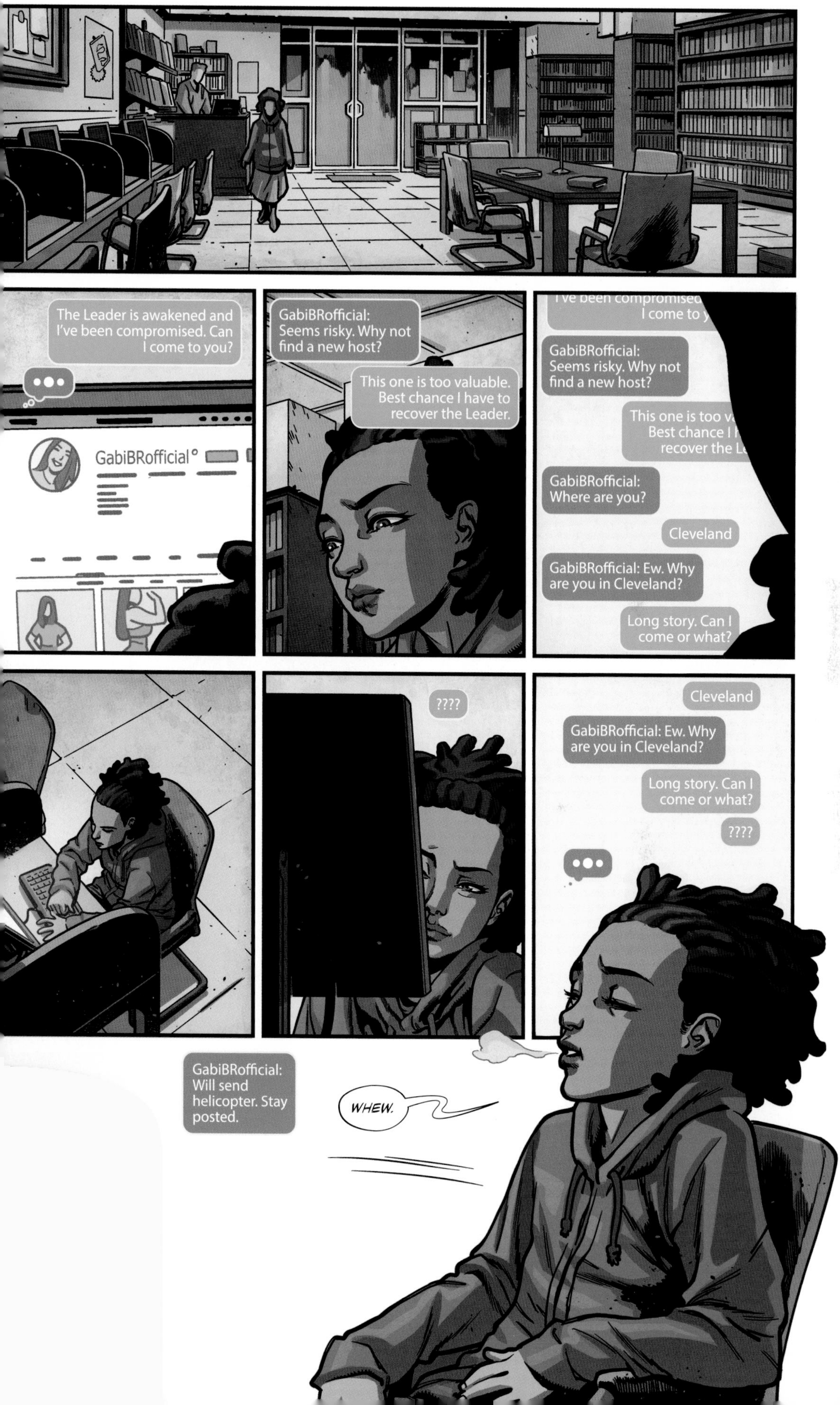

The Leader is awakened and I've been compromised. Can I come to you?
GabiBRofficial
GabiBRofficial: Seems risky. Why not find a new host?
This one is too valuable. Best chance I have to recover the Leader.
I've been compromised I come to y
GabiBRofficial: Seems risky. Why not find a new host?
This one is too va Best chance I h recover the Le
GabiBRofficial: Where are you?
Cleveland
GabiBRofficial: Ew. Why are you in Cleveland?
Long story. Can I come or what?
????
Cleveland
GabiBRofficial: Ew. Why are you in Cleveland?
Long story. Can I come or what?
????
GabiBRofficial: Will send helicopter. Stay posted.
WHEW.

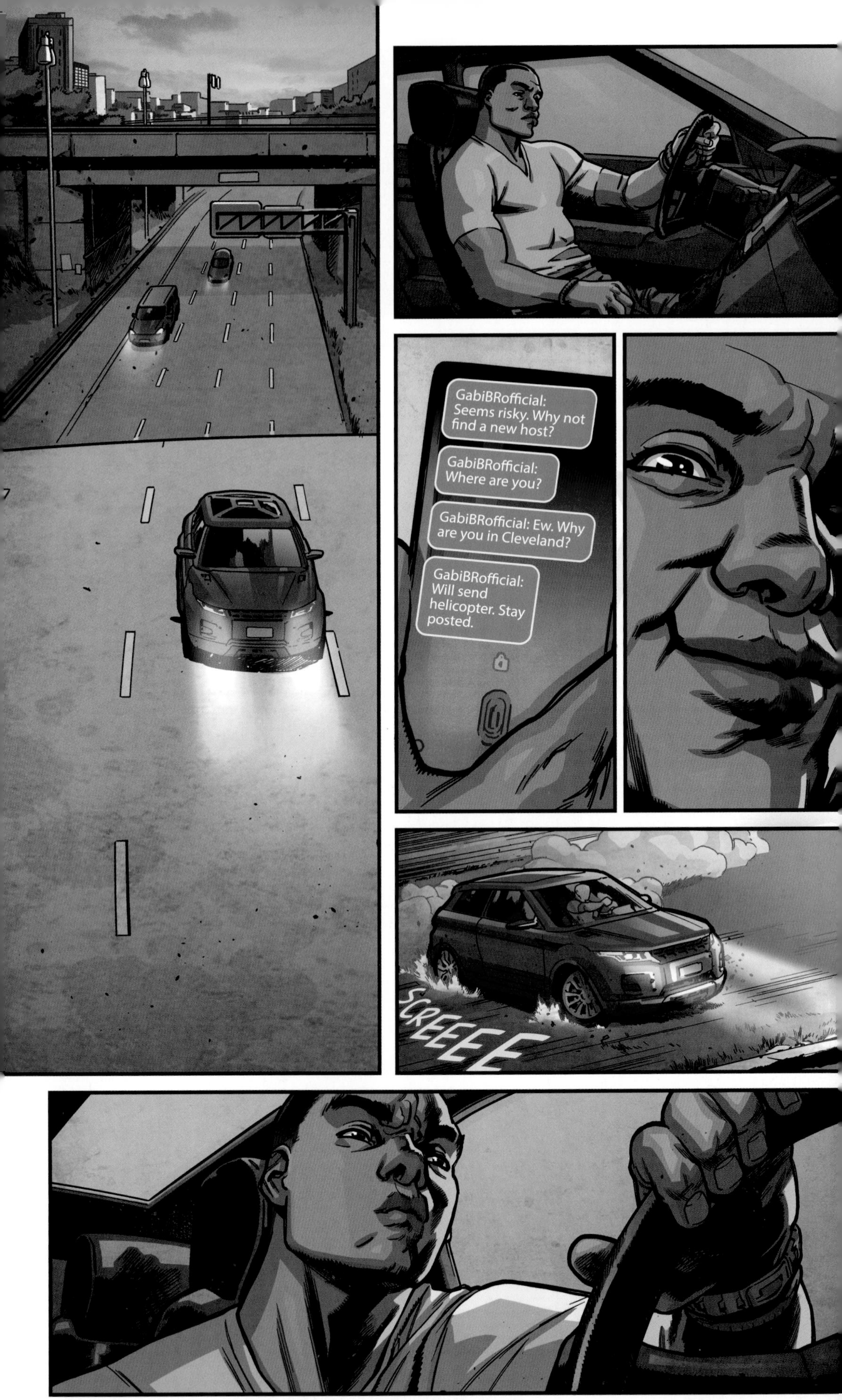
GabiBRofficial: Seems risky. Why not find a new host?
GabiBRofficial: Where are you?
GabiBRofficial: Ew. Why are you in Cleveland?
GabiBRofficial: Will send helicopter. Stay posted.
SCREEEE

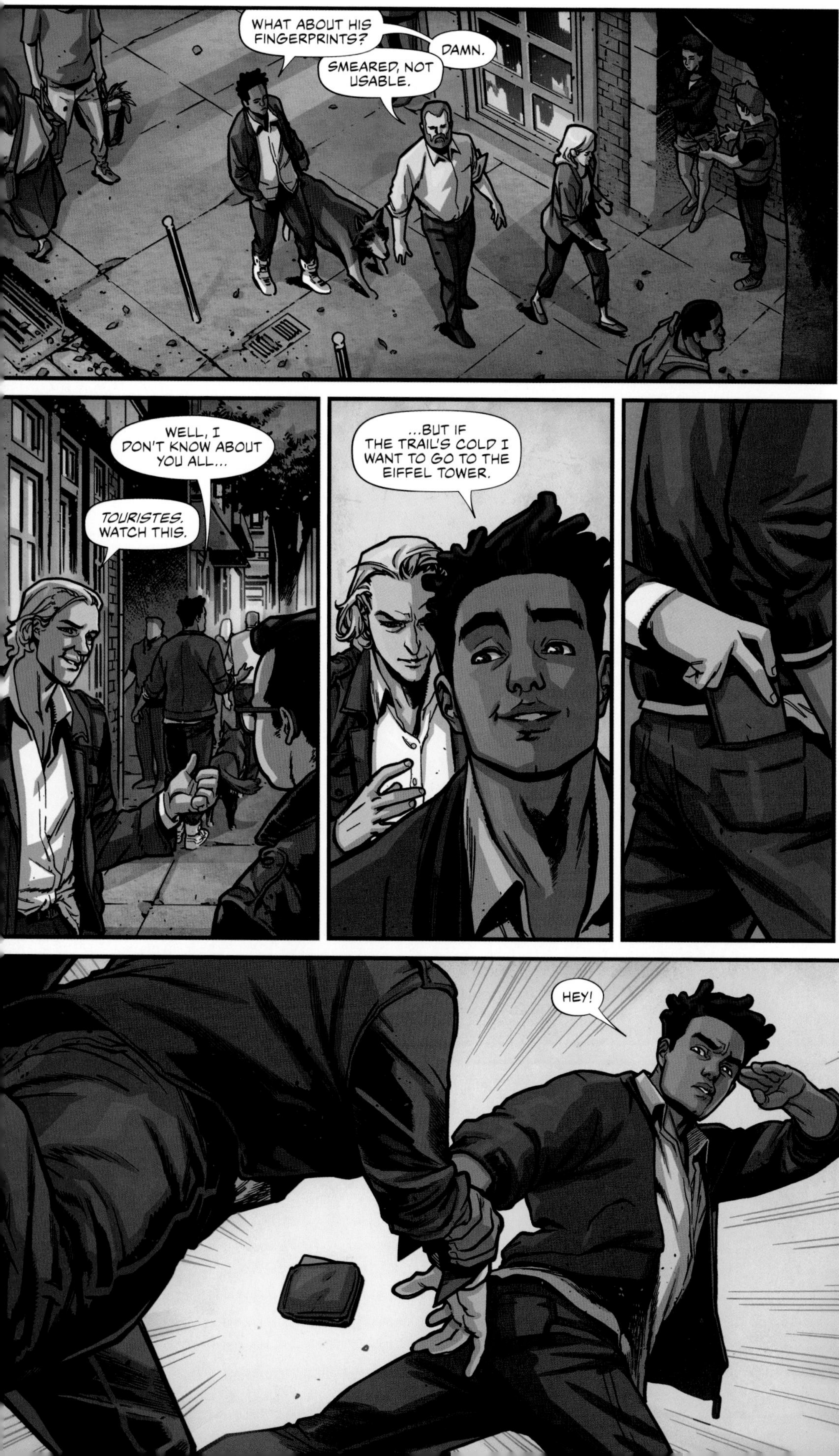
WHAT ABOUT HIS FINGERPRINTS?
SMEARED, NOT USABLE.
DAMN.
WELL, I DON'T KNOW ABOUT YOU ALL...
TOURISTES. WATCH THIS.
...BUT IF THE TRAIL'S COLD I WANT TO GO TO THE EIFFEL TOWER.
HEY!

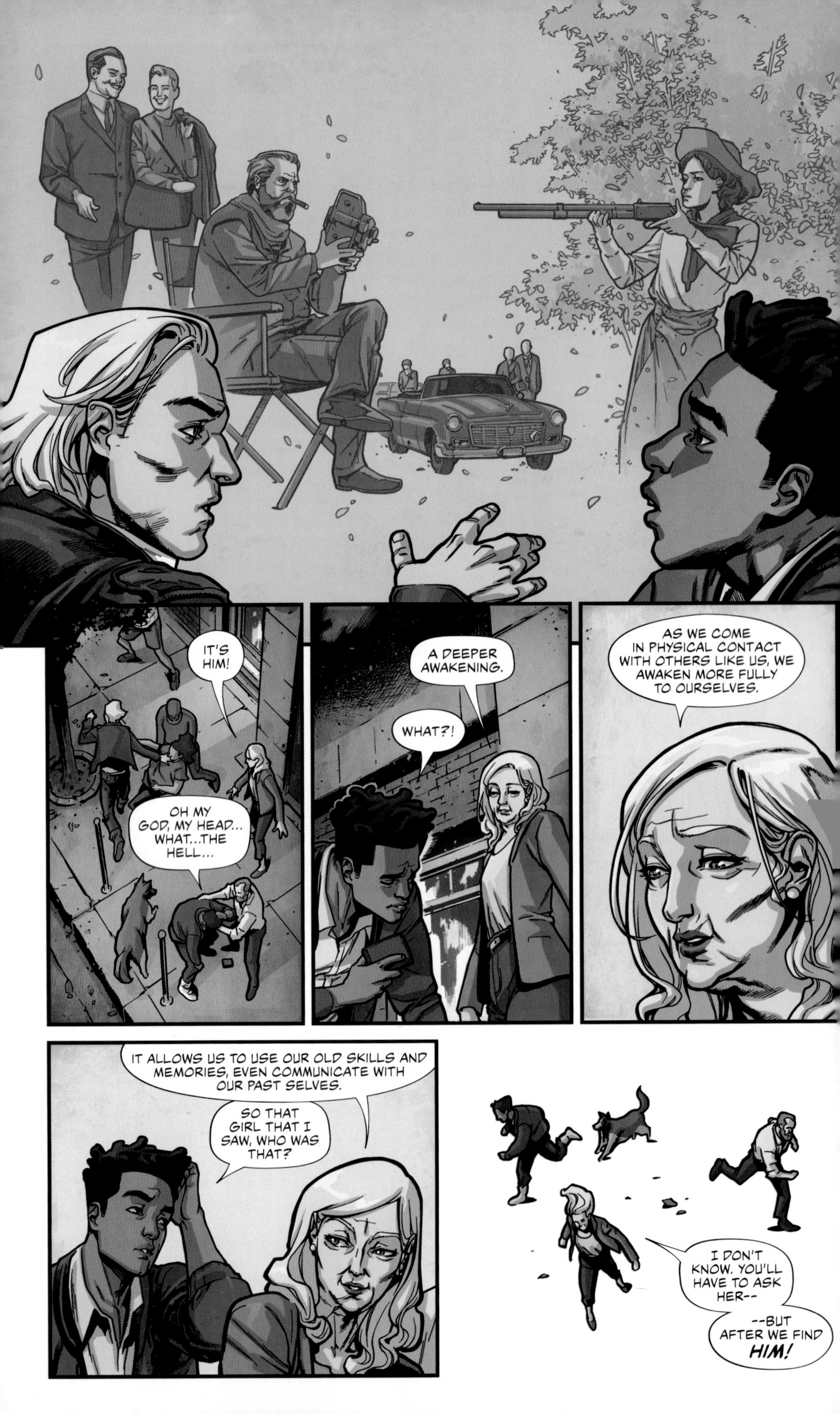
IT'S HIM!
OH MY GOD, MY HEAD... WHAT...THE HELL...
A DEEPER AWAKENING.
WHAT?!
AS WE COME IN PHYSICAL CONTACT WITH OTHERS LIKE US, WE AWAKEN MORE FULLY TO OURSELVES.
IT ALLOWS US TO USE OUR OLD SKILLS AND MEMORIES, EVEN COMMUNICATE WITH OUR PAST SELVES.
SO THAT GIRL THAT I SAW, WHO WAS THAT?
I DON'T KNOW. YOU'LL HAVE TO ASK HER--
--BUT AFTER WE FIND HIM!

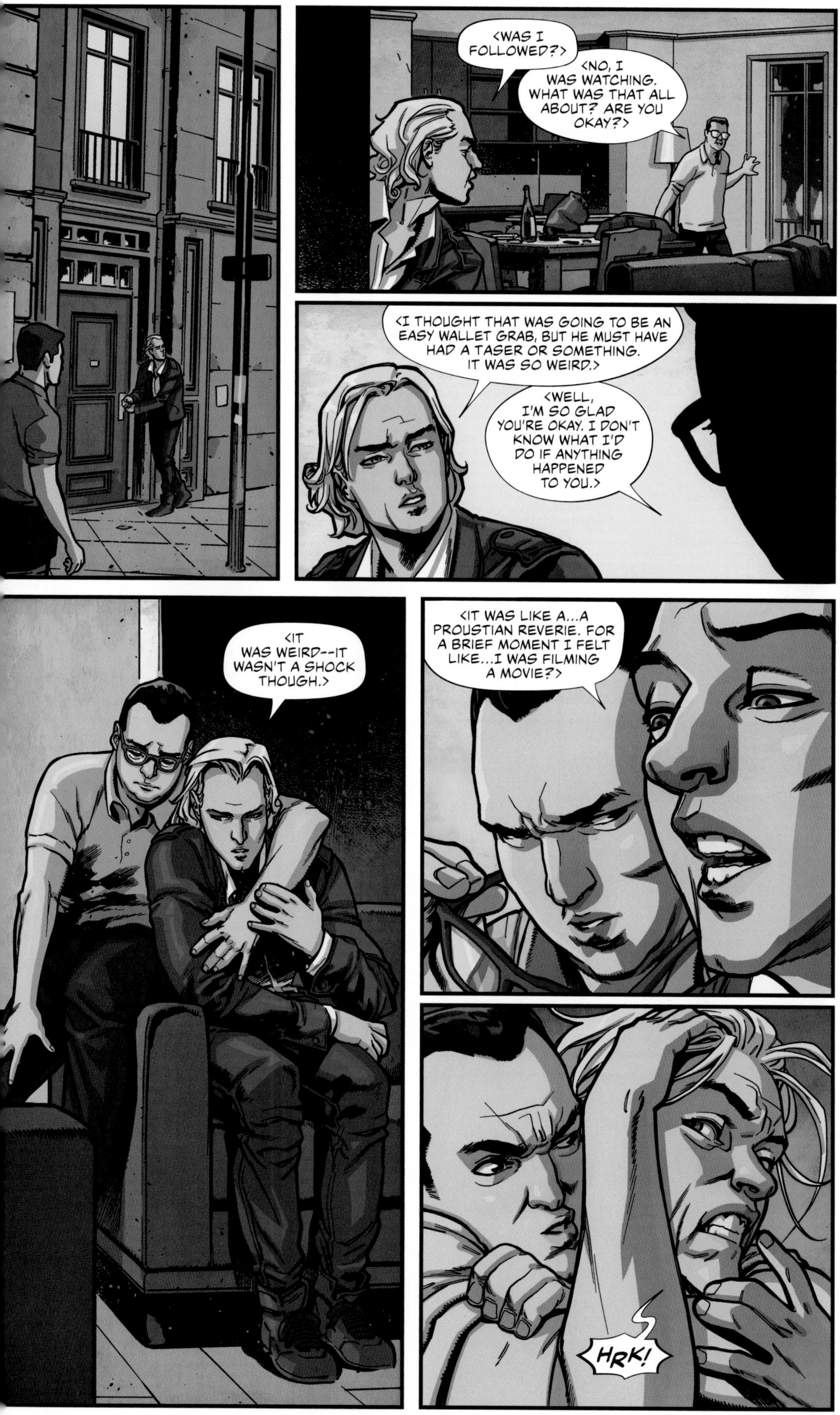

<WAS I FOLLOWED?>
<NO, I WAS WATCHING. WHAT WAS THAT ALL ABOUT? ARE YOU OKAY?>
<I THOUGHT THAT WAS GOING TO BE AN EASY WALLET GRAB, BUT HE MUST HAVE HAD A TASER OR SOMETHING. IT WAS SO WEIRD.>
<WELL, I'M SO GLAD YOU'RE OKAY. I DON'T KNOW WHAT I'D DO IF ANYTHING HAPPENED TO YOU.>
<IT WAS WEIRD--IT WASN'T A SHOCK THOUGH.>
<IT WAS LIKE A...A PROUSTIAN REVERIE. FOR A BRIEF MOMENT I FELT LIKE...I WAS FILMING A MOVIE?>
HRK!

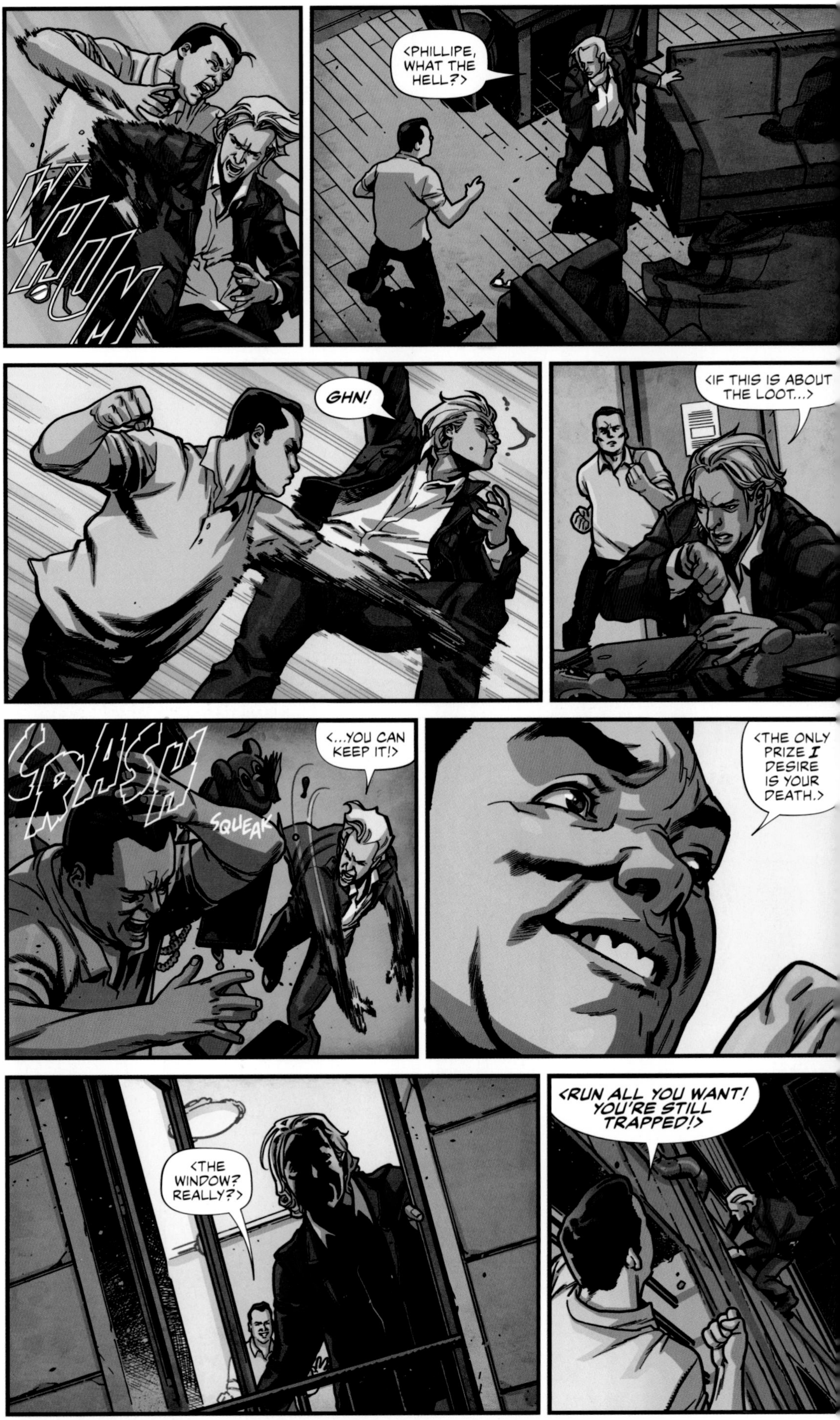
<PHILLIPE, WHAT THE HELL?>
GHN!
<IF THIS IS ABOUT THE LOOT...>
CRASH
SQUEAK
<...YOU CAN KEEP IT!>
<THE ONLY PRIZE *I* DESIRE IS YOUR DEATH.>
<THE WINDOW? REALLY?>
<RUN ALL YOU WANT! YOU'RE STILL TRAPPED!>

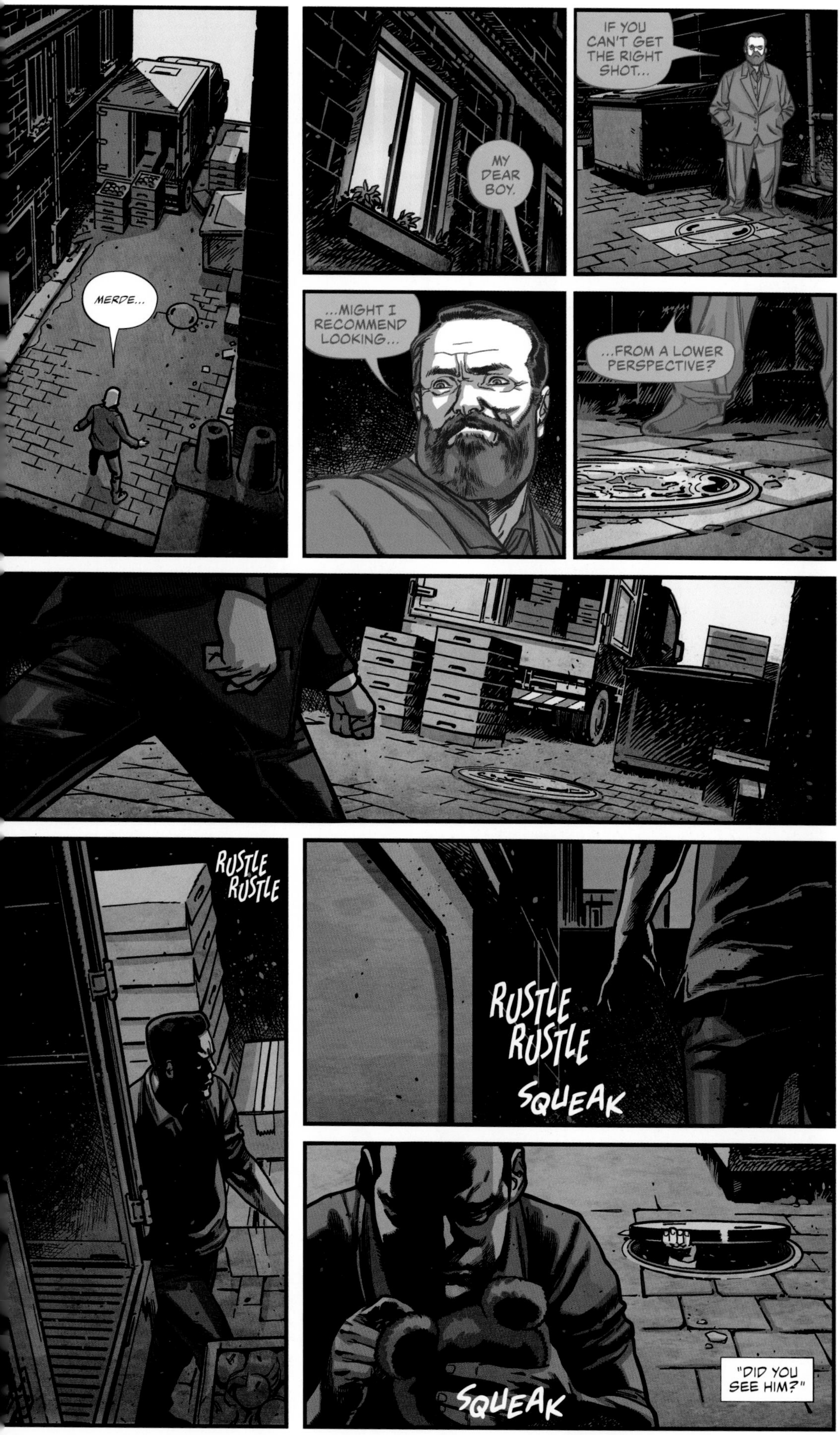
MERDE...
MY DEAR BOY.
IF YOU CAN'T GET THE RIGHT SHOT...
...MIGHT I RECOMMEND LOOKING...
...FROM A LOWER PERSPECTIVE?
RUSTLE RUSTLE
RUSTLE RUSTLE
SQUEAK
SQUEAK
"DID YOU SEE HIM?"

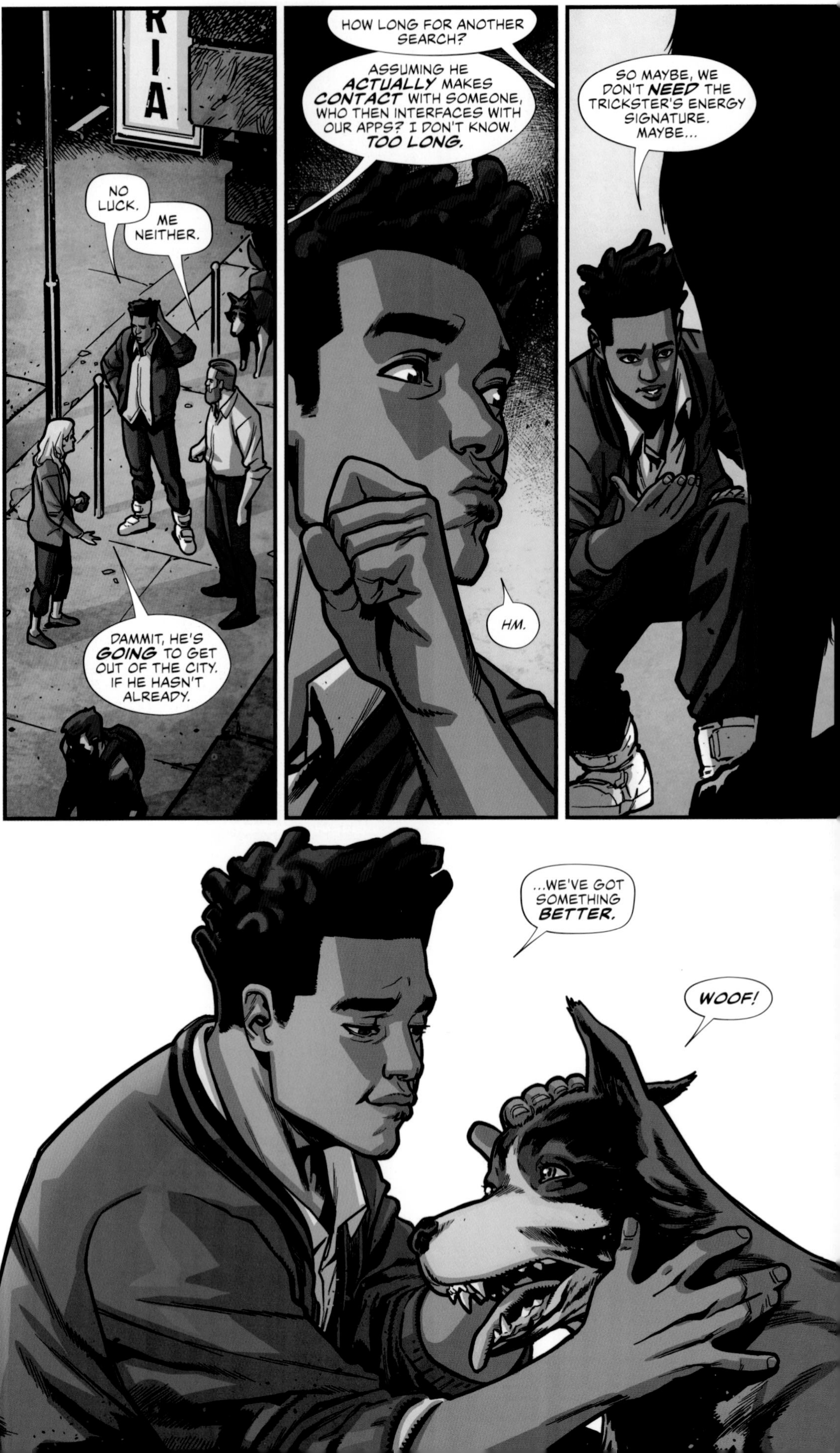
NO LUCK.
ME NEITHER.
DAMMIT, HE'S GOING TO GET OUT OF THE CITY. IF HE HASN'T ALREADY.
HOW LONG FOR ANOTHER SEARCH?
ASSUMING HE ACTUALLY MAKES CONTACT WITH SOMEONE, WHO THEN INTERFACES WITH OUR APPS? I DON'T KNOW. TOO LONG.
HM.
SO MAYBE, WE DON'T NEED THE TRICKSTER'S ENERGY SIGNATURE. MAYBE...
...WE'VE GOT SOMETHING BETTER.
WOOF!

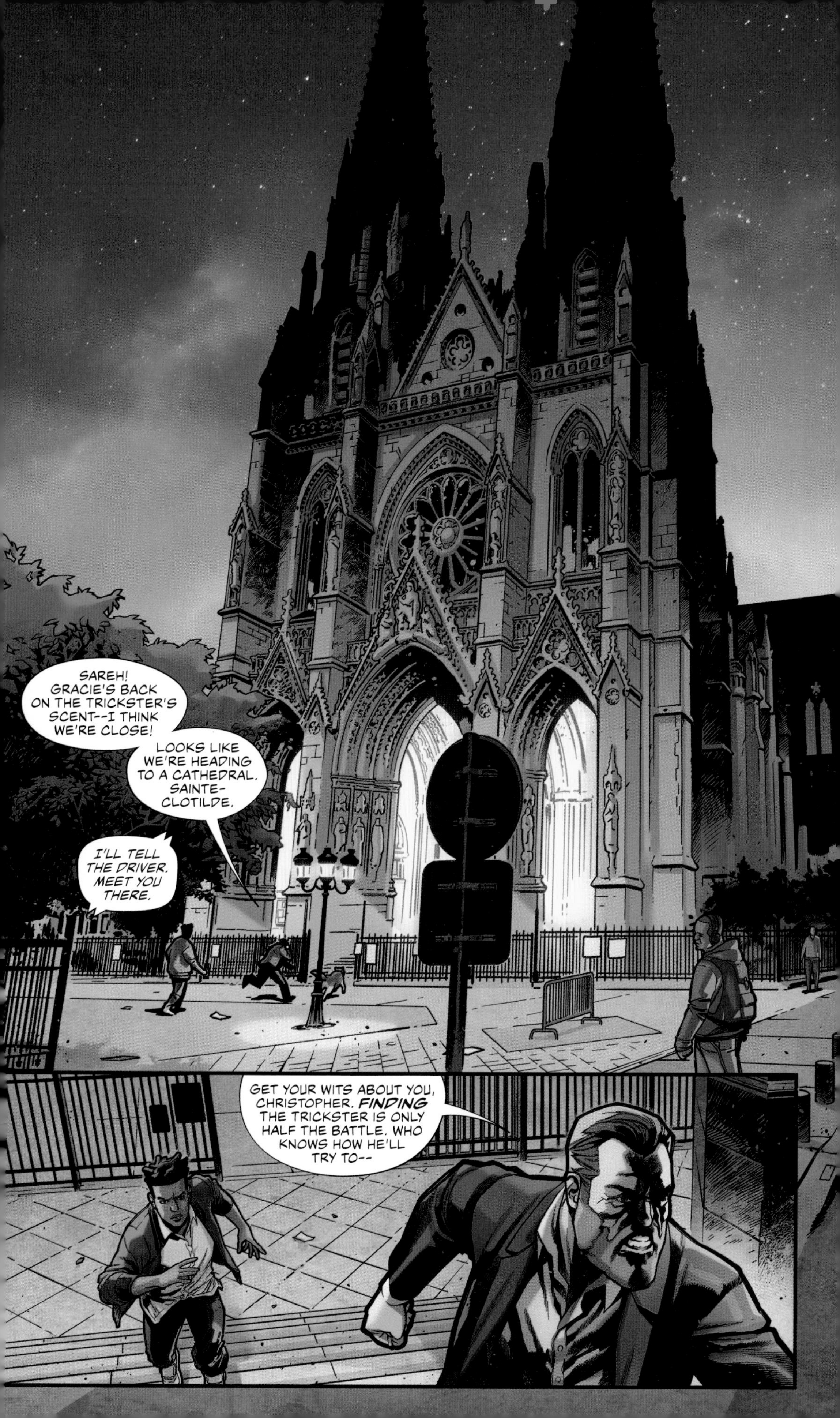
SAREH! GRACIE'S BACK ON THE TRICKSTER'S SCENT--I THINK WE'RE CLOSE!
LOOKS LIKE WE'RE HEADING TO A CATHEDRAL. SAINTE-CLOTILDE.
I'LL TELL THE DRIVER. MEET YOU THERE.
GET YOUR WITS ABOUT YOU, CHRISTOPHER. FINDING THE TRICKSTER IS ONLY HALF THE BATTLE. WHO KNOWS HOW HE'LL TRY TO--

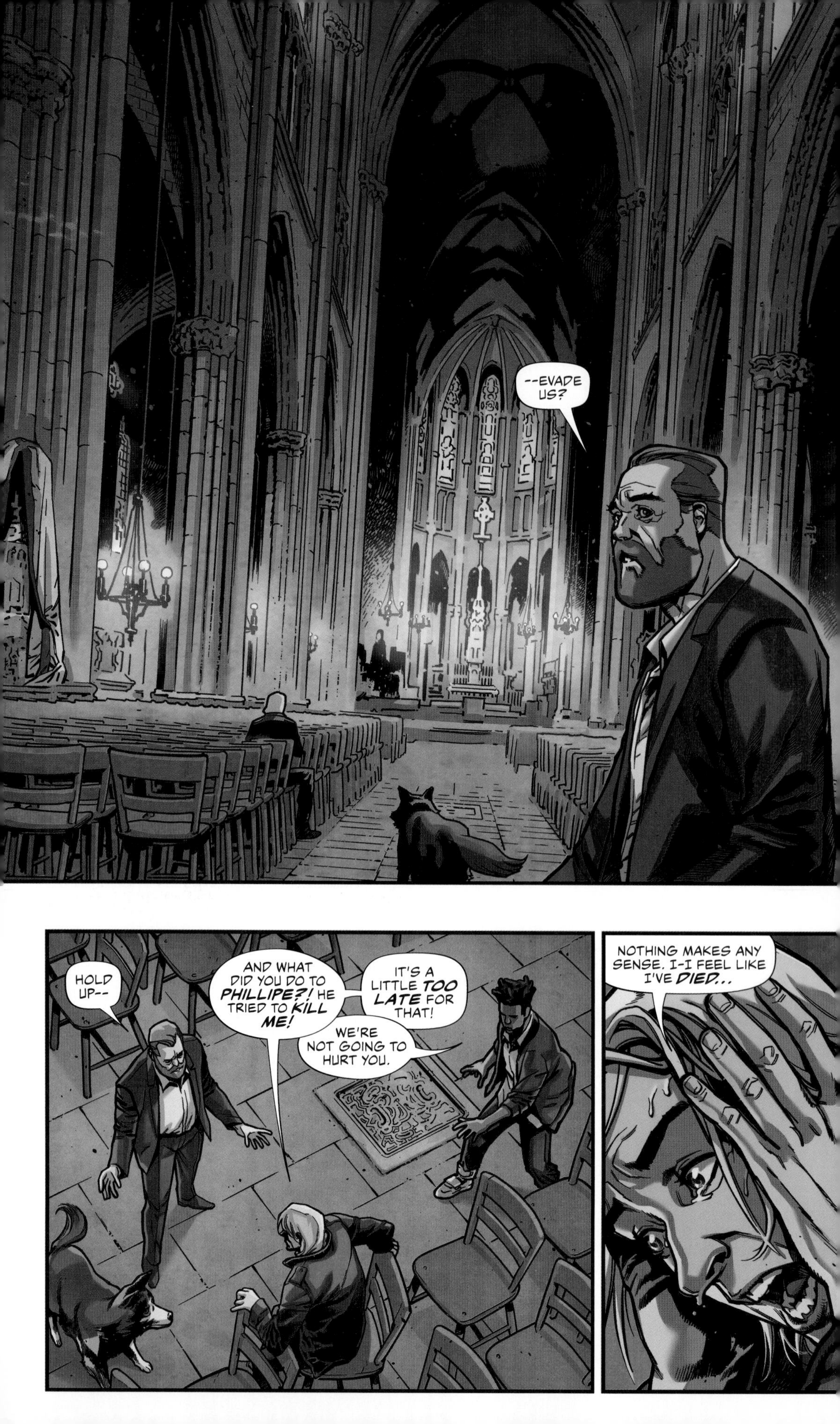
--EVADE US?
HOLD UP--
AND WHAT DID YOU DO TO PHILLIPE?! HE TRIED TO KILL ME!
IT'S A LITTLE TOO LATE FOR THAT!
WE'RE NOT GOING TO HURT YOU.
NOTHING MAKES ANY SENSE. I-I FEEL LIKE I'VE DIED...

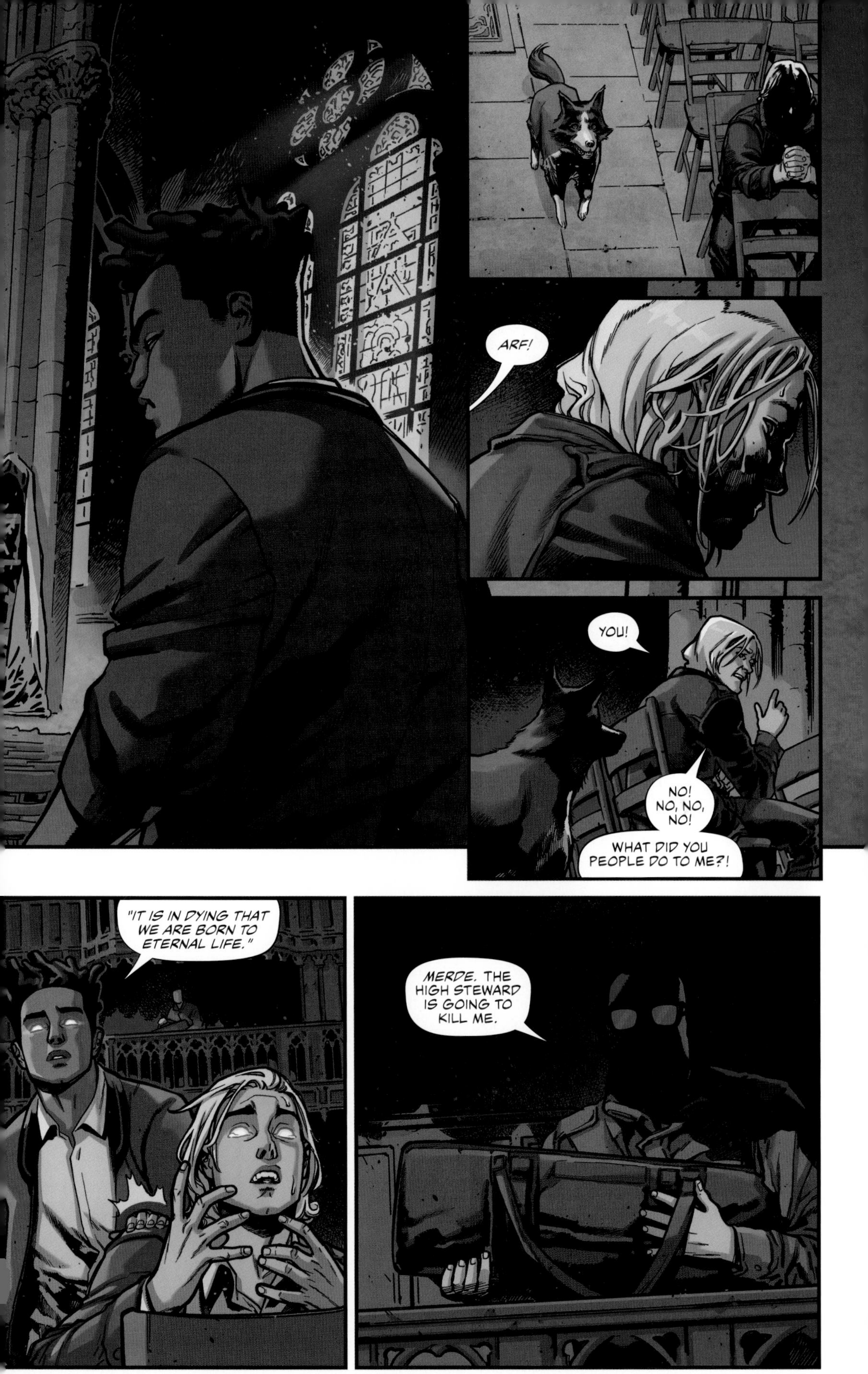
ARF!
YOU!
NO! NO, NO, NO!
WHAT DID YOU PEOPLE DO TO ME?!
"IT IS IN DYING THAT WE ARE BORN TO ETERNAL LIFE."
MERDE. THE HIGH STEWARD IS GOING TO KILL ME.

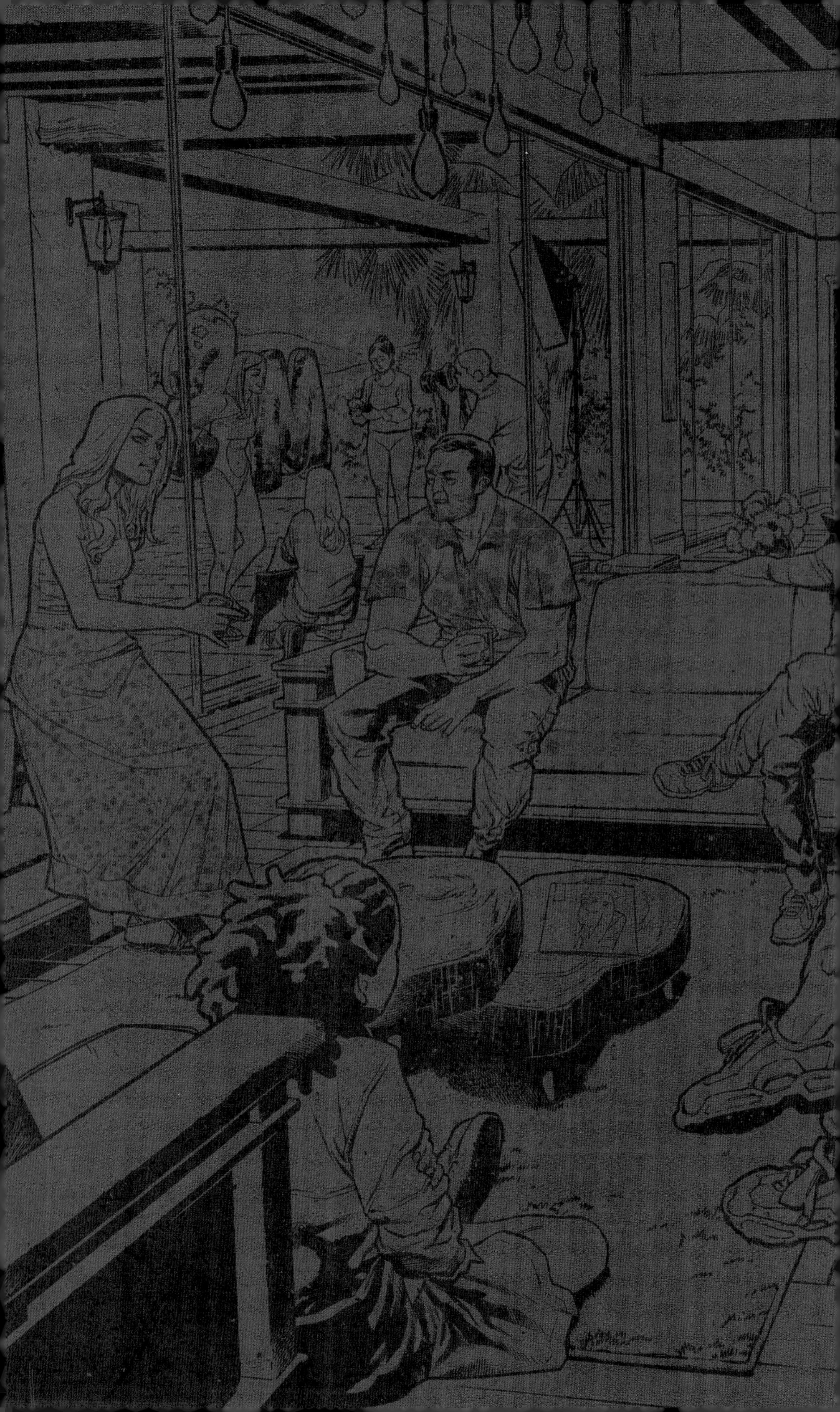

CHAPTER V
Advaya

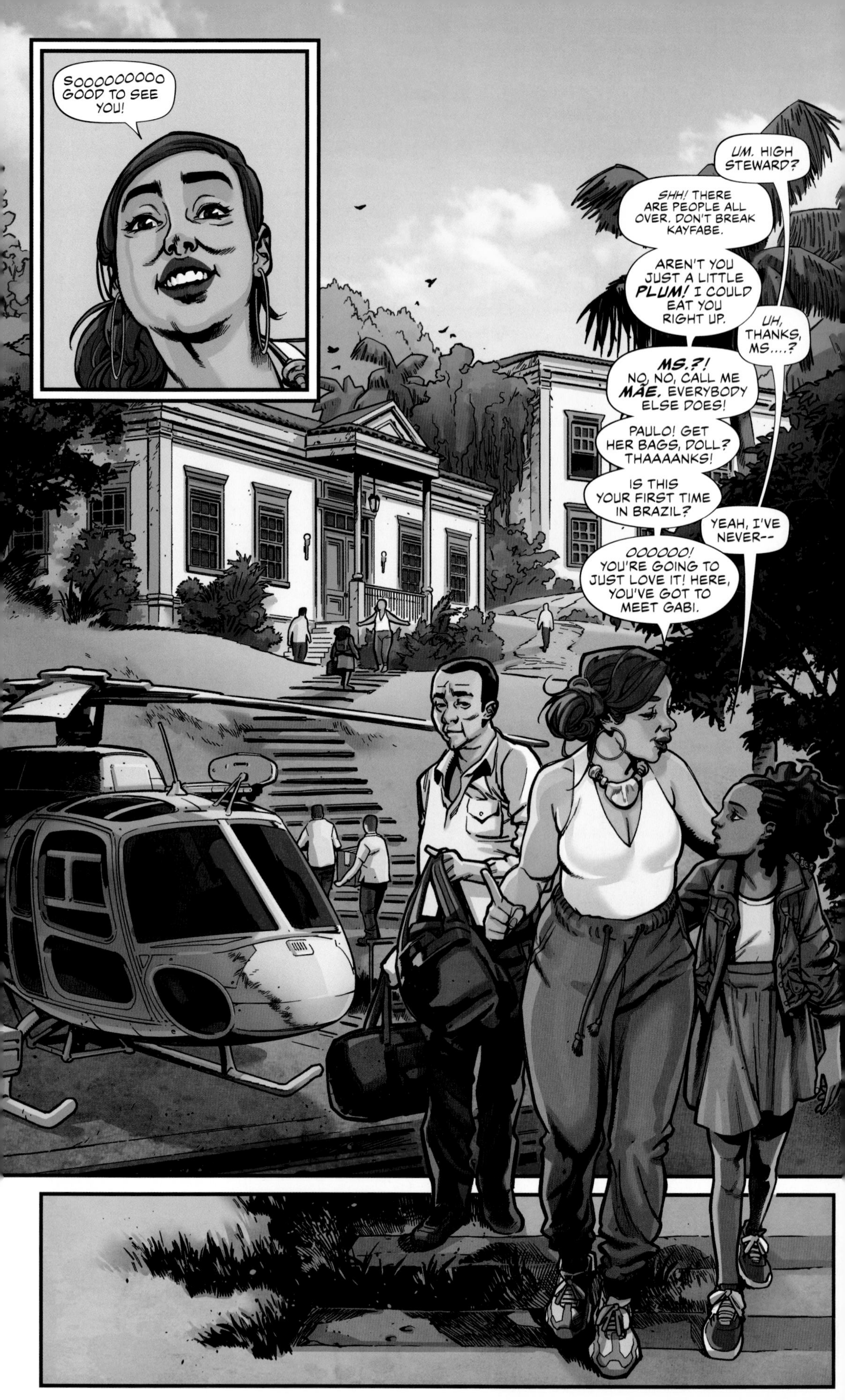
SOOOOOOOOO GOOD TO SEE YOU!
UM. HIGH STEWARD?
SHH! THERE ARE PEOPLE ALL OVER. DON'T BREAK KAYFABE.
AREN'T YOU JUST A LITTLE PLUM! I COULD EAT YOU RIGHT UP.
UH, THANKS, MS....?
MS.?! NO, NO, CALL ME MÃE. EVERYBODY ELSE DOES!
PAULO! GET HER BAGS, DOLL? THAAAANKS!
IS THIS YOUR FIRST TIME IN BRAZIL?
YEAH, I'VE NEVER--
OOOOOO! YOU'RE GOING TO JUST LOVE IT! HERE, YOU'VE GOT TO MEET GABI.

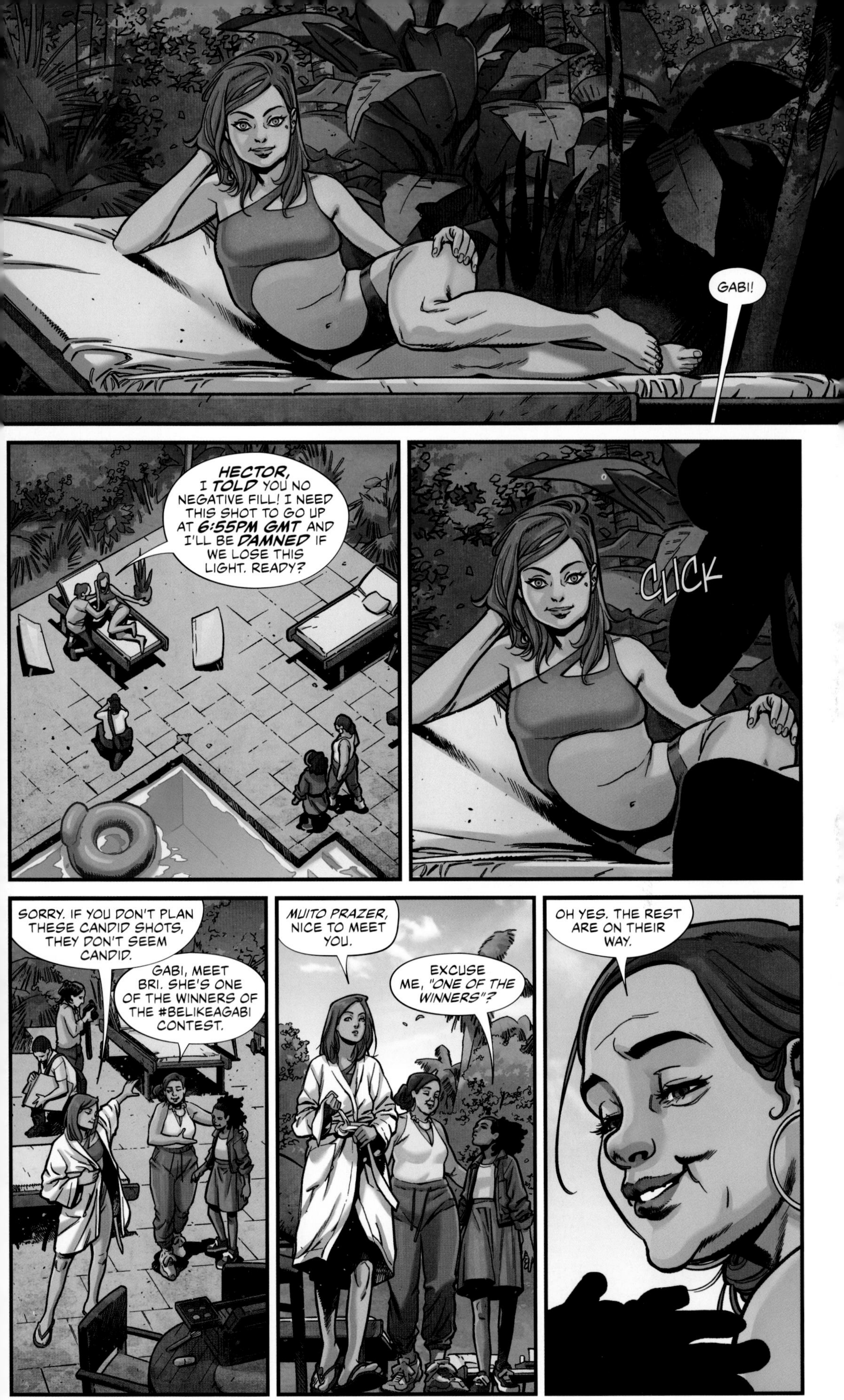
GABI!
HECTOR, I TOLD YOU NO NEGATIVE FILL! I NEED THIS SHOT TO GO UP AT 6:55PM GMT AND I'LL BE DAMNED IF WE LOSE THIS LIGHT. READY?
CLICK
SORRY. IF YOU DON'T PLAN THESE CANDID SHOTS, THEY DON'T SEEM CANDID.
GABI, MEET BRI. SHE'S ONE OF THE WINNERS OF THE #BELIKEAGABI CONTEST.
MUITO PRAZER, NICE TO MEET YOU.
EXCUSE ME, "ONE OF THE WINNERS"?
OH YES. THE REST ARE ON THEIR WAY.

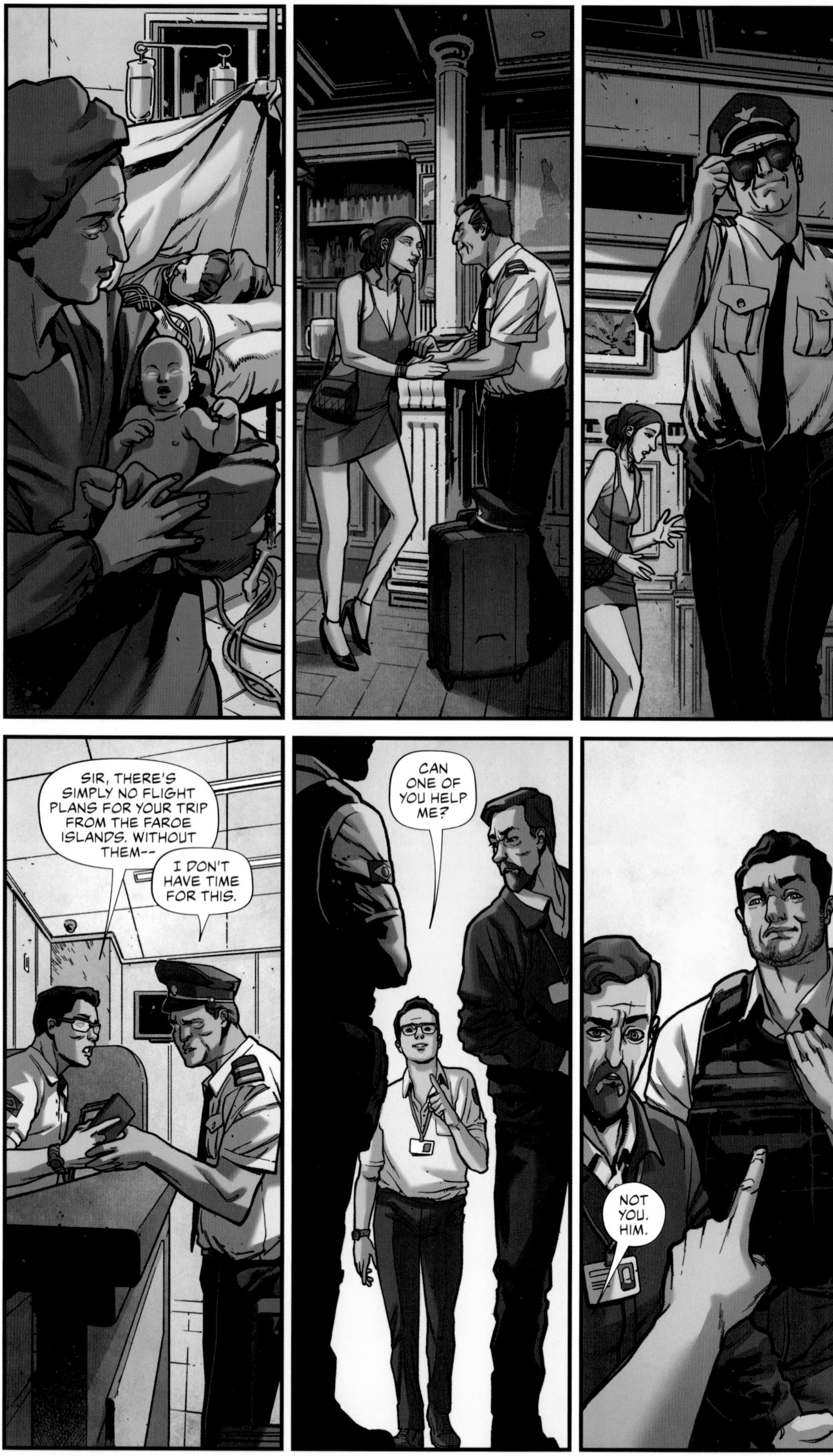
SIR, THERE'S SIMPLY NO FLIGHT PLANS FOR YOUR TRIP FROM THE FAROE ISLANDS. WITHOUT THEM--
I DON'T HAVE TIME FOR THIS.
CAN ONE OF YOU HELP ME?
NOT YOU. HIM.

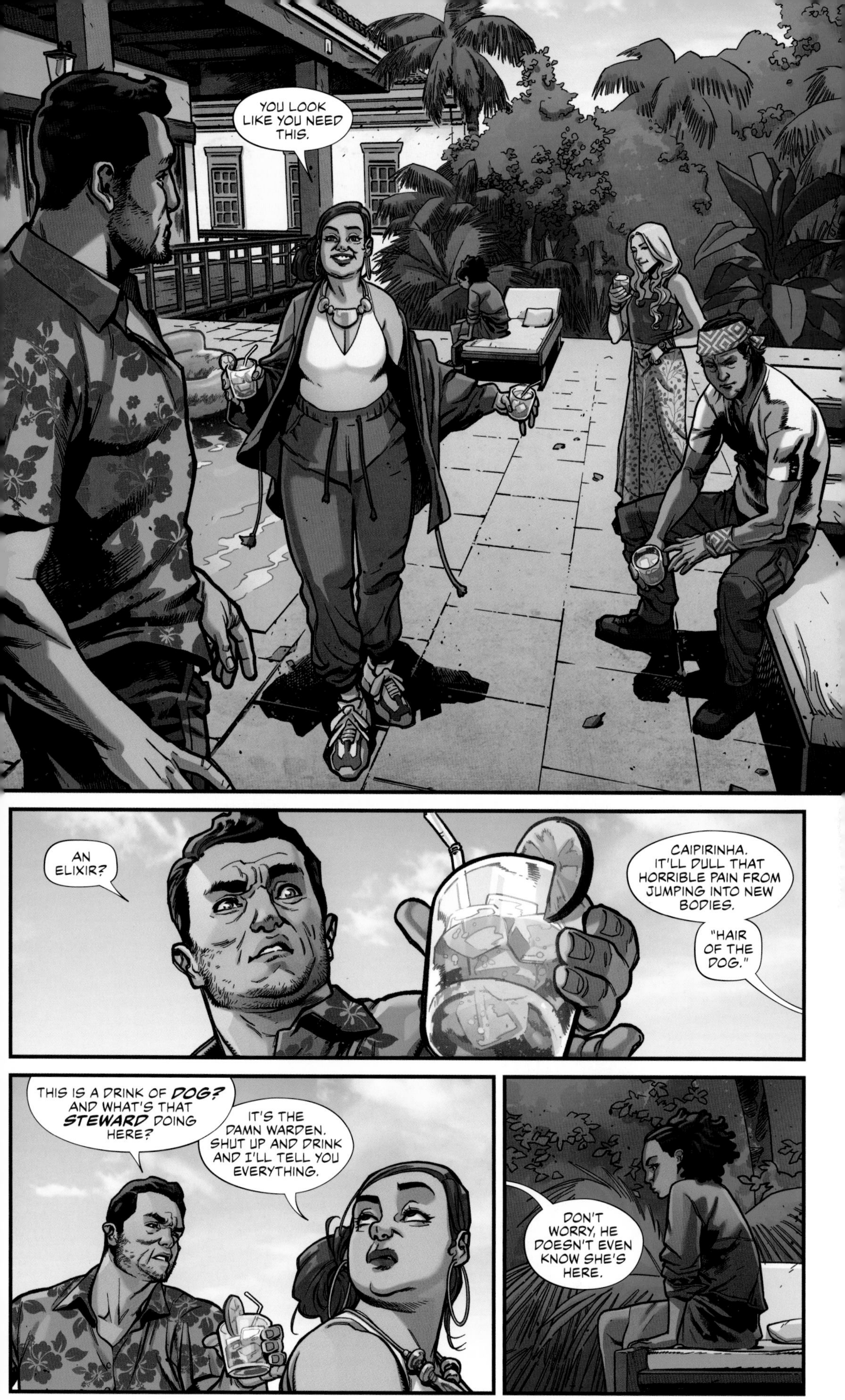

YOU LOOK LIKE YOU NEED THIS.
AN ELIXIR?
CAIPIRINHA. IT'LL DULL THAT HORRIBLE PAIN FROM JUMPING INTO NEW BODIES.
"HAIR OF THE DOG."
THIS IS A DRINK OF DOG? AND WHAT'S THAT STEWARD DOING HERE?
IT'S THE DAMN WARDEN. SHUT UP AND DRINK AND I'LL TELL YOU EVERYTHING.
DON'T WORRY, HE DOESN'T EVEN KNOW SHE'S HERE.

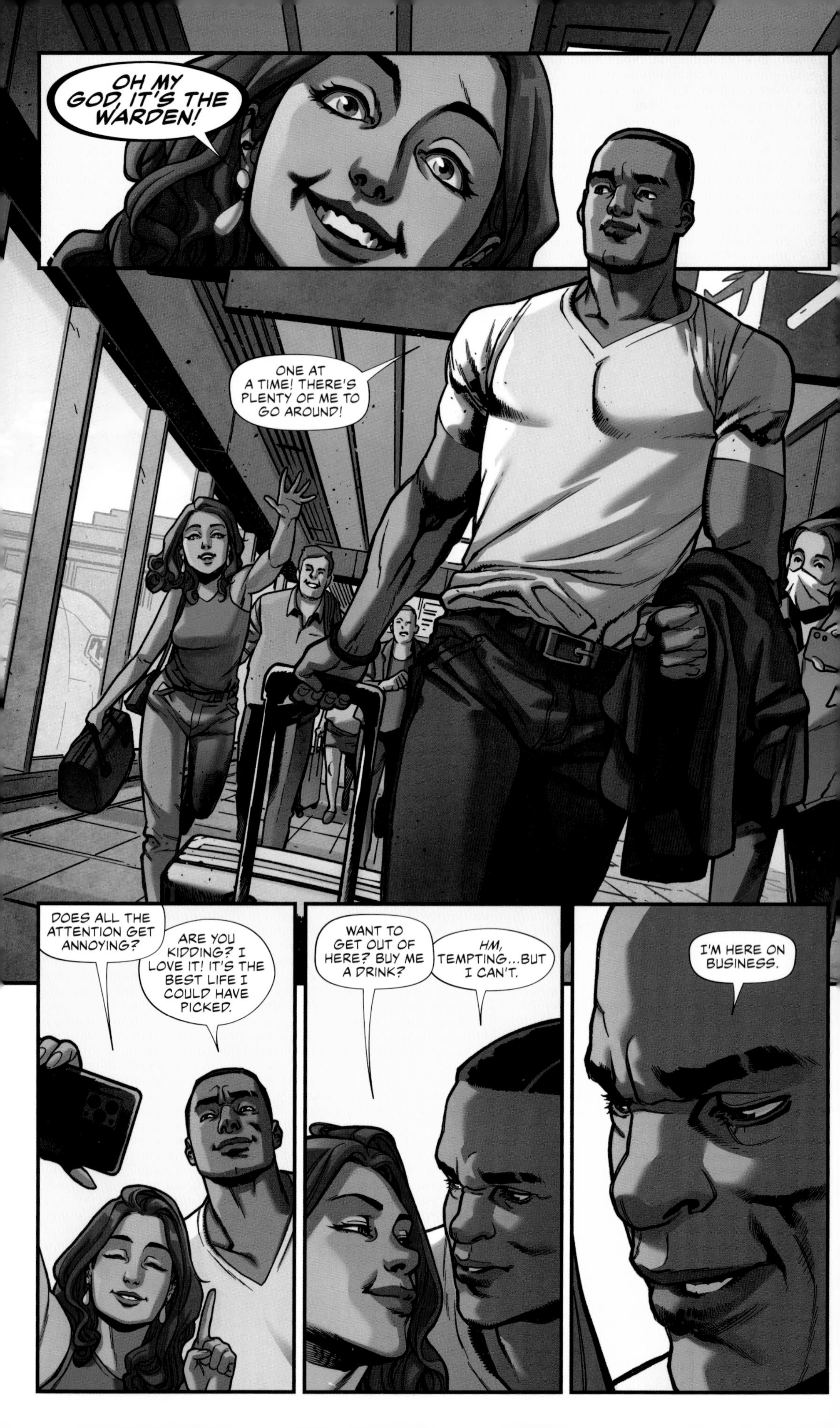
OH MY GOD, IT'S THE WARDEN!
ONE AT A TIME! THERE'S PLENTY OF ME TO GO AROUND!
DOES ALL THE ATTENTION GET ANNOYING?
ARE YOU KIDDING? I LOVE IT! IT'S THE BEST LIFE I COULD HAVE PICKED.
WANT TO GET OUT OF HERE? BUY ME A DRINK?
HM, TEMPTING...BUT I CAN'T.
I'M HERE ON BUSINESS.

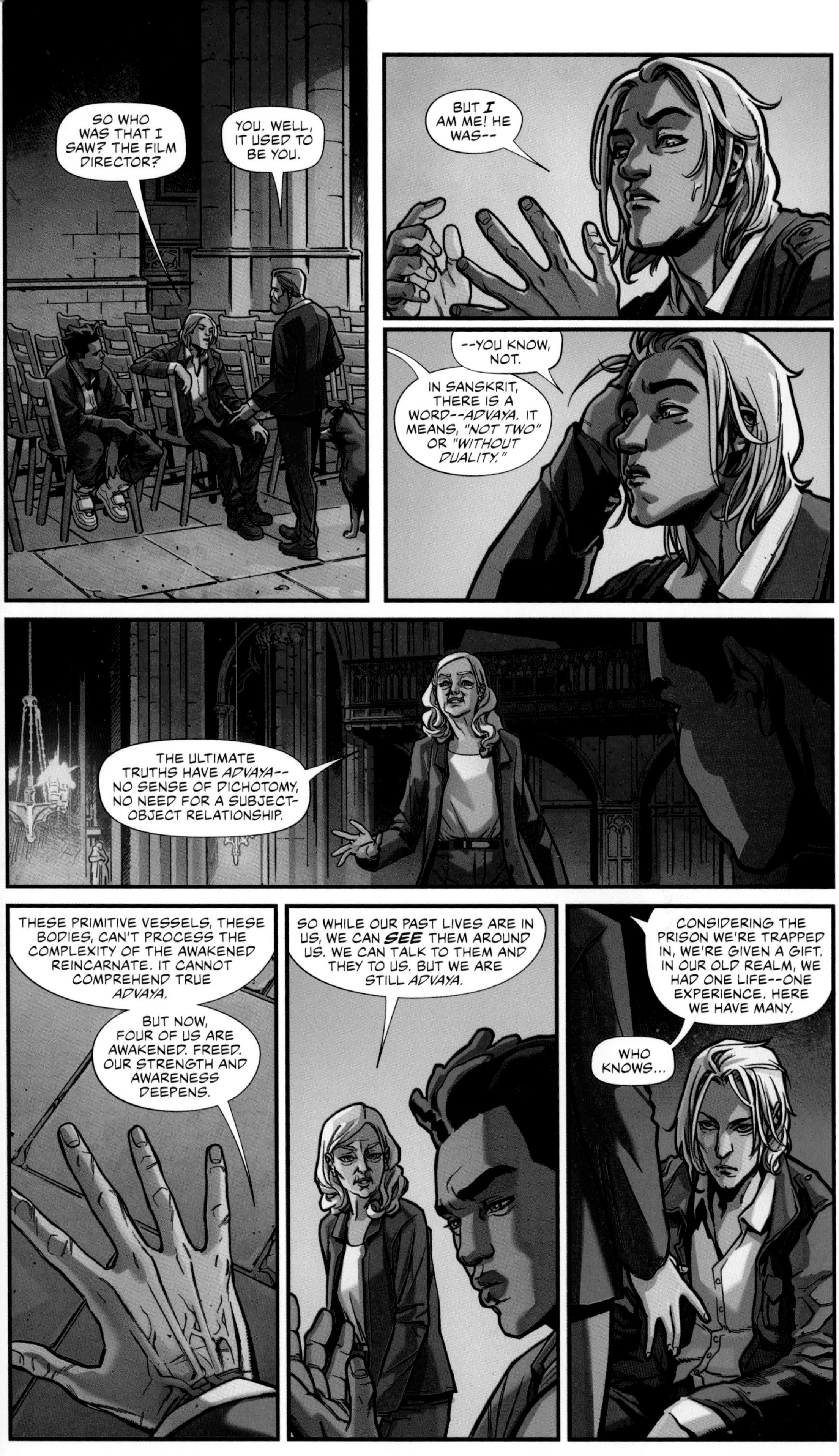
SO WHO WAS THAT I SAW? THE FILM DIRECTOR?
YOU. WELL, IT USED TO BE YOU.
BUT *I* AM ME! HE WAS--
--YOU KNOW, NOT.
IN SANSKRIT, THERE IS A WORD--*ADVAYA*. IT MEANS, *"NOT TWO"* OR *"WITHOUT DUALITY."*
THE ULTIMATE TRUTHS HAVE *ADVAYA*-- NO SENSE OF DICHOTOMY, NO NEED FOR A SUBJECT-OBJECT RELATIONSHIP.
THESE PRIMITIVE VESSELS, THESE BODIES, CAN'T PROCESS THE COMPLEXITY OF THE AWAKENED REINCARNATE. IT CANNOT COMPREHEND TRUE *ADVAYA.*
BUT NOW, FOUR OF US ARE AWAKENED. FREED. OUR STRENGTH AND AWARENESS DEEPENS.
SO WHILE OUR PAST LIVES ARE IN US, WE CAN ***SEE*** THEM AROUND US. WE CAN TALK TO THEM AND THEY TO US. BUT WE ARE STILL *ADVAYA.*
CONSIDERING THE PRISON WE'RE TRAPPED IN, WE'RE GIVEN A GIFT. IN OUR OLD REALM, WE HAD ONE LIFE--ONE EXPERIENCE. HERE WE HAVE MANY.
WHO KNOWS...

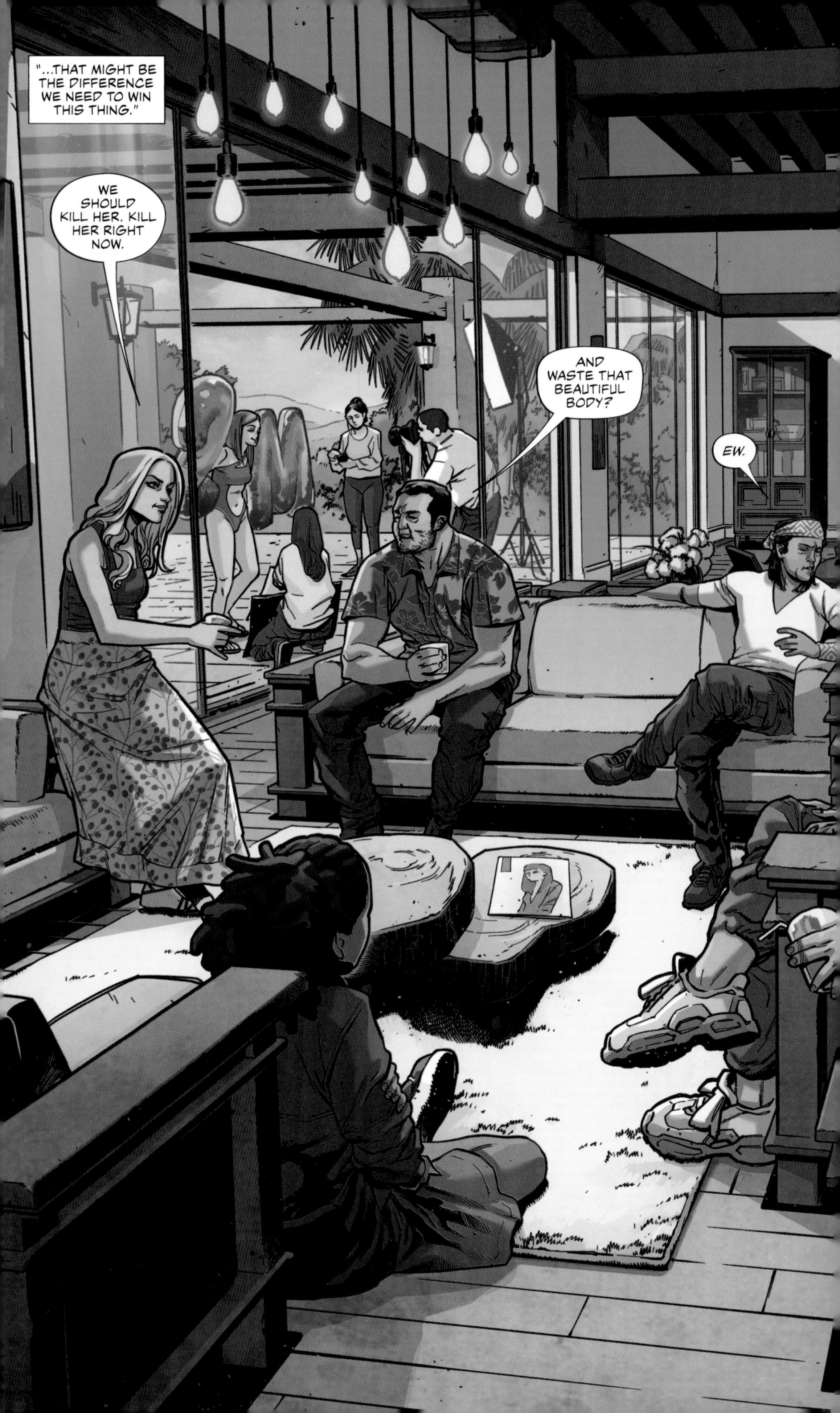
"...THAT MIGHT BE THE DIFFERENCE WE NEED TO WIN THIS THING."
WE SHOULD KILL HER. KILL HER RIGHT NOW.
AND WASTE THAT BEAUTIFUL BODY?
EW.

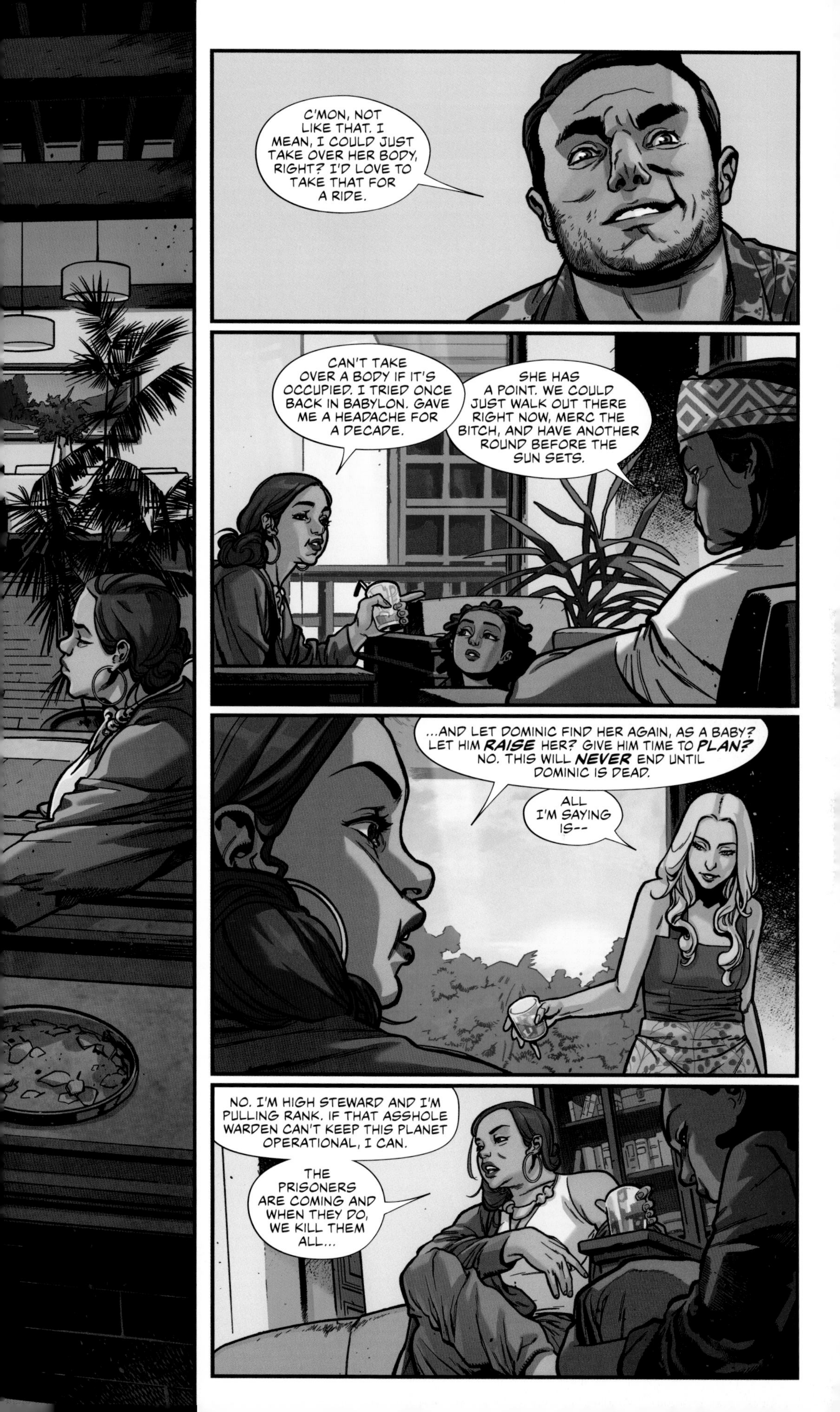
C'MON, NOT LIKE THAT. I MEAN, I COULD JUST TAKE OVER HER BODY, RIGHT? I'D LOVE TO TAKE THAT FOR A RIDE.
CAN'T TAKE OVER A BODY IF IT'S OCCUPIED. I TRIED ONCE BACK IN BABYLON. GAVE ME A HEADACHE FOR A DECADE.
SHE HAS A POINT. WE COULD JUST WALK OUT THERE RIGHT NOW, MERC THE BITCH, AND HAVE ANOTHER ROUND BEFORE THE SUN SETS.
...AND LET DOMINIC FIND HER AGAIN, AS A BABY? LET HIM RAISE HER? GIVE HIM TIME TO PLAN? NO. THIS WILL NEVER END UNTIL DOMINIC IS DEAD.
ALL I'M SAYING IS--
NO. I'M HIGH STEWARD AND I'M PULLING RANK. IF THAT ASSHOLE WARDEN CAN'T KEEP THIS PLANET OPERATIONAL, I CAN.
THE PRISONERS ARE COMING AND WHEN THEY DO, WE KILL THEM ALL...

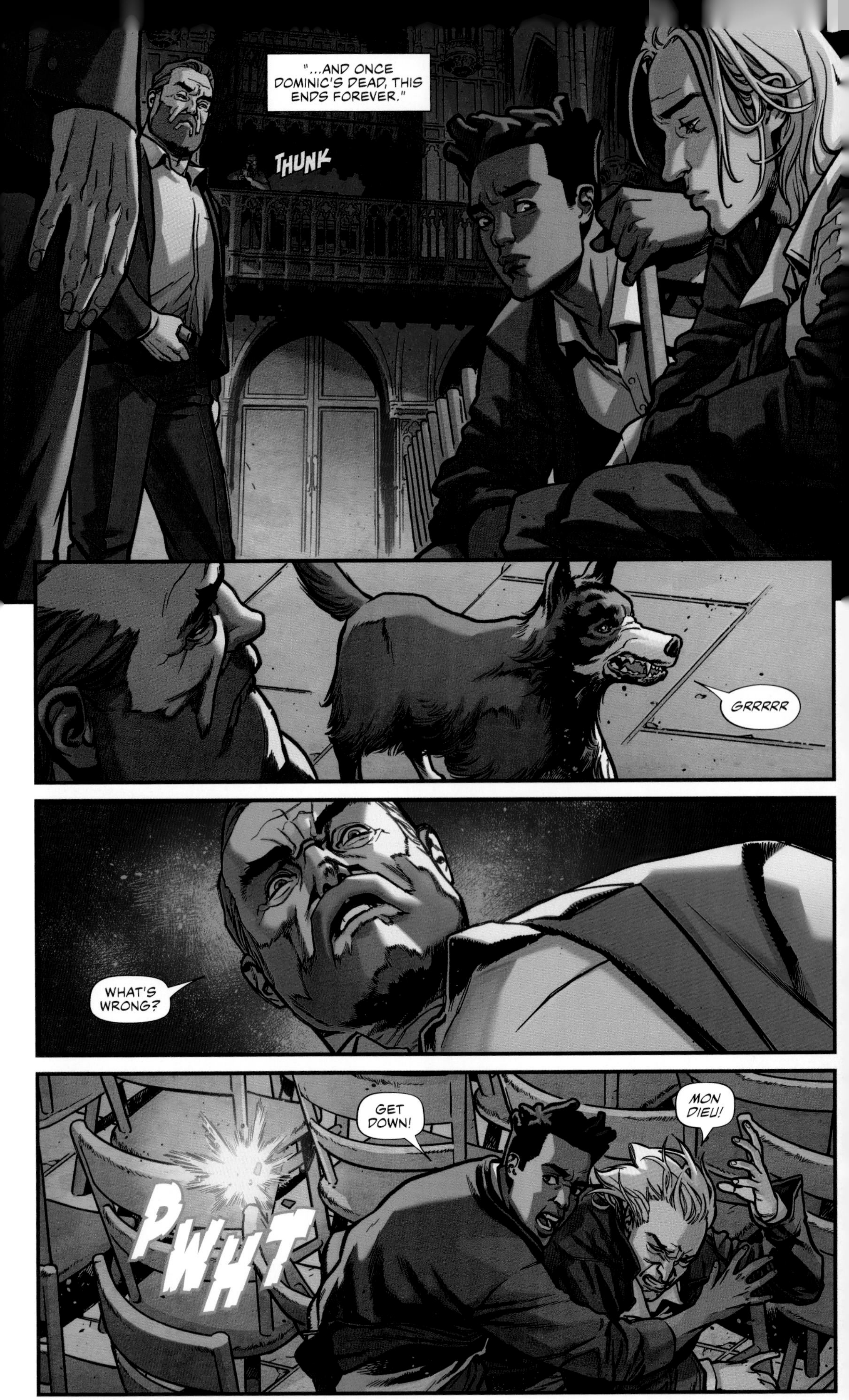
"...AND ONCE DOMINIC'S DEAD, THIS ENDS FOREVER."
THUNK
GRRRRR
WHAT'S WRONG?
GET DOWN!
MON DIEU!
PWHT

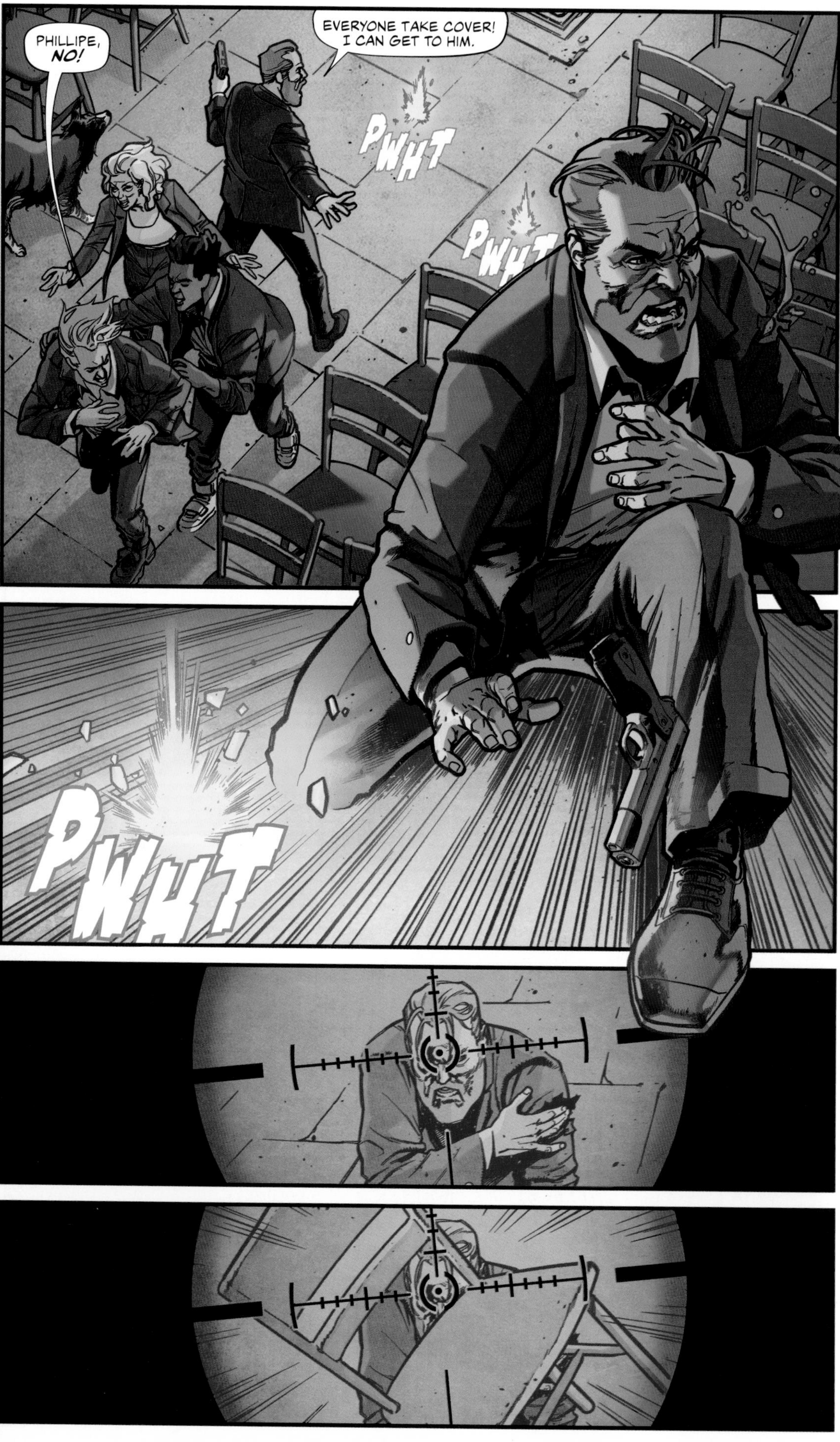
PHILLIPE, NO!
EVERYONE TAKE COVER! I CAN GET TO HIM.
PWHT
PWHT

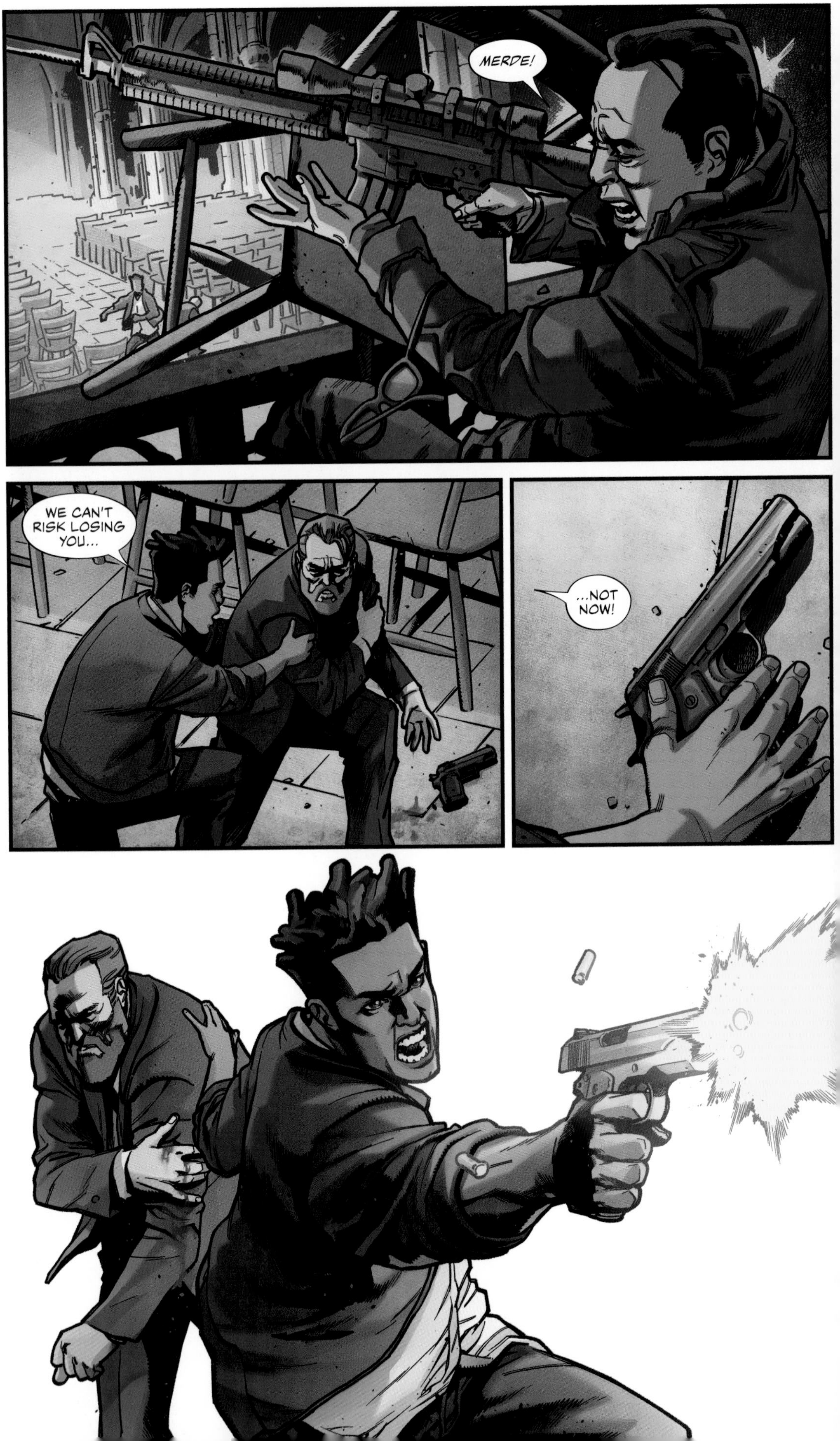
MERDE!
WE CAN'T RISK LOSING YOU...
...NOT NOW!

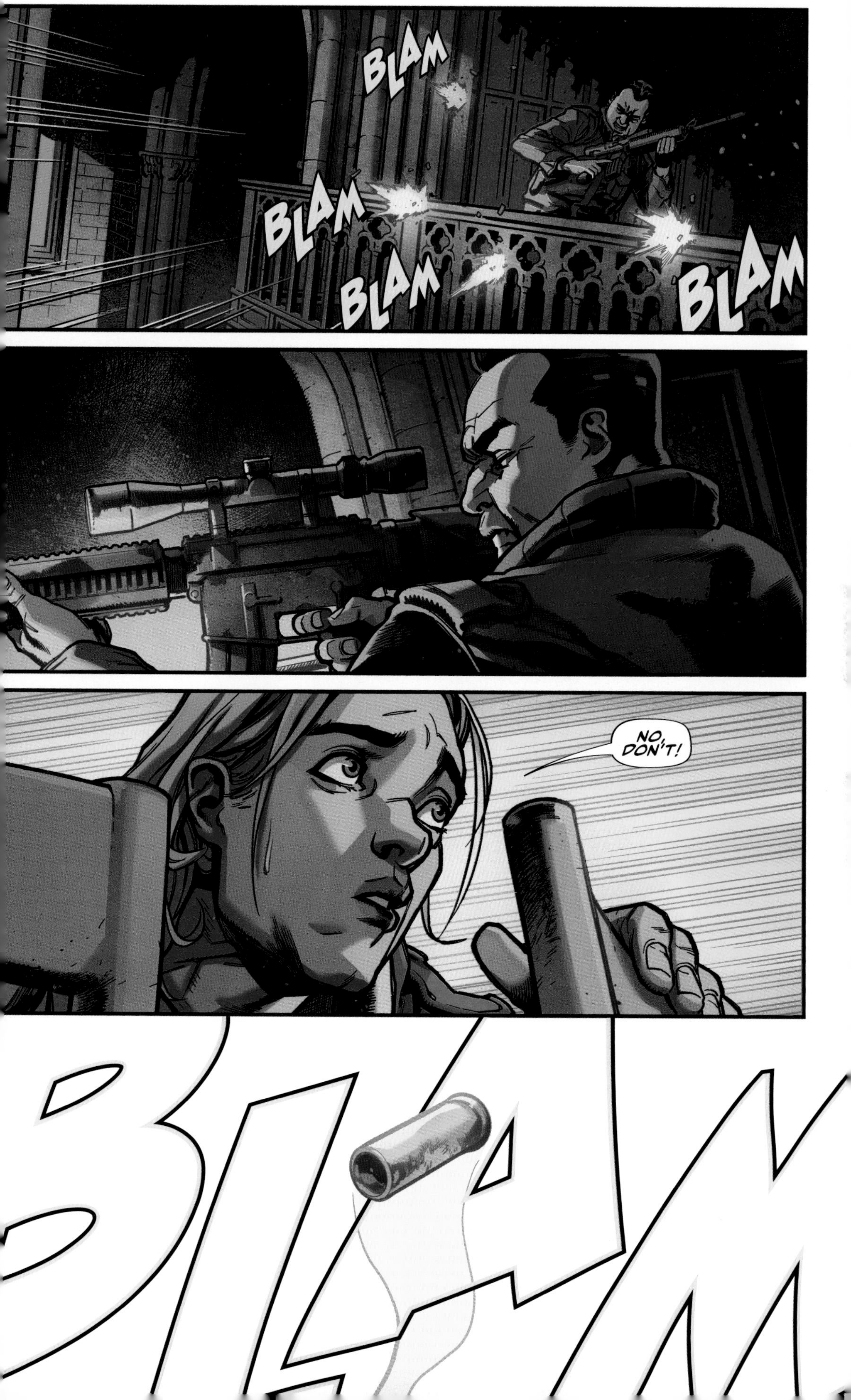
BLAM
BLAM
BLAM
BLAM
NO, DON'T!
BLAM

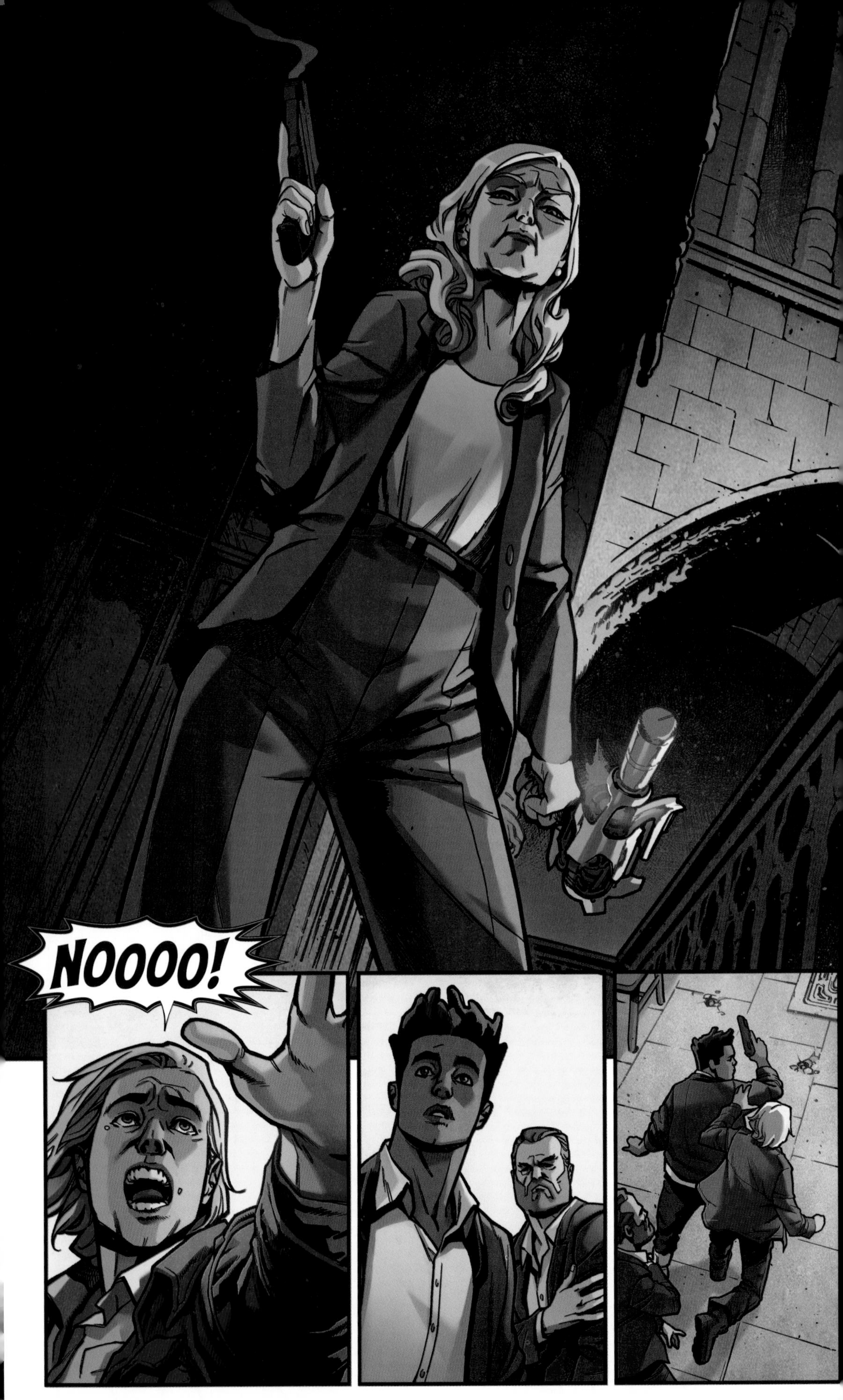
NOOOO!

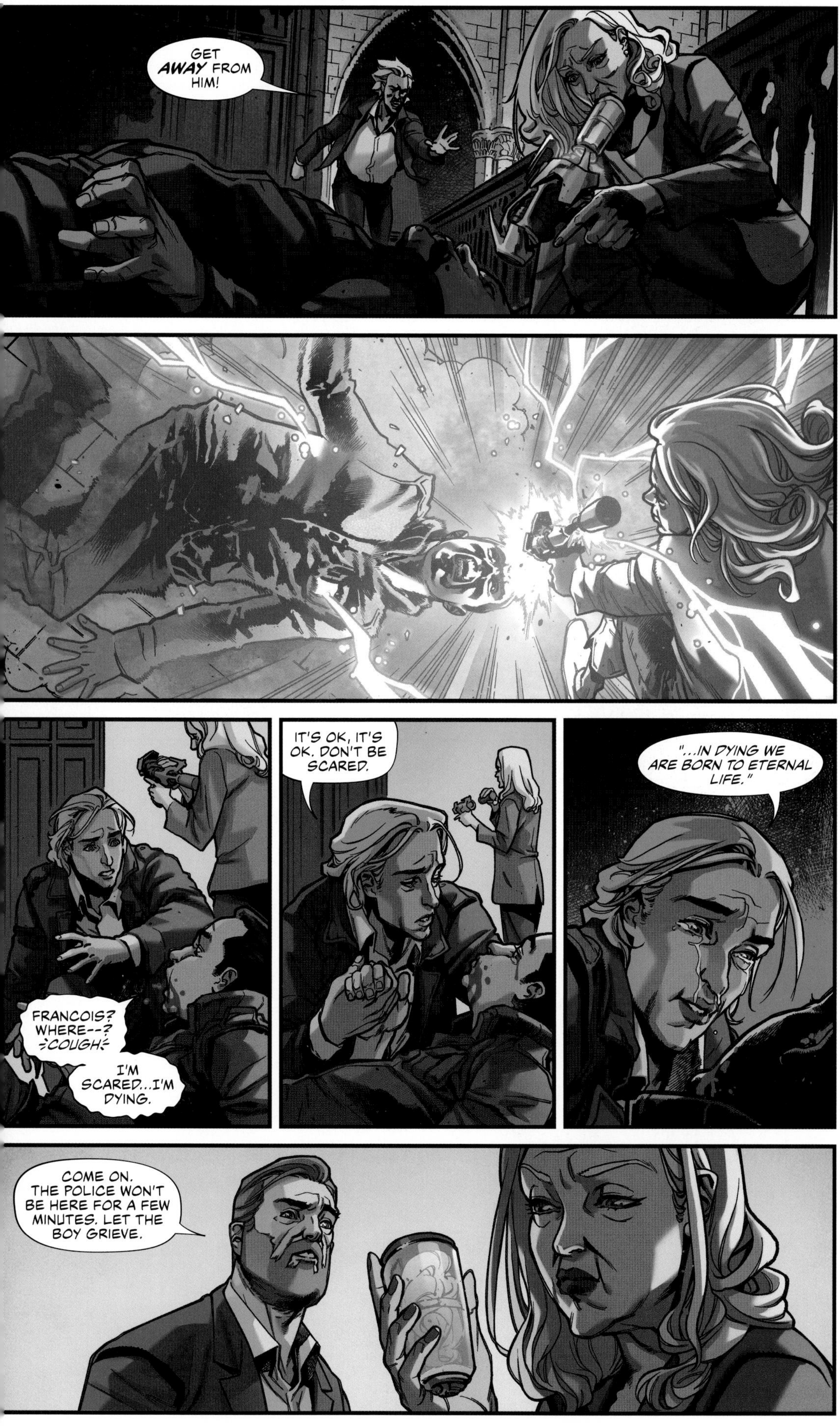
GET AWAY FROM HIM!
IT'S OK, IT'S OK. DON'T BE SCARED.
FRANCOIS? WHERE--? ≠COUGH≠
I'M SCARED...I'M DYING.
"...IN DYING WE ARE BORN TO ETERNAL LIFE."
COME ON. THE POLICE WON'T BE HERE FOR A FEW MINUTES. LET THE BOY GRIEVE.

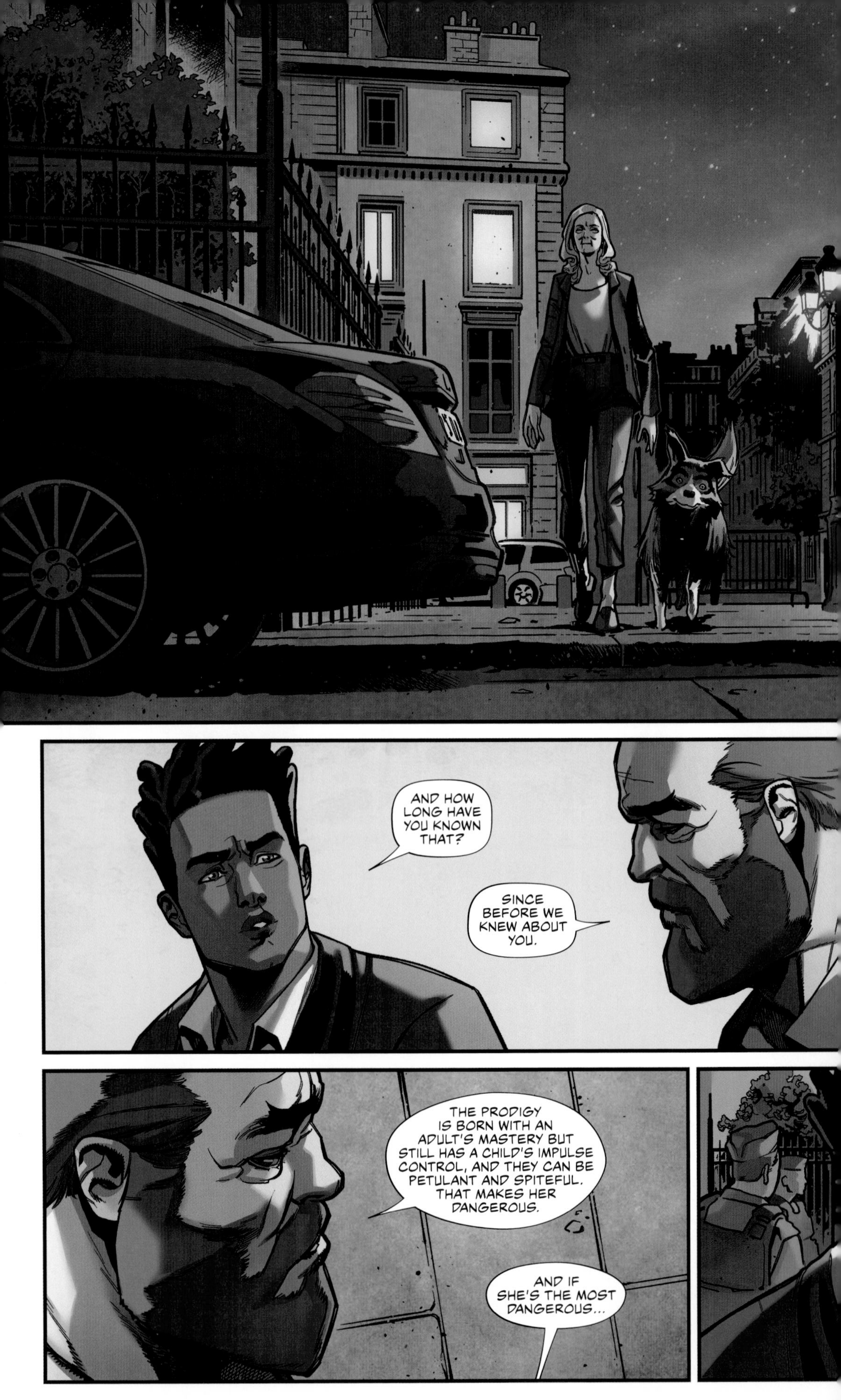

AND HOW LONG HAVE YOU KNOWN THAT?
SINCE BEFORE WE KNEW ABOUT YOU.
THE PRODIGY IS BORN WITH AN ADULT'S MASTERY BUT STILL HAS A CHILD'S IMPULSE CONTROL, AND THEY CAN BE PETULANT AND SPITEFUL. THAT MAKES HER DANGEROUS.
AND IF SHE'S THE MOST DANGEROUS...

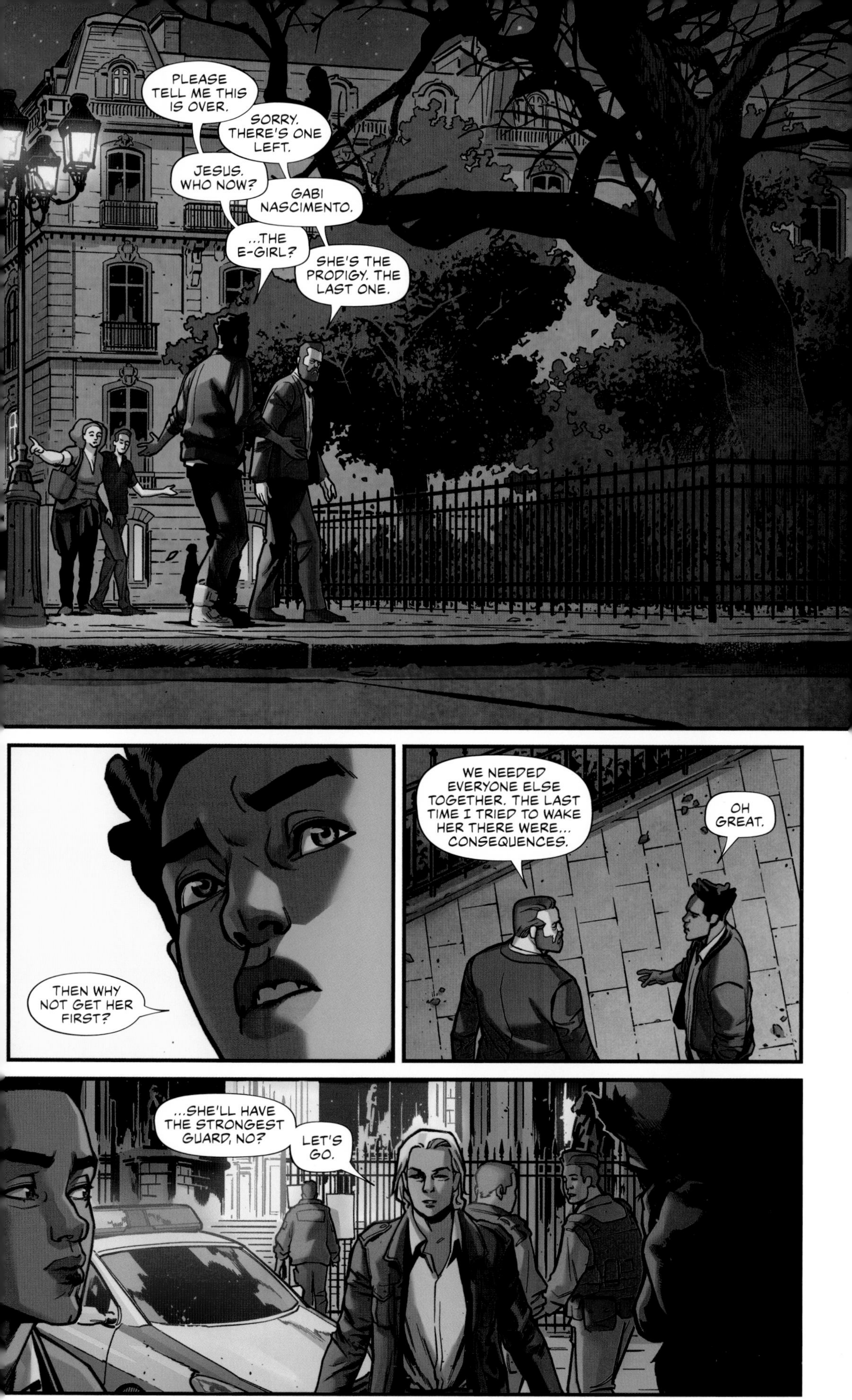
PLEASE TELL ME THIS IS OVER.
SORRY. THERE'S ONE LEFT.
JESUS. WHO NOW?
GABI NASCIMENTO.
...THE E-GIRL?
SHE'S THE PRODIGY. THE LAST ONE.
THEN WHY NOT GET HER FIRST?
WE NEEDED EVERYONE ELSE TOGETHER. THE LAST TIME I TRIED TO WAKE HER THERE WERE... CONSEQUENCES.
OH GREAT.
...SHE'LL HAVE THE STRONGEST GUARD, NO?
LET'S GO.

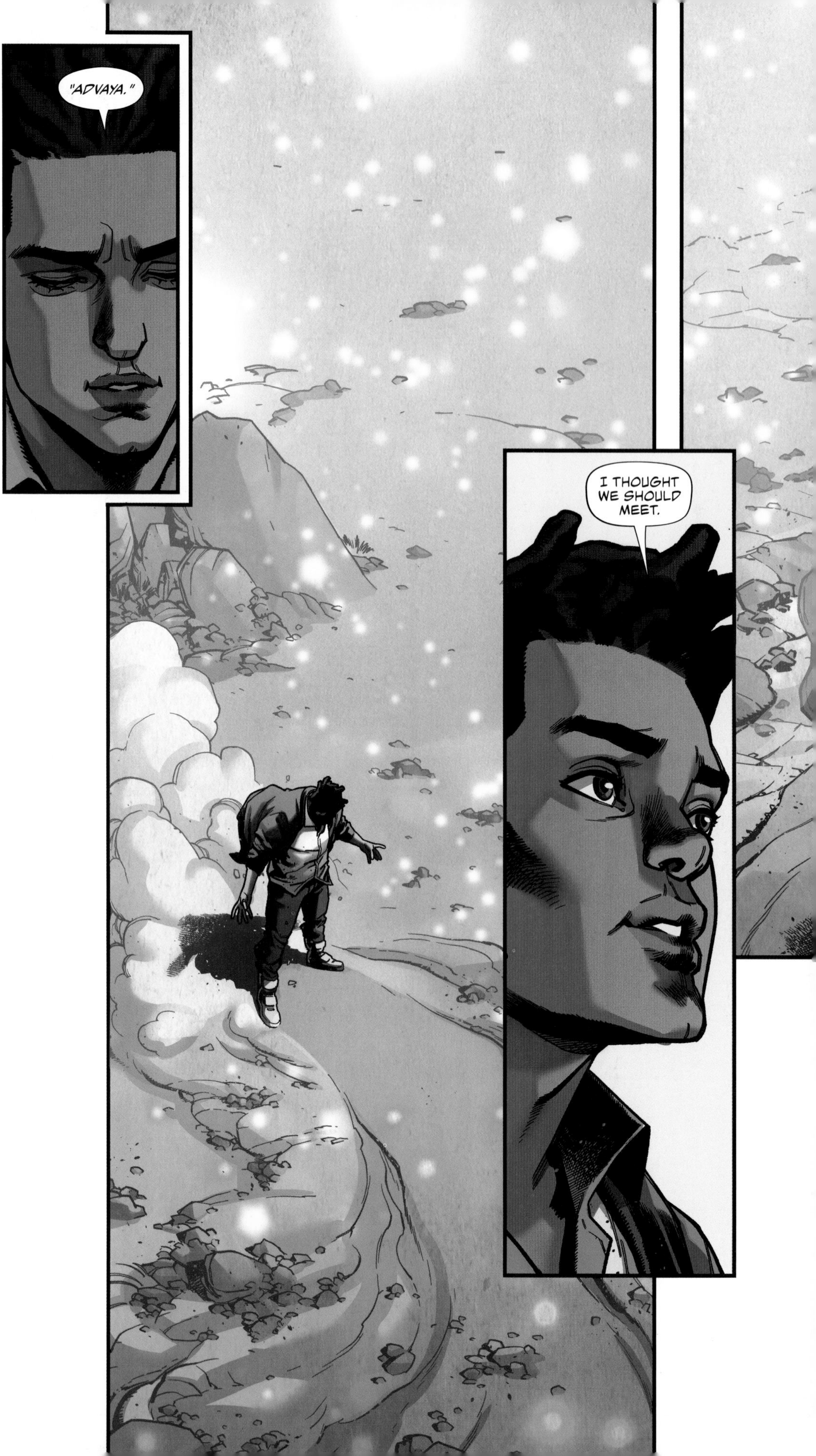
"ADVAYA."
I THOUGHT WE SHOULD MEET.

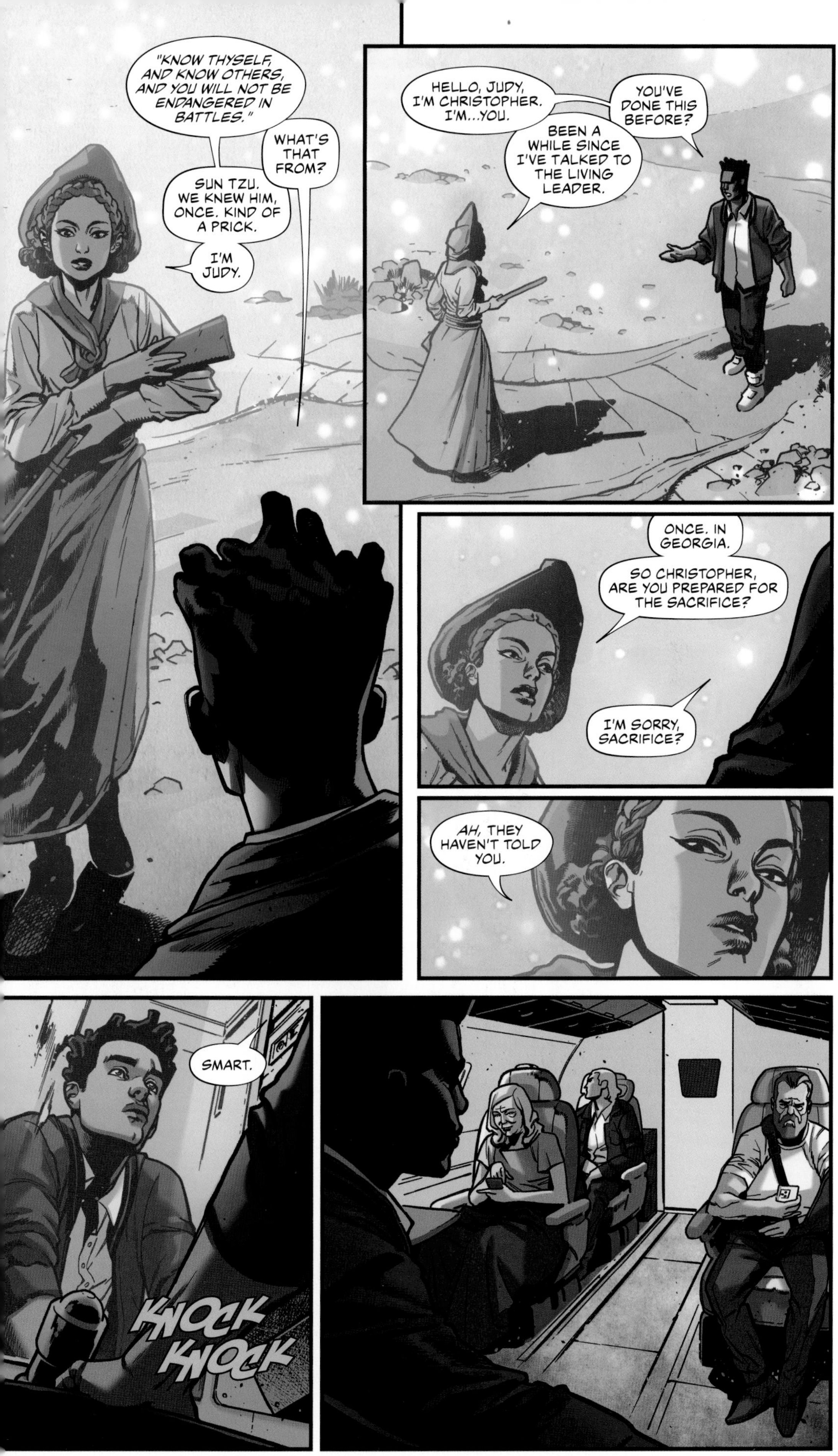
"KNOW THYSELF, AND KNOW OTHERS, AND YOU WILL NOT BE ENDANGERED IN BATTLES."
WHAT'S THAT FROM?
SUN TZU. WE KNEW HIM, ONCE. KIND OF A PRICK.
I'M JUDY.
HELLO, JUDY, I'M CHRISTOPHER. I'M...YOU.
YOU'VE DONE THIS BEFORE?
BEEN A WHILE SINCE I'VE TALKED TO THE LIVING LEADER.
ONCE. IN GEORGIA.
SO CHRISTOPHER, ARE YOU PREPARED FOR THE SACRIFICE?
I'M SORRY, SACRIFICE?
AH, THEY HAVEN'T TOLD YOU.
SMART.
KNOCK KNOCK

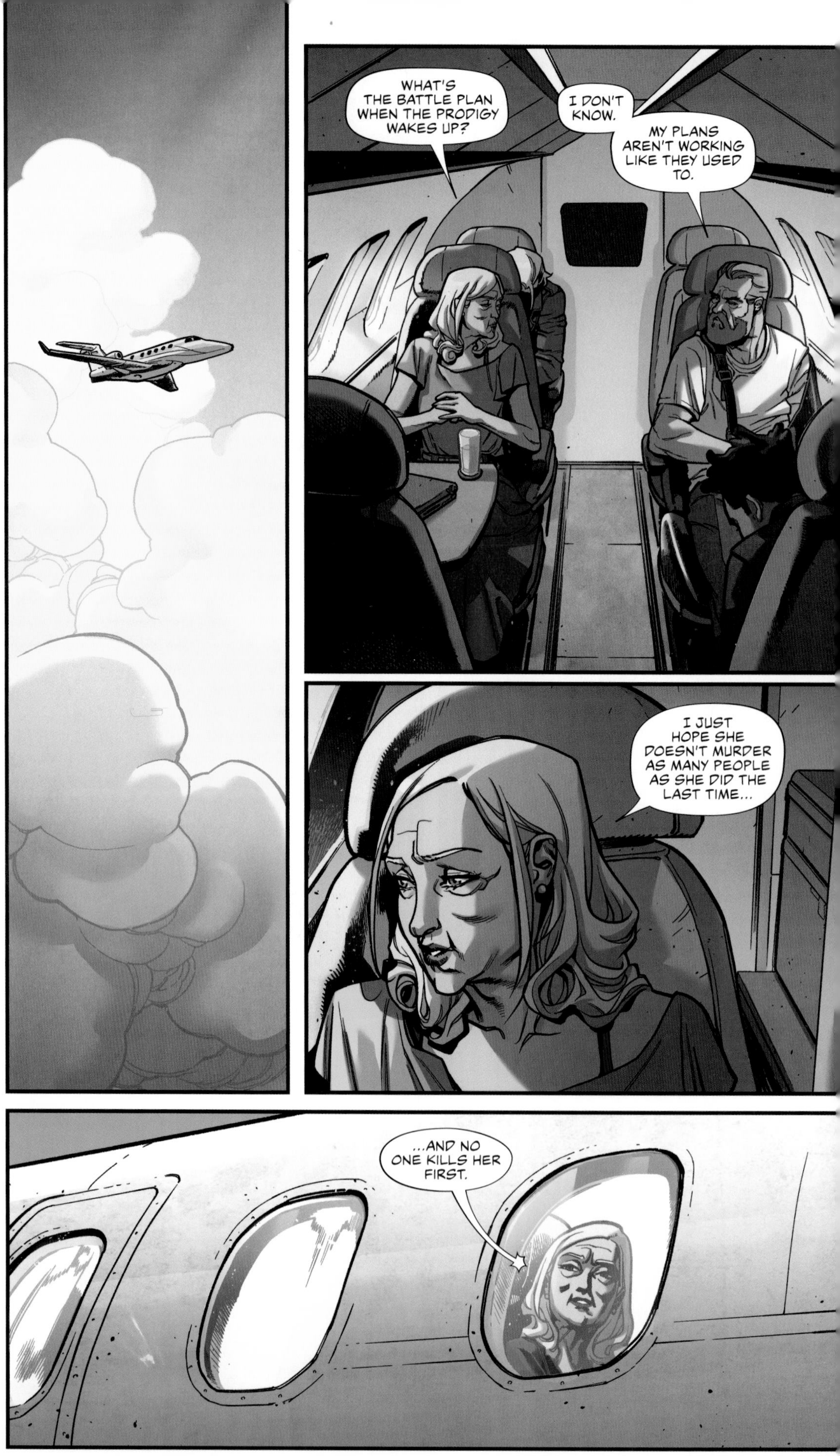
WHAT'S THE BATTLE PLAN WHEN THE PRODIGY WAKES UP?
I DON'T KNOW.
MY PLANS AREN'T WORKING LIKE THEY USED TO.
I JUST HOPE SHE DOESN'T MURDER AS MANY PEOPLE AS SHE DID THE LAST TIME...
...AND NO ONE KILLS HER FIRST.

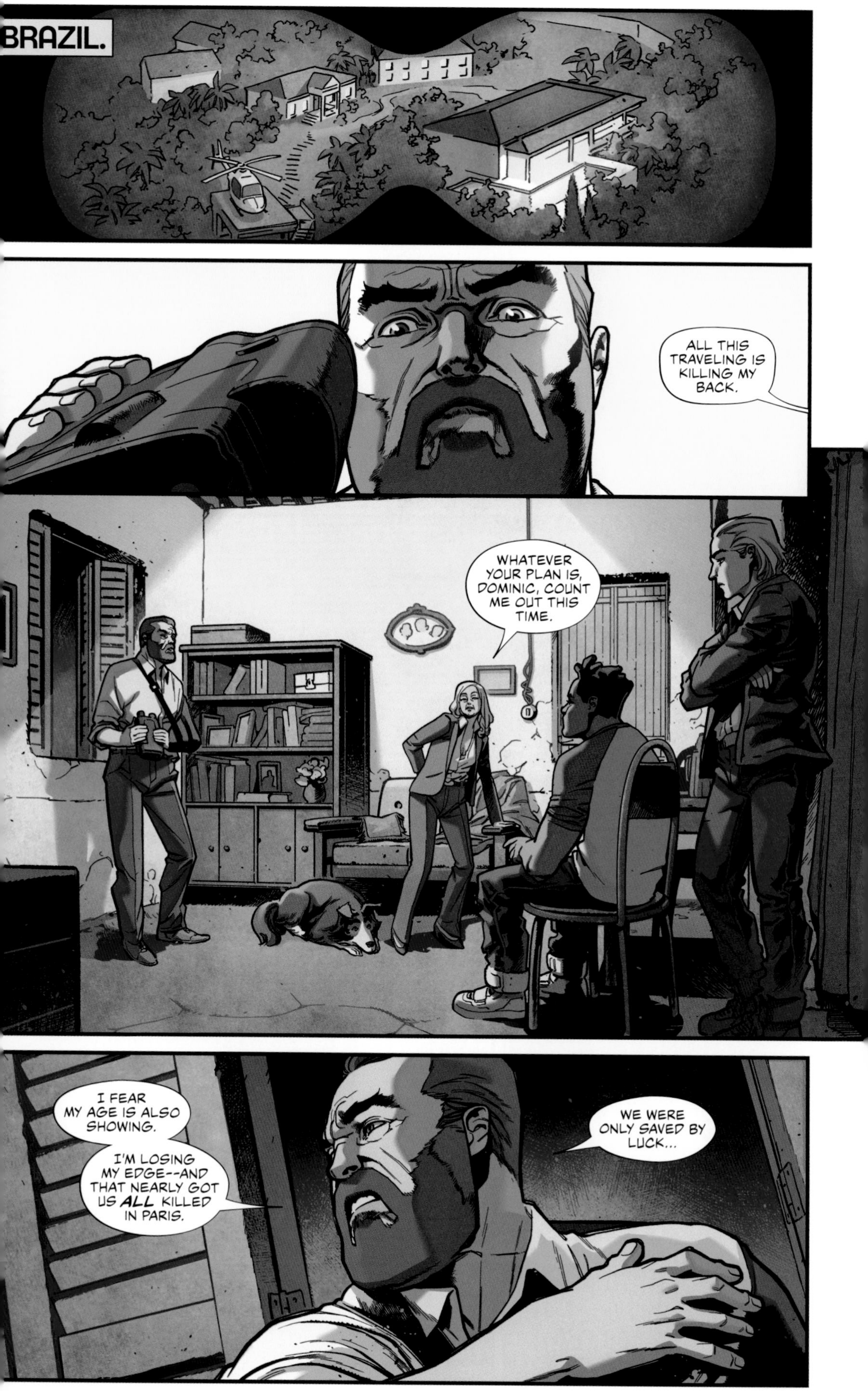
BRAZIL.
ALL THIS TRAVELING IS KILLING MY BACK.
WHATEVER YOUR PLAN IS, DOMINIC, COUNT ME OUT THIS TIME.
I FEAR MY AGE IS ALSO SHOWING.
I'M LOSING MY EDGE--AND THAT NEARLY GOT US ALL KILLED IN PARIS.
WE WERE ONLY SAVED BY LUCK...

...AND CHRISTOPHER'S QUICK THINKING.

HE SHOULD BE LEADING.

EXCUSE ME?

YOU'RE **THE LEADER**. THIS IS WHAT YOU DO.

I-I HAVE **NO IDEA** WHAT TO DO!

YOU DEFEATED THE LOVER'S HOARDS WITH A FEW DOZEN WARRIORS AT THE ISTHMUS OF WOE.

YOU NEGOTIATED THE FIVEFOLD TRUCE TO END THE WARS OF COVETOUSNESS.

YOU STOPPED HITLER FROM CONQUERING ASIA.

I TRUST YOUR LEADERSHIP MORE THAN ANY PERSON WHO HAS EVER BEEN BORN.

IF THERE'S A WAY TO AWAKEN THE PRODIGY WITH MINIMAL BLOODSHED, IT'LL BE YOUR PLAN.

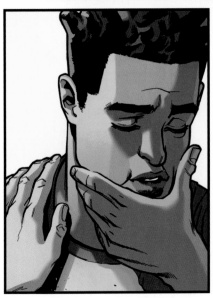

OK. LET'S START WITH A DISTRACTION. IF WE DO THIS RIGHT...

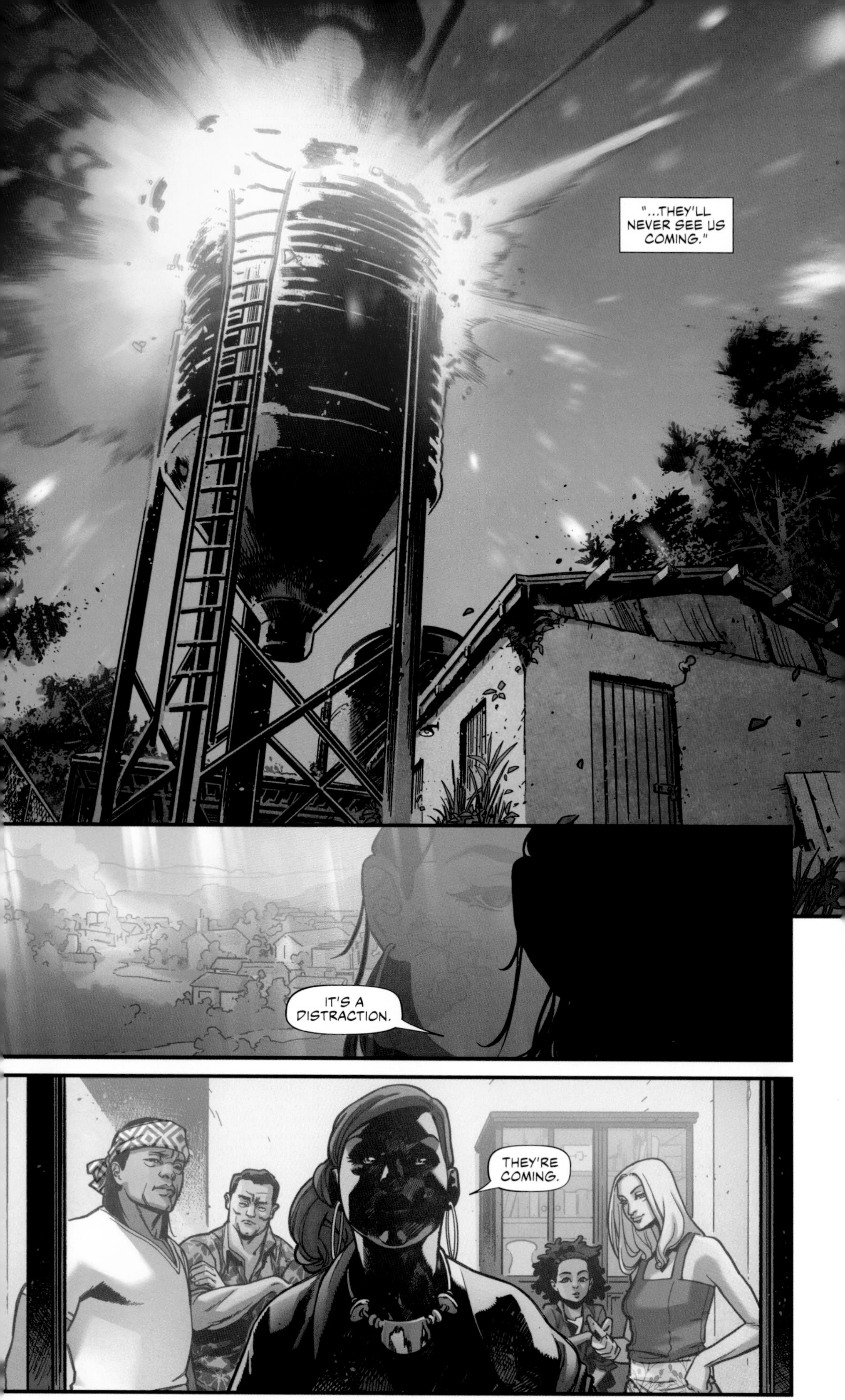
"...THEY'LL NEVER SEE US COMING."
IT'S A DISTRACTION.
THEY'RE COMING.

CHAPTER VI

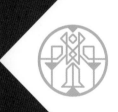

God Spark

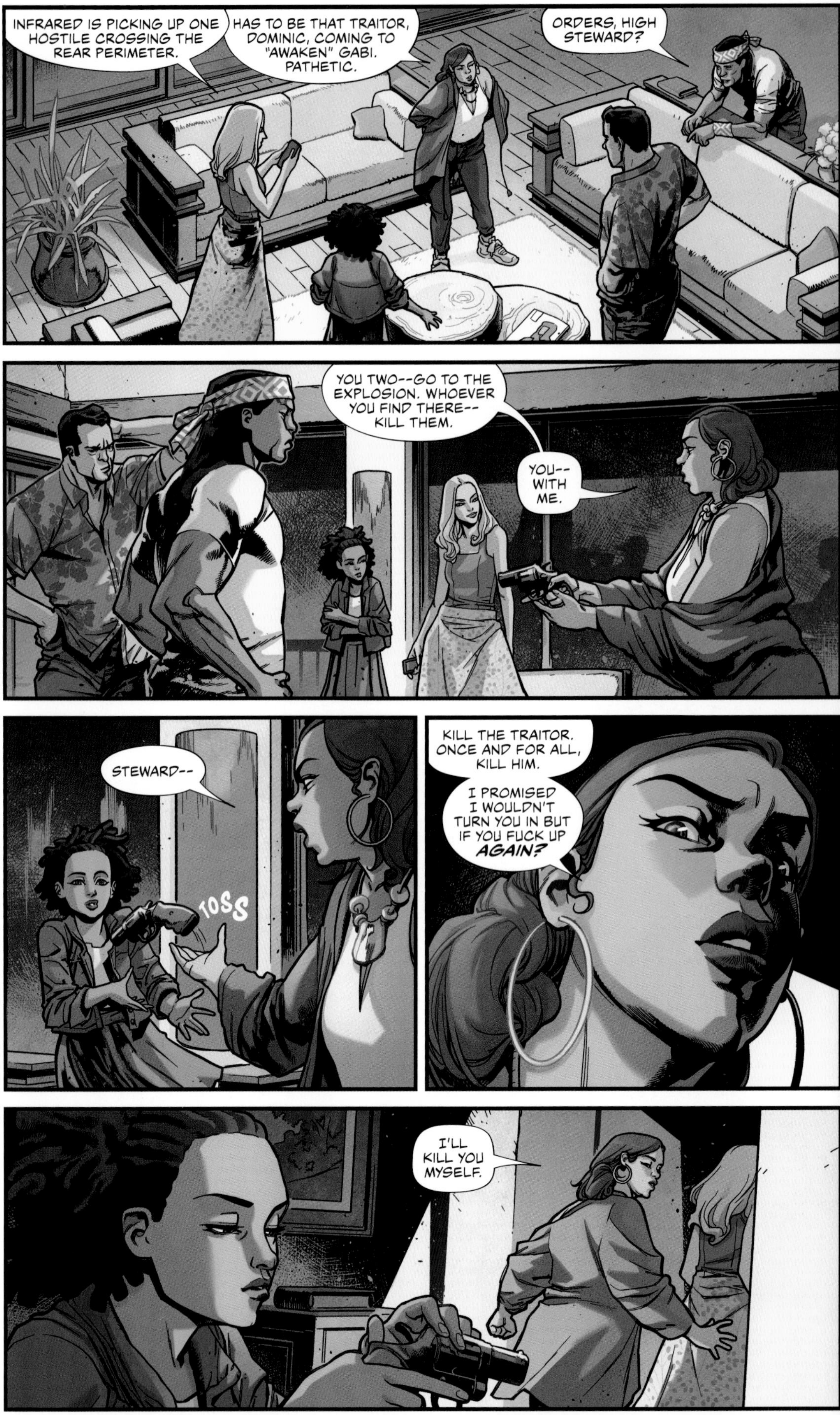
INFRARED IS PICKING UP ONE HOSTILE CROSSING THE REAR PERIMETER.
HAS TO BE THAT TRAITOR, DOMINIC, COMING TO "AWAKEN" GABI. PATHETIC.
ORDERS, HIGH STEWARD?
YOU TWO--GO TO THE EXPLOSION. WHOEVER YOU FIND THERE--KILL THEM.
YOU--WITH ME.
STEWARD--
TOSS
KILL THE TRAITOR. ONCE AND FOR ALL, KILL HIM.
I PROMISED I WOULDN'T TURN YOU IN BUT IF YOU FUCK UP **AGAIN?**
I'LL KILL YOU MYSELF.

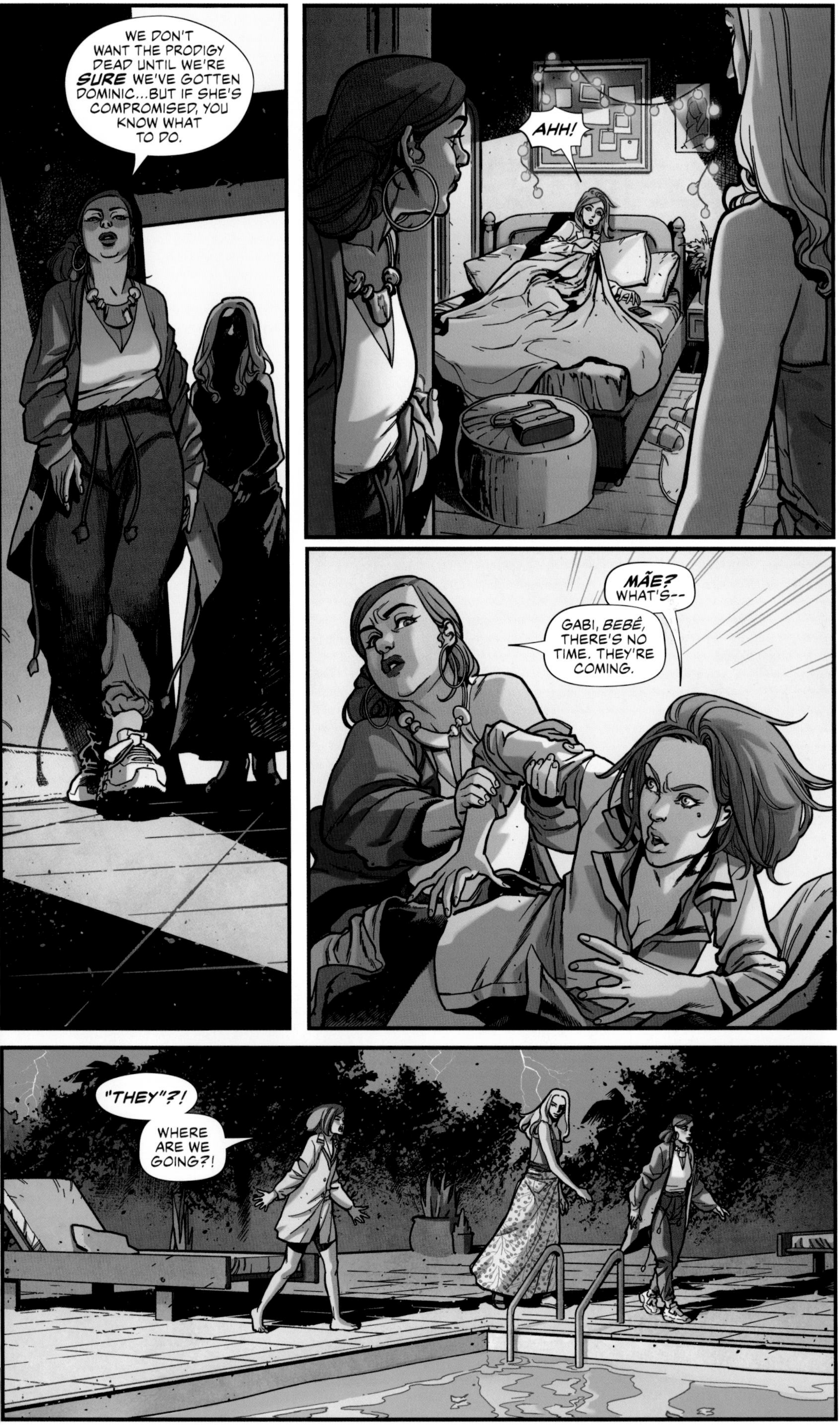
WE DON'T WANT THE PRODIGY DEAD UNTIL WE'RE *SURE* WE'VE GOTTEN DOMINIC...BUT IF SHE'S COMPROMISED, YOU KNOW WHAT TO DO.
AHH!
MÃE? WHAT'S--
GABI, *BEBÊ*, THERE'S NO TIME. THEY'RE COMING.
"THEY"?!
WHERE ARE WE GOING?!

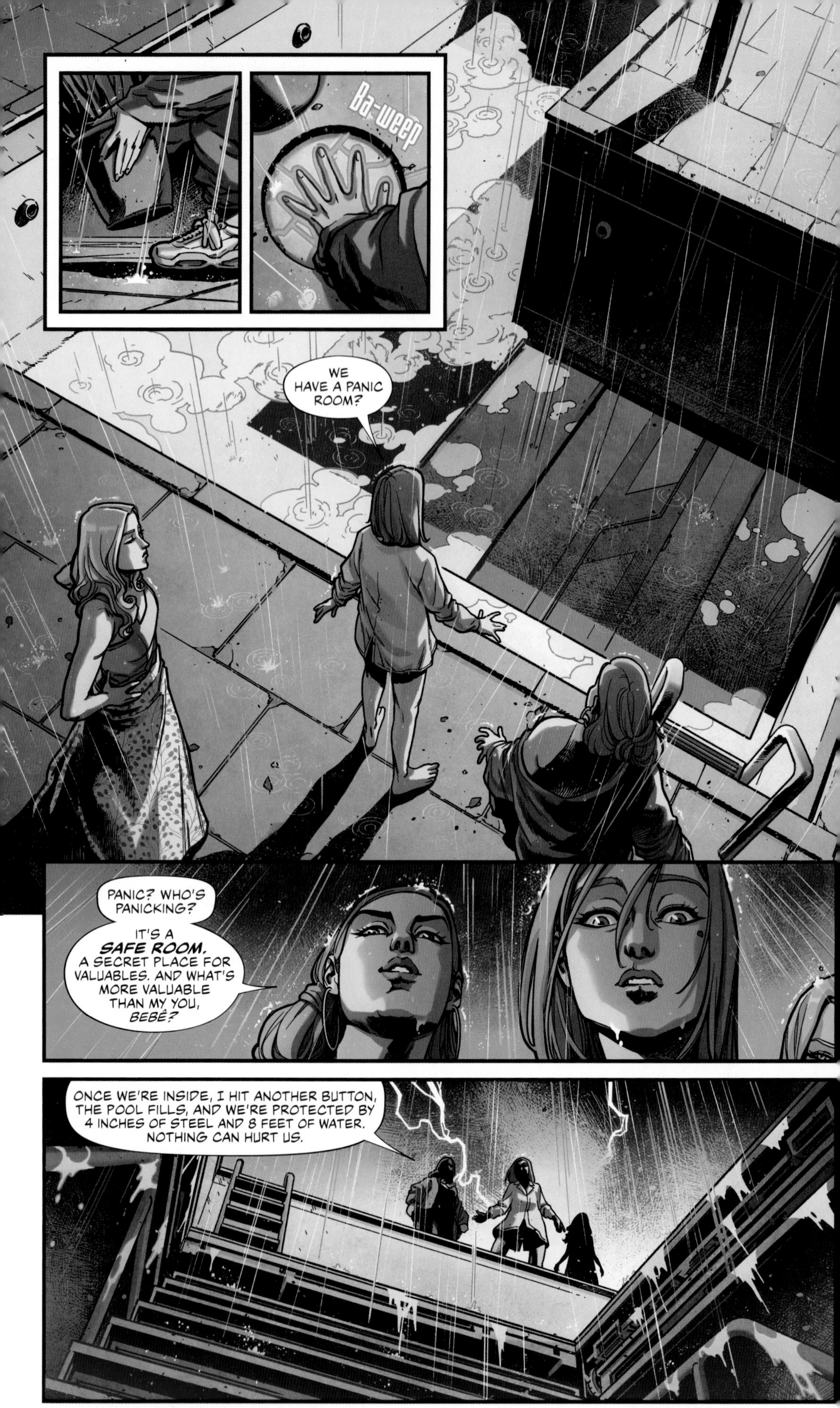
Ba-weep
WE HAVE A PANIC ROOM?
PANIC? WHO'S PANICKING?
IT'S A *SAFE ROOM.* A SECRET PLACE FOR VALUABLES. AND WHAT'S MORE VALUABLE THAN MY YOU, *BEBÊ?*
ONCE WE'RE INSIDE, I HIT ANOTHER BUTTON, THE POOL FILLS, AND WE'RE PROTECTED BY 4 INCHES OF STEEL AND 8 FEET OF WATER. NOTHING CAN HURT US.

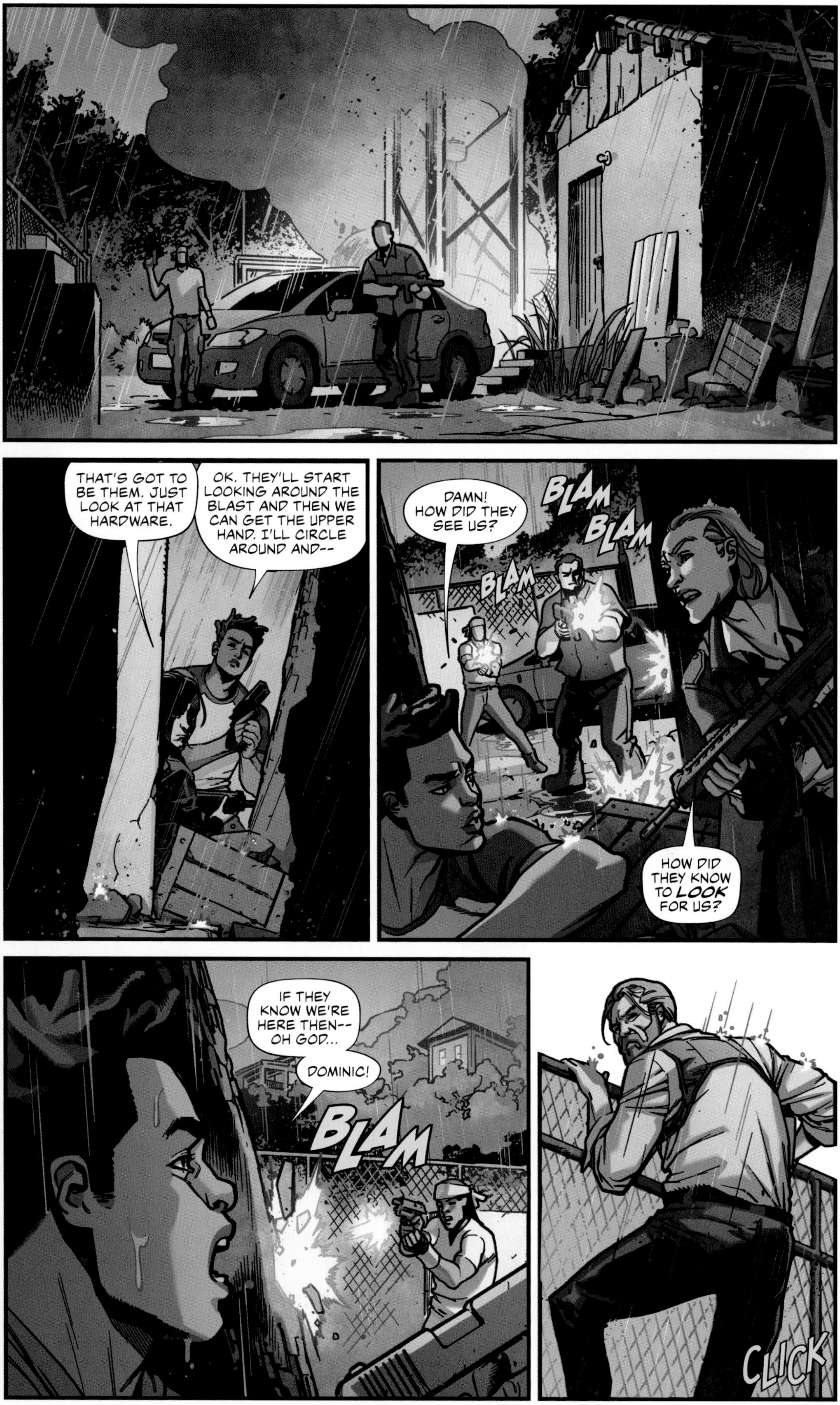

THAT'S GOT TO BE THEM. JUST LOOK AT THAT HARDWARE.
OK. THEY'LL START LOOKING AROUND THE BLAST AND THEN WE CAN GET THE UPPER HAND. I'LL CIRCLE AROUND AND--
DAMN! HOW DID THEY SEE US?
BLAM
BLAM
BLAM
HOW DID THEY KNOW TO LOOK FOR US?
IF THEY KNOW WE'RE HERE THEN-- OH GOD...
DOMINIC!
BLAM
CLICK

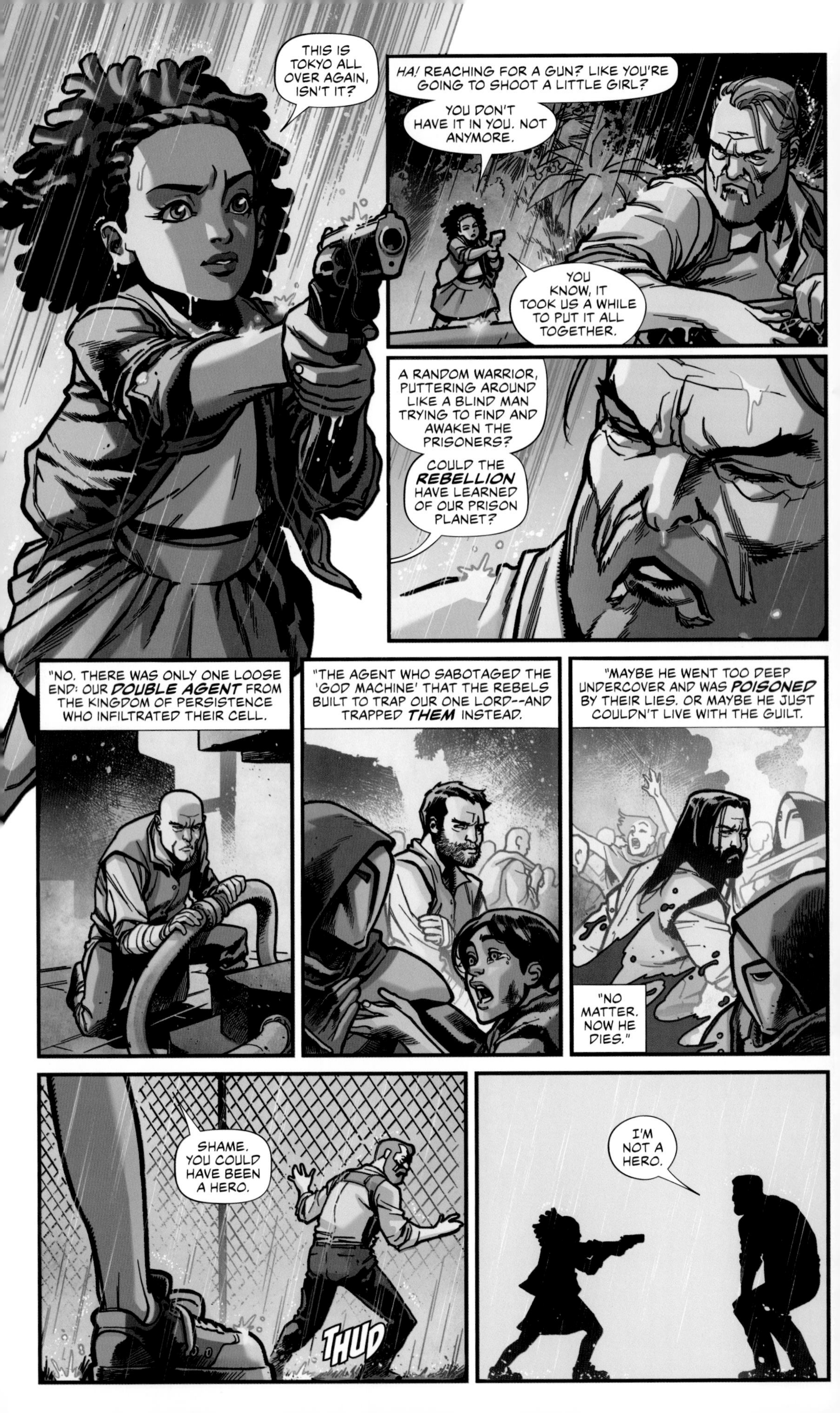
THIS IS TOKYO ALL OVER AGAIN, ISN'T IT?
HA! REACHING FOR A GUN? LIKE YOU'RE GOING TO SHOOT A LITTLE GIRL?
YOU DON'T HAVE IT IN YOU. NOT ANYMORE.
YOU KNOW, IT TOOK US A WHILE TO PUT IT ALL TOGETHER.
A RANDOM WARRIOR, PUTTERING AROUND LIKE A BLIND MAN TRYING TO FIND AND AWAKEN THE PRISONERS?
COULD THE REBELLION HAVE LEARNED OF OUR PRISON PLANET?
"NO. THERE WAS ONLY ONE LOOSE END: OUR DOUBLE AGENT FROM THE KINGDOM OF PERSISTENCE WHO INFILTRATED THEIR CELL.
"THE AGENT WHO SABOTAGED THE 'GOD MACHINE' THAT THE REBELS BUILT TO TRAP OUR ONE LORD--AND TRAPPED THEM INSTEAD.
"MAYBE HE WENT TOO DEEP UNDERCOVER AND WAS POISONED BY THEIR LIES. OR MAYBE HE JUST COULDN'T LIVE WITH THE GUILT.
"NO MATTER. NOW HE DIES."
SHAME. YOU COULD HAVE BEEN A HERO.
THUD
I'M NOT A HERO.

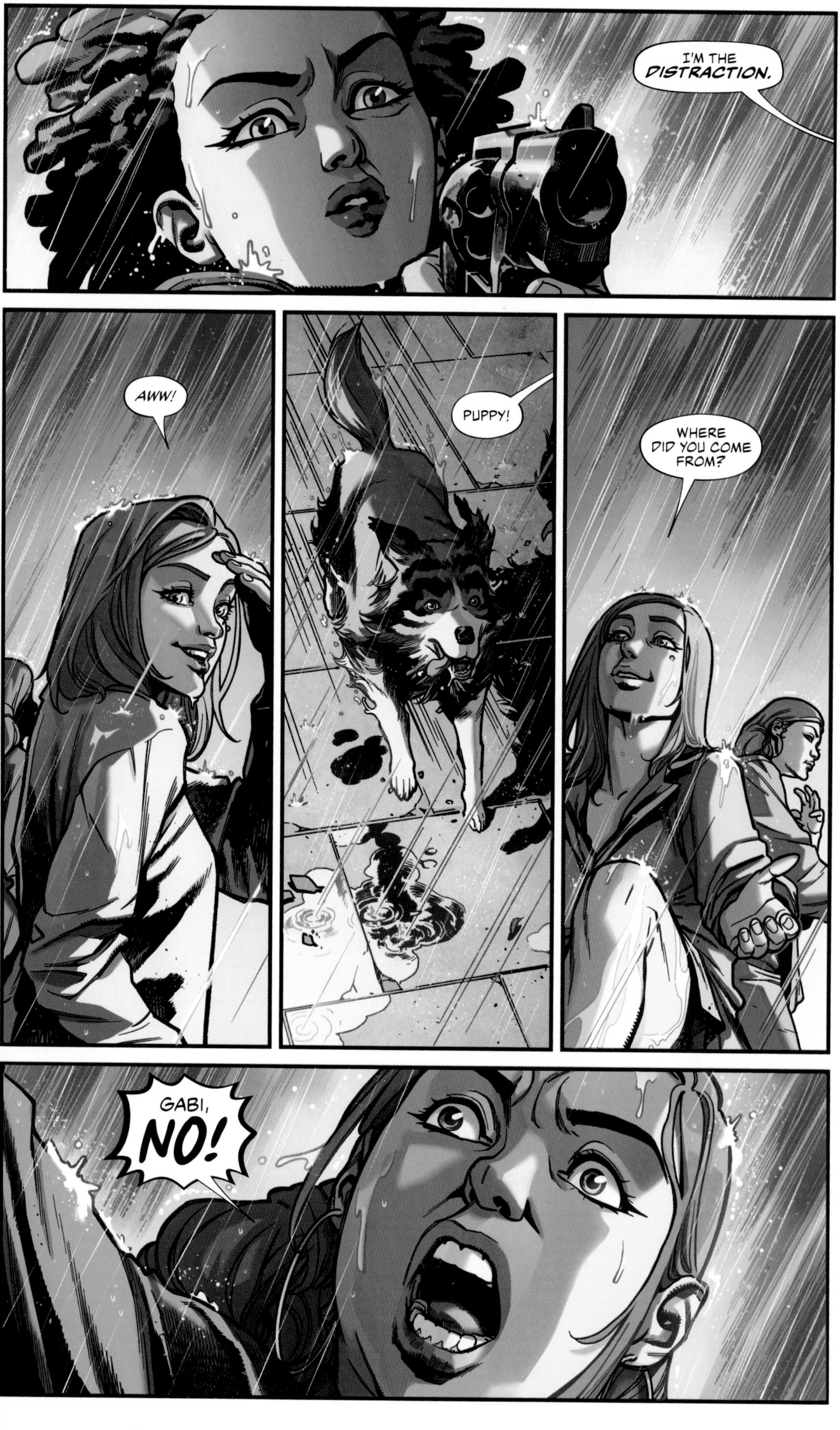
I'M THE DISTRACTION.
AWW!
PUPPY!
WHERE DID YOU COME FROM?
GABI, NO!

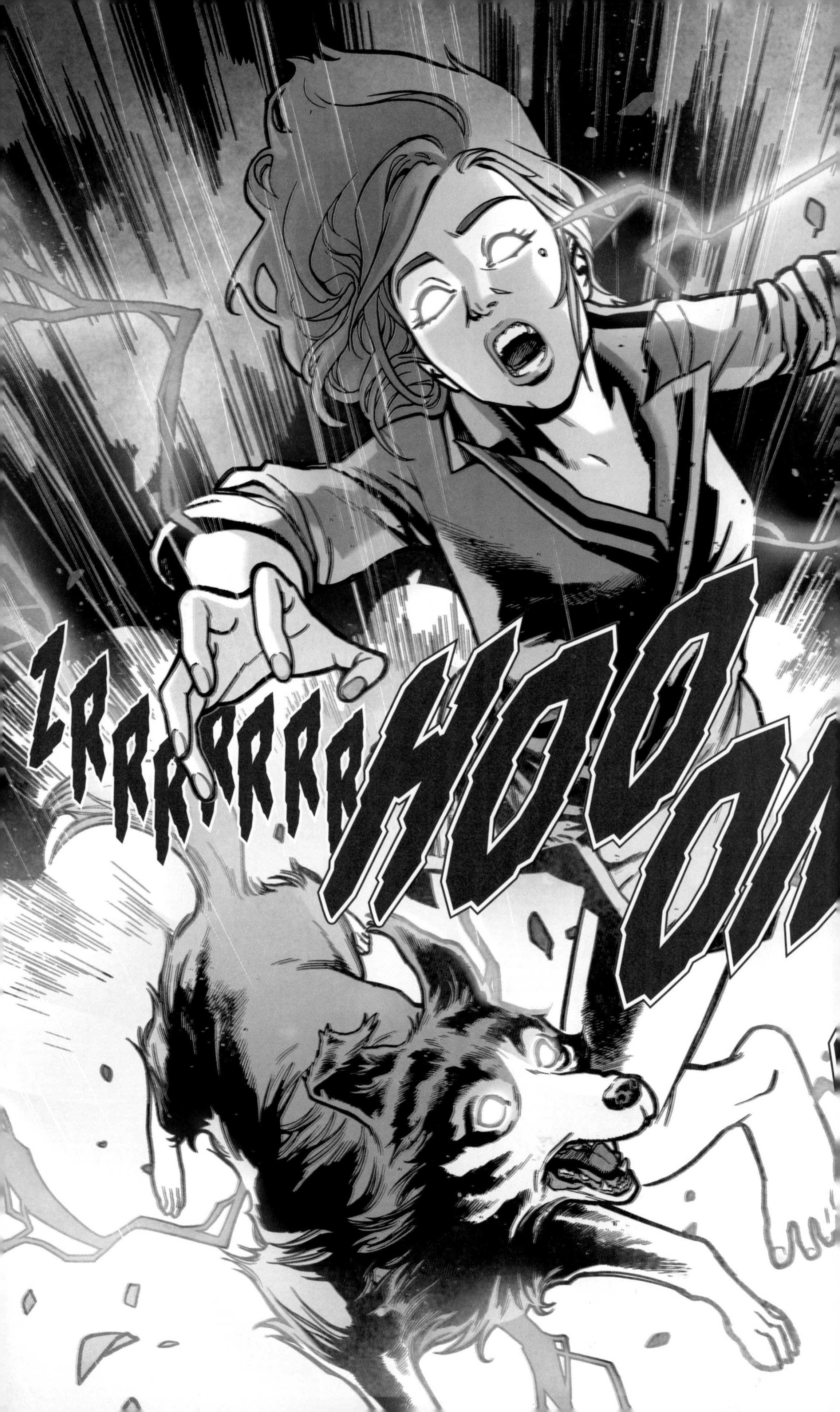
ZRRRRRRRHOOOO

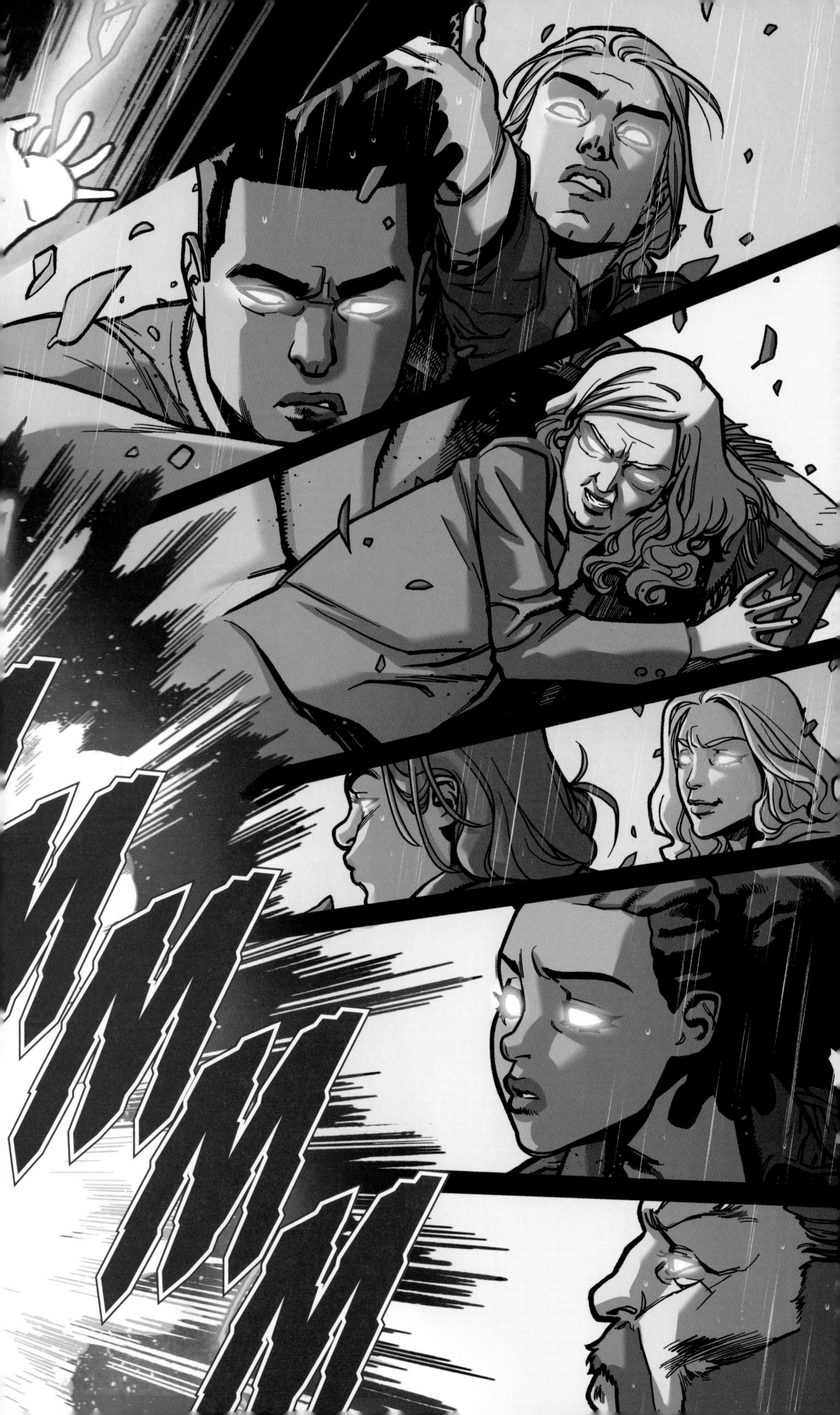

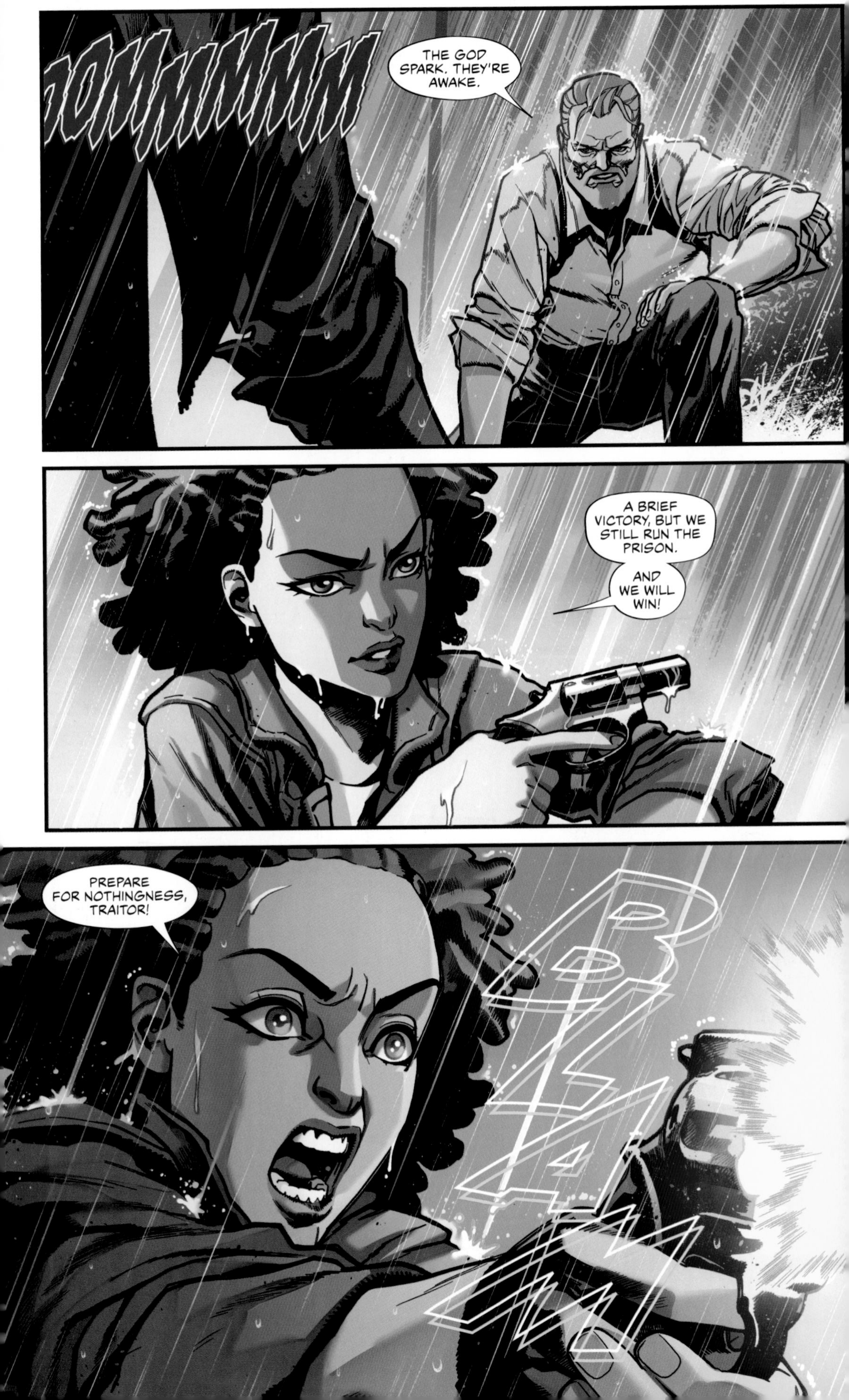

THE GOD SPARK. THEY'RE AWAKE.
A BRIEF VICTORY, BUT WE STILL RUN THE PRISON.
AND WE WILL WIN!
PREPARE FOR NOTHINGNESS, TRAITOR!

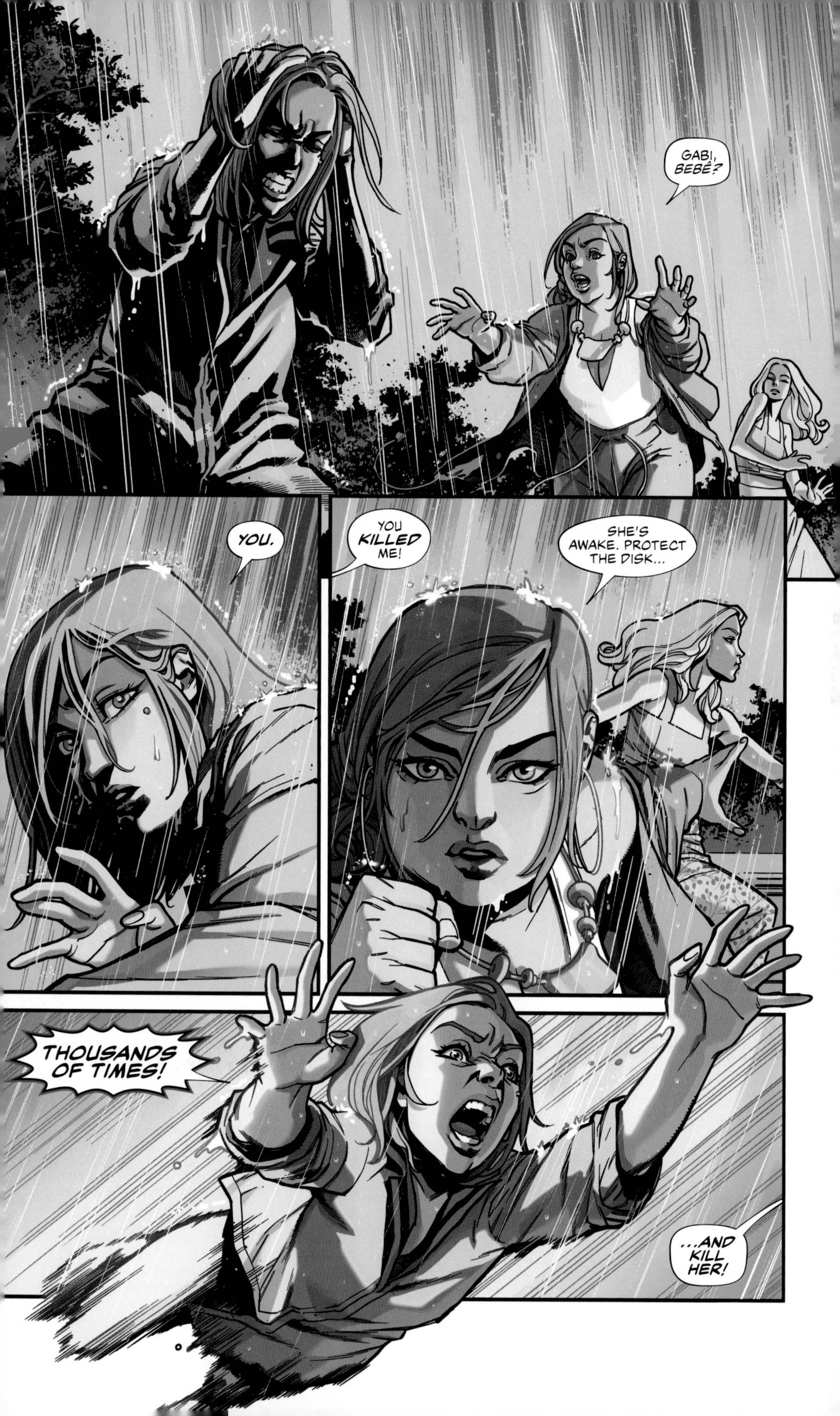
GABI, BEBÊ?
YOU.
YOU KILLED ME!
SHE'S AWAKE. PROTECT THE DISK...
THOUSANDS OF TIMES!
...AND KILL HER!

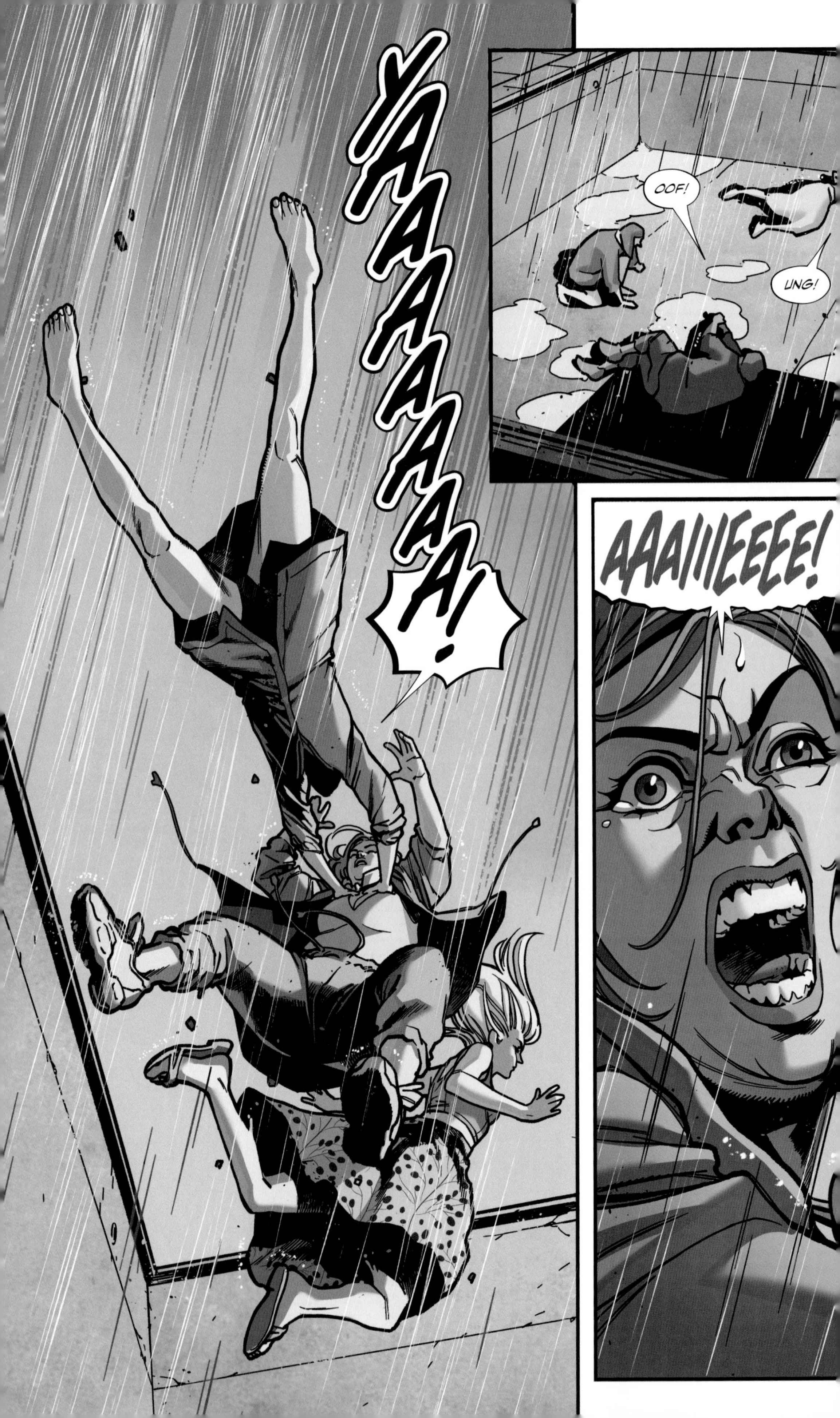
YAAAAAAAA!
OOF!
UNG!
AAAIIIEEEE!

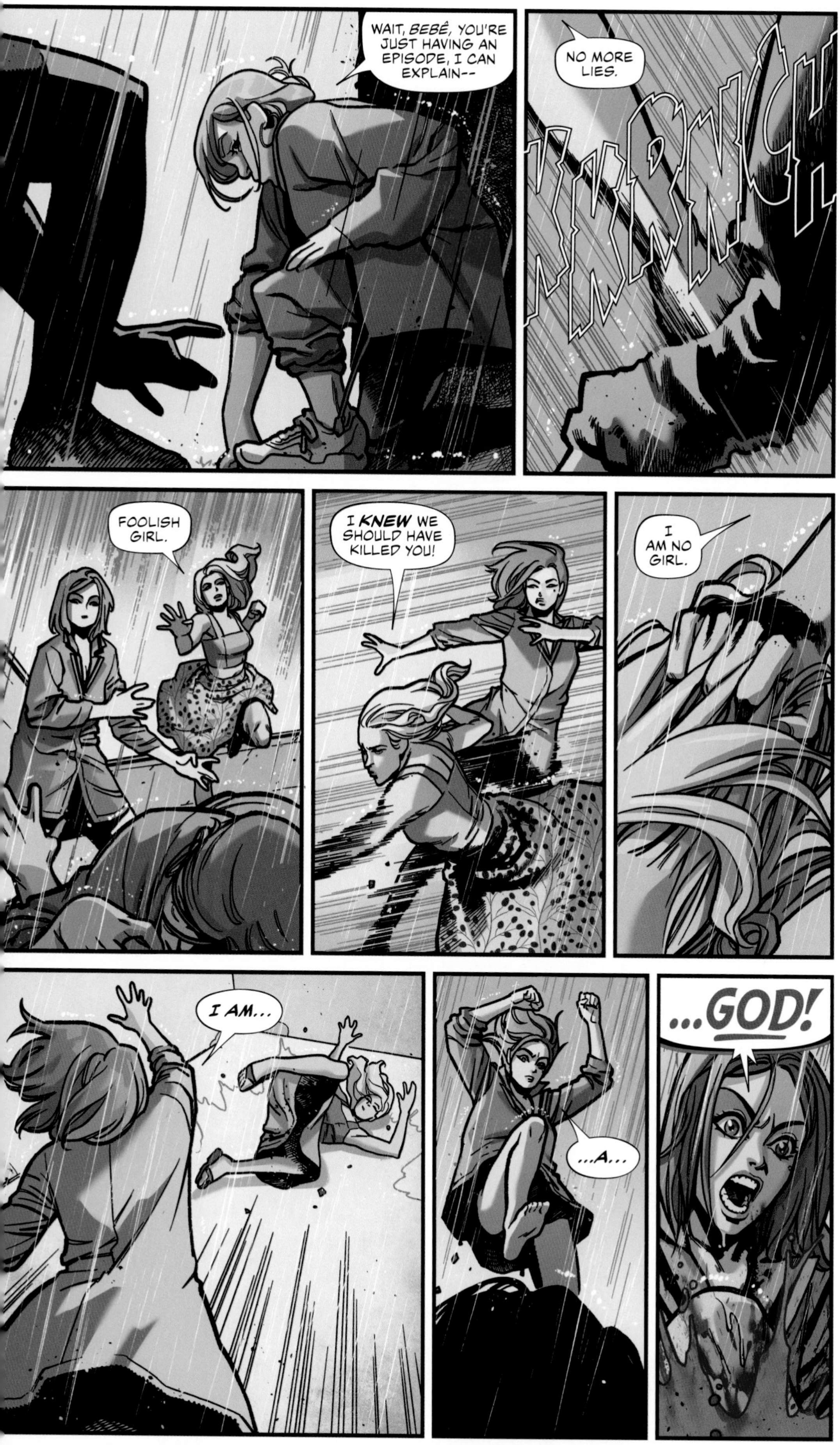
WAIT, *BEBÊ*, YOU'RE JUST HAVING AN EPISODE, I CAN EXPLAIN--
NO MORE LIES.
KRRRNCH
FOOLISH GIRL.
I **KNEW** WE SHOULD HAVE KILLED YOU!
I AM NO GIRL.
I AM...
...A...
...GOD!

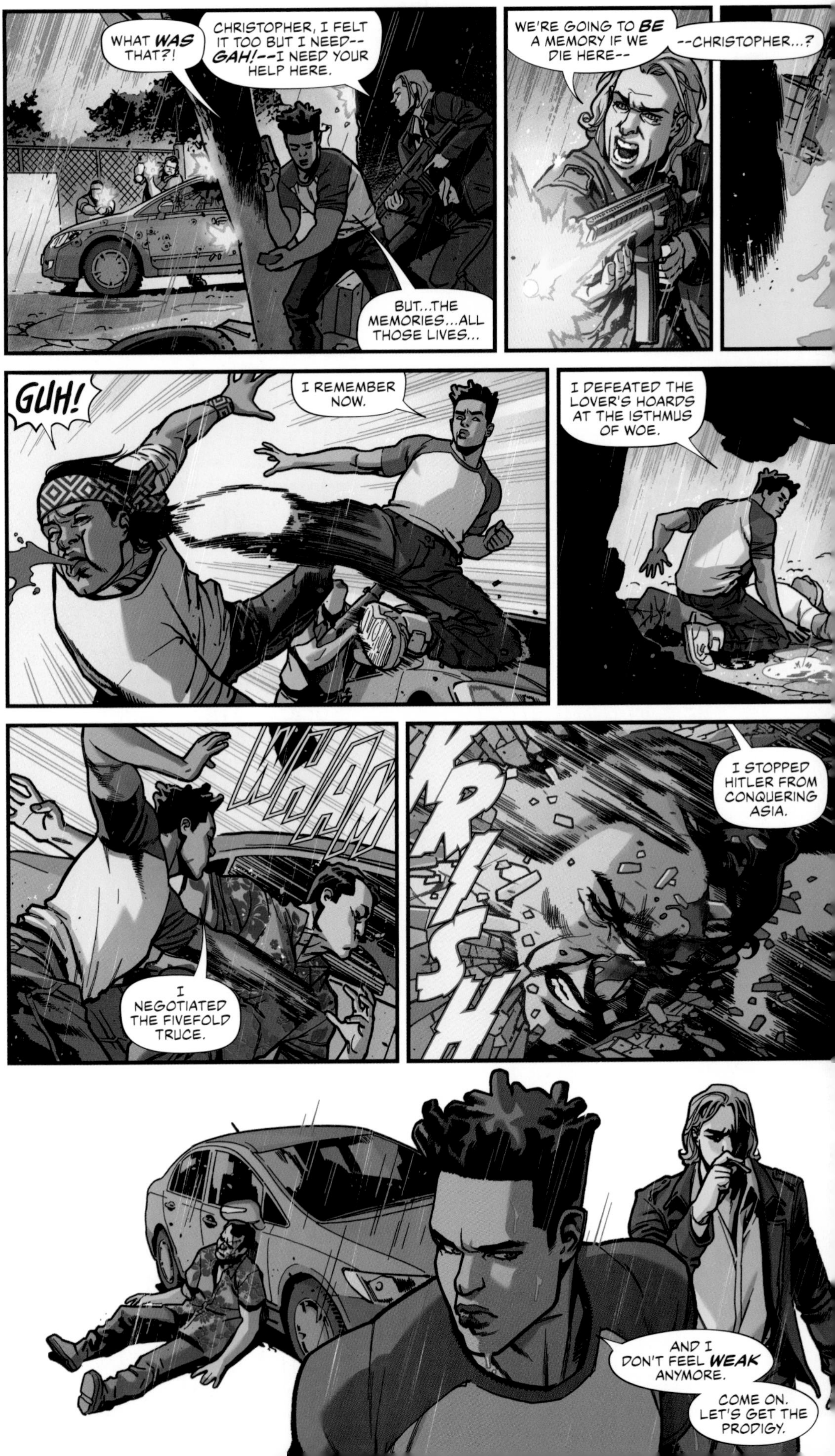
WHAT *WAS* THAT?!
CHRISTOPHER, I FELT IT TOO BUT I NEED-- *GAH!*--I NEED YOUR HELP HERE.
BUT...THE MEMORIES...ALL THOSE LIVES...
WE'RE GOING TO *BE* A MEMORY IF WE DIE HERE--
--CHRISTOPHER...?
GUH!
I REMEMBER NOW.
I DEFEATED THE LOVER'S HOARDS AT THE ISTHMUS OF WOE.
WHAM
I NEGOTIATED THE FIVEFOLD TRUCE.
KRISH
I STOPPED HITLER FROM CONQUERING ASIA.
AND I DON'T FEEL *WEAK* ANYMORE.
COME ON. LET'S GET THE PRODIGY.

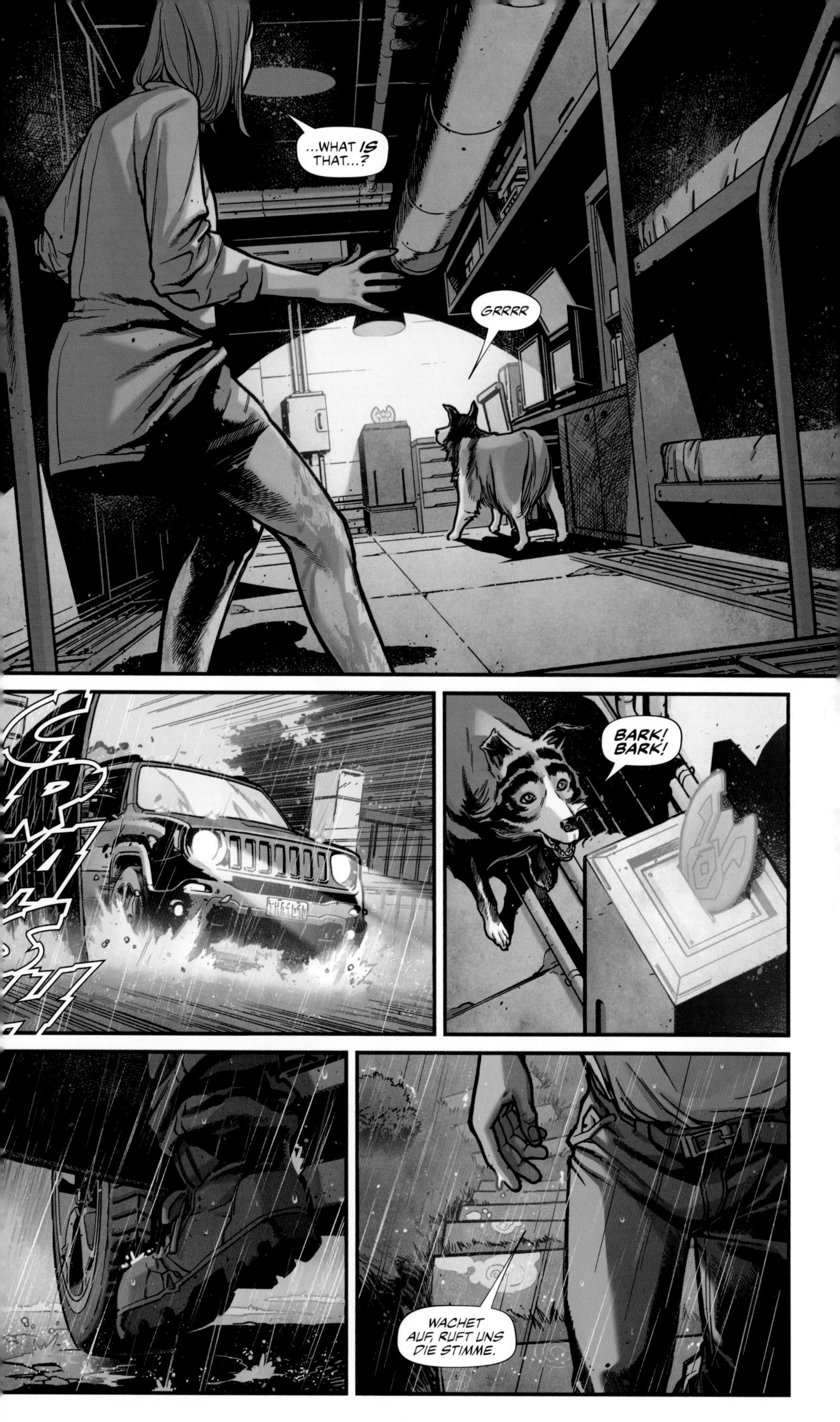
...WHAT IS THAT...?
GRRRR
BARK! BARK!
WACHET AUF, RUFT UNS DIE STIMME.

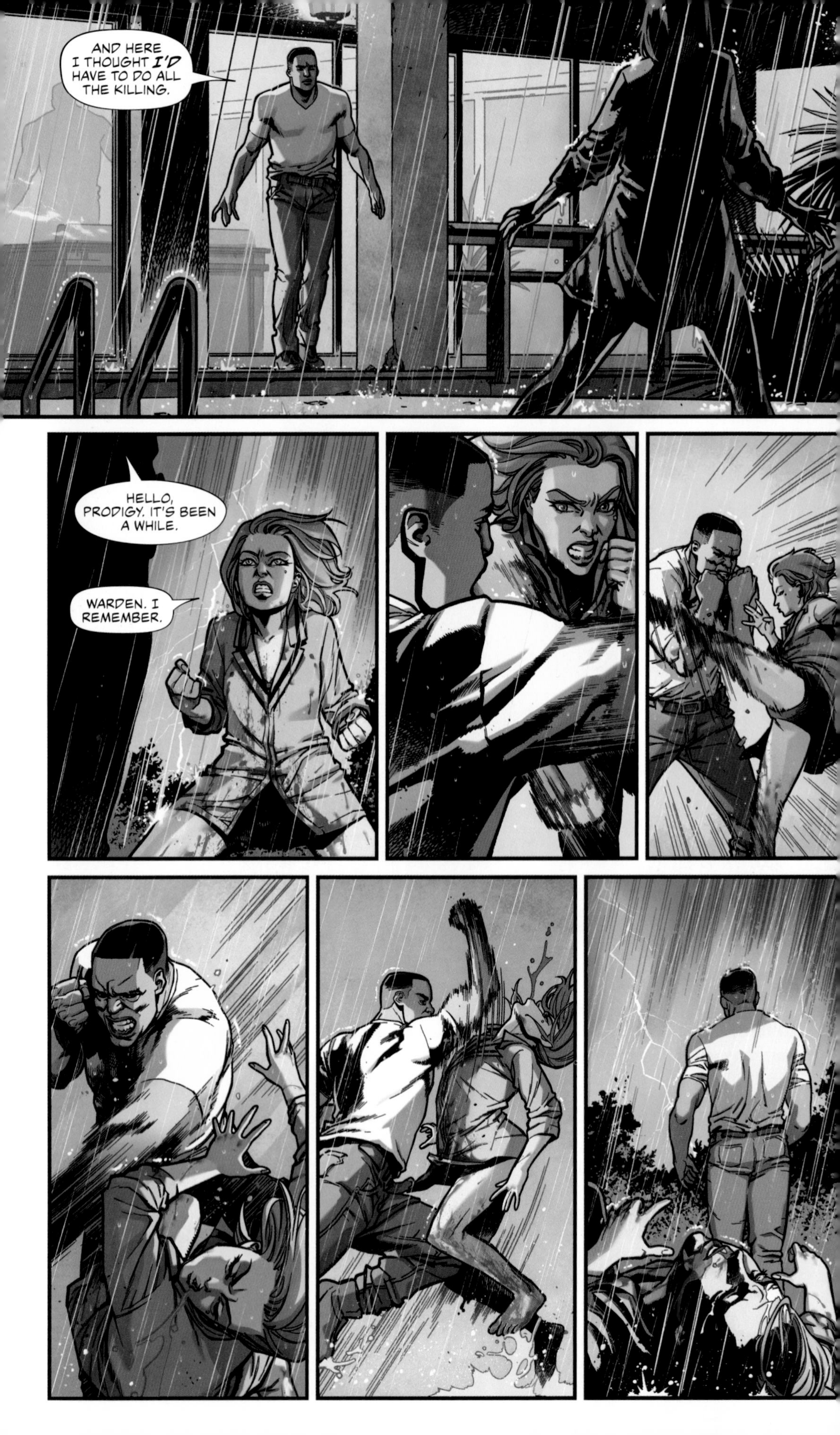
AND HERE I THOUGHT *I'D* HAVE TO DO ALL THE KILLING.
HELLO, PRODIGY. IT'S BEEN A WHILE.
WARDEN. I REMEMBER.

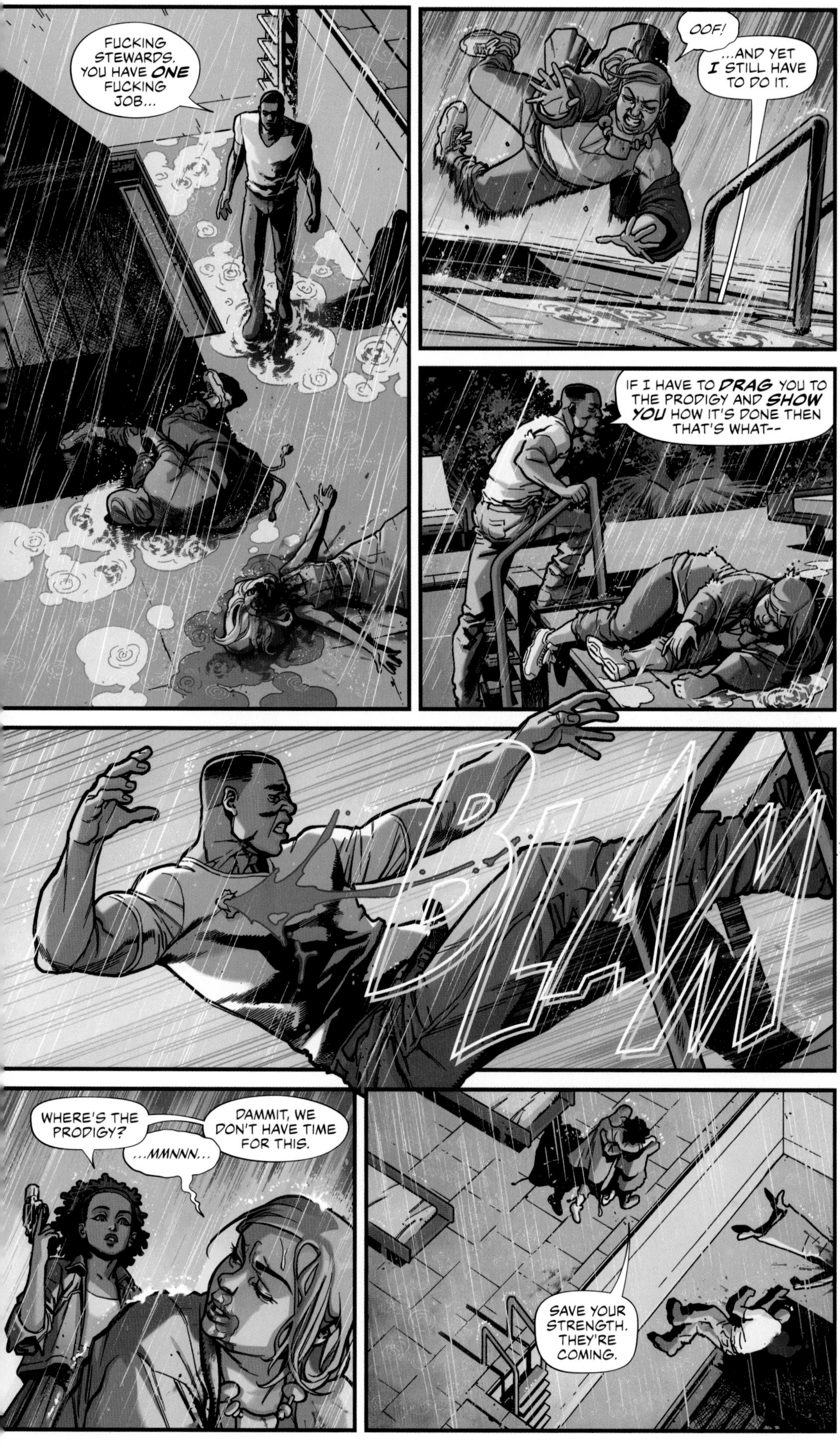
FUCKING STEWARDS. YOU HAVE ONE FUCKING JOB...
OOF!
...AND YET I STILL HAVE TO DO IT.
IF I HAVE TO DRAG YOU TO THE PRODIGY AND SHOW YOU HOW IT'S DONE THEN THAT'S WHAT--
BLAM
WHERE'S THE PRODIGY?
...MMNNN...
DAMMIT, WE DON'T HAVE TIME FOR THIS.
SAVE YOUR STRENGTH. THEY'RE COMING.

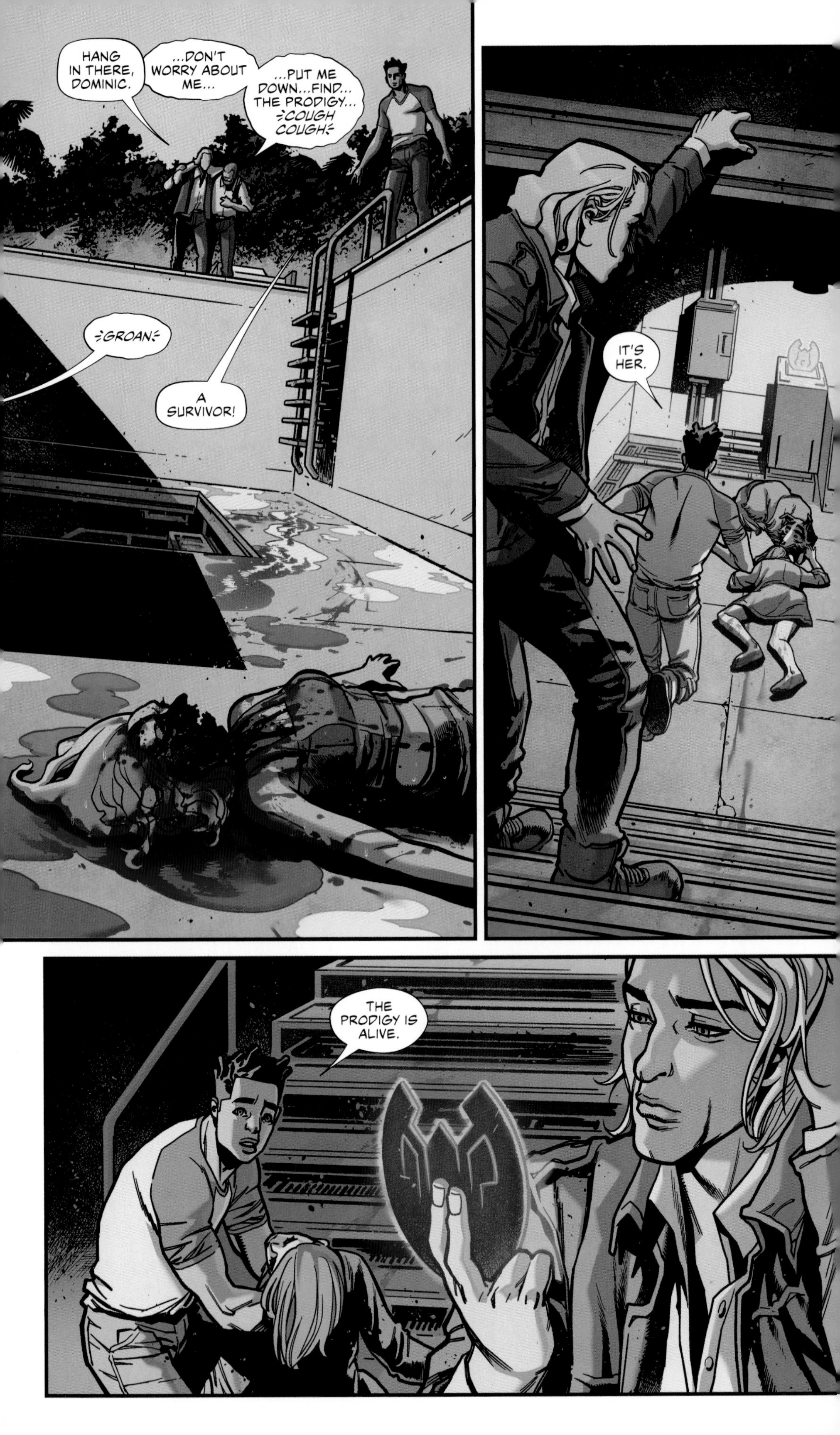
HANG IN THERE, DOMINIC.
...DON'T WORRY ABOUT ME...
...PUT ME DOWN...FIND... THE PRODIGY... *COUGH COUGH*
GROAN
A SURVIVOR!
IT'S HER.
THE PRODIGY IS ALIVE.

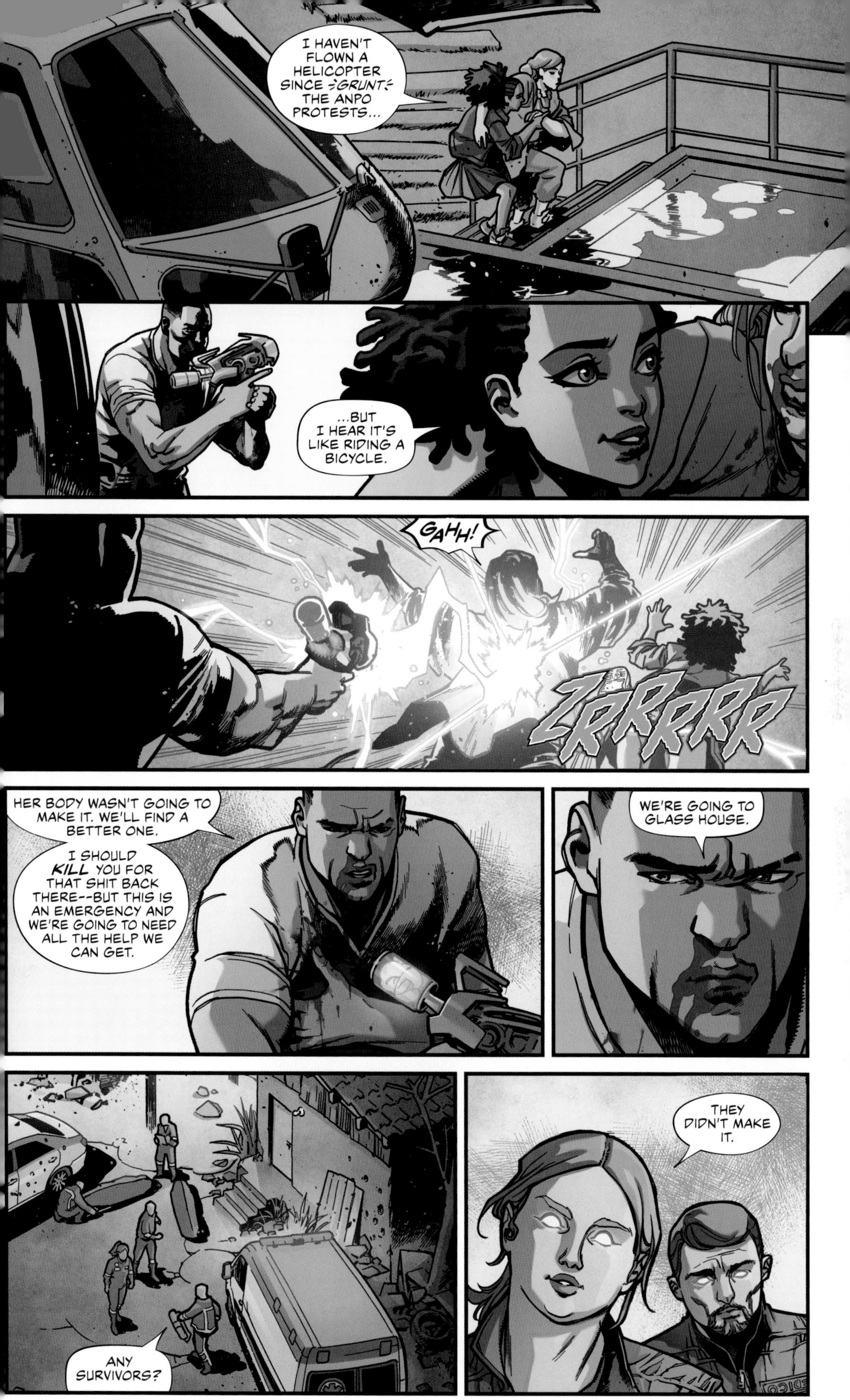
I HAVEN'T FLOWN A HELICOPTER SINCE -GRUNT- THE ANPO PROTESTS...
...BUT I HEAR IT'S LIKE RIDING A BICYCLE.
GAHH!
ZRRRRR
HER BODY WASN'T GOING TO MAKE IT. WE'LL FIND A BETTER ONE.
I SHOULD KILL YOU FOR THAT SHIT BACK THERE--BUT THIS IS AN EMERGENCY AND WE'RE GOING TO NEED ALL THE HELP WE CAN GET.
WE'RE GOING TO GLASS HOUSE.
ANY SURVIVORS?
THEY DIDN'T MAKE IT.

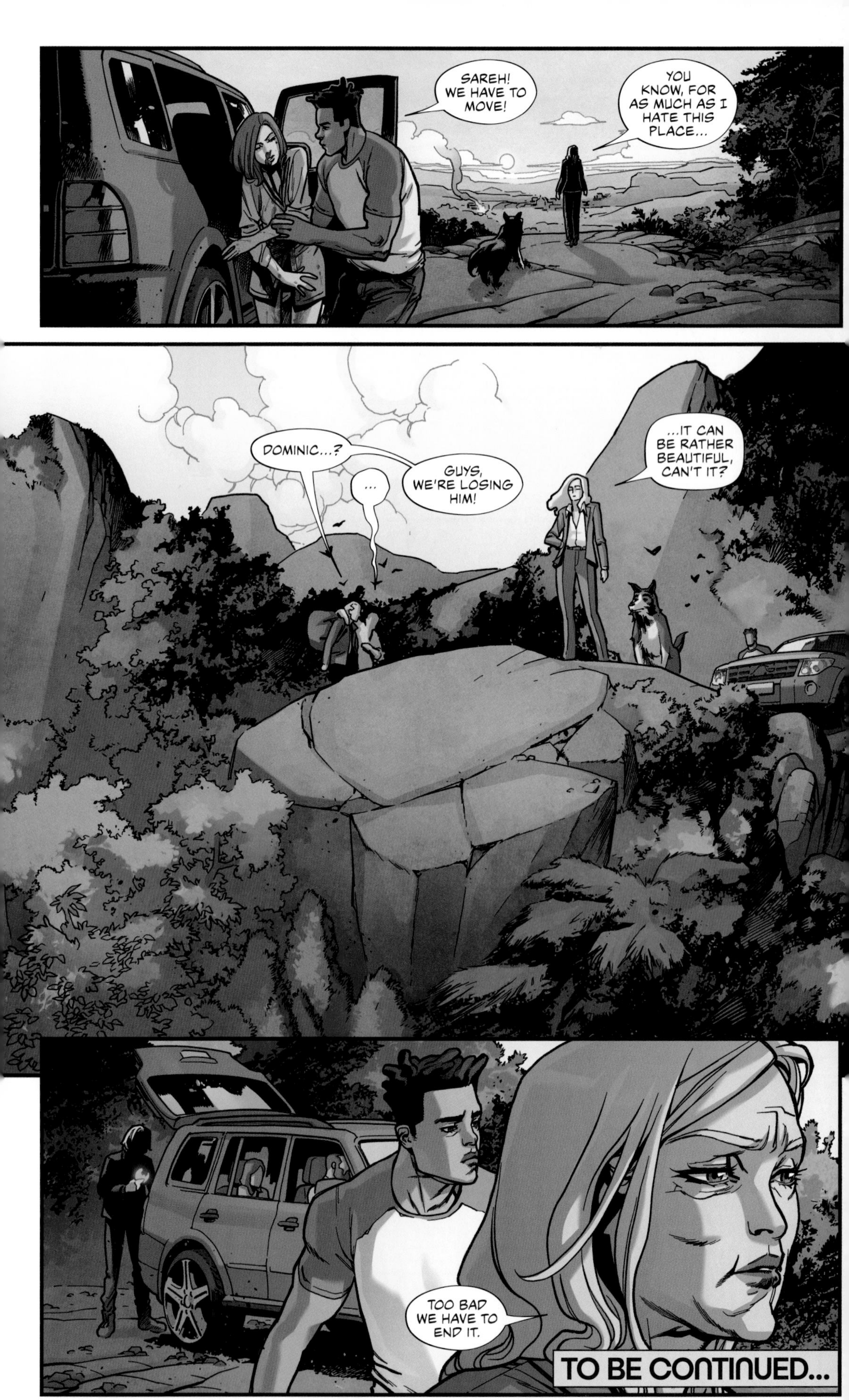
SAREH! WE HAVE TO MOVE!
YOU KNOW, FOR AS MUCH AS I HATE THIS PLACE...
DOMINIC...?
...
GUYS, WE'RE LOSING HIM!
...IT CAN BE RATHER BEAUTIFUL, CAN'T IT?
TOO BAD WE HAVE TO END IT.
TO BE CONTINUED...

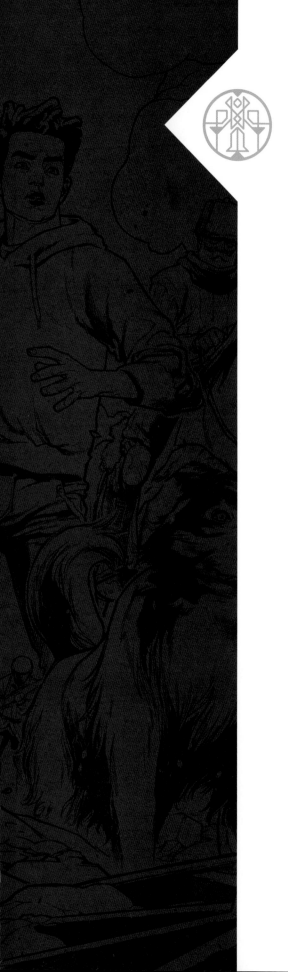

Cover Gallery

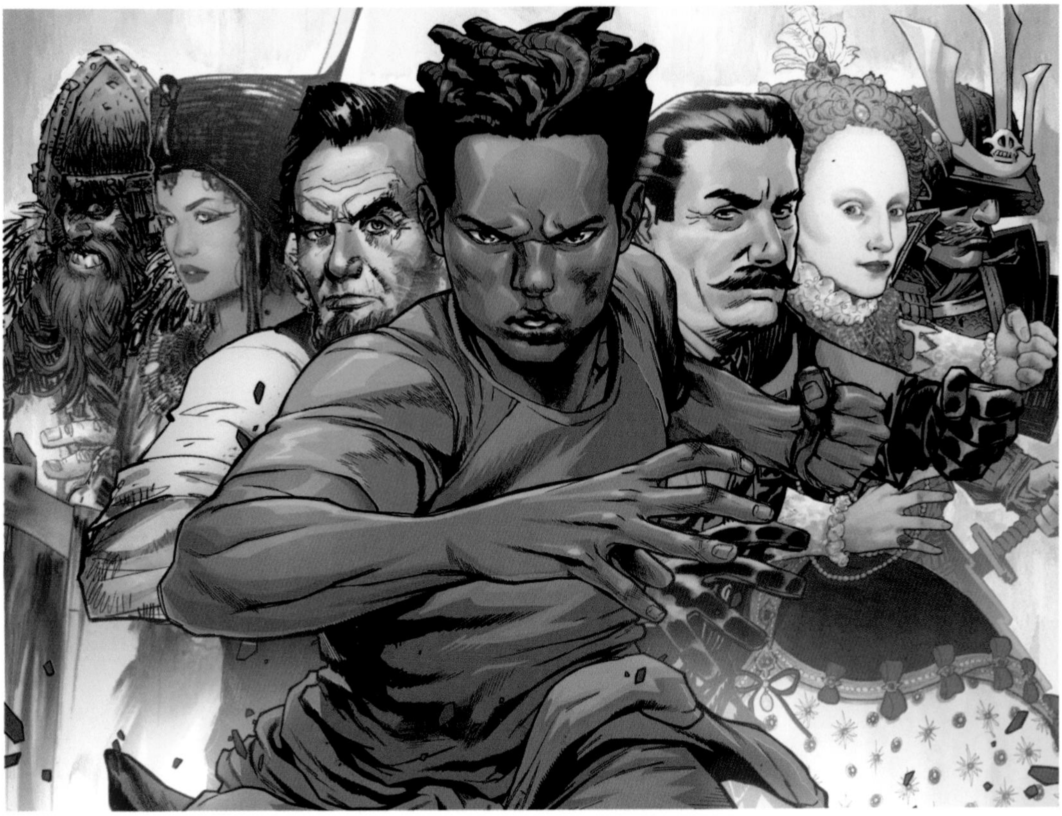

CHAPTER I

Dave Johnson, Tula Lotay, Rod Reis, Felipe Watanabe, Dan Panosian, Nicola Scott, and Declan Shalvey w/ Matt Wilson

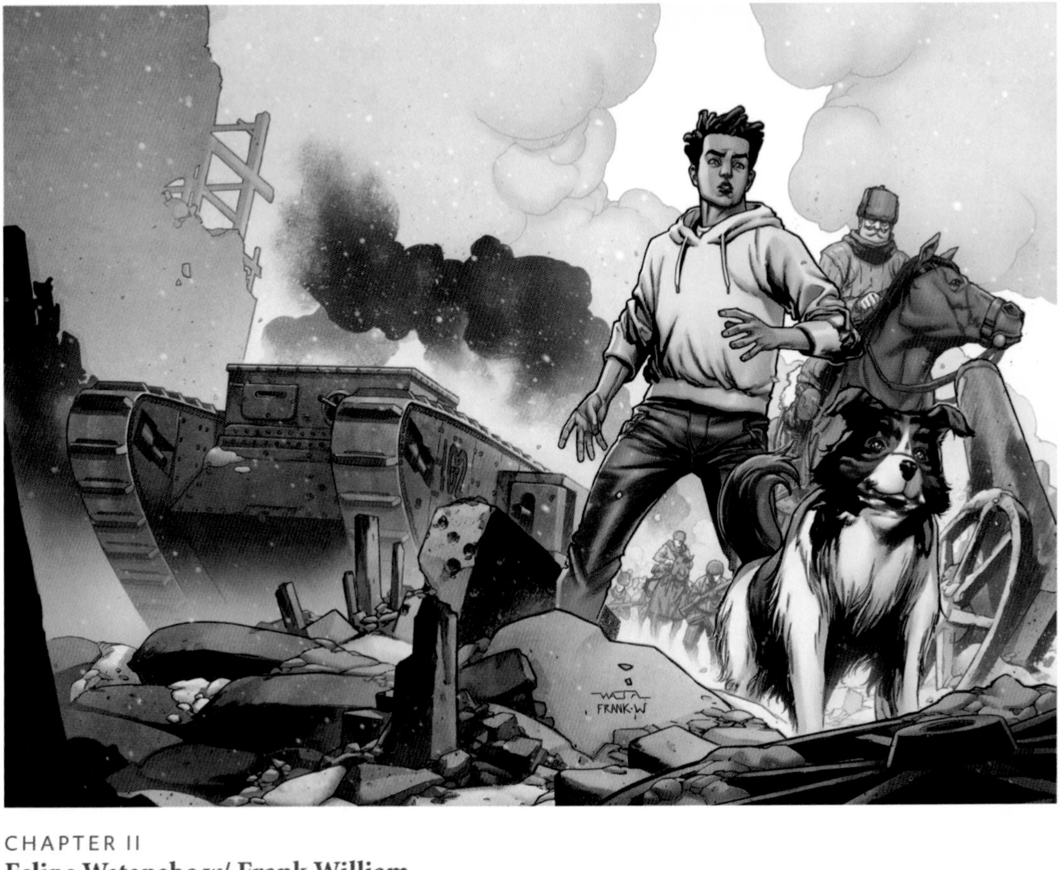

CHAPTER II

Felipe Watanabe w/ Frank William

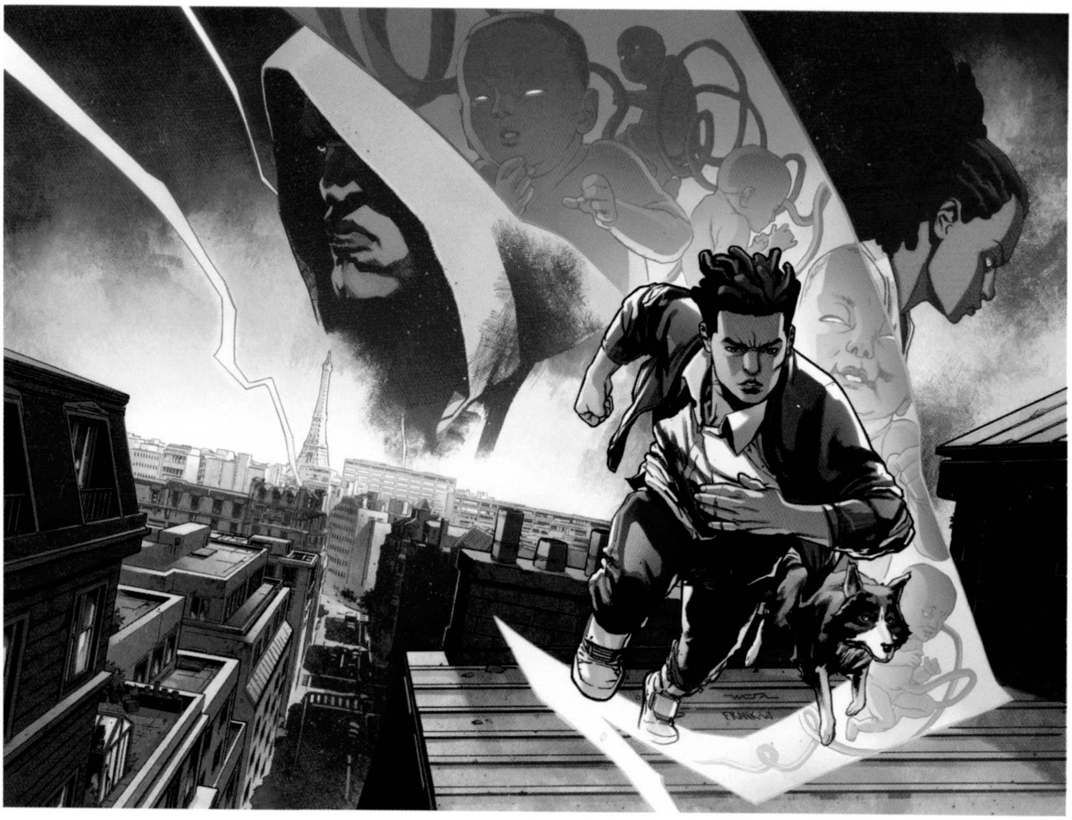

CHAPTER III
Felipe Watanabe w/ Frank William

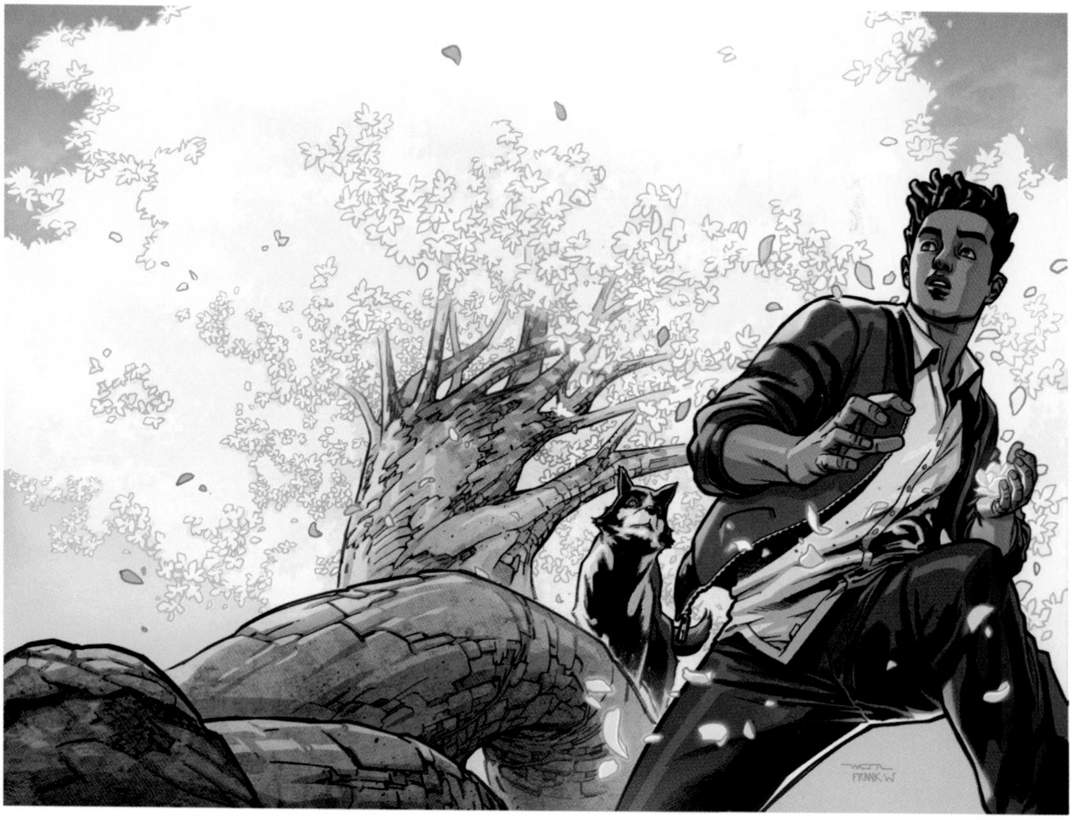

CHAPTER IV
Felipe Watanabe w/ Frank William

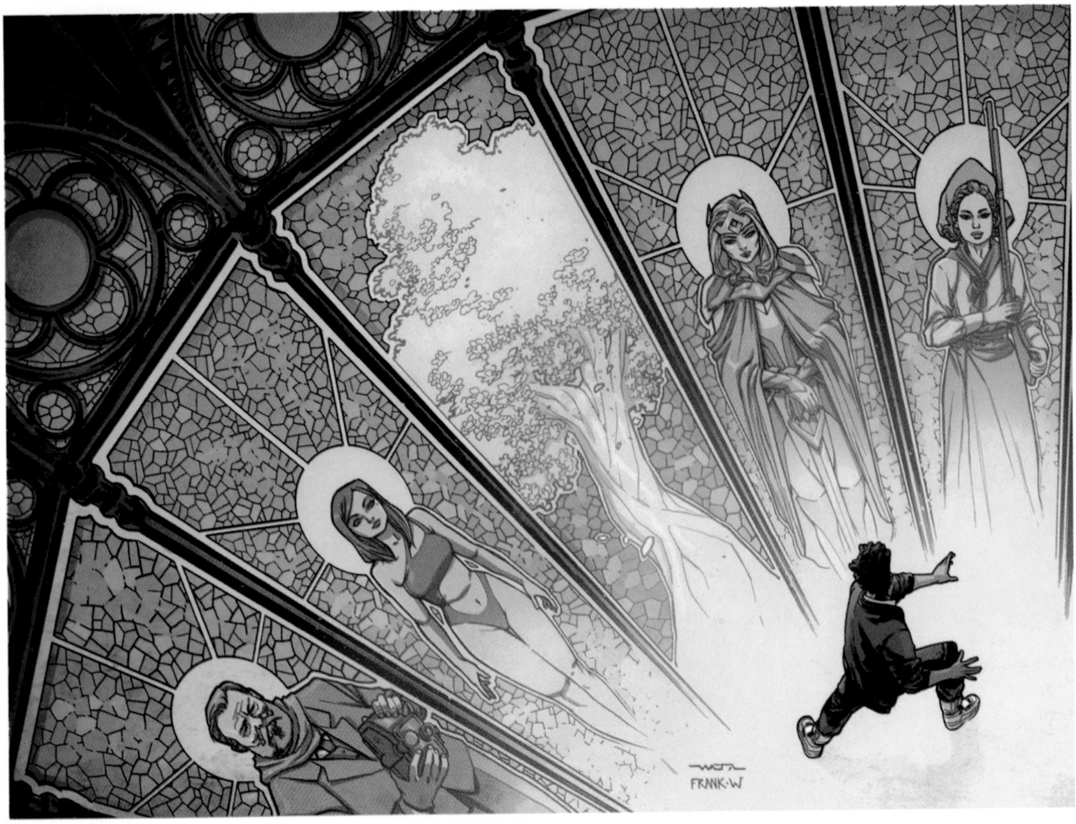
FRNK·W

CHAPTER V
Felipe Watanabe w/ Frank William

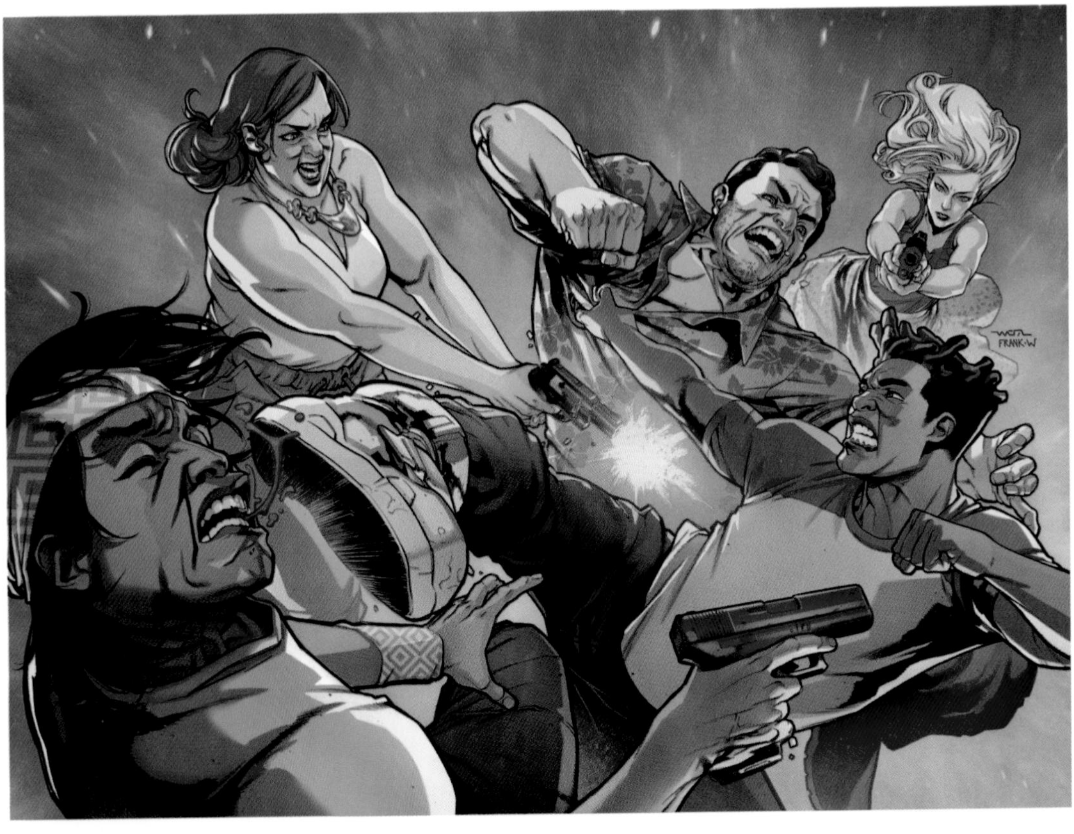
FRNK·W

CHAPTER VI
Felipe Watanabe w/ Frank William

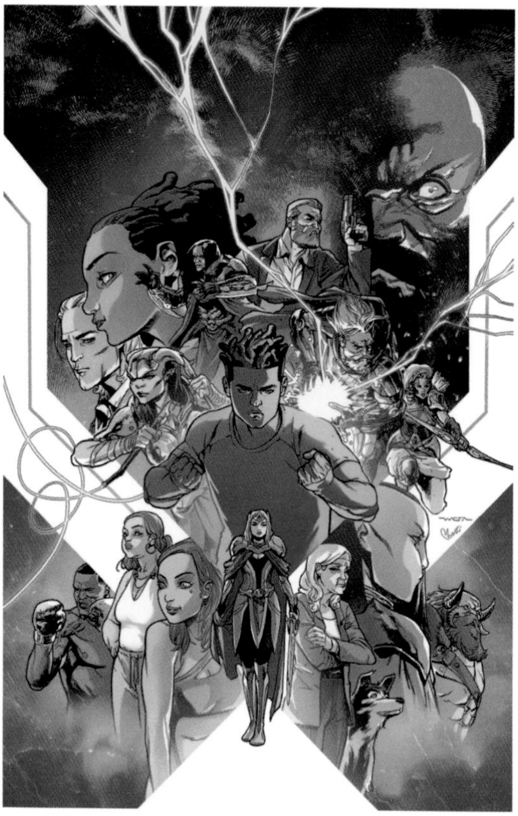

CHAPTER I [SECOND PRINTING]
Felipe Watanabe w/ Igor Monti

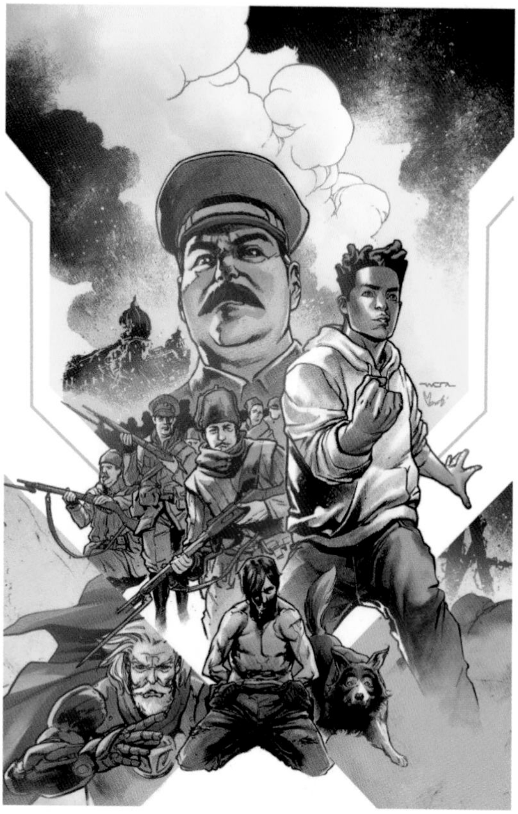

CHAPTER II [SECOND PRINTING]
Felipe Watanabe w/ Igor Monti

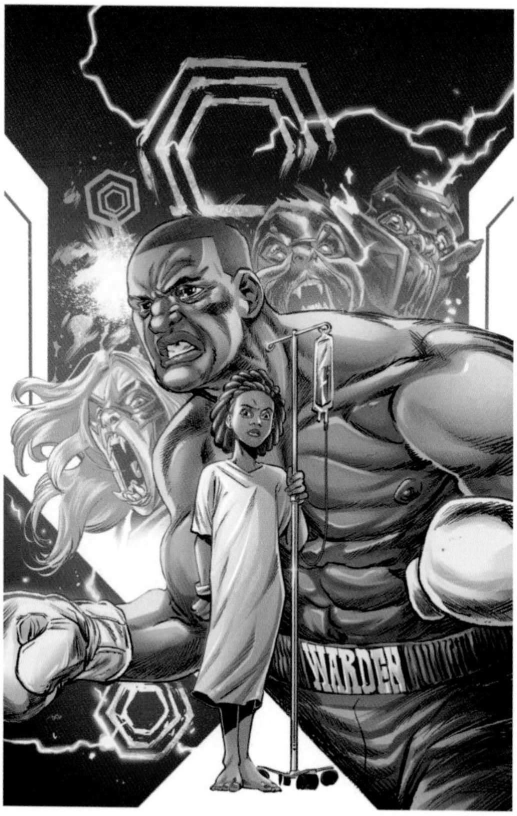
WARDEN

CHAPTER III [SECOND PRINTING]
Danilo Beyruth w/ Dijjo Lima

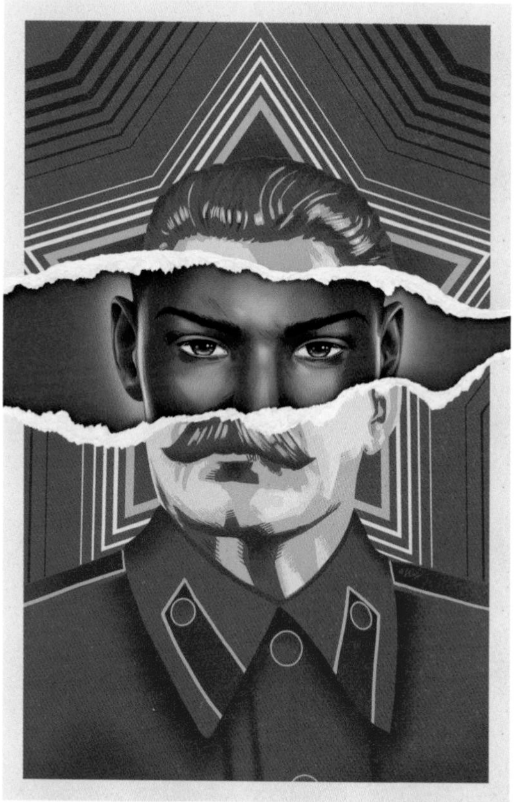

CHAPTER II [1:25]
Doaly

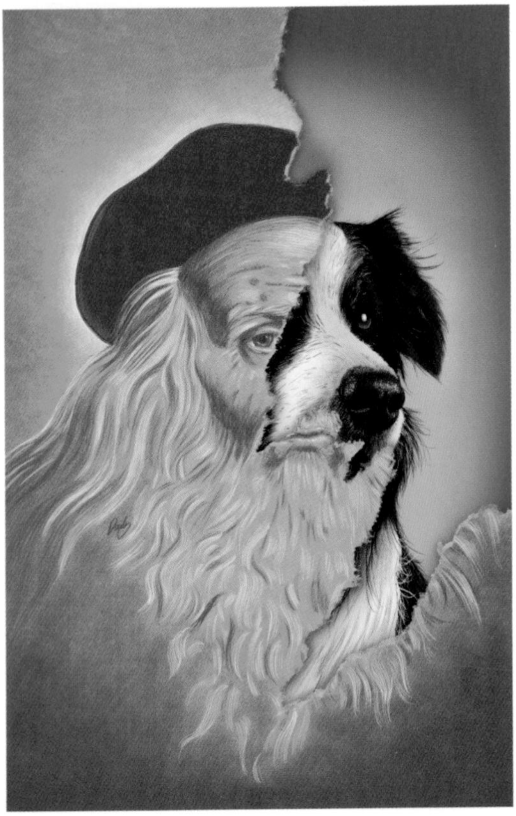

CHAPTER III [1:25]
Doaly

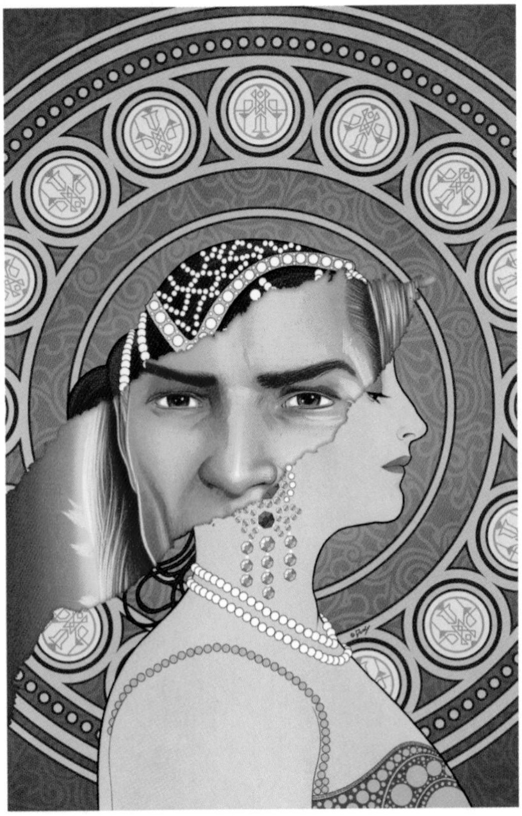

CHAPTER IV [1:25]
Doaly

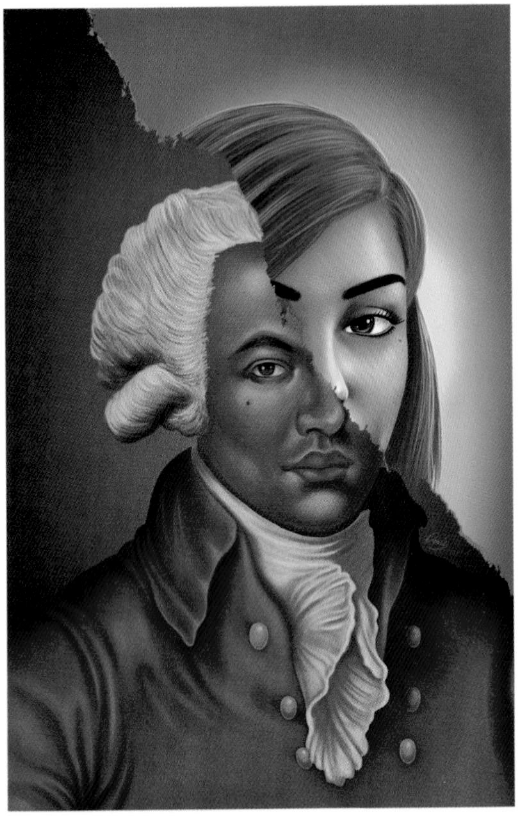

CHAPTER V [1:25]
Doaly

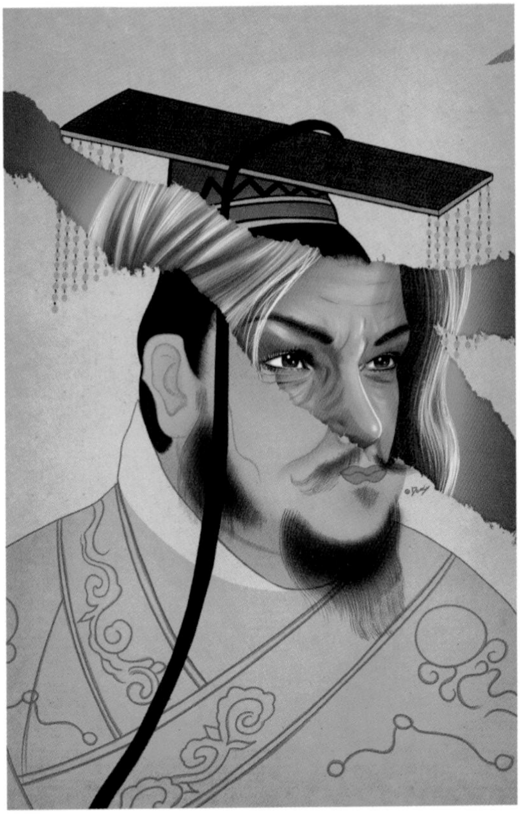

CHAPTER VI [1:25]
Doaly

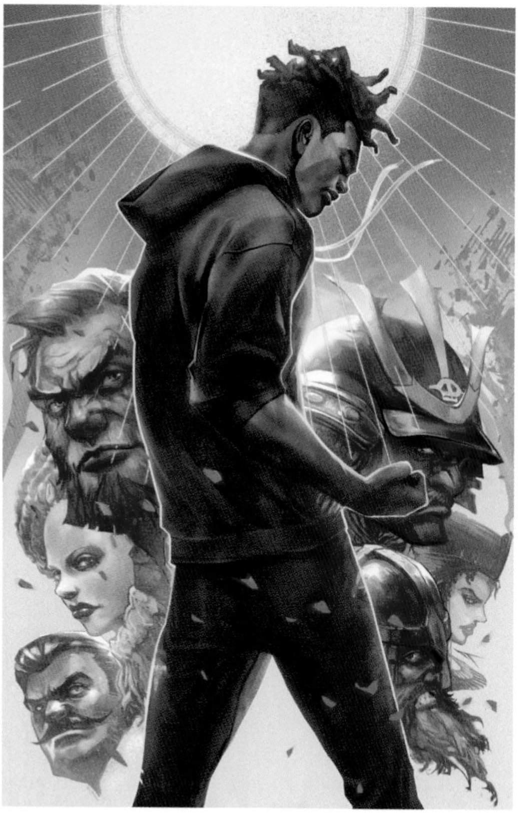

CHAPTER I [YELLOW SNOW]
Ivan Tao

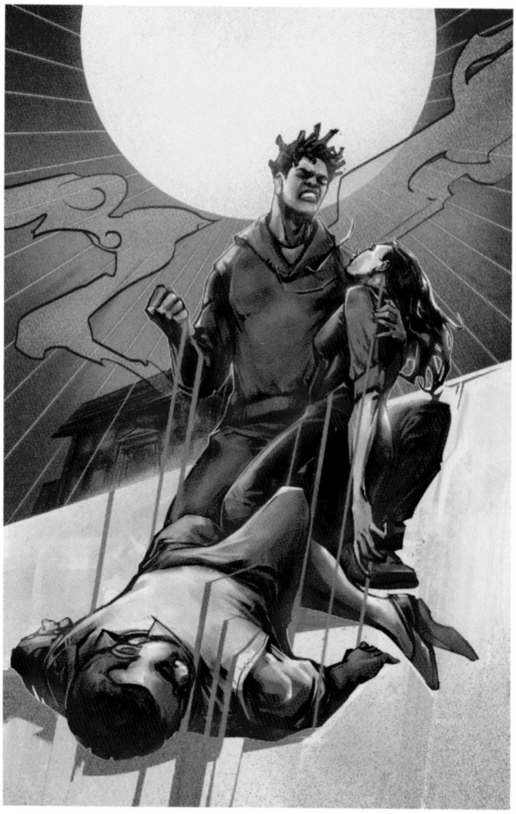

CHAPTER II [YELLOW SNOW]
Ivan Tao

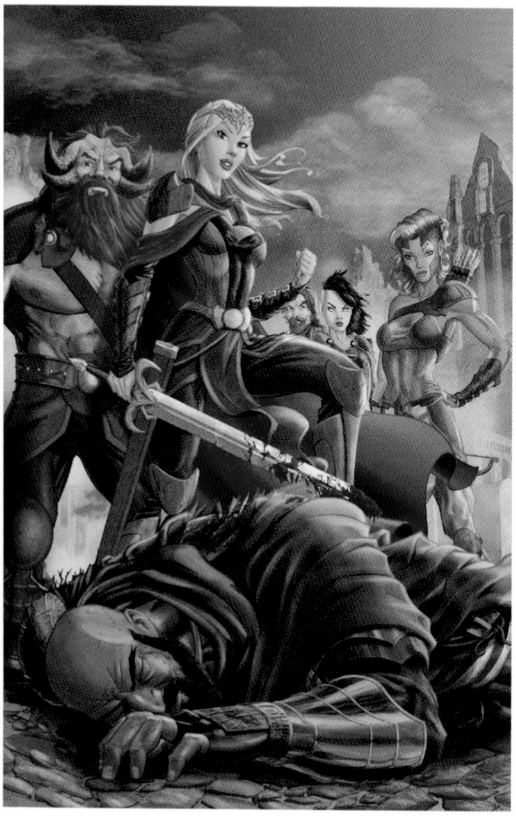

CHAPTER I [MODERN ERA]
Chris Ehnot

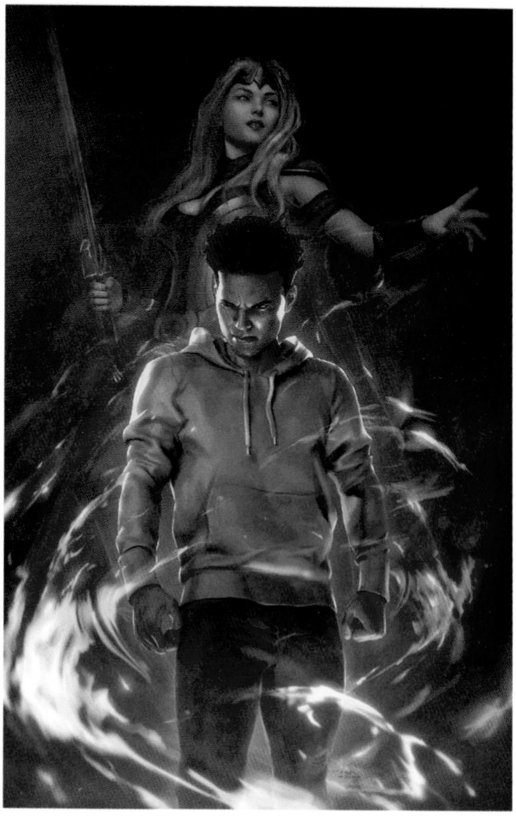

CHAPTER I [THE COMIC BOOK DEALER]
Tiago da Silva

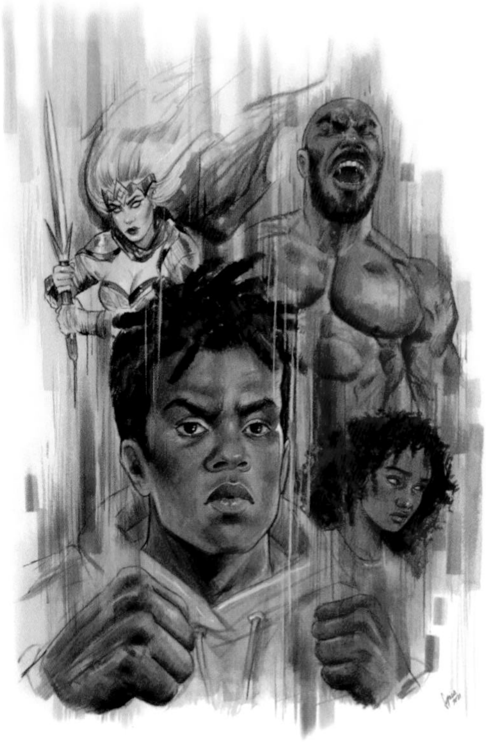

CHAPTER I [GALAXYCON]
Suspirialand

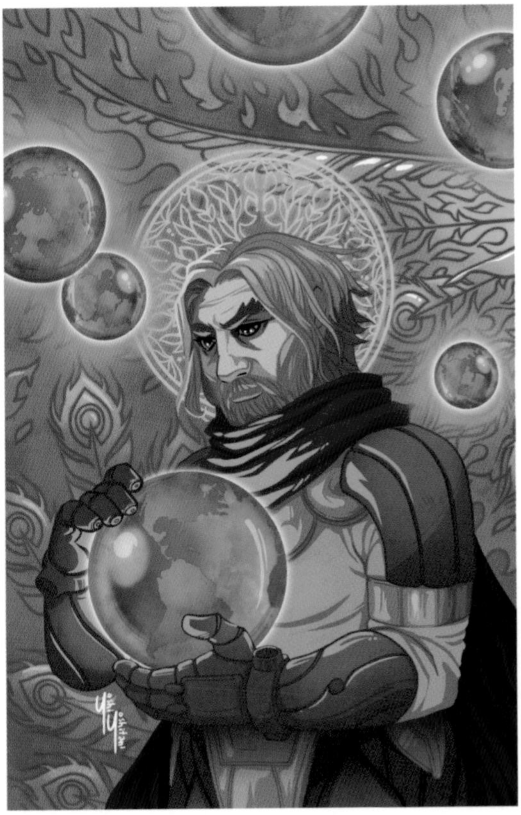

CHAPTER I [LINEBREAKERS]
Yoshi Yoshitani

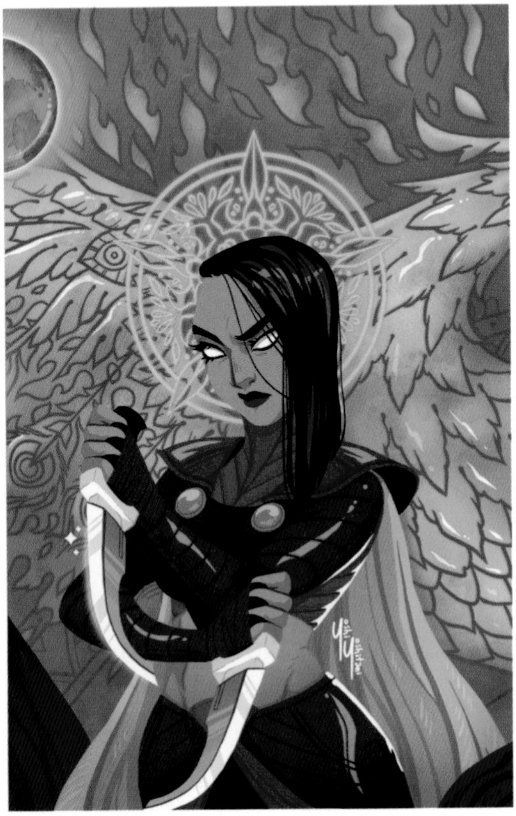

CHAPTER II [LINEBREAKERS]
Yoshi Yoshitani

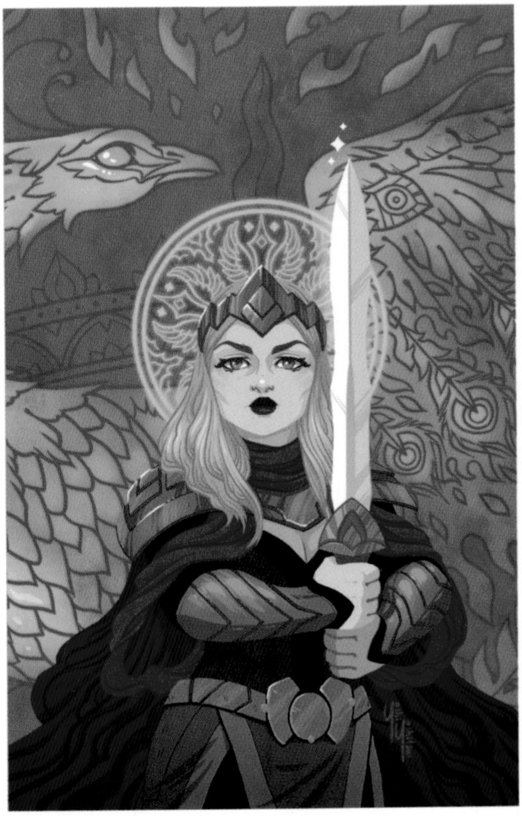

CHAPTER III [LINEBREAKERS]
Yoshi Yoshitani

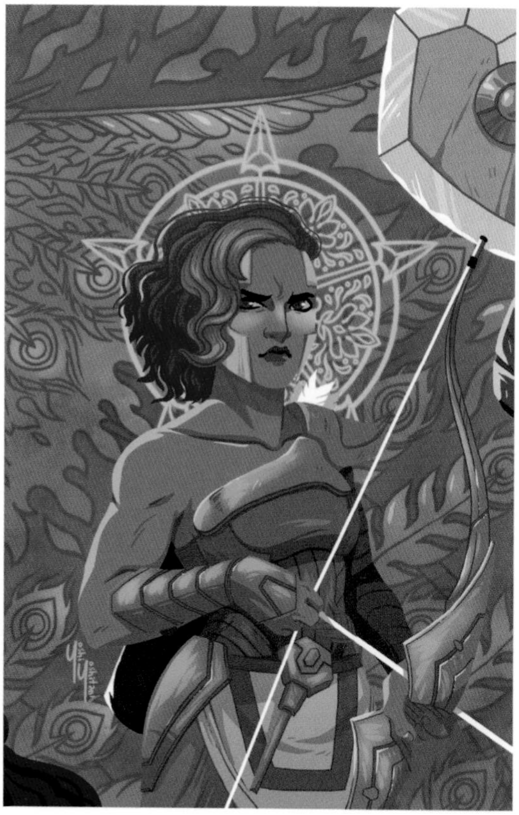

CHAPTER IV [LINEBREAKERS]
Yoshi Yoshitani

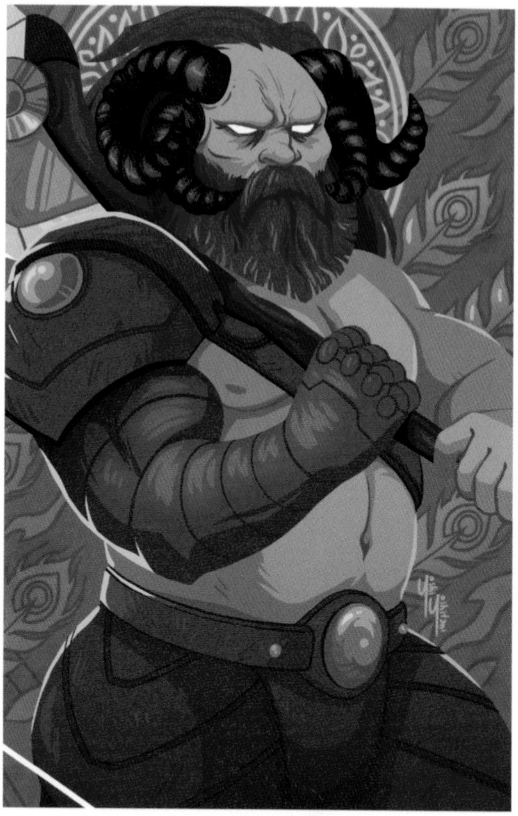

CHAPTER V [LINEBREAKERS]
Yoshi Yoshitani

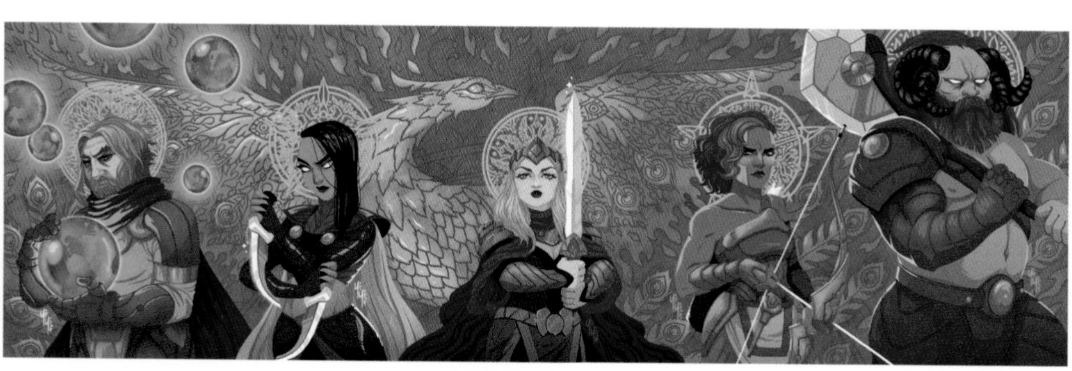

CHAPTERS I THROUGH V [LINEBREAKERS]
Yoshi Yoshitani

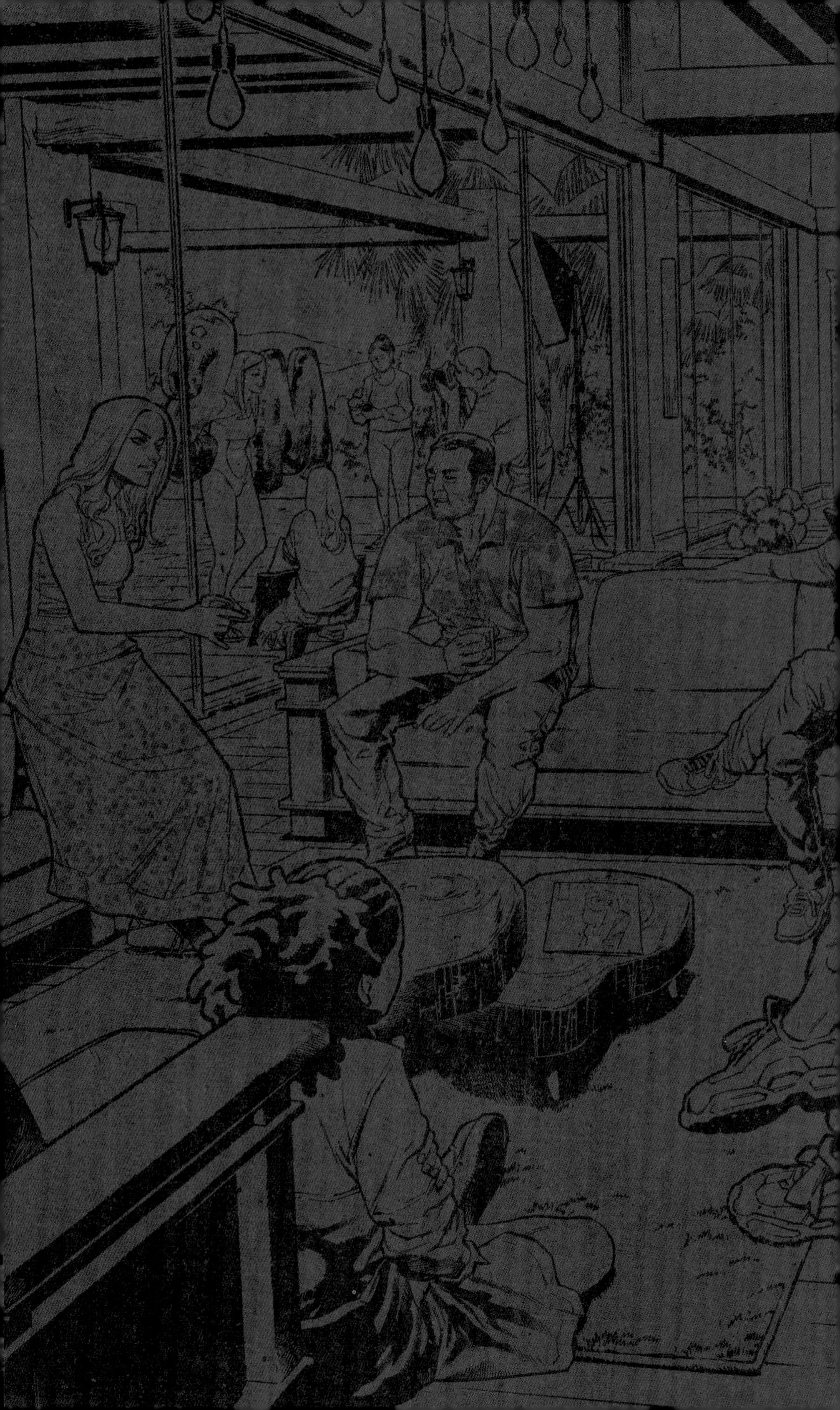

Stories

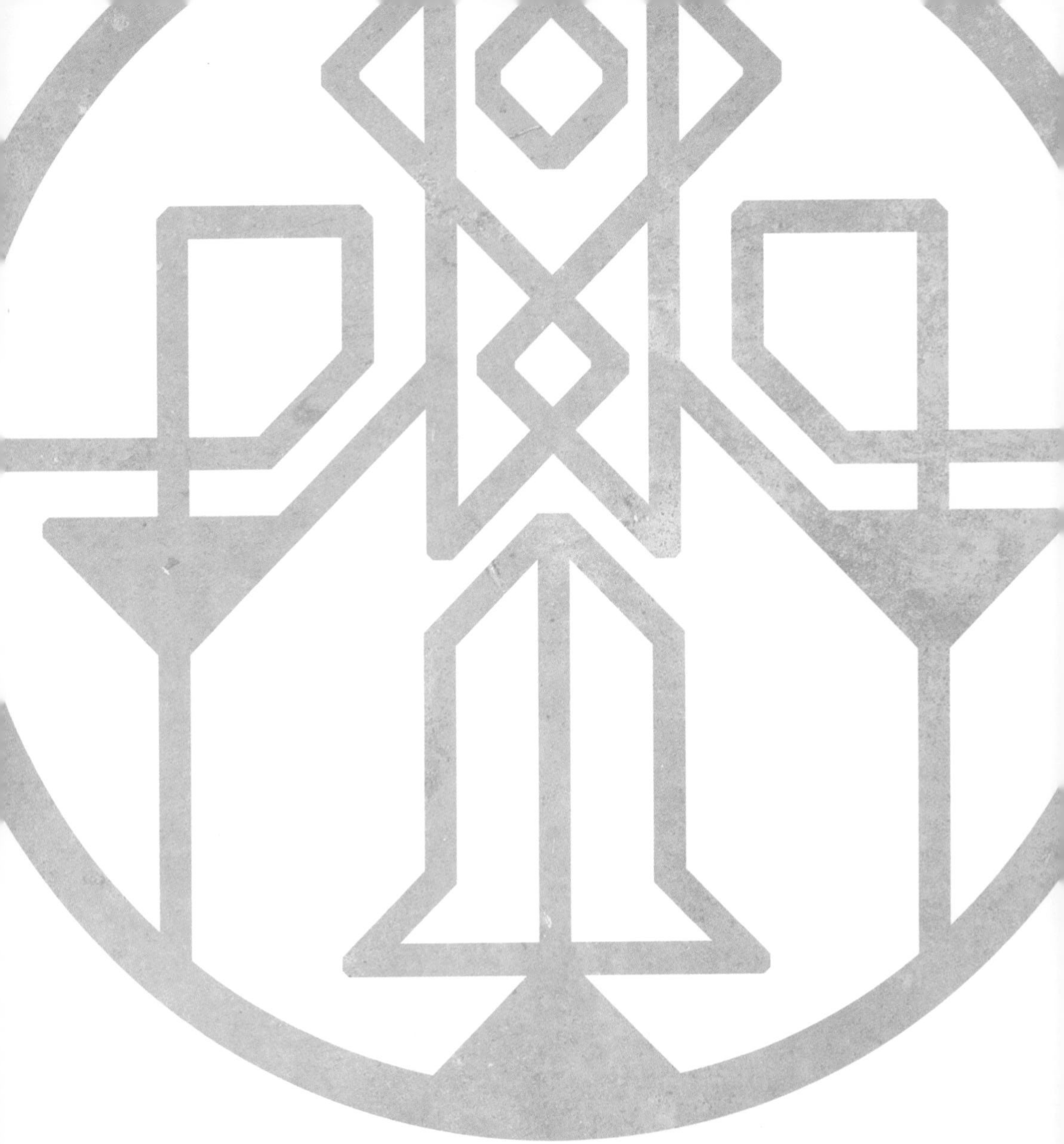

Flip of a Coin

ORIGINALLY PUBLISHED IN CHAPTER I

It wasn't the first time Masato Taoka had flipped a coin to decide a man's fate.

Taoka ran the bloody 100 yen piece across his knuckles as he considered the puddle of weakness at his feet. He was called Hideki, and his time with the family had been brief. Taoka saw the other half dozen young men shifting at the edges of the dusty pachinko parlor, the bright lights from the illuminated machines highlighting their furtive glances to one another. Almost everyone there had joined the family within the last month, and for many of them, it was the first time they were seeing Taoka up close.

This was intentional. It would be the first time they saw the repercussions of failure, what it meant to be committed to the yakuza.

He looked to his bodyguard, Matsuda, who was swallowed and looked away from the kneeling traitor. This was an opportunity to demonstrate firm leadership to his loyal friend. Though Matsuda had never said a word against Taoka's decisions, the yakuza boss could tell that his bodyguard did not have the stomach for doling out consequences.

"Tell me," Taoka said, as he rubbed the coin between his thumb and pointer finger. The boy wiped his bloody nose with his shoulder and strained against the taut rope binding his wrists. He wished Matsuda hadn't tied up the boy; it would make the others think Taoka was afraid of this pathetic child. But Matsuda had been paranoid in recent weeks about someone following them, worried someone was targeting Taoka, and had likely erred on the side of caution. Hideki had an impulsive temper, and perhaps the power tools left around the parlor from the construction workers would prove to be too tempting. A prudent maneuver for a bodyguard. A sign of frailty in a leader.

"The girl, she-- she would not pay. I told her to get her father, and she started yelling. She pushed me, she's the one that started--"

"я не будут торговать лейтенанта для фельдмаршала."

"--and she kept screaming... I- I know the partnership with the Hayashi family has been... been... an example needed to be set--"

A figure in a military uniform stood, no, flickered in the doorway. He wore a red armband with a black manji, his left hand gripping a holstered gun.

"он не мой сын. вы ничего не получите."

The language was Russian, Georgian maybe. A man's voice. Furious. Disgusted. Echoing through Taoka's skull and drowning out the boy's petulant mewling.

"--the blood, so I told Matsuda he had to--"

Taoka held up one hand, and Hideki's words stopped. The figure in the doorway was gone, and his mind, too, fell silent, though his stomach lurched. His vision swam for a moment, and he reached out his other hand for the back of a chair to catch himself.

The men straightened but did not move forward to help him. They took his stumble as an act of aggression. Good.

Taoka breathed slowly, deeply. That had been the most disorienting one yet.

He looked at each of the young men surrounding him, balanced the slick 100 yen piece on his thumb, and flipped it. The same as always: flowers for mercy, numbers for retribution. He flipped the coin in the air and let it fall to the ground.

Without looking, he stepped on it.

"Free his hands."

Hideki's shoulders slumped in relief as Matsuda stepped forward to cut the rope. The boy bowed so deeply Taoka could hardly hear the muffled gratitude.

"Thank you, sir. I knew you would understand. I only wanted to protect--" Hideki's voice dropped off as Matsuda slammed the boy's left hand onto a sawhorse, sending a billow of dust into the air. The boy struggled only briefly then stopped, watering eyes staring down at his left hand, lips trembling.

"Kaida Hayashi was the contact for her family. She has made every payment on time since her father died six years ago, and she's transported our girls through her hotel. You put your pride ahead of the family. You gave orders to someone you are in no position to command. And you may have killed a woman who is our sister." Taoka nodded to Matsuda, who stepped forward, presenting a blade.

"Should there be another transgression, no coin will be consulted. Consider yourself fortunate to be shown this mercy."

~

Two days later, Taoka and Matsuda sat in the restaurant above the near complete pachinko parlor, sharing a celebratory sake. The parlor would open by the end of the week, if all stayed on schedule, and one more line of income would be secured for the family. This was essential as Taoka expected Kaida Hayashi's medical bills to be significant.

Matsuda had been trying to convince Taoka to cancel the opening day's events and take time away from the city, and considering the visions - hallucinations, Matsuda insisted - were coming more rapidly, even twice a day, he was considering a postponement.

"I can't tell if it's the Takagi clan, the police, or someone from higher up, but it is a certainty; we are being followed," Matsuda said, looking over his shoulder, as though they may burst in any minute. Taoka smirked, but his stomach clenched. He had glimpsed one of the men himself earlier in the day, an American shouting for pedestrians to move out of his way, and the brief, intense eye confirmed that he was indeed a target.

Taoka sipped his drink and placed it carefully on the table, stretching the silence.

"How is Hideki?"

"Stronger. He will receive his prosthetics from Dr. Takei within the month."

"And the others?"

"They understand. They have volunteered to provide assistance at the hotel until Ms. Hayashi is... well again." Matsuda shifted uncomfortably in his seat.

Taoka sipped his sake, and as he moved to put the glass back down, he saw rings on his fingers - one laid with rubies around the band and a diamond letter E and the other featuring a large central ruby encircled with diamonds. His- the hands appeared smooth, small, foreign.

"I HAVE TESTED NEITHER YOUR LOYALTY NOR YOUR SILENCE; WHY SHOULD YOU HAVE MY TRUST?"

This voice was much louder, female, English. He gritted his teeth, forced his eyes closed. When he opened them, his hands were his own again, and Matsuda was standing, pulling his cell phone from his pocket.

"No, no need," Taoka said. "We must be saving the good stuff for the grand opening." Matsuda sat but kept his phone in hand.

It was too much. The visions, hallucinations, memories, whatever they were - they were too much, especially while dodging a nameless pursuer. He pulled out a coin and flipped it on the table, quickly slammed his hand down to stop the spinning, and closed his eyes again for a moment. When he opened them, he slid the coin off the table and back into his pocket. Matsuda watched him expectantly.

"We leave in the morning," he said finally. "Tell the doctor to meet us at the Okutama safe house."

"Taoka-san, why do you flip the coin if you never look at it?"

Taoka paused. Though he had adopted this practice when he first joined the family over ten years before, no one had ever asked. He had never needed to put into words why this ritual fueled his rapid ascent in the yakuza. Russian and English echoed in his mind, but the voices were an overlapping, dull murmur.

"When I flip the coin, I am not looking to any force of nature to rule an absolute truth. There is no absolute truth. I flip the coin because as it spins in the air, I find I am hoping for the numbers or the flowers. There is no need to look at the upturned side of the coin, because that is not where the answer lies. The moments of the turning coin reveal what I have already decided but am only now ready to know."

Matsuda nodded slowly, thoughtfully, then raised his glass.

The voices fell quiet.

~

Half an hour later, in the split second between hearing the gunfire so close to his skull and the darkness descending, Taoka thought perhaps he should have checked the coin.

Deathbed

ORIGINALLY PUBLISHED IN CHAPTER 11

A glass of water would be lovely.

No, nothing else. Thank you, dear.

I heard your father asking your mother to fetch the priest, so I know there isn't time for much else. I only ask that you stay with me for a few minutes before I sleep.

Did I ever tell you how much you look like my Terrence? He was such a lovely boy. Everyone, even the newspapers, called me "Mother," but the word sounded sweetest from him. He was so little when we lost him to the fever, he only could say, "Ma." More than sixty years later, I can still hear his voice. Ma.

Four. And all of them and my husband lost to the fever. No time to grieve, though. That's not true. Only time to grieve and wash my babies before they were laid to rest while we all stayed huddled in our homes waiting for it to pass or take us. For a time I wanted to follow them, my children, my husband, but God did not will it. So I put myself in the lion's jaws and helped others who had fallen ill. And still, God did not will it.

I do know. He saved me so that I would save all the little babies. All the children who used to be babies. All the men and women who used to be children who used to be babies. I knew it was His will because He sent me visions. He chose me to be strong for those who couldn't, and He chose me to show people they had their own strength, so that it was not merely a battle fought but a war won.

Don't scoff now, boy. There are more things in this world than your science books can tell you. How do I survive a fever that takes the last breath of thousands and leaves me to tend to the most scorching heat without a moment's pause? How do I survive a fire that takes down a great city and lets me walk out unburnt like Shadrach, Meshach, and Abednego? I was chosen to be strong. The strength was--is a gift. One it seems I have nearly used up.

Because the visions showed me. I saw myself pressing swords to the throats of enemies. I commanded large crowds in languages I never spoke. I withstood torture I could not dream of surviving in this body. Although this body has survived quite a lot, hasn't it?

One more pillow, just on my left side here, thank you.

I saw the first vision when I helped the railworkers in Pennsylvania. You see, I worked with the Knights of Labor. They aren't around anymore, but they were a force to be reckoned with. They started work in secret, because if talk of things like strikes and boycotts reached the ears of the owner… They wouldn't bother with the charade of taking people behind a building for a beating. But consensus, even in large groups, is nothing without will. A majority means nothing in silence.

Oh, aye, plenty of nights. Jail wasn't the horror I imagined it would be. Then again, the men I was thrown in with would take the shirts from their backs to make me a soft place to sit. No one dared touch me except to help me. Those men, many of whom could have crushed my throat with one hand, others who I had seen take lives themselves, would never raise a hand to me, a frail woman. That, darling, is strength.

Aye, the first vision. When the Great Fire burnt through Chicago, I stood in the street with nothing but the dish towel I had been holding when I heard the cries from my window. There was nothing, no one, coming to help. I thought, hoped, prayed, those plumes would take me back to my husband and babies. But as the smoke enveloped me, I saw in my hands a massive axe, and I was using it to break chains of the colored men and women and babies packed together like cattle. They did not belong in the belly of that ship. The babies belonged in schools, not in a field. The women and men belonged together with their families, free from the shackles on their wrists, embedded in their skin, chained to their future.

Remember Genesis. "Now Joseph had a dream, and when he told it to his brothers they hated him even more." My purpose was to save those babies, save their parents, save those who did not know their own strength and watch them rise against the greedy and depraved who would make themselves comfortable in excess and opulence on the backs of others. You will find your own purpose, and you will know you can fulfill it, because you will be given visions of its fulfillment. God is good, child. He willed it, and it was so.

I will see my babies soon. I will hear my Terrence and his sweet voice.

Another glass of water would be wonderful. And then, I think, to sleep.

Come the Fuck On

ORIGINALLY PUBLISHED IN CHAPTER III

So riding shotgun in someone's body is pretty goddamn boring for the most part, especially when the immortal is still stuck in a kid. I mean, even the Prodigy has to get someone to wipe their ass for the first few years. I know some of the others go into this sleep mode for a bit to pass the time, because a watched pot never boils, right? But it's gotten so crazy in the last hundred years or so that I can't risk stepping out for a smoke, if you know what I mean.

You know, this used to be so much easier before there were domesticated horses and ships and covered wagons and trains and telegraphs and phones and cars and airplanes and don't even get me started on the fucking internet. We hopped bodies once, maybe twice per job, and the whole thing reset before anything got crazy. But now? Fuck.

Anyway, this host isn't too bad, all things considered. I mean, things have gotten a lot more comfortable since I originally got here; clean clothing and water, indoor plumbing are all nice. The fucking measles are back, so that's wild, but daily life still overall seems to be getting easier. More comfortable for humans, anyway. So as much of job hazards as the mobility and media are, they do let me take a little stroll outside my host's immediate world in a way that wasn't even a dream when this immortal was reborn. Oh, that reminds me, I got stuck in a movie projector operator once, and it made me want to light myself on fire (which pretty much sums up what it feels like to hop to a new body), but it was only for about two years before the immortal's host died right in the third row, so you know, win-win.

Shit, where was I? Oh, yeah, this body I'm in has a cute suburban life with a solid husband, two sweet kids, fenced-in yard, blah blah blah. She blows off her family for "self-care" and sneaks off to - get this - watch old foreign horror movies. Some of them are classics, and others are pretty fucked up amateur stuff. Most seem legit, and it's a trip to see these grainy old films on her giant screen in all their 4k HDR OLED glory. I was actually on set as a camera operator for a Japanese flick. Small world, right? Anyway, she'll throw some American stuff in there, too. One of the ones she's watched at least twice a year since I've been checked in was one that came up last night in the rotation. It has the creepy little guy who talks about how a boy's best friend is his mother.

Which got me thinking… when does that end? It makes sense when the boy is a baby, because human babies have weak survival skills and take years to stop doing stupid suicidal shit on accident, so yeah, Mom shows up to make sure things keep rolling. And if one thing hasn't changed in these past few hundred thousand years, it's that the women are typically the ones most connected from the get-go. But at some point, unless the mom wants to be a skeleton in a spinny chair, they start facilitating other relationships to make sure they branch out, learn independence, and do their own goddamn laundry.

Kid is twenty-two. Guess he's not a kid anymore. Shit, hadn't even thought of that. It's true; they really do grow up fast. Time flies when you're poised to kill.

Like I was saying, it got me thinking. Who's the best friend now? Who is he connected to the most? Who would he take a bullet to save? Who would he allow to fuck up over and over again and still let into his life with open arms? That's what I'm trying to sort out now. Christopher still lives at home and has a pretty shit job, no relationship, barely any friends. Just a family-oriented kid. I can feel his mom's waves of pride in his work ethic and dedication to family but also the worry that he's spinning his wheels.

I don't think his mom is seeing that he's getting restless. That's never a good sign. And when he tried to get himself reborn the other day and called his sister's name? I don't know if one of the other immortals got close and triggered something or maybe the legacies are revealing themselves in his dreams and freaked him out or if it's just ordinary young adulthood bullshit.

But Christopher yelling out his sister's name during his flip out really threw me for a loop. Then later he was telling his mom he wanted to make sure he could borrow her car to bring Brianna and her friend out to the mall, and when asked why he didn't use his own car, he said his mom's car had better safety features.

Shit. Shit shit shit.

The only reason I'm talking to myself through this so much and stalling like a pissant is because it just hurts so fucking bad when I have to switch. I don't want to leap over and then find out oops, his car smells like weed, and he didn't want his sister to rat him out, and he's still a mama's boy. But fuck, yeah, I know that's not it. Between Christopher's little stunt and a weakening in the earthly presence of the other Stewards, it's enough to go on. They happened years apart, but when you've been around as long as I have, they're basically on top of each other. The message isn't clear yet, but I feel an electricity in the air, like just before a storm.

Yeah, it'll hurt like hell, but it's nothing compared to my punishment if I fail.

Here goes nothing.

*****PROPERTY OF YORK SCHOOL OF DRAMATIC ART**
INTERVIEW TRANSCRIPT BY BEATRICE LEONARD
3 DECEMBER 1950
ORSON WELLES, FILMMAKER AND ACTOR / DAVI

SAREH.

Research team dug this up. Worth a read.

ELLIOT Thank you, Mr. Welles, for agree
I know Othello is taking up much of your time, so I promise to limit myself to only an hour or three of fawning.

WELLES That's very kind of you, David. I do have a 6:30 flight to Rome, so please feel free to write if there's anything you neglect to compliment during our time together.

ELLIOT I will be certain to do that. In the interests of keeping you on schedule, let's get started, shall we?

WELLES Of course. I apologize if I'm a bit… scattered. I've been flying back and forth across the pond, and I'm not sure what day it is or which way is up. The little I've been able to sleep has been--that is all immaterial. Please carry on.

ELLIOT You're known worldwide for your incredible films such as The Magnificent Ambersons and Citizen Kane and of course you've been generous enough to speak to our aspiring actors about your stage work on Broadway in Julius ~~Caesar~~ Caesar and Romeo and Juliet, but what I would love to tell our readers about is your work on the radio, particularly your War of the Worlds broadcast.

WELLES Hmm. I don't know that there is much to say. It did not have the outcome I expected.

ELLIOT I-- um, well, it was quite widely covered in America as--

WELLES   Coverage is not a mark of quality, David. One mustn't
          reward the barest of observational skills lest we
          become utterly blind rather than merely myopic.

ELLIOT   Of-- of course not, sir. I am merely commenting on
          what a great impact the War of the Worlds had on the
          American people. There were reports of thousands of
          citizens calling in to local police stations, believing
          that Martians were attacking Earth.

WELLES   And why do you suppose that was?

ELLIOT   The writing and, of course, the acting was
          extraordinary. I was able to listen to a recording,
          and--

WELLES   And were you fooled?

ELLIOT   Well, no, but I knew before I listened that it was a
          dramatisation.

WELLES   Ah, the ~~slight~~ sleight of hand is not so slight when
          your eyes are open to the truth. Then it all seems like
          paper tigers. Shadows on the cave wall.

ELLIOT   I'm sorry. What cave?

WELLES   I've pulled us a bit off course, haven't I? To be
          perfectly candid, as I find it a struggle not to be, I
          go through cycles, particularly when under pressure,
          where my very poor sleep is rife with powerfully vivid
          dreams. It's nearly like living two lives, I imagine.
          The strangest thing. You've unfortunately caught me
          in the height of such a cycle. I do not always take
          my conversation partners along with me as I move from
          point to point.

ELLIOT   That sounds quite exhausting, frankly.

WELLES   You can't imagine.

ELLIOT   If you're up for it, we can continue.

WELLES   Of course. Go on.

ELLIOT   I was saying earlier that I hoped to discuss War of the
          Worlds. You mentioned that it did not have the outcome
          you hoped for. Can you speak more on that?

WELLES   What is the purpose of storytelling, David?

ELLIOT   Well, I think--

WELLES   It's a rhetorical question, son. I'm building a moment.

ELLIOT   Apologies.

WELLES   The purpose of storytelling, David, is to tell the
          truth wrapped in a lie. Ordinary minds cannot cope with
          a dramatic paradigm shift. It would be like explaining
          an elevator - a lift, as you call it - to a cat.
          You may show them the mechanics and give them every
          possible angle to examine, but it means nothing to
          them. The doors simply close in front of them, and when
          they open again, the world has changed. They accept
          that the world works as it does without deriving any
          truth from how things become the way they are.

ELLIOT   So you had hoped that by writing and performing War
          of the Worlds as a realistic radio broadcast that you
          might open peoples' eyes to a, what, great and terrible
          truth?

WELLES   Yes! Yes, my boy! Can you imagine souls traveling here
          from the heavens? Viewing us with no more interest
          than a hunter to an ant colony? Knowing those ants,
          burdened with nothing more than errant corn kernels

and scavenged animal bits are convinced they carry the greatest sustenance in the universe?

ELLIOT   I'm not certain I--

WELLES   No one would believe a single scientist, no matter how well-respected and accomplished he was. But wrap the same story in flying saucers and news reports, and the switchboards catch fire. Do you understand now? Does this mean something to you?

ELLIOT   I'm afraid it doesn't.

WELLES   Are we humans who dream of being butterflies? Or butterflies who dream to live as humans?

         four minutes of silence on recording

ELLIOT   Are you all right, Mr. Welles?

WELLES   I am... as I expected to be. I had hoped that among all the fervor following the broadcast that there would be a connection established with others seeking the truth. But, as it appears to be my fate, I am disconnected.

ELLIOT   I apologize. I hope I didn't say anything to offend.

WELLES   No, David, the apologies are mine. My expectations were not managed. I must again apologize and excuse myself. I will send word when I am able to complete our interview.

END OF TRANSCRIPT

NOTE: Hold article. Just received word that Welles was admitted to hospital shortly after interview. Full recovery expected, but manager requests waiting on publication until after Othello wraps. -DE

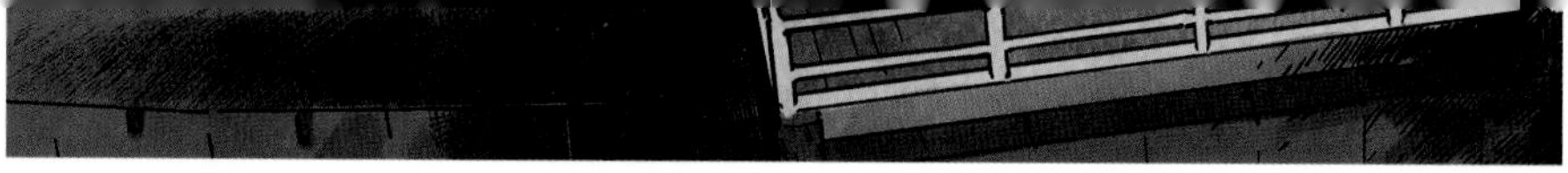

Liked by **thewarden** and **182 others**

all_aussies 100% Purebred Australian Shepherds - AKC Registered
Raised IN HOME with love!!

Puppies available 6/10/13
Starting at $1500

6 males, 2 females
Mix of Merle and Tricolor

Please email to request information/pictures for specific puppies. Link in bio.

View all 347 comments

billlymarvellous dugs

radiantblk good boys!

5 YEARS AGO

Add a comment... Post

prev next

favorite hide flag share Posted: 5 years ago

Need a Christmas pup???

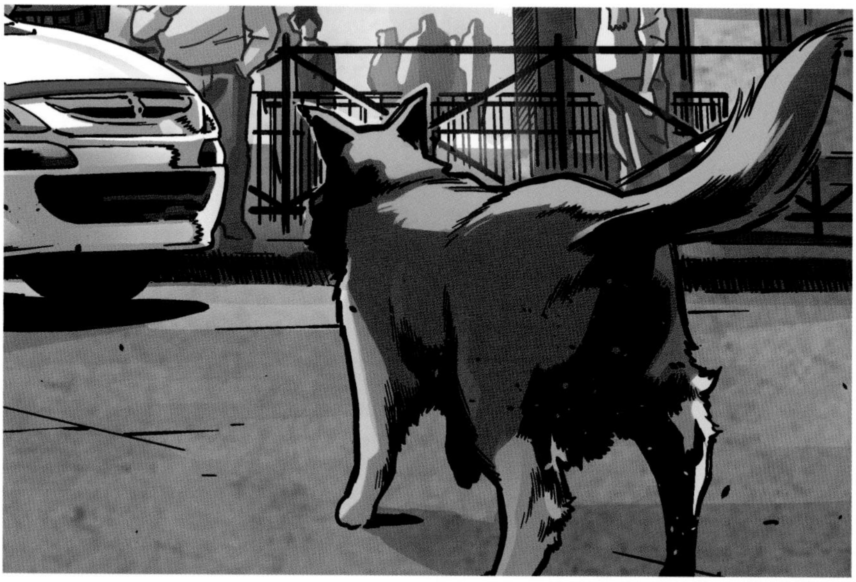

We have to rehome our PUREBREED AUSTRALIAN SHEPARD due to personal reasons. No mean messages pls. Dog is healthy and super soft, we're just a really busy family. She's crate trained and good w/ kids. Originally cost $1700, asking for at least $1K.

DON'T contact me with services or offers

post id: 15190502 posted: 5 years ago

Donate!

ked

● date

te

hipped

Meet Noel!

Meet Noel! She is an approximately one year old Australian Shepherd mix. She was found by herself last Christmas hiding under a dumpster near a restaurant by New Haven Forest Preserve. She has spent a few months recovering with one of our loving foster families due to leg injuries, possibly from being confined to a small space over a long period of time. She wore a collar but had no identifying tags or microchip.

Noel is a sweet dog who loves to be near her humans. She's also a very smart pup who has figured out how to open cabinets and pantry doors to get extra snacks, so a childproof home is a must. She particularly enjoys lying on the couch while her people listen to music or watch TV. The way she tilts her head during the evening news makes her quite the "newshound!"

She can become anxious and scratch at doors when she is left alone for long periods of time, so ideally she can be adopted by a family who has someone who can stay with her during the day. She also would make a great therapy or emotional support animal, as she can sense when people are stressed out or sad and cuddles extra close.

A property check may be necessary before adoption to ensure the safety and welfare of our animals. Proof of a rental agreement allowing pets is required for an adoption into a rental property.

This website updates frequently. There is a chance that by the time you arrive at our location, the animal you are interested in may have been adopted already. We cannot put animals on hold over the phone.

Our Sponsors and Partners

PURPOSE

ABOUT US OUR STORIES DONATE CONTACT US

TILLY

ID	15041452
GENDER	F
BREED	Australian Shepherd
AGE	4-5 years
PRICE	$300

Tilly came to us when her owner recently passed away unexpectedly. She was found near her recently deceased owner and became defensive when emergency services attempted to intervene. However, she calmed down when a more familiar family member approached. We share this with you to let you know she is a loyal companion, even though she may need time to grieve the loss of her owner. Unfortunately, the owner's family is unable to care for a dog at this time, and they approached Paws for a Purpose to help find the perfect family.

Per family report, Tilly is a good girl who enjoys being around other people more than other dogs but is not aggressive to other pets in the household (although she prefers to be the closest one to her human family members). She is clever and reportedly can identify over 20 different household items and retrieve them. She was clearly very loved by her owner, but we're sure in time she will become the happy, energetic puppy her extended family remembers her to have been.

ENQUIRE NOW SPONSOR ME

Gracie ♡

Australian Shepherd

Rescue Group	FOREVER HOME DOG RESCUE
Rescue Pet ID	ML1506
Age	5 years
Adoption Fee	$400.00
Microchip Number	55342113853211
Desexed?	Yes

Overview

Gracie was found by West Prairie Animal Control, who scanned her for a microchip. After contacting her owner, it was decided she would be surrendered to the county animal control due to her frequent escapes as well as the family's decision to discontinue entering her into dog shows.

All that said, Gracie is a loving dog who takes treats carefully, follows all basic commands (and some unexpected ones like "watch out" when a box fell down in the office area), and does not show any signs of aggression toward other dogs or humans when approached slowly. She has been trained in retrieval, agility, and scent work, per the previous owner's report, and has won several national titles. Based on her microchip information, she has had several families, but for one reason or another, they weren't the right fit. Perhaps you and your family are!

We decided to rename her Gracie to send her into her new life, because we believe she deserves grace after everything she has been through. If you're interested in a dedicated, brilliant, and sweet companion (and have good security against this little Houdini's escape tricks), Gracie is the dog for you!

DR MARK THOMAS
BMed, Dip Paediatrics

CASE NOTES

PATIENT: DOMINIC MONTAGUE

DATE OF BIRTH: 11/11/1969

VISIT NOTES

Mother (Celeste Montague) reports unremarkable but unplanned pregnancy and birth.

Child reportedly demonstrated paroxysmal fussing ("colic") for first six months of life, only soothed by listening to TV or radio news.

Per parent report, child spoke first at 10 months, putting together three words at a time, but appears embarrassed to speak in front of other adults? Concerns re: mother's mental health in light of doubtful claims.

DOMINIC

Trees

There are lots of types of trees. Some types of tree include **oak**, **ash**, and **birch**.

What is your favourite type of tree?

~~I feel a call to the aspen,~~
~~tender twigs reaching as a~~
~~man's fingers to a distant~~
~~realm - just as desperate~~
~~and just as vain.~~

I like the aspen tree because it is white.

CRESCENT CITY PRIMARY SCHOOL

STUDENT	DATE
MONTAGUE, DOMINIC	12-22-1979

GRADE	PERIOD	TEACHER
FIFTH	HALF-TERM	B. SPAGNOLI

COMMENTS

Dominic is a bright boy who completes work quickly and without error. He rarely socializes with peers, preferring the company of adults at lunch time or recess. He is polite and appears to have exceptional academic skills, but when he has taken the state achievement tests for gifted programs, he has done uncharacteristically poorly.

He spends all free time in the library and has special interests in history and literature. He has recently been asking for all of the published works of Sarojini Naidu, which our library does not carry.

For the rest of the school year, I would like to see him continue to work on engaging with his classmates and being more age appropriate in his social interactions.

FROM THE DESK OF
ROBERT M. ULRICH

To Whom it May Concern:

In my thirty-seven years in education, I have taught students who have gone on to produce groundbreaking research in bioengineering, serve in presidential cabinets, and create art that hangs in the Museum of Modern Art. Not one of their achievements compares to the potential I see in Dominic Montague. Dominic has a wisdom beyond his years, connecting significant historical eras and events with achievements in science and literature. I have no doubt that admitting him to your political science program would be an incredible opportunity for Dominic and that Harvard University would benefit from having such an inspired mind among its prestigious alumni.

While Dominic's academic achievements are remarkable for any student his age, I believe it is important for this committee to note that he has done so without the support of close family, having never known his father and having lost his mother very recently and unexpectedly. He has always been a serious student who took every educational endeavor as seriously as Shackleton, but his laser focus on completing higher education despite his personal situation has been nothing short of miraculous. I am confident that his dedication, ingenuity, strength, cleverness, and leadership qualities will make him an asset to your university.

In his personal statement, Dominic mentions that he has always felt he has had a purpose and that he has been put on this earth to correct the mistakes of the past. He is quick to cite military and political leaders as the ones making mistakes, but I can tell there is a particular connection there where, even at his young age, I can see he may have some regrets of his own.

Bearing all of this in mind, I wholeheartedly and without caveat recommend Dominic Montague to your institution.

Best,

R. Ulrich

Mr. Robert Ulrich

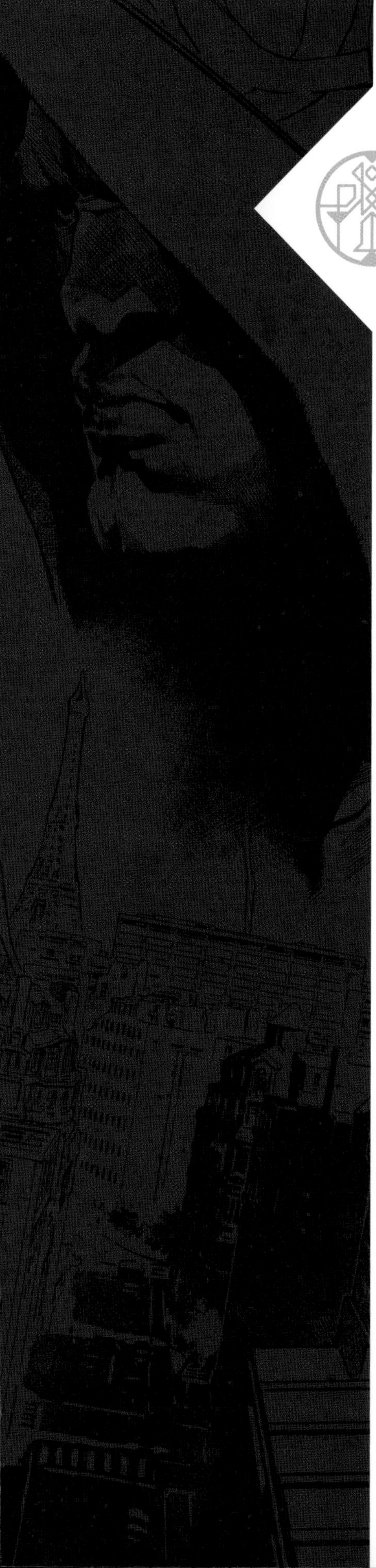

Concept Art

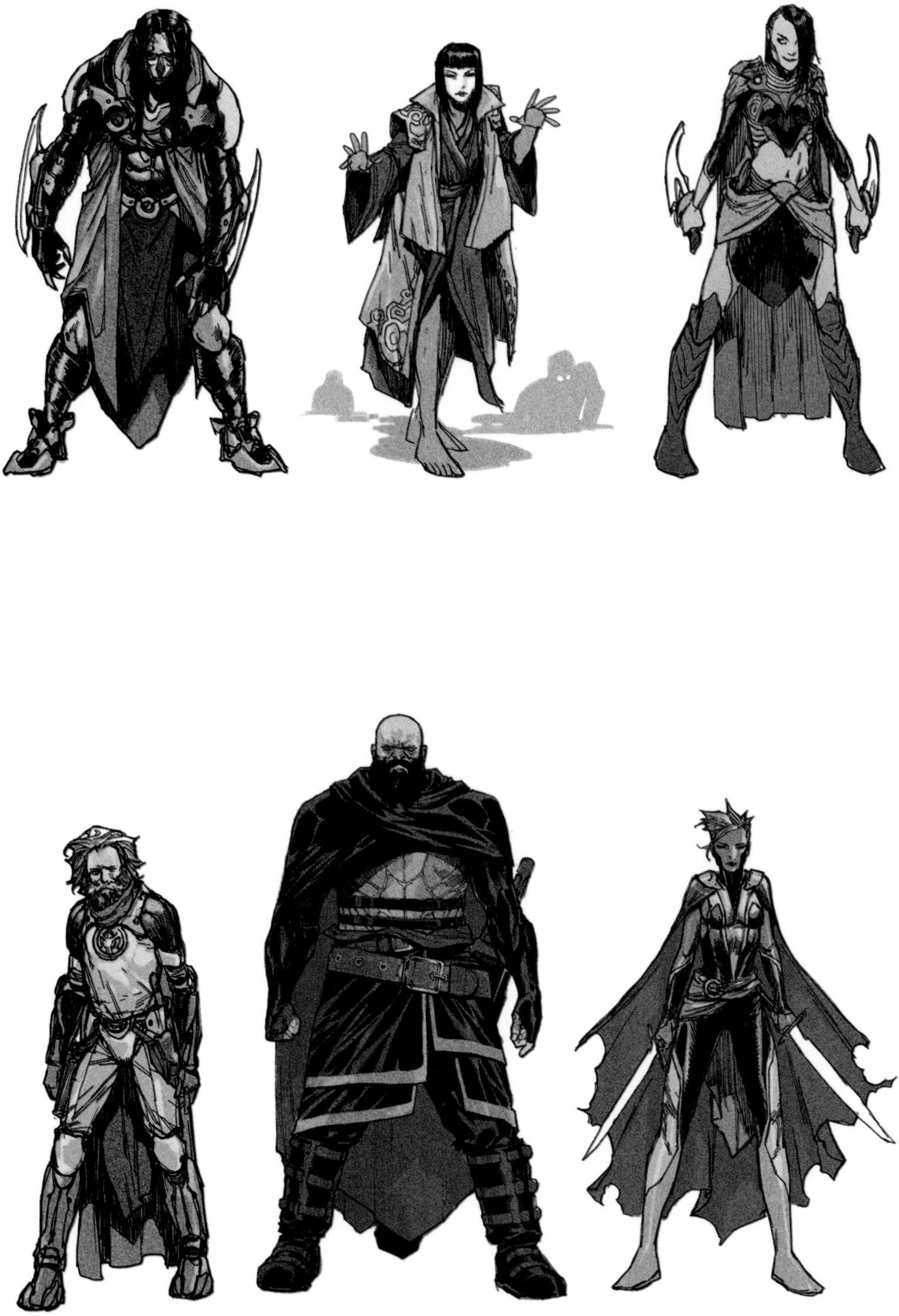

THE GODS
Felipe Watanabe

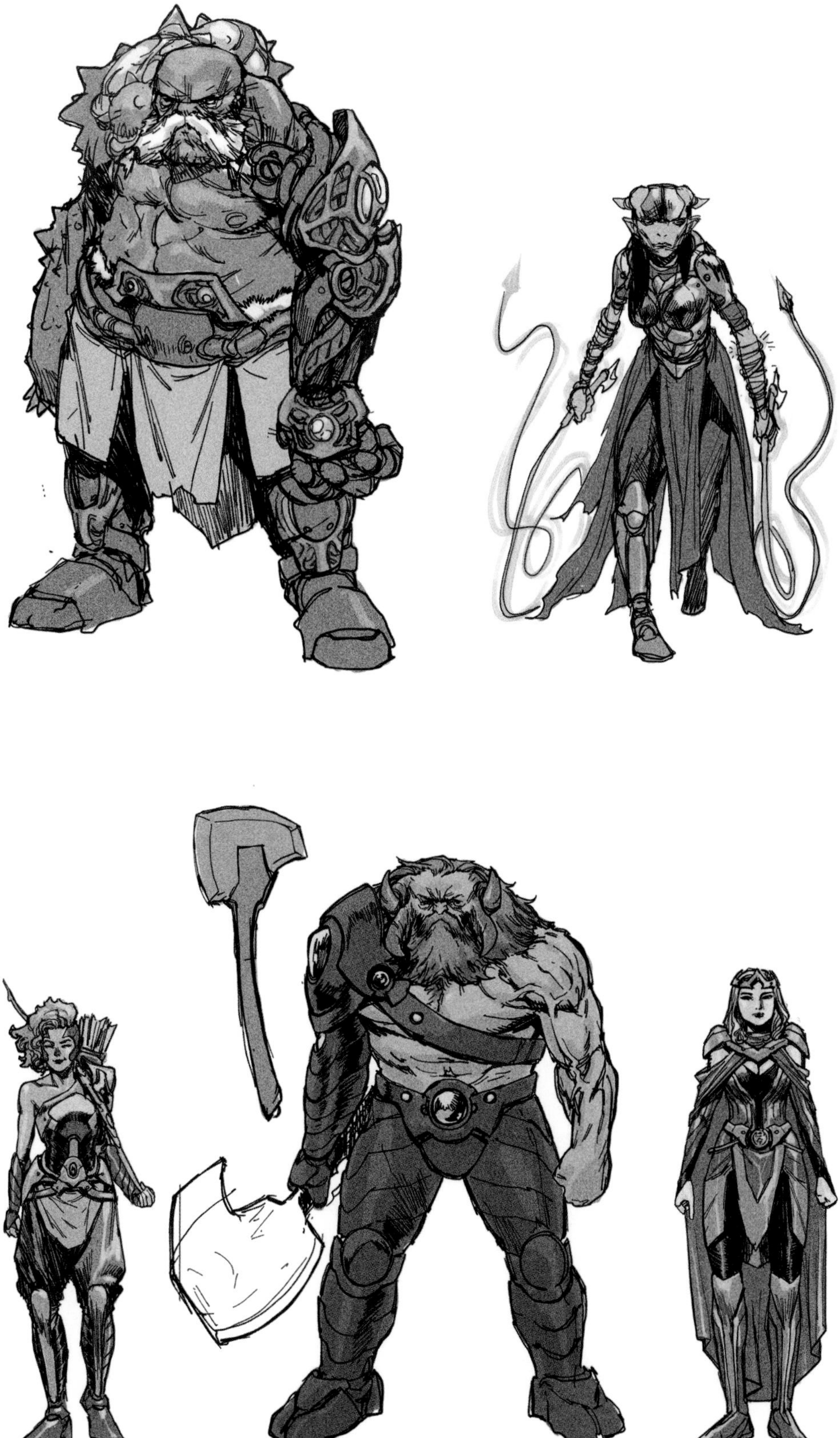

THE MORTALS
Felipe Watanabe

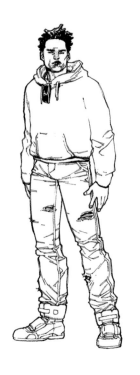

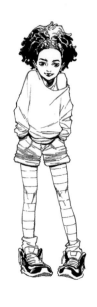

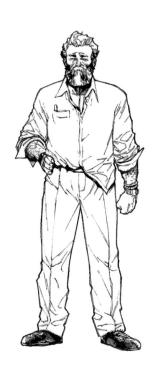

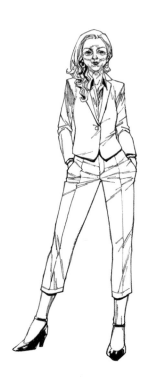

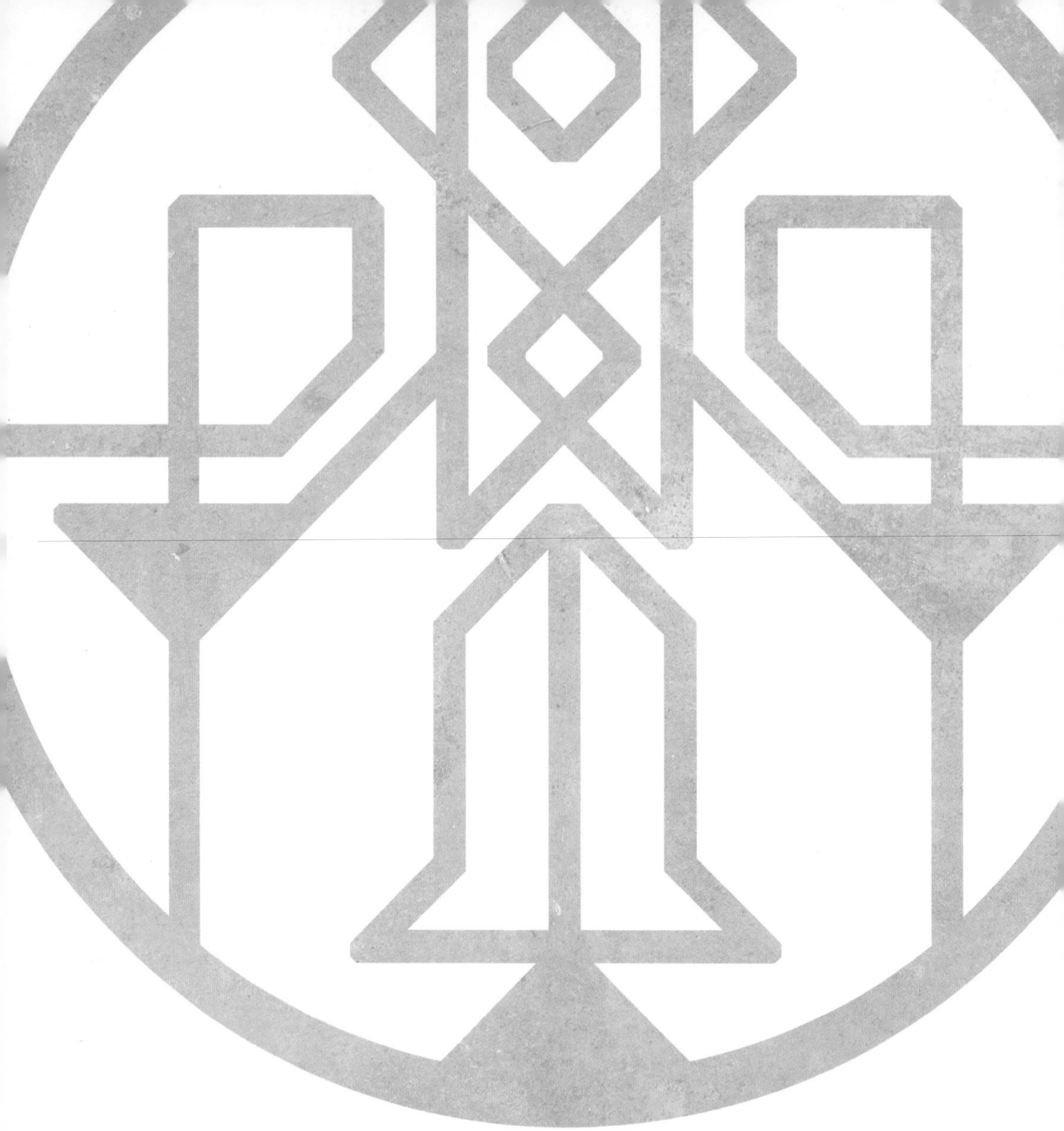